Spring 92

ERANOS

Its Magical Past and Alluring Future: The Spirit of a Wondrous Place

A Journal of
Archetype
and
Culture

Spring 2015

SPRING JOURNAL
New Orleans, Louisiana

SPRING: A JOURNAL OF ARCHETYPE AND CULTURE

Nancy Cater, Editor-in-chief
Riccardo Bernardini, Guest Editor

Jungiana Editor: Riccardo Bernardini   Film Review Editor: Helena Bassil-Morozow

Book Review Editor: Emilija Kiehl

Spring is the oldest Jungian psychology journal in the world. Published twice a year, each issue explores from the perspective of depth psychology a theme of contemporary relevance and contains articles as well as book and film reviews by a wide range of authors from Jungian psychology, the humanities, and other interrelated disciplines.

Founded in 1941 by the Analytical Psychology Club of New York, *Spring* was edited by Jane Pratt until 1969. With the 1970 issue, James Hillman became the editor of *Spring* and moved it to Zürich. When Hillman left Zürich and became the Dean of Graduate Studies at the University of Dallas in 1978, he transferred the editing and publishing of *Spring* there. It was edited in Dallas until 1988 when Hillman and *Spring* moved to Connecticut. Hillman retired as Publisher and Senior Editor of the journal in 1997. From 1997 until 2004 *Spring* remained in Connecticut and was edited by Charles Boer. *Spring* moved its offices to New Orleans, Louisiana in 2004 and has been edited by Nancy Cater since there.

Cover Image:
The monument dedicated "to the unknown spirit of the place" (*genio loci ignoto*), sculpted in 1949 by Paul Speck (1896-1966) and placed on the terrace of Casa Gabriella, in a picture from the mid 1950s.
(Ph. Tim Gidal. Eranos Foundation Archives).

Editorial and production assistance:
Dr. Jeff Borchers, MS, PhD, LPC, borchers@commensa.org
Dr. Gay Bradshaw, PhD, PhD, bradshaw@kerulos.org
Erica Mattingly, eemattingly@gmail.com

Cover design, typography, and layout:
Northern Graphic Design & Publishing, info@ncarto.com

© 2015 Spring Journal, Inc.   ISSN: 0362-0522   ISBN: 978-1-935528-69-2

CONTENTS

JUNGIANA

BOOK REVIEWS

BIBLIOGRAPHICAL APPENDICES

A Note from
the Editor

NANCY CATER

*S*pring is delighted to publish this special issue on Eranos, founded in Ascona, Switzerland by Olga Fröbe-Kapteyn in 1933. *Spring* has had a longing-standing connection to Eranos, and has published through the decades articles by many of the key figures who presented at the Eranos conferences, including works by C. G. Jung, Karl Kerényi, Mircea Eliade, Heinrich Zimmer, Erich Neumann, Henry Corbin, Adolf Portmann, Alfred Ziegler, Gilbert Durand, James Hillman, Rudolf Ritsema, David Miller, and Wolfgang Giegerich.

We would like to extend our deep appreciation to Riccardo Bernardini, Ph.D., Psy.D, the Scientific Secretary of the Eranos Foundation and the Jungiana editor of this journal, for kindly accepting our invitation to guest edit this volume. As Adjunct Professor at the Turin University Faculty of Psychology, Italy, Dr. Bernardini previously taught Analytical Psychology and Educational Psychology. He is an Associate of the Associazione per la Ricerca in Psicologia Analitica (ARPA) in Turin and a Member of the Board of The Fellow Traveller Foundation in Lugano. His research interests focus on the history of the Eranos phenomenon. His writings in this field include *Carl Gustav Jung a Eranos 1933–1952*, edited with Gian Piero Quaglino and Augusto Romano (2007), and *Jung a Eranos. Il progetto della psicologia complessa* (2011), with an up-coming English edition (*Jung at Eranos—The Complex Psychology Project*). He also brought to publication Carl Gustav Jung's *The Solar Myths and Opicinus de Canistris—Notes of the Seminar given at Eranos in 1943*, edited with Gian Piero Quaglino and Augusto Romano (2014), which was preceded by a number of studies in *The Journal of Analytical Psychology* (2010–2013), as well as the Carl Gustav Jung–Henry Corbin correspondence (2013). For the Eranos Foundation, he is now editing Olga Fröbe-Kapteyn's *Visions*, Emma von Pelet's *Analytic Diaries*, and Alwine von Keller's *Paintings of the Unconscious*, among other works. Since 2006, he has served as co-editor of the *Eranos Yearbooks* series, together with Fabio Merlini.

We hope you enjoy learning more about Eranos—past, present, and future—in this issue and also share our enthusiasm for having the opportunity to see the large number of previously unpublished photographs from the Eranos Archives made available to *Spring* through the Eranos Foundation for this celebratory event.

Nancy Cater, J.D., Ph.D.
Editor-in-Chief, *Spring: A Journal of Archetype and Culture*
New Orleans, Louisiana
May 22, 2015

GUEST EDITOR'S
INTRODUCTION

RICCARDO BERNARDINI

More than eighty years have passed since the founding of Eranos in 1933. This pioneering endeavor of interdisciplinary conferences has been properly recognized as "one of the most creative cultural experiences in the modern Western world" and "one of the richest centers of intellectual and spiritual interchange known to our century."[1,2] Its influence has been documented in a number of fields of knowledge ranging from psychology to the history of religions, from philosophy to Eastern studies, from theology to anthropology, and from biology to physics. A myriad of writings bear witness to this influence, more than seven-hundred articles in over seventy *Yearbooks*.[3] The value of those proceedings themselves has been recognized as "truly incalculable. A fabulously rich store of learning."[4] It has been also highlighted that, "there is hardly anything comparable to them; the *Corpus Eranos* will remain as one of the few encyclopedias of our time."[5]

Many of the talks given at Eranos took on the shape of works of some of most influential scholars of the twentieth century. Among the contributions that were developed from lectures delivered at Eranos, we can mention here Carl Gustav Jung's *Archetypes of the Collective Unconscious* (1934/1954) and *On Synchronicity* (1951), Károly Kerényi's *Hermes, Guide of Souls* (1944), Mircea Eliade's *Images and Symbols* (1952), Henry Corbin's *Creative Imagination in the Sufism of Ibn 'Arabî* (1958) and *Temple and Contemplation* (1980), Gershom Scholem's *On the Kabbalah and its Symbolism* (1960) and *The Messianic Idea in Judaism* (1971), James Hillman's *The Myth of Analysis* (1972) and *The Dream and the Underworld* (1979), and Heinrich Zimmer's *The Indian World Mother* (1980). Moreover, the Eranos Archive for Research in Symbolism served as the iconographic support for fundamental studies, such as Carl Gustav Jung's *Psychology and Alchemy* (1944), Mircea Eliade's *The Forge and the Crucible* (1956), and Erich Neumann's *The Origins and History of Consciousness* (1954) and *The Great Mother* (1955).[6] In some cases, the Eranos talks were first published in the *Yearbooks* and, then, republished in special series.[7] In other cases, the Eranos essays were reprinted in monographic collections, collective volumes, and specialized journals, translated (generally, from German) into English, French, Italian, Spanish, Russian, Hebrew, and Japanese.[8,9,10]

Despite the enormous amount of intellectual work, thus far only three journals have published special issues dedicated to Eranos. The famous Swiss magazine, *Du*, edited by Walter Robert Corti, celebrated Eranos in the April 1955 issue, gathering contributions by Olga Fröbe-Kapteyn, Adolf Portmann, Carl Gustav Jung, Aniela Jaffé, Henry Corbin, Károly Kerényi, Daniel Brody, Jolande Jacobi, Mircea Eliade, Hans Conrad Bänziger, and Gershom Scholem.[11] More recently, the Spanish journal, *Anthropos*, dedicated the February 1994 issue to Eranos. That book, published with a supplementary volume, includes an in-depth examination of Eranos's philosophical contribution to modern thought. The Italian analytical psychology journal, *Klaros*, edited by Ida Regina Zoccoli Francesini, also celebrated Eranos in the 2003 issue.[12,13]

Aside from these three special issues, it is surprising that there are relatively few historical studies dedicated to the Eranos phenomenon.[14] There has been, in fact, a singular lack of balance between Eranos's cultural importance and the attention paid to it in scholarly literature. Hans Thomas Hakl pointed this out clearly, when he was preparing the draft of his important book on the subject, commenting:

> I could not understand why there was hardly any information to be found about such an important and longstanding intellectual forum. There is no reference to Eranos in any of the relevant reference books on the history of religion (including the sixteen-volume *Encyclopedia of Religions*, edited by Mircea Eliade, or in the second edition edited by Lindsay Jones), or in standard works on anthropology, psychology, and philosophy (not even in the index to the truly comprehensive *Encyclopédie Philosophique Universelle*, published by the Presses Universitaires Françaises, with its 11,000 large-format pages and its countless cross-references) or in numerous dictionaries of esotericism, symbolism, and mythology. I was able to find only

two entries on the subject. The first one, in the third volume of the *Lexikon für Theologie und Kirche* (*Dictionary of Theology and the Church*), although very brief, does at least mention Rudolf Otto's description of Eranos as "a place of encounter between East and West." The second, somewhat longer, entry was written by Magda Kerényi and appears in the six-volume *Schweizer Lexikon* (*Swiss Lexicon*). One might argue that the thematic range of Eranos is too wide for a specialized dictionary, but even the twenty-five-volume *Meyers Enzyklopädisches Wörterbuch* (*Meyer's Encyclopedic Dictionary*) and the twenty-four-volume *Brockhaus* mention only the ancient Greek word, *eranos*, meaning a banquet, without saying a single word about the meetings. The world-famous *Encyclopedia Britannica* … also contains not a single entry.[15]

As Hakl noted, this situation could probably be attributed, among other factors, to that

particular mental climate that gave rise to the frequent critical comments about Eranos … First of all there is the accusation of irrationalism (because of a too pronounced sympathy for esotericism of whatever hue), and secondly there are the alleged links to authoritarian … currents of thought. This might, incidentally, be one of the reasons why Eranos has been given such an unfairly small amount of space in academic literature.[16]

There are some, including authoritative scholars, who even thought that they detected a form of modern "gnosis" in Eranos.[17] This type of judgment had already been made about Jung's thought and Jung had been the principal inspirer and *spiritus rector* of Eranos for the first twenty years.[18,19] Henry Corbin himself warned against a simplistic reading of Eranos as a purely sociological and cultural phenomenon, emphasizing instead its "esoteric" aspect.[20,21] Even so, this "aura" probably contributed to limiting any interest in historical research, which would have granted Eranos its rightful place in the history of ideas.

There is, indeed, a distinct characteristic in the Eranos experience that probably contributed to its relative marginalization in specialized studies. It is, however, to be sought neither in its "mysteriosophic" background, although this is tangible, nor in its unlikely alleged "traditionalist," or even "authoritarian" sympathies.[22,23] Rather, the distinct characteristic is probably the difficulty of positioning Eranos in a zone of "edge," "margin," or "limit" of the disciplines. This "borderland" makes up in fact precisely the area, one might say, that Eranos took on for its explorations from the beginning as its distinct and paradigmatic task. As David L. Miller points out, in fact, the scholars at the Eranos Conferences are always invited

> to speak at the very *edge* of their disciplines ... The perspectives of the speakers, even those who came out of monotheistic traditions, were situated at the *edges* of the religious traditions of Christianity, Judaism, and Islam. For example, the theological arguments were not those of main-line or orthodox Christian theology, but those of "gnostic" Christianity ... not conventional Jewish theology, but Kabbalah or mystical traditions ... not Shi'ite or Sunni theology, but Sufism in Islam ... Eranos represented an openness to understanding theological studies beyond those of monotheistic traditions, a fundamental understanding of *theologia* as "talk about gods."[24]

James Hillman also recalls:

> Many of those who were steadily at Eranos were ... in a very peculiar position in their own fields. They ... were adventurous, they ... were an avant-garde in the field, and were true scholars, but they were trying to re-imagine their work. They were concerned with the loss, the fall, or what [Henry] Corbin calls, "the exile."[25]

And Richard Tarnas remarks:

> Invited participants in the Eranos meetings are encouraged to explore beyond the borders of their academic specializations while remaining grounded in that critical knowledge ... Eranos seeks to nourish that "fertile crescent" of the overlap between mainstream and alternative cultural-intellectual circles, anchored in each yet reaching out to both.[26]

From an historiographical point of view, it is interesting to mention here a series of works dedicated to Eranos, which, for a variety of reasons, have never been published. First is *Die Geschichte von Eranos* (*The History of Eranos*), which includes a miscellaneous series of typescripts written by Eranos founder Olga Fröbe-Kapteyn (1881–1962) mainly between 1952 and 1958 from the point of view of her "inner" experience. Like many other of her manuscripts, they have never been published.[27] A second work is *Eranos in seiner Geschichte* (*Eranos in Its History*) by Gerhard Wehr. This book was to be published around 1996–1997, but it never saw the light of day.[28,29] A third work, *L'Oeuvre d'Eranos et Vie d'Olga Fröbe-Kapteyn* (*The Work of Eranos and Olga Fröbe-Kapteyn's Life*) by Catherine Ritsema-Gris, was never completed because of the author's advanced age and infirmity.[30,31] A fourth work is *The Periplus of the Eranos Archetype*, to which Rudolf Ritsema dedicated the last years of his life.[32,33]

Thus, from the point of view of the scholarly literature on Eranos, there has been no adequate treatment for a long time. In particular, of the about 180 works (articles, chapters in volumes, books, congress proceedings, and book reviews) dedicated to Eranos that were published between 1935 and 2015, only a few are historical. For example, there is a chapter dedicated to Eranos in the catalog of the exhibition entitled, "Monte Verità—The Breasts of Truth," curated by Harald Szeemann in 1978. There, the Eranos experience was seen as part of that radical social and cultural change with beginnings that could be traced to the last quarter of the nineteenth century, a change that touched the "ahistorical and pedagogical region of upper Lake Maggiore."[34] Four years later, in William McGuire's *Bollingen—An Adventure in Collecting the Past* (1982), the first decades of Eranos were retraced in the light of the support granted to it by the Bollingen Foundation. Both Maggy Anthony's *The Valkyries—The Women Around Jung* (1990) and Nadia Neri's *Oltre l'Ombra* (*Beyond the Shadow*, 1995) included a chapter dedicated to Olga Fröbe-Kapteyn. A proper biography on the Eranos's founder is however still missing.[35] In 1999, the contribution of three leading figures at Eranos—Gershom Scholem, Mircea Eliade, and Henry Corbin—was examined in Steven M. Wasserstrom's *Religion after Religion*.[36] In 2000, the Associazione Amici di Eranos (Association of the Friends of Eranos) organized a conference on the topic, "Eranos, Monte Verità, Ascona," with the idea of "placing the Eranos Conferences into the wider frame of the different cultural phenomena, which alternated and interacted in Ascona during the 1900s."[37] In a volume published the same year, *Kreise, Gruppen, Bünde* (*Circles, Groups, Confederations*), the Eranos phenomenon was presented in the context of several modern intellectual associations.[38]

Only in 2001 was the rich essay by Hans Thomas Hakl, *Der verborgene Geist von Eranos* (*The Hidden Spirit of Eranos*), finally published.[39] His book, preceded and followed by a number of significant publications by the same author, is a landmark among studies of the Eranos phenomenon. It was recently re-published, in a greatly enlarged English edition, as *Eranos—An Alternative Intellectual History of the Twentieth Century* (2013), as well as in a new German one, *Eranos: Nabel der Welt. Glied der goldenen Kette. Die alternative Geistesgeschichte* (*Eranos: Navel of the World. Link in the Golden Chain. The Alternative Intellectual History*, 2015).[40] There, the author opens with these words:

> Originally I planned to write an introduction of some twenty pages to a selection of Eranos lectures with distinctly esoteric themes. I felt such an introduction to be necessary in order to make the reading public familiar with the history and significance of the Eranos meetings … Then came the first surprise: there appeared to be no published reports or historical information about the meetings and how they came into being … After some initial research, however, there began to come my way— at first slowly and then ever faster—information that was highly intriguing and evidently important. When I then tried to squeeze all the facts that I had gathered into the prescribed parameters, I realized how much highly interesting material simply could not be accommodated … as it was the seeking and finding of material that I most enjoyed, more and more stuff accumulated, and gradually it became clear to me that in Eranos I was dealing with something far more important than I had originally assumed. My rather general interest in the meetings began to deepen. Having initially concentrated on printed material, albeit including published primary sources such as diaries and conference reports, I extended the search to unpublished manuscripts, letters, and diary entries. This led to conversations and correspondence with a number of Eranos speakers and participants. The leading figures in the story came more and more clearly into focus, becoming real human beings rather than just world- famous names from diverse academic disciplines. They came to life again in all their feelings and emotions—envy and joy, pride and vanity—but also in their self-sacrifice and their metaphysical longing. Their long forgotten hopes and disappointments

were revived—if only in my mind. Furthermore, what had
previously been for me a purely intellectual sympathy for
spiritual and cultural strivings in general, now became more
and more emotionally tinged and increasingly focused on
Eranos in particular.[41]

Building also on Hakl's outstanding research, other publications
came to light in the following years. At the occasion of the sixteenth
Congress of the International Association for Analytical Psychology
(IAAP) held in Barcelona in 2004, for example, a series of lectures,
"Walking in the Footsteps of Eranos," was presented. The
proceedings included contributions from the Eranos lecturers,
Hayao Kawai, David L. Miller, and Gilles Quispel, as well as from
Robert Hinshaw, who—through James Hillman and the C. G. Jung
Institute in Zürich—has a longstanding connection with Eranos,
and Paul Kugler, who displayed previously unpublished photographs
of the Conferences.[42,43] Still among the Jungian conferences, at the
time of preparation of the present issue, the Jung–Neumann Letters
Conference, held in Tel Aviv (Israel) on April 24–26, 2015 at the
occasion of the publication of the Carl Gustav Jung–Erich Neumann
correspondence, hosted a panel on the theme, "Neumann at
Eranos." On that occasion, it was also shown the *Eranos 1951* movie,
directed by Ximena de Angulo-Roelli and Willy Roelli and
produced by the C. G. Jung Institute of Los Angeles in 1951.
Furthermore, the Third European Congress of Analytical
Psychology, entitled, "Encounters, Traditions, Developments:
Analysis at the Cultural Crossroads", and to be held in Trieste (Italy)
on August 27–30, 2015, will host a panel on the topic, "Eranos
and the European Spirit."

In 2007, the photographic catalogue, *Carl Gustav Jung at Eranos
1933–1952*, the testimony of an exhibition that marked the tenth
anniversary of the Turin University Faculty of Psychology, included
a number of photographic and documentary materials belonging
to the Eranos archives, which were still unpublished at that
time.[44,45] In 2009, the Fetzer Institute organized a symposium in
Ascona on the topic, "Love in the History of Eranos," chaired by
the theologian, anthropologist, and historian of religions, Lawrence
E. Sullivan. The proceedings also gathered some historical contributions
based on primary sources.[46]

Based on the above and other unpublished documents belonging
to the Eranos archives, a 2011 work of mine, *Jung a Eranos*. *Il progetto
della psicologia complessa* (*Jung at Eranos—The Complex Psychology
Project*), attempted to track more closely Jung's participation in
Eranos in the light of his project of psychology. In fact, it was at
Eranos that Jung most clearly outlined the idea of "complex
psychology." In *Jung and the Making of Modern Psychology* (2003),
a seminal work that also sheds light on the meaning of the Eranos
project, Sonu Shamdasani pointed out how, with that expression, Jung
was not describing a school of psychotherapy but, rather, an exhaustive
"general psychology," which would converse with the other
disciplines—the history of religions, philosophy, theology,
anthropology, history of the arts, and natural sciences.[47] Jung used
the expression, "complex psychology," particularly from the 1930s,
to differentiate the theoretical and cultural perspective of his own
thinking from its clinical application.[48] The name never disappears.
In contemporary thought, the expression, "analytical psychology," has
been however preferred instead of "complex psychology." This may
suggest that current teaching somehow still obscures one aspect of what
Jung wished to achieve, which was instead core to the Eranos
program: an ambitious, pioneering, and in many aspects unrepeated
"comparative study of the individuation process."[49,50,51]

In the meantime, the publication of various biographies and
exchanges of letters have also contributed to shed more light on the
history of the Eranos Conferences. Biographical works include, for
example, those on Louis Massignon, Adolf Portmann, Mircea Eliade,
Jakob Wilhelm Hauer, Heinrich Zimmer, Roland Holst, Raffaele
Pettazzoni, Elémire Zolla, Hermann Hesse, and James Hillman,
among others.[52] In addition, of course, there are the numerous "lives"
of Carl Gustav Jung.[53] The critical editions of correspondences
include those of Kurt Wolff, Carl Gustav Jung, Heinrich Zimmer,
Mircea Eliade, Gershom Scholem, and André Jolles.[54] Moreover,
there is a series of publications of letters—complete or partial—
between the following pairs of scholars: Mircea Eliade–Raffaele
Pettazzoni, Carl Gustav Jung–Mary Mellon, Carl Gustav Jung–
Wolfgang Pauli, Carl Gustav Jung–Ernst Bernhard, Olga
Fröbe-Kapteyn–Ludwig Derleth, Mircea Eliade–Károly Kerényi,
Mircea Eliade–Rudolf Ritsema, Hermann Hesse–Josef Bernhard

Lang, Carl Gustav Jung–Victor White, James Hillman–Rudolf Ritsema, Carl Gustav Jung–Henry Corbin, Walter Friedrich Otto–Károly Kerényi, Martin Buber–Gerardus van der Leeuw, and the most recent one, the long awaited Carl Gustav Jung–Erich Neumann correspondence.[55] Other letters are still in the pre-publication state—those of Carl Gustav Jung–Jakob Wilhelm Hauer, Carl Gustav Jung–Heinrich Zimmer, and Carl Gustav Jung–Mircea Eliade, for example.[56] The publication of further exchanges of letters relevant to the history of Eranos is now in preparation, such as the Erich Neumann–Olga Fröbe-Kapteyn correspondence, now being jointly edited by the Eranos Foundation and Erich Neumann's heirs.

Among the research projects connected to Eranos that have recently been developed, the main one is surely the 2014 edition of Carl Gustav Jung's *The Solar Myths and Opicinus de Canistris—Notes of the Seminar given at Eranos in 1943*. By agreement with the Foundation of the Works of C. G. Jung and in collaboration with the heirs, it was possible to publish notes from the seminar taken by two of Jung's students, Alwine von Keller and Rivkah Schärf Kluger. This material was drawn from the archives—respectively—of the Eranos Foundation in Ascona and of the Swiss Federal Institute of Technology (ETH) in Zürich. Also significant was the handwritten outline that Jung prepared for his seminar, which was found in the attic of his former home in Küsnacht.[57] The edition of this seminar, which is the result of numerous studies that preceded that publication, allowed us all to witness Jung's creative work at Eranos virtually "live."[58] In our mind's eye we could see and hear his fertile dialogue with other scholars and get closer and closer to the almost "magic" atmosphere of the Eranos Conferences. This enabled us to understand better what his student, Aniela Jaffé, meant: "These were the most impressive and the liveliest teachings in psychology that we were ever to experience."[59]

Further editorial projects are still being prepared by the Eranos Foundation, projects that also will shed more light on the Eranos experience itself. In the case of Jung, the publication of *The Red Book* helped people realize all the more (if they needed to at all) that there was a strict connection between his personal and his intellectual paths. Up to now, several of Olga Fröbe-Kapteyn's allusions have sounded in that sense much more hermetic. For example, she stated, "The deepest things in human life ... can only be expressed in images."[60] Twenty years after, she also wrote: "I beg your pardon if I am speaking through images! This is the way my mind works."[61] These are words that become much clearer now in the light of her *Visions*, an impressive collection of over three-hundred images drawn by Olga Fröbe-Kapteyn, using the Jungian technique of the active imagination, between 1934 and 1938.[62] These were the crucial beginning years of her cultural enterprise, her relationship with Jung, and her research into iconographic material entrusted to her by Jung. Olga Fröbe-Kapteyn's *Visions* testifies to the intimate bond between inner reality and the outer world, as well as between psychological processes and the creative dimension. It is this bond that yields perhaps the deepest meaning of Eranos, which Olga Fröbe-Kapteyn herself alluded to:

> The history of Eranos can be found in a *book* that has no writing, which I often go through, read, examine, and compare. I observe the *images* too, in that there are many in this book, and I look for the connections that form the whole in a meaningful and unifying way. The overall image, the model that has become visible, is so wound around and interwoven with the model of my life that it is really hard to separate them.[63]

Between Jung and Olga Fröbe-Kapteyn, it must be clear, there was never an analytical relationship *stricto sensu*. At least initially, she may have wished this, but—apart from few sessions held in the mid '30s— it did not take place.[64] Even in the absence of a formal analytical contract, she however continued to go to Jung, beyond matters linked to Eranos, to ask his advice on personal problems, as she did later with other analysts, such as Léopold Szondi and Erich Neumann. The latter, in particular, has been a longstanding and intimate confidant for Olga Fröbe-Kapteyn. Jung suggested that she write down her dreams and that she try to interpret them, offering to have a personal meeting when she did not know how to work with the material from her own unconscious.[65] Some paintings by Olga Fröbe-Kapteyn will be shown at the occasion of the exhibition entitled, "The Great Mother," organized by the Trussardi Foundation and the City of Milan at the Royal Palace of Milan on August 25–November 15, 2015, in conjunction with the 2015 Universal Exhibition (Expo Milano 2015) on the theme, "Feeding the Planet. Energy for Life." "The Great Mother" exhibition is directed by Massimiliano Gioni, assisted by Roberta Tenconi, who already curated the 55ᵗʰ Venice Biennale (2013), "The Encyclopedic Palace," inspired by Jung's *Red Book*.

Emma Hélène von Pelet-Narbonne's (1892–1967) *Analytic Diaries* (1935–1966) attest to her analysis with Carl Alfred Meier, in 1940–1941, and then with Jung, from 1941.[66] Writer, poet, and translator of authors like Swami Vivekananda, Sri Ramakrishna, Mircea Eliade, Daisetsu Teitarō Suzuki, Jean Herbert, Denis de Rougemont, Mary Esther Harding, Marie Bonaparte, Akihisa Kondo, and Howard Littleton Philp, she spent most of her life at Eranos. She had in fact decided to leave Germany when Hitler took power. She had purchased Casa Shanti in 1937, where Olga Fröbe-Kapteyn had been putting up friends and Eranos lecturers before then, but which she had been obliged to a put up for sale to cover the ever more onerous costs of her project. In her diaries, Emma von Pelet collected dreams, personal reflections, and notes about her analytical work with Jung. Moreover, she included personal memories of her encounters with Jung at Eranos and in Küsnacht. In fact, he used to come to Eranos not only to discuss questions regarding the Conferences with Olga Fröbe-Kapteyn, but also to spend some periods of leisure and to enjoy the splendid terrace of Casa Shanti looking onto Lake Maggiore.[67]

In 1937, Alwine (Alwina) von Keller (1878–1965) joined Emma von Pelet at Casa Shanti, which the two women would share from that moment on. Alwine von Keller herself translated works of authors such as Sri Aurobindo and Swami Vivekananda from English into German. According to Catherine Ritsema, Alwine von Keller's "relationship and her work with C. G. Jung, her bond and friendship with Olga Fröbe-Kapteyn, played a minor role, certainly, but one not without importance in the development of Eranos."[68] Alwine von Keller underwent analysis with Ernst Bernhard, the pioneer of analytical psychology in Italy, and then with Jung.[69] As analytical psychologist, she subsequently used the ground floor of Casa Shanti as a professional consulting room, where she received the patients sent to her from Zürich by Jung. Alwine von Keller began creating a series of "unconscious pictures, glorious paintings, which evoked complementary images like one dream interpreting another one, till a succession showed the different aspects of a subject and the hidden meaning shone forth in a beautiful process of self-realization."[70] Alwine von Keller's *Paintings of the Unconscious*, together with Olga

Fröbe-Kapteyn's *Visions* and Emma von Pelet's *Analytic Diaries*, are now being prepared for publication as a substantial and critical edition for the Eranos Foundation.

Ultimately, even without gathering strictly historiographical works on the topic, this issue of *Spring* is meant to propose a reflection and a discussion on Eranos from various points of view. A first series of contributions, gathered under the title, "The Eranos Phenomenon," mainly offers an interpretation of Eranos from a historical perspective. Eranos Foundation President Fabio Merlini's *Eranos: A Space and a Time for Thought*, in particular, examines not only the past history of Eranos as an institution, but also its present interests, current projects, and future perspectives on research and scholarship. Hans Thomas Hakl's *Eranos: A Counter Current to The Common Intellectual History of the 20th Century?* features instead a "wide ranging" panorama on Eranos, from its "pre-history" to the present. In addition, Olga Fröbe-Kapteyn's *The Psychological Background of Eranos*, originally presented as a lecture at the New York Analytical Psychology Club in 1939, appears in print in this issue for the first time.

A second series of essays, grouped under the title, "Eranos and the Psychological Tradition," deal with Eranos's contribution to Jung's thought and then to the development of analytical psychology. Gian Piero Quaglino's *Carl Gustav Jung: His Life Before His Works* provide a key to understand the meaning and the motivations of the involvement in the Conferences of one of its leading figures. Antonio Vitolo's *The Analytical Leitmotif of the Eranos Conferences* focuses on the constant presence of the analytical dimension thoughout all the decades of the gatherings, the result of Jung's marked influence on Olga Fröbe-Kapteyn's project from the beginning. Stephen Aizenstat's *Eranos as Dream* is instead a more imaginative look at Eranos, fruit of his own years of attendance and personal seminar experiences there. This section also include a historical essay by Carl Gustav Jung, *American Eranos Volume: Introduction* (1939), originally published in this journal in 1984.

A third section, entitled, "Eranos and the Idea of the Sacred," gathers a series of articles that deal with Eranos's view of the religious issues and the study of the sacred. David L. Miller's *On the Edge of the Round Table: Eranos and Theological Studies* surveys Eranos's approach to theological studies. Miller was a leading figure in the

Eranos circle from the mid-1970s to the late 1980s. In *Eranos: The Study of Religion as a Religious Phenomenon*, Bernardo Nante treats Eranos's approach to the study of religions and provides at the same time an interpretation of Eranos as an "experience," which goes beyond a purely "academic" phenomenon. Moreover, Moshe Idel's *Archetypes and Androgynes at Eranos* covers interest in the topics of androgyny and the *coniunctio oppositorum*, which have been treated by several Eranos lecturers. Also this section includes a contribution from the past, i.e., Mircea Eliade's *Encounters at Ascona* (1960).

A fourth group of articles deal with the "Philosophical Perspectives of Eranos." More historically oriented, Michel Cazenave's *Some Remembrances of Eranos* is a recollection of meetings with some of the leading figures at Eranos, such as Henry Corbin, Gilbert Durand, and James Hillman. From a theoretical point of view, Romano Màdera's *The Missing Link: From Jung to Hadot and Vice Versa* discusses the Eranos dialogue between psychological and philosophical perspectives, an issue that is very much other than linear and often taken for granted. Grazia Shōgen Marchianò's *Non-Duality: The Deep Challenge of Bringing Together Ancient and Modern Ways of Knowledge in an Epistemic World View* deals instead with the European reception of Far-Eastern thought, a topic that lies in the founding of Eranos itself as a "Meeting Place for East and West" (*Begegnungsstätte für Ost und West*), but one that was not free of misunderstandings. Re-published here is also Henry Corbin's *The Time of Eranos* (1956).

A fifth series of writings, collected under the title, "Eranos and the Unity of Psyche and Matter," delve into Eranos's contribution to the dialogue between human sciences and natural sciences as well as between the theoretical speculation and the need for concrete answers to some crucial problems of the world we are living. The section includes *The Enlightening Role of Adolf Portmann*, in which Adolf Portmann student Sigurd von Boletzky focuses on some aspects of the Swiss biologist's thought, which were later crucial for the Eranos's approach to natural sciences and for Portmann's (unresolved) dialogue with Jung on the problem of psychic inheritance. Augusto Shantena Sabbadini's *Eranos, Synchronicity, and the I Ching: A Personal Journey* reviews instead interest at Eranos in the ancient Chinese oral text, *I Ching*, and the ambitious *I Ching* project later developed by the Eranos Foundation. Finally, Her Royal

Highness Princess Irene of the Netherlands, Princess of Orange-Nassau, Princess of Lippe-Biesterfeld's note, *Our Relation to Nature Determines Our Worldview: Eranos and Today's Great Cultural Challenge*, reflects on the possible contribution of Eranos in relation to some of the most important challenges that humanity finds itself facing in the coming decades. The section also includes a historical contribution by Adolf Portmann and Rudolf Ritsema, entitled, *Eranos and its Meaning* (1978).

Moreover, the Jungiana section of this issue hosts an article by Beth Darlington dedicated to Kristine Mann, entitled, *Jung's "Miss X" and a Pioneer in Psychoanalysis*. Jung examined in depth Kristine Mann's *maṇḍalas* in his first talk at Eranos in 1933, *A Study in the Process of Individuation* (1934/1950), which represented the first extended case description of the individuation process.[71]

This issue of *Spring* also includes an ample iconographic section with more than fifty photographs from the Eranos Foundation Archives, many never before published. They are products of Eranos photographers Margarita Marianne (Margarethe) Fellerer (1886–1961), Tim N. Gidal (1909–1996), and Luciano Soave.

The volume closes with a bibliographical appendix comprising a list of the *Eranos Yearbooks* (1933–2014) and of the *Eranos Round Table Sessions* (1990–2002), as well as of the proceedings of the Associazione Amici di Eranos (1990–2012) and of the Verein zur Förderung der wissenschaftlichen Tagungen von Eranos (2001–2014).

I would like to conclude this introductory note by thanking those who, in one way or another, have contributed to the preparation and realization of this publication: Fabio Merlini, Gianni Aprile, Maurizio Checchi, Claudio W. Metzger, Luca Pissoglio, Sandro Rusconi, and Gisela Binda (Eranos Foundation, Ascona), for their trust, collaboration, and support in all stages of this editorial project; Thomas Fischer and Ulrich Hoerni (Foundation of the Works of C. G. Jung, Zürich), for permission to republish Carl Gustav Jung's article and handwritten dedication, as well as Annkathrin Wollert (Paul & Peter Fritz AG, Literary Agency, Zürich), for the kind administrative assistance; Daniel Gastambide (Association des Amis de Henry et Stella Corbin, Paris), for permission to republish Henry Corbin's article; Sorin Alexandrescu, for permission to republish Mircea Eliade's article; Elisabeth von Orelli-Schütz and Augusto Shantena Sabbadini, for permission to republish the article by Adolf Portmann and Rudolf Ritsema; Franziska Fellerer-

Wistuba, for permission to publish Margarethe Fellerer's photographs; Renée Nieuwendijk Hoek, for providing the photographic portrait of Her Royal Highness Princess Irene of the Netherlands; Shanti Pappu, for the continuing collaboration on the edition of Alwine von Keller's materials; Romano Màdera and Paolo Mottana, assisted by Marina Barioglio and Alessandra Indelicato, for giving a prominent space to Eranos in the Symbolic Cultures post-graduate program at the University of Milano-Bicocca; Erel Shalit, Tamar Kron, and Murray Stein, for the great attention given to Eranos at the occasion of the Jung–Neumann Letters Conference; Ralli Neumann-Löwenthal and Nancy Furlotti, for their continuing interest on the Erich Neumann–Olga Fröbe-Kapteyn correspondence; Vincent Marsicano, for the English translation of Fabio Merlini's article and this Introduction; Robert Hinshaw, for the expert advice on some historical issues; Gay Bradshaw and Jeff Borchers, for careful editorial work; and, above all, the authors, who have made this publication possible through their generous intellectual contribution. I especially would like to thank Nancy Cater, Editor of *Spring—A Journal of Archetype and Culture*, for her longstanding interest in Eranos, her trust in this project, and the enthusiasm she has showed since its inception.

NOTES

1. Mircea Eliade, *Journal II, 1957–1969* (Chicago, IL: University of Chicago Press, 1989), p. xiii.

2. Michel Cazenave, *Jung. L'expérience intérieure* (Paris: Éditions du Rocher, 1997), p. 122. (English translation from Hans Thomas Hakl, *Eranos—An Alternative Intellectual History of the Twentieth Century* (Montreal/Kingston: McGill-Queen's University Press, 2013), p. 7.)

3. The *Eranos Yearbooks* were published by Rhein-Verlag (volumes I/1933–XXXVIII/1969), E.J. Brill (XXXIX/1969–XLV/1976), Insel Verlag (XLVI/1977–LVII/1988), Eranos Foundation (LVIII/1989–LX/1991), Spring Journal, Inc. (LXI/1992 and LXV/1996–LXVIII/1999). Currently the proceedings are published by Daimon Verlag (LXIX/2006–2007–2008–LXXII/2013–2014).

4. Fritz L. Kunz in *Main Currents in Modern Thought* (1954), quoted on the dust jacket of the *Eranos-Jahrbuch* 23 (1954). (English translation from Hakl, *Eranos*, p. 11.)

5. This was the opinion of North German Radio, as reported on the dust jacket of the *Eranos-Jahrbuch* 27 (1958). (English translation from Hakl, *Eranos*, p. 11.)

6. On the history of this project, see Riccardo Bernardini, *Jung a Eranos. Il progetto della psicologia complessa* (Milan: FrancoAngeli, 2011), § 3; see also Jessie A. Fraser, "ARAS: Archive for Research in Archetypal Symbolism," *Spring* (1964): 60–67; and Torben Gronning, Patricia Sohl, and Thomas Singer, "ARAS: Archetypal Symbolism and Images," *Visual Resources* 23 (3, 2007): 245–67.

7. In English language, Joseph Campbell, ed., *Papers from the Eranos Yearbooks* (Princeton, NJ: Princeton University Press, 1954–1868, 6 volumes), and the *Eranos Lectures* (Dallas, TX: Spring Publications, Inc., 1984–1989, 9 volumes). In Italian, Claudio Risé, ed., *Quaderni di Eranos* (Como: Red, 1989–1999, 9 volumes), and Fabio Merlini, ed., *Saggi di Eranos* (Turin: Rosenberg & Sellier, 2013–2014, 2 volumes, with further ones in preparation). In Japanese, Rudolf Ritsema and Toshihiko Izutsu, eds., *Eranos Series* (Ascona/Tokyo: Eranos Foundation/ Heibonsha Ltd., 1990–1995, 11 volumes). In Spanish, Andrés Ortiz-Osés, ed., *Círculo Eranos (Cuadernos de Eranos)* (Barcelona: Anthropos, 1994–2004, 3 volumes).

8. We list here, among others, Ernst Benz's *Urbild und Abbild. Der Mensch und die mythische Welt* (1974); Ernesto Buonaiuti's *Die exkommunizierte Kirche* (1966); Gilbert Durand's *Structures* (2003), *La crisis espiritual en occidente* (2011), and *La beauté comme présence* (2014); James Hillman's *Le figure del mito* (2014); Toshihiko Izutsu's *The Structure of Oriental Philosophy* (2008); Carl Gustav Jung's *The Integration of the Personality* (1939); Hayao Kawai's *Dreams, Myths, and Fairy Tales in Japan* (1995); Erich Neumann's *Umkreisung der Mitte* (1953–1954, 3 volumes), *Art and the Creative Unconscious* (1959), *Creative Man* (1979), *The Place of Creation* (1989), *The Fear of the Feminine and Other Essays on Feminine Psychology* (1994), *Die Psiche als Ort der Gestaltung* (1992), *Eranos-Voträge* (2007–2009, 5 volumes), and *Man and Meaning* (2013); Adolf Portmann's *Das Tier als soziales Wesen* (1953), *Biologie und Geist* (1956), and *Aufbruch der Lebensforschung* (1965); Gilles Quispel's *Gnostic Studies* (1974); Hugo Rahner's *Griechische Mythen in Chrislicher Deutung* (1957); Herbert Read's *The Forms of Things Unknown* (1960); Gershom Scholem's *Judaica* (1963–1997, 6 volumes), *Concetti fondamentali dell'Ebraismo* (1986), and *La figura mistica della divinità* (2010); Hellmut Wilhelm's *Heaven, Earth, and*

Man in the Book of Changes (1958); and Victor Zuckerkandl's *Vom musikalischen Denken* (1964).

9. See, e.g., VV.AA., *Aspekte des Lebendigen* (Freiburg im Breisgau: Herder, 1965); VV.AA., *Gibt es Grenzen der Naturforschung?* (Freiburg im Breisgau: Herder, 1966); VV.AA., *Color Symbolism*, eds. S. Haule and R. Weening (Dallas, TX: Spring Publications, Inc., 1977), rpt. as *Color Symbolism*, ed. K. Ottman (Putnam, CT: Spring Publications, Inc., 2005); and VV.AA., *Vida y Trascendencia* (Caracas: Monte Avila, 1970).

10. Such as the journals *Diogénès*, *L'Immaginale*, and *Anima*.

11. *Du. Schweizerische Monatsschrift* 15 (4, 1955).

12. VV.AA., *Suplementos. Materiales de trabajo intellectual. Una interpretación evaluativa de nuestra cultura. Análisis y lectura del almacén simbólico de Eranos. Antología y estudios*, vol. 42 (Barcelona: Anthropos, 1994); VV.AA., *El Círculo de Eranos: una hermenéutica simbólica del sentido. Anthropos. Boletín de información y documentación* 153 (1994).

13. VV.AA., *Jung Eranos. Klaros. Quaderni di psicologia analitica* 16 (1–2, 2003).

14. For a detailed and up-dated bibliography on the Eranos phenomenon, see Bernardini, *Jung a Eranos*, pp. 363–407, and Hakl, *Eranos*, pp. 391–422.

15. Hakl, *Eranos*, p. 8.

16. *Ibid.*, p. 3.

17. See Hans Heinz Holz, "Eranos – eine moderne Pseudo-Gnosis," in J. Taubes, ed., *Gnosis und Politik. Religionstheorie und Politische Theologie* (Munich: Wilhelm Fink/Ferdinand Schöningh, 1984), vol. II, pp. 249–63; Giovanni Filoramo, *Il risveglio della gnosi ovvero diventare dio* (Rome-Bari: Laterza, 1990), pp. 21–27; Giovanni Filoramo, *Figure del sacro. Saggi di storia religiosa* (Brescia: Morcelliana, 1993), pp. 305ff.; Flavio Cuniberto, "Ecumenismo e nuova era. Riflessioni sul paradigma planetario," *Filosofia e teologia* 7 (2, 1993): 397–414; Steven M. Wasserstrom, *Religion after Religion—Gershom Scholem, Mircea Eliade, and Henry Corbin at Eranos* (Princeton, NJ: Princeton University Press, 1999); and Bernardo Nante, "Eranos: The Study of Religion as a Religious Phenomenon," published in this issue of *Spring*.

18. See George Steiner, *Nostalgia for the Absolute* (Toronto: CBC, 1974), § 2; Giovanni Filoramo, *L'attesa della fine. Storia della gnosi* (Rome-Bari: Laterza, 1983), pp. X–XI; Giovanni Filoramo, *Religione*

e ragione tra Ottocento e Novecento (Rome-Bari: Laterza, 1985), pp. 243ff.; Massimo Introvigne, *Il cappello del mago. I nuovi movimenti magici, dallo spiritismo al satanismo* (Carnago: SugarCo, 1990), pp. 254ff.; Massimo Introvigne, *Il ritorno dello gnosticismo* (Carnago: SugarCo, 1993), pp. 41ff.; and Massimo Introvigne and Pier Luigi Zoccatelli, eds., *Le religioni in Italia* (Turin: CESNUR/Elledici/Velar, 2006), p. 981.

19. On Jung's involvement in the Eranos project, see Bernardini, *Jung a Eranos*.

20. See Henry Corbin, "The Time of Eranos," in J. Campbell, ed., *Man and Time. Papers from the Eranos Yearbooks* (London: Routledge and Kegan Paul, 1959), p. xiii, published also in this issue of *Spring*.

21. See, e.g., Henry Corbin, "A Olga Fröbe Kapteyn" (1951), in C. Jambet, ed., *Henry Corbin. L'Herne* (Paris : L'Herne, 1981), pp. 264–65; and Henry Corbin, "De l'Iran à Eranos," *Du. Schweizerische Monatsschrift* 15 (4, 1955): 29.

22. In the recently published *Lament of the Dead*, for example, James Hillman remembers: "I used to go to Eranos and they'd ask and I'd say I'm talking to the dead. Every year I'd give a lecture there but I never thought I was talking to the audience." (James Hillman and Sonu Shamdasani, *Lament of the Dead—Psychology after Jung's Red Book* (New York, NY: W. W. Norton & Company, Inc., 2013), p. 27.)

23. Furio Jesi, *Cultura di Destra* (Milan: Garzanti, 1979), p. 58.

24. David L. Miller, "On the Edge of the Round Table: Eranos and Theological Studies," published in this issue of *Spring*. See also David L. Miller, "At the Edges of the Round Table: Jung, Religion, and Eranos," in L. Cowan, ed., *Barcelona 2004—Edges of Experience: Memory and Emergence—Proceedings of the Sixteenth International Congress for Analytical Psychology* (Einsiedeln: Daimon, 2006), pp. 129–44.

25. Hillman and Shamdasani, *Lament of the Dead*, p. 146.

26. Richard Tarnas, "The Eranos Coordinating Council's Vision Statement," *Eranos Yearbook* 69 (2006–2007–2008): 40–41.

27. Some excerpts were published in Bernardini, *Jung a Eranos*, pp. 90–110.

28. Gerhard Wehr, *Jean Gebser. Individuelle Transformation vor dem Horizont eines neuen Bewußtseins* (Petersberg: Via Nova, 1996), p. 273; see also Hakl, *Eranos*, pp. vi, 10–11, 235, and 297; Hans Thomas Hakl, "Prefazione," in Bernardini, *Jung a Eranos*, p. 19; and Riccardo Bernardini, "The Secret of Eranos," *Spring* 88 (2012): 335.

29. Hakl, *Eranos*, pp. 10–11.

30. Catherine Ritsema, *L'Œuvre d'Eranos et Vie d'Olga Froebe-Kapteyn* (Ascona: unpublished typescript, undated); see also Hakl, *Eranos*, pp. vi and 11; and Hakl, "Prefazione," p. 19.

31. Hakl, *Eranos*, pp. 220 and 296.

32. Rudolf Ritsema, "The Periplus of the Eranos Archetype" (Ascona: unpublished typescript, 2002; personal copy).

33. *Ibid.*, p. 243; Hakl, "Prefazione," p. 19.

34. Harald Szeemann, "Monte Verità. La montagna della verità," in H. Szeemann, ed., *Monte Verità. Antropologia locale come contributo alla riscoperta di una topografia sacrale moderna* (Locarno/Milan: Armando Dadò/Electa, 1978), pp. 5–6; see, in particular, Sybille Rosenbaum-Kroeber, "Eranos e Olga Fröbe-Kapteyn," in Szeemann, *Monte Verità*, pp. 119–21.

35. William McGuire, *Bollingen—An Adventure in Collecting the Past*, Bollingen Series (Princeton, NJ Princeton University Press, 1982); Maggy Anthony, *The Valkyries—The Women Around Jung* (Shaftesbury, Dorset: Element Books, Ltd., 1990); Nadia Neri, *Oltre l'Ombra. Donne intorno a Jung* (Rome: Borla, 1995). See also William McGuire's articles: "The Arcane Summer School," *Spring* (1980): 146–56; "Jung and Eranos in America," *Spring* (1984): 51–59; and "Firm Affinities: Jung's Relations with Britain and the United States," *Journal of Analytical Psychology* 40 (3, 1995): 301–26.

36. Steven M. Wasserstrom, *Religion after Religion—Gershom Scholem, Mircea Eliade, and Henry Corbin at Eranos* (Princeton, NJ: Princeton University Press, 1999). For the controversies on this book, see Hakl, *Eranos, passim.*

37. Elisabetta Barone, Adriano Fabris, and Flavia Monceri, eds., *Eranos. Monte Verità. Ascona* (Pisa: ETS, 2003); German edition: Elisabetta Barone, Matthias Riedl, and Alexandra Tischel, eds., *Pioniere, Poeten, Professoren. Eranos und der Monte Verità in der Zivilisationsgeschichte des 20. Jahrhunderts* (Würzburg: Königshausen & Neumann, 2004). In 2012, the same association organized a conference on the topic, "The Eranos Movement." See Tilo Schabert, ed., *The Eranos Movement* (Würzburg: Königshausen + Neumann, 2015; forthcoming).

38. See, in particular, Barbara von Reibnitz, "Der Eranos-Kreis. Religionswissenschaft und Weltanschauung oder der Gelehrte als Laien-Priester," in R. Faber and C. Holste, eds., *Kreise, Gruppen, Bünde. Zur*

Soziologie moderner Intellektuellenassoziation (Würzburg: Könighausen + Neumann, 2000), pp. 425–40. (Rpt. in: R. Schleiser and R. S. Martinez, eds., *Neuhumanismus und Anthropologie des griechischen Mythos. Karl Kerényi im europäischen Kontext des 20. Jahrhunderts* (Locarno: Rezzonico, 2006), pp. 107–23.)

39. Hans Thomas Hakl, *Der verborgene Geist von Eranos. Unbekannte Begegnungen von Wissenschaft und Esoterik. Eine alternative Geistesgeschichte des 20. Jahrhunderts* (Bretten: Scientia nova-Neue Wissenschaft, 2001).

40. Hans Thomas Hakl, "Der verborgene Geist von Eranos. Unbekannte Begegnungen von Wissenschaft und Esoterik - Beitrag zu einer alternativen Geistesgeschichte des 20. Jahrhunderts," *Gnostika. Zeitschrift für Wissenschaft & Esoterik* 5 (17, 2001): 21–42; Hans Thomas Hakl, "Eranos im Spiegel der Geistesgeschichte des 20. Jahrhunderts," *Archævs. Études d'Histoire des Religions/Studies in the History of Religions* 6 (1–2, 2002): 183–200, rpt. in *Zeitschrift für Ganzheitsforschung* 1 (2004): 31–47; Hans Thomas Hakl, "Anmerkungen des Autors Dr. H.T. Hakl [zur Rezension von Friedrich Niewöhner]," *Gnostika. Zeitschrift für Wissenschaft & Esoterik* 6 (20, 2002): 62–63; Hans Thomas Hakl, "Plauderei über C.G. Jung und die Eranos-Tagungen," in Psychologischer Club, *Jahresbericht* (2002–2003), pp. 19–20; Hans Thomas Hakl, Review of: Riccardo Bernardini, "Da Monte Verità a Eranos. Elementi per lo studio della psiche e della complessità umana" [M.A. diss., Turin University, 2003], *Gnostika. Zeitschrift für Wissenschaft & Esoterik* 8 (26, 2004): 4–22; Hans Thomas Hakl, Review of: Barone, Riedl, and Tischel, *Pioniere, Poeten, Professoren*, *Aries* 5 (2, 2005): 284–87; Hans Thomas Hakl, Review of: Riccardo Bernardini, "Carl Gustav Jung a Eranos. Il contributo junghiano al Circolo di Eranos. Ideazione, contributi e iniziative dal 1933 al 1952" [Ph.D. diss., University of Bologna, 2010], *Gnostika. Wissenschaft. Esoterikforschung. Lebenswelt* 14 (44, 2010): 10–11; Hans Thomas Hakl, "Prefazione," in Bernardini, *Jung a Eranos*, pp. 19–20. For a bibliography of the author up-dated to 2007, see Hans Thomas Hakl, *"Die wahre Magie ist ein Akt der Liebe." 3 Aufsätze und Bibliographie von Hans Thomas Hakl zum 60. Geburtstag* (Sinzheim: AAGW, 2007). A forthcoming, miscellaneous volume, now in preparation, will be dedicated to Hakl's library in Graz: Hans Thomas Hakl, ed., *Octagon—The Quest For Wholeness Mirrored in a Library*

Dedicated to Religious Studies, Philosophy, and Esotericism in Particular (Gaggenau: scientia nova, 2015–2016).

41. Hakl, *Eranos*, p. 1. The new German edition: Hans Thomas Hakl, *Eranos: Nabel der Welt. Glied der goldenen Kette. Die alternative Geistesgeschichte* (Bretten: Scientia nova-Neue Wissenschaft, 2015), pp. 16–17.

42. Robert Hinshaw, "Walking in the Footsteps of Eranos. Introduction," in L. Cowan, ed., *Barcelona 2004, Edges of Experience: Memory and Emergence, Proceedings of the Sixteenth International Congress for Analytical Psychology* (Einsiedeln: Daimon, 2006), pp. 93–98.

43. Paul Kugler, "Eranos and Jungian Psychology: A History in Images," in Cowan, *Barcelona 2004*, pp. 99–114. (Rpt. as: "Eranos and Jungian Psychology: A Photographic History," in C. Downing, eds., *Disturbances in the Field—Essays in Honor of David L. Miller* (New Orleans, LA: Spring Journal, Inc., 2006), pp. 69–112.)

44. Turin, October 19–November 9, 2007. A previous exhibition was set up in 2006 in Ascona, with the title, "Eranos—Images of a Mythical Journey into Our Times" (Eranos Foundation, Fondazione Monte Verità, Isole di Brissago, Museo Comunale d'Arte Moderna, Museo Epper, Ascona and Brissago Islands, June 6–September 2, 2006). A third exhibition, entitled, "Margarethe Fellerer. Photographer," was set up in Ascona in 2012 (Museo Epper, Ascona, March 31–May 28, 2012).

45. Gian Piero Quaglino, Augusto Romano, and Riccardo Bernardini, eds., *Carl Gustav Jung a Eranos 1933-1952* (Turin: Antigone, 2007).

46. See, in particular, Giovanni Sorge, "Love as Devotion. Olga Fröbe-Kapteyn's Relationship with Eranos and Jungian Psychology," *Eranos-Jahrbuch* 70 (2009–2010–2011): 388–434.

47. Sonu Shamdasani, *Jung and the Making of Modern Psychology—The Dream of a Science* (Cambridge: Press Syndicate of the University of Cambridge, 2003), pp. 13ff.

48. Toni Wolff, "Einführung in die Grundlagen der Komplexen Psychologie," in Psychologischer Club, *Die kulturelle Bedeutung der komplexen Psychologie* (Berlin: Julius Springer, 1935). Rpt. in *Studien zu C.G. Jungs Psychologie* (Einsiedeln: Daimon, 2003), pp. 15ff.

49. The reasons regarding the prevalence of the expression, "analytical psychology," over "complex psychology" may likely be found

in the need for Jungian thought to differentiate itself from other schools of psychotherapy, in particular, Freud's psychoanalysis, as well as simply the difficulty in translating this term from German. (See, e.g., Carl Alfred Meier, *Die Empirie des Unbewußten. Lehrbuch der komplexen Psychologie C.G. Jungs* (Zürich: Daimon, 1968; 1994), pp. 11–12.) Shamdasani highlighted that, in the passage from the *Psychologische Abhandlungen* (*Psychological Treatises)*—a first and partial systematization of Jung's works in German—to the *Collected Works*, the expression, "complex psychology," was substituted thirteen times with "analytical psychology," or simply omitted (Shamdasani, *Jung and the Making of Modern Psychology*, p. 14, fn. 19).

    50. Eugene Taylor, *The Mystery of Personality—A History of Psychodynamics Theories*, Library of the History of Psychology Theories (Dordrecht/Heidelberg/London/New York, NY: Springer, 2009), p. 131.

    51. Sonu Shamdasani, *"Liber Novus*: The 'Red Book' of C.G. Jung," in Carl Gustav Jung, *The Red Book. Liber Novus*, Philemon Series (New York, NY/London: W. W. Norton Company, 2009), p. 219.

    52. Jean-François Six, *Louis Massignon* (Paris: L'Herne, 1970); Giulio Basetti-Sani, *Louis Massignon (1883–1962). Christian Ecumenist, Prophet of Inter-Religious Reconciliation* (Chicago, IL: Franciscan Herald, 1974); Joachim Illies, *Das Geheimnis des Lebendigen. Leben und Werk des Biologen Adolf Portmann* (Munich: Kindler, 1976); for a critical examination of the biographical studies on Eliade, see Natale Spineto, *Mircea Eliade storico delle religioni. Con la corrispondenza inedita Mircea Eliade - Károly Kerényi* (Brescia: Morcelliana, 2006); Margarete Dierks, *Jakob Wilhelm Hauer 1881–1962. Leben, Werk, Wirkung* (Heidelberg: Lambert Schneider, 1986); Margaret H. Case, *Heinrich Zimmer— Coming into His Own* (Princeton, NJ: Princeton University Press, 1994); Jan van der Vegt, *A. Roland Holst. Biografie* (Baarn: de Prom, 2000); Mario Gandini, "Raffaele Pettazzoni negli anni 1949-1950. Materiali per una biografia," *Strada maestra* 60 (2006): 19–237; Grazia Marchianò, *Elémire Zolla. Il conoscitore di segreti. Una biografia intellettuale* (Venice: Marsilio, 2012); Carlo Zanda, *Un bel posticino. La Spoon River di Hermann Hesse* (Milan: Marcos y Marcos, 2012); Dick Russell, *The Life and Ideas of James Hillman—The Making of a Psychologist* (New York, NY: Skyhorse, 2013).

53. On the situation of the biographical studies on Jung, including Barbara Hannah's *Jung. His Life and Work. A Biographical Memoir* (1976), Paul Stern's *C. G. Jung. The Haunted Prophet* (1976), Vincent Brome's *Jung. Man and Myth* (1978), Gerhard Wehr's *Jung. A Biography* (1983), Frank McLynn's *Carl Gustav Jung* (1996), Ronald Hayman's *A Life of Jung* (1999), and, more recently, Deirdre Bair's *Jung. A Biography* (2003), see Sonu Shamdasani, *Jung Stripped Bare: By His Biographers, Even* (London: Karnac, 2005).

54. Kurt Wolff, *Briefwechsel eines Verlegers 1911–1963,* eds. Bernhard Zeller and Ellen Otten (Frankfurt am Main: H. Scheffler, 1966); Carl Gustav Jung, *Letters: 1906–1961*, eds. G. Adler and A. Jaffé, Bollingen Series XCV:1–2 (Princeton, NJ: Princeton University Press, 1973–1975, 2 volumes); Maya Rauch and Dorothee Mußgnug, "Briefe aus dem Exil: Aus der Korrespondenz von Heinrich Zimmer 1939–1943," *Heidelberger Jahrbücher* 35 (1991): 219–43; *Mircea Eliade și corespondenții săi*, ed. M. Handoca (Bucharest: Minerva, 1993–2007, 5 volumes); Gershom Scholem, *Briefe, 1914–1982*, ed. I. Shedletzky and T. Sparr (Munich: Beck, 1994–1999, 3 volumes); Gershom Scholem, *A Life in Letters, 1914–1982*, ed. and trans. A. D. Skinner (Cambridge, MA: Harvard University Press, 2002); Walter Thys, *André Jolles (1874–1946), "Gebildeter Vagant." Brieven en documenten* Amsterdam/Leipzig: Amsterdam University Press/Leipziger Universität GmbH, 2000).

55. Natale Spineto, ed., *Mircea Eliade–Raffaele Pettazzoni. L'histoire des religions a-t-elle un sens? Correspondance 1926–1959* (Paris: Éditions du Cerf, 1994); William Schoenl, *C. G. Jung—His Friendships with Mary Mellon and J. B. Priestley* (Wilmette, IL: Chiron, 1998); Carl Gustav Jung and Wolfgang Pauli, *Atom and Archetype—The Pauli/Jung Letters, 1932–1958*, ed. C. A. Meier (London/New York, NY: Routledge, London, 2001); Carl Gustav Jung and Ernst Bernhard, *Lettere tra Ernst Bernhard e Carl Gustav Jung. 1934/1959*, ed. G. Sorge (Milan: La biblioteca di Vivarium, 2001); Georg Dörr, "Archetipo e storia ovvero Monaco-Ascona: prossimità tipologica e umana (con lettere di Olga Fröbe a Ludwig Derleth)," in E. Barone, A. Fabris, and F. Monceri, *Eranos. Monte Verità. Ascona*, pp. 105–21; Natale Spineto, *Mircea Eliade storico delle religioni. Con la corrispondenza inedita Mircea Eliade-Károly Kerényi*; Riccardo Bernardini, Review of: Spineto, *Mircea*

Eliade storico delle religioni, Annali di Storia dell'Esegesi 23 (2, 2006): 569–73; Hermann Hesse and Josef Bernhard Lang, *"Die dunkle und wilde Seite der Seele." Briefwechsel von Hermann Hesse mit seinem Psychoanalytiker Josef Bernhard Lang. 1916–1944,* ed. T. Feitknecht (Frankfurt am Main: Suhrkamp, 2006); Carl Gustav Jung and Victor White, *The Jung–White Letters,* eds. A. C. Lammers and A. Cunningham (London/New York, NY: Philemon Series, Routledge, 2007); Riccardo Bernardini, "Hillman a Eranos," *Anima* (2012): 47–93; Riccardo Bernardini, "La corrispondenza Carl Gustav Jung-Henry Corbin," *Historia religionum* 5 (2013): 93–108; Alessandro Stavru, "Eine wesentliche Gemeinsamkeit." Il sodalizio intellettuale tra Walter F. Otto e Karl Kerényi alla luce del carteggio (1940–1958) conservato presso il 'Deutsches Literaturarchiv'," *Historia religionum* 5 (2013): 63–74; Riccardo Nanini, "Von Ihnen aber erwarte ich die eigene Sicht..." Il carteggio Martin Buber-Gerardus van der Leeuw (1938–1950): un Sammelwerk e un manoscritto da tagliare," *Historia religionum* 5 (2013): 49–61; Carl Gustav Jung and Erich Neumann, *Analytical Psychology in Exile: The Correspondence of C. G. Jung and Erich Neumann,* ed. M. Liebscher (Princeton, NJ: Princeton University Press, 2015).

56. Carl Gustav Jung, Jakob Wihelm Hauer, Heinrich Zimmer, and Mircea Eliade, *Jung and the Indologists—Jung's Correspondences with Wihelm Hauer, Heinrich Zimmer, and Mircea Eliade,* ed. G. Sorge (Philemon Series, forthcoming).

57. Carl Gustav Jung, *The Solar Myths and Opicinus de Canistris—Notes of the Seminar given at Eranos in 1943,* eds. R. Bernardini, G. P. Quaglino, and A. Romano, forewords by T. Fischer and F. Merlini, with a contribution by N. Kluger-Nash (Einsiedeln: Daimon, 2015). The Italian edition: *I miti solari e Opicino de Canistris. Appunti del Seminario tenuto a Eranos nel 1943* (Bergamo: Moretti&Vitali, 2014).

58. In particular, excerpts from the following writings appear there: Gian Piero Quaglino, Augusto Romano, and Riccardo Bernardini, "Un seminario ritrovato di Jung su Opicino de Canistris," in Quaglino, Romano, and Bernardini, *Carl Gustav Jung a Eranos 1933-1952,* pp. 161–97; Riccardo Bernardini, "Una lettura junghiana dell'amore nell'arte di Opicino de Canistris," *Psicologi a confronto* 3 (2, 2009): 24–42; Gian Piero Quaglino, Augusto Romano, and Riccardo Bernardini, "Opicinus de Canistris: some notes from Jung's unpublished Eranos Seminar on the medieval *Codex Palatinus Latinus*

1993," *Journal of Analytical Psychology* 55 (3, 2010): 398–422; Gian Piero Quaglino and Augusto Romano, *Nel giardino di Jung* (Milan: Raffaello Cortina, 2010), pp. 106–10; Bernardini, *Jung a Eranos,* pp. 213–17; Gian Piero Quaglino, Augusto Romano, and Riccardo Bernardini, "A visit paid to Jung by Alwine von Keller," *Journal of Analytical Psychology* 56 (2, 2011): 232–54; Bernardini, "Hillman a Eranos," p. 64; Riccardo Bernardini, "*Amor carnalis, amor spiritualis.* Notes on Jung's Treatment of Love from an Eranos Seminar on Opicinus de Canistris," *Eranos Yearbook* 70 (2009–2010–2011): 339–71; Riccardo Bernardini, "Prospettive di ricerca storica in psicologia analitica," *Tempo d'analisi. Paradigmi junghiani comparati* 1 (0, 2012): 151–75; Riccardo Bernardini, Gian Piero Quaglino, and Augusto Romano, "Preface to Opicinus de Canistris: concluding lecture by C. G. Jung, Eranos, Ascona, 1943 and Further studies on Jung's Eranos seminar on Opicinus de Canistris," *Journal of Analytical Psychology* 58 (2, 2013): 162; Carl Gustav Jung, "Opicinus de Canistris: Concluding Lecture by C. G. Jung, Eranos, Ascona, 1943. Notes taken [probably] by Rivkah Schärf Kluger," *Journal of Analytical Psychology* 58 (2, 2013): 163–83; Riccardo Bernardini, Gian Piero Quaglino, and Augusto Romano, "Further studies on Jung's Eranos Seminar on Opicinus de Canistris," *Journal of Analytical Psychology* 58 (2, 2013): 184–99.

59. Aniela Jaffé, "C. G. Jung and the Eranos Conferences," *Spring* (1977): 202.

60. Olga Fröbe-Kapteyn, "Gleichnisse" (Ascona: Eranos Foundation Archives, unpublished typescript, 1933), quoted in Hakl, *Eranos,* p. 33.

61. Olga Fröbe-Kapteyn, "An Attempt at Definition and Description of Eranos and of the *Eranos-Jahrbücher*" (Ascona: Eranos Foundation Archives, unpublished typescript, 1953), p. 1.

62. See Riccardo Bernardini, "Jung nel giardino di Eranos: il paesaggio dell'analisi," in F. Vigna, ed., *L'Ombra del flâneur. Scritti in onore di Augusto Romano* (Bergamo: Moretti&Vitali, 2014), pp. 35–46.

63. Olga Fröbe-Kapteyn, "Eranos Vortrag" (Ascona: Eranos Foundation Archives, unpublished typescript, 1939), p. 1.

64. Bernardini, *Jung a Eranos,* p. 101.

65. In a letter to Jung dated March 11, 1960, Olga Fröbe-Kapteyn wrote: "I have never been through an analysis but have just followed

all your seminars (as the books were mostly too difficult for me), and I found the vividness of the seminars more meaningful to me." (Quoted in Hakl, *Eranos*, p. 300.)

66. Ritsema, *L'Œuvre d'Eranos*, p. 83. See also Riccardo Bernardini, "'Picnic' del sogno: una matrice di sogno sociale a Eranos," *Anamorphosis* 4 (4, 2006): 71, fn. 4; Maurizio Gasseau and Riccardo Bernardini, "Il sogno: prospettive di Eranos," in M. Gasseau and R. Bernardini, eds., *Il sogno. Dalla psicologia analitica allo psicodramma junghiano* (Milan: FrancoAngeli, 2009), p. 21; Christa Robinson, "Eranos: A Place, an Encounter, a Story," *Spring* 86 (2011): 169; Quaglino, Romano, and Bernardini, "A visit paid to Jung," p. 237; Bernardini, *Jung a Eranos*, pp. 215–16, fn. 207; Riccardo Bernardini, "The Secret of Eranos," *Spring* 88 (2013): 336 and 339; Riccardo Bernardini, Gian Piero Quaglino, and Augusto Romano, "Introduction. Carl Gustav Jung's Eranos Seminar on *The Solar Myths and Opicinus de Canistris*," in Jung, *The Solar Myths*, p. 29; Riccardo Bernardini, Gian Piero Quaglino, and Augusto Romano, "Appendix II. Alwine von Keller (1878–1965). A Biographical Memoir," in Jung, *The Solar Myths*, p. 131; and Riccardo Bernardini, "In analisi con Jung: i diari di Emma von Pelet," *Rivista di Psicologia Analitica* 90 (2015; forthcoming).

67. Ritsema, *L'Œuvre d'Eranos*, p. 83.

68. *Ibid.*, p. 59.

69. Alwina von Keller, *My Story* (Madras: ADART, undated), "Introduction." See also Ritsema, *L'Œuvre d'Eranos*, p. 83; Robinson, "Eranos," p. 169; Bernardini, "'Picnic' del sogno," p. 71, fn. 4; Bernardini and Gasseau, "Il sogno," pp. 20–21; Quaglino, Romano, and Bernardini, "A visit paid to Jung," p. 236; Bernardini, *Jung a Eranos*, pp. 215–16, fn. 207; Bernardini, "The Secret of Eranos," p. 336; Quaglino, Romano, and Bernardini, "Introduction. Carl Gustav Jung's Eranos Seminar on *The Solar Myths and Opicinus de Canistris*," p. 33; and Quaglino, Romano, and Bernardini, "Appendix II. Alwine von Keller (1878–1965). A Biographical Memoir," pp. 129–39.

70. Von Keller, *My Story*, "Introduction."

71. Shamdasani, "*Liber Novus*: The 'Red Book' of C.G. Jung," p. 220.

I.

THE ERANOS PHENOMENON

Freunde sammeln an gepflegter Stätte,
und durch die Freunde den Menschen einen
Weg bereiten.

Confucius

Eranos zur 25. Tagung
Seattle, April 1957

Hellmut Wilhelm

A dedication written by the Sinologist, Hellmut Wilhelm (quoting Confucius), on the occasion of the 25th anniversary of the Eranos Conferences, in 1957, which reads: "Friends gather at a well-tended place, and together prepare a way for humanity."

OLGA FRÖBE-KAPTEYN

Olga Frobe-Kapteyn was born on October 19, 1881 in London to Dutch parents from a culturally diverse background. She moved to Zurich in 1900, where she studied at the School of Applied Arts and then at the University of Zürich. In 1909, she married the orchestra conductor, Iwan Fröbe, with whom she lived in Berlin and then, from 1914, in Zürich. She became widow of Iwan Fröbe in 1915. In 1920, together with her daughter, Bettina Gertrude, she moved to the South of Switzerland and settled down in the charming Casa Gabriella (Gabriella House) in Ascona-Moscia, on the shores of Lake Maggiore. It was there that, during a long period of solitude, she familiarized herself with oriental philosophies, meditation, and depth psychology. In 1928, she built a lecture hall near her Casa Gabriella. It was called, Casa Eranos (Eranos House), and was used as "a place of encounter and experience," where Eastern and Western philosophies could meet. In 1933, Olga Fröbe-Kapteyn founded there the Eranos Conferences, which attracted some of the most influential scholars of the twentieth century. In the following years, she focused on further enriching the Conferences, which were becoming like a "ritual," a "dance," which started anew each year, but always with different "dancers." From the mid-1930s, initially at Carl Gustav Jung's request, Olga Fröbe-Kapteyn also travelled to European and American libraries—in London, Paris, Rome, Munich, Zürich, Athens, Stuttgart, Oxford, Crete, Berlin, Bonn, Trier, and New York, among others—in order to acquire symbolical images. She thus formed a rich archive, which became very important for the research of many scholars. The Eranos Archive for Research in Symbolism is now part of the collections of the Warburg Institute (University of London). Olga Fröbe-Kapteyn edited the first thirty *Eranos Yearbooks* (1933–1961) and dedicated all her life to nurture her cultural enterprise. She passed away in Casa Gabriella on April 25, 1962.

Olga Fröbe-Kapteyn's "The Psychological Background of Eranos," presented in the following pages for the first time, was originally written in English in September 1939. It was presented as a lecture at the Analytical Psychology Club in New York on October 27, 1939. The paper was delivered at the occasion of the opening of an exhibition of the Eranos Archive for Research in Symbolism on the "Great Mother," containing about three hundred images, which Olga Fröbe-Kapteyn organized on Hildegard Nagel's invitation and with Mary and Paul Mellon's financial support. The exhibition and the lecture represented the "debut" of Eranos in the United States.

The Psychological Background
of Eranos

OLGA FRÖBE-KAPTEYN

In speaking to you of Eranos, I am giving you a report of its work
since 1933, and my own observations and realizations concerning
its origin, the nature of the central or archetypal *idea* that energizes
it, and the way in which this *idea* has used individuals and a group for
its own ends.

Outwardly, it looks as if Eranos were a personal undertaking of
mine, a personal experiment. But behind the scenes, this impression
disappears and the true nature, value, and facts of the Eranos work stand
out as they really are. This changes the picture to a very great degree.
The only person in the Eranos group who has spent most of her
time behind the scenes is myself, and I have studied things from
that point of view as thoroughly as I could. I have, therefore, a story
to tell of an archetype that gripped me some twelve years ago, and
with which I was identified for a long time, as anyone has to be,
who carries through a piece of work of this kind. It is a story of archetypal
possession. This identification, or at least partial disidentification, was
essential or I should not be telling it.

Eranos has come into existence at a time when the collective
unconscious is peculiarly disturbed, and is breaking through all
over the world in religious, political, social, and other
manifestations. Historically and astrologically, we live in a
period of transition from one age to another—from one sign of
the Zodiac to another—from the sign of Fishes into that of
Aquarius, and this constellation causes all the upheavals in the world
today. No group or individual remains untouched by this
underground, dynamic movement of the whole archetypal realm.
Everywhere, groups and individuals are responding to it, mostly
quite unconsciously, and as a consequence there is chaos.

The background of Eranos is linked up with the entire collective unconscious, out of which the material handled at the conferences has emerged. Eranos represents the reaction of a group of scholars and of their audiences to a vital and powerful urge, which they all feel, but cannot yet define. They register the fact that something draws them into the Eranos work, something that is stronger than themselves—an irrational and magnetic force that is integrating the Eranos group from within, not without.

As I have seen this force at work for over ten years and come to understand how it works, I have given up any thought of making Eranos into an organization with a committee and a president and all the rules belonging to such outer organizations. If the central *idea* of Eranos is strong enough, and our attempts at keeping in line with it unwavering enough, then it will integrate and hold the group together without any outer organization. If not, the group will disintegrate, and rightly so. It is a first attempt at a new kind of group work, and it depends for the time being on my own realization of certain laws and facts that come under my observation in the work.

If we compare the subjects of each congress since 1933, it becomes clear that there is continuity among them. When we started in 1933 with the subject of Yoga and Meditation in East and West, no one, including myself, had any idea where that subject was going to lead us. And yet in that first conference the archetypal *idea* behind Eranos was clearly visible as the *Idea of the Quest,* the Way of Man, the Middle Way, or the Way of Individuation, and the methods of approach to that Way in East and West.

We had, and we have, no program. We have never made a plan of the ground that we intend to cover, nor a pattern to which we intend to keep. That Pattern exists somewhere beyond space and time, just as the pattern of an individual life is pre-existent to the birth of a human being. All we can do is to try and sense the Pattern by degrees, keeping our own intentions out of the picture. That, of course, is extremely difficult, as anyone knows who has ever tried to discover the pattern of his or her individual life in a psychological sense, and has learned that personal will is the greatest hindrance to that realization.

Eranos moves with the times. It is feeling its way along a current, which never flows in a straight line, but in a serpentine way. One can never see farther ahead than the next curve, and when one gets there it surprisingly turns in an opposite direction. By moving with the times, Eranos is able to reflect those human problems that today are demanding a solution. These problems are all rooted in religious experience, even those that seem to us most material, and it is therefore essential to provide those who seek answers or solutions with an adequate orientation in the field of comparative religion and the history of the great tides of culture through which humanity has passed. Without this background we can have no connection to religious experience of past ages or ability to understand ourselves and the deepest human problems of today.

Scientific research of the past fifty years has laid bare the entrance to a vast archive of human records, architectural and pictorial remains of ancient civilizations, and fragments of the scriptures of many peoples. It is a treasure-house of symbolic values, the extent of which cannot even be surmised. This research has built a bridge between our times and the past, between the man of today and man of past ages, and has made a relationship between these possible. Psychology, as interpreted by C. G. Jung, has discovered many sign-posts of the ancient Way of the Midst, and owes much to the work of archeologists, orientalists, and other specialists.

At the Eranos Meetings, an attempt is being made to present the fruits of specialist research in the various fields of archeology, comparative religion, theology, the history of art, ethnology, and others. The synthesis that results from the cooperation of research workers in all these departments will gradually build up a picture of past ages and of man's inner transformations.

This historical and comparative study of the records of man's quest, as it was understood and formulated in different cycles of civilization, brings much material to the surface that belonged to the esoteric doctrines of diverse races and peoples. Archeological discoveries have lately made many original texts available (Manichean, Gnostic, Babylonian, Syrian, and others), and a selection of the most important are presented at the Eranos meetings, usually by scholars who have either made the discoveries, or have worked over and translated them into modern languages. The scattered links of the Golden Chain, the *Catena Aurea*, of religious tradition are being collected in this way and its continuity restored.

The work of C. G. Jung, although never especially emphasized, represents the synthetic force at the heart of Eranos. It works, we might say, underground, invisibly, yet it holds the whole together and embodies the real significance of these meetings. It establishes a net of relationships between the different fields of research, between the speakers, and between all members of the conferences, whether they are aware of it or not.

Eranos is an international meeting place, a place where Eastern and Western Teaching of the science of the soul is studied and compared. It is the *first and only platform* that brings psychology, as represented by C. G. Jung, into direct contact with many other fields of scientific research and with the greatest specialists of Europe.

As the name Eranos indicates, all of these scholars gather around a chosen subject, and bring their special contributions. In ancient Greece, Eranos stood for a banquet to which the guests each brought their individual offering. This spirit of international collaboration is one of the outstanding features of these meetings. Nowhere in the Europe of today does this exist to the same extent.

At the last Eranos meeting in August, I think everyone felt how exceptional it was that scholars and students from Germany, France, England, Holland, and Switzerland should meet at Eranos in peace and harmony, whilst most of the European countries were waiting, armed to the teeth, for the signal of war! It often looks as if Eranos has created a magic circle, a *maṇḍala* in which the work can proceed in spite of the difficulties of the times. Within this circle, freedom of speech is possible, and I know that many who were present last August were profoundly touched by this experience, which took place, as Jung one day called it, "in the island beyond time." Many of these specialists consider Eranos as their meeting place, and have discovered that their work is related after all (quite a discovery for specialists!).

An integrating and synthetic force is working here in a collective form. The integration of the group is directed from the center of the circle, by the archetypal idea that is creating something in its own impersonal and irrational way and continuing that, which for ages, has sought to express. Once again, its pressure is intensified, once again, its magnetic force is attracting a group of human beings who lend themselves to this urge, and once again, the quest of the human soul is to be formulated as it has been so often through the centuries.

Might not therefore Eranos be compared to the Gnostic Schools of Mystery Teaching, to groups like the Essenes and others, to the schools of Plato and Pythagoras, to eastern schools of Yoga, which were all concerned with the sciences of the soul, with man's Quest, and with the extension of consciousness? Later, the alchemical groups continued this tradition, and today, psychology is gathering up all these threads and is but repeating the ancient teaching in a modern form.

The same archetypal idea is behind all these manifestations. Its projection into time necessarily adapts itself to the various ages in which it finds expression. It has always taken the form of an esoteric science, and it remains so today, with the difference being that its scientific aspect is stressed, and its relationship to other sciences is revealed. The mystery aspect, which is that of inner experience, is an individual realization and only valid for that man or woman who goes through the experience.

You will realize by what I have said concerning the archetypal background of Eranos, that the *same archetypal idea* is activating both C. G. Jung's teaching of individuation and the Eranos work. This explains Jung's close cooperation with Eranos in the last seven years. Many of the greatest scientific specialists of Europe have come into contact with the work of C. G. Jung for the first time at Eranos meetings or through its yearbooks. This is one of the most important aspects of Eranos. It means that Jung's teaching is entering into a relationship with many fields of research through the men and women who represent them. Their attitude towards their own work begins to change, as we note at the yearly meetings. They begin to feel that their respective departments of research, which once seemed isolated and absolutely specialized, are linked with others, including psychology, the youngest of the sciences.

They begin to feel that things *happen* to them at the Eranos meetings, things that do not happen elsewhere. They are moved, touched and wish to come back again. They feel that they *belong* to this group for some mysterious reason or other. (It often makes it very difficult for me as organizer, because nearly all the speakers want to come every year!). All this is, of course, registers, not only in the speakers, but in most of the audience. Those of us who have learned to examine what happens to us, see it most clearly. To us, the ten days of the conference are a period of intense psychological experience. We have an audience of about two hundred people. I think we can safely say that not one of these individuals remains unmoved. Why?

I have watched these things for many years, and I believe that the reason is the following. We have a group in which an archetype is working out its purpose. This means that those who partake in this work whether unconsciously or consciously, make contact with this archetype, and are as a consequence moved and shaken by the deeper life force of the archetypal world. Their depths are stirred, both by the archetypal material handled in the lectures, and by the invisible spirit of these meetings, a spirit that is simply abroad, that is present, that is almost a presence, and that is linked to those who speak and to those who listen. It is linked to the landscape and to the garden in which the lecture-hall stands. Nature plays a large role at these meetings, as do the elements of wind, water, sunshine, and an exceptionally fertile earth. No other conference takes place in such a setting. I have seen people come into this work for the first time, swept off their feet by the power of the experience, elated, even alarmed, filled by something greater than themselves. All of this gives us the great opportunity to study what happens in a group and discover which law binds it together and rules it, and the nature of the psychic realities involved.

In the sense that all outer happenings are a reflection, as in a mirror, of an inner reality, Eranos reflects something that already exists in the inner world. That something is using Eranos as the path of least resistance and is seeking to express itself and to function through the Eranos group. Originally, twelve years ago, it seized upon myself, and I became its servant. For the first few years I knew little more than that I was a pawn upon a chessboard used by an invisible player for its own ends. Year by year, I have seen more clearly, and have been able to disidentify up to a certain point, so that I can observe a good deal that happens to me and to others in this work. I still serve, but I *know* what I am serving. I still sit back and watch during the Eranos meetings, but I have begun to understand what I see. I watch the changes, the growth, and the transformations in the group.

The fact that we have no outer organization makes the whole enterprise very flexible. The central idea, therefore, is in no way hampered, and its energy is free to flow as it will, attracting those people who can further its ends. In so doing, it automatically casts out those who hinder the work, thus building up a group of workers according to a plan of its own. I have watched this building process for many years and accepted its unseen director and the law that governs its movements. The irrational plays a big part in this method of organization and often looks irresponsible. Yet responsibility is merely shifted to another level, a more powerful reality than any personal mode of action could ever be.

I have found that we must stay aligned with that reality and that I must watch the signs very carefully so as not to diverge from it. Any personal intent, plan, or purpose has had to be given up. This excludes the personal will entirely and means complete submission to the greater, impersonal Will. We all know what that implies, even whilst we are unable to continually comply with it. It means that here the problem of Self comes in—not just the individual Self, but also the Self of a group. Organization then becomes a living reality and a constant readjustment to the direction of the undercurrent. This requires close attention to the signs and happenings in the outer world. I doubt whether any scientific group in the world except Eranos is managed along these lines.

Now, all this talk about an archetype may seem too much of a concretization to you. But remember that we are not handling a fantasy or a dream that is beyond space and time, but a very tangible reality *within* space and time. Eranos is the incorporation or incarnation of the archetype. It is the body of an idea. When an archetype breaks through into our world, it has to *take shape*, that is, embody, and through this shape, work out its purpose. All art proves this, and a new study of art from this standpoint will be the task of the next generation.

In closing I want to mention an aspect of Eranos that is beginning to become visible and tangible, but which perhaps only a few of us have grasped. In the last few years a group of quite young people has been forming within the bigger group, and it is clear to me that they are the nucleus of the young generation within the Eranos work that will have to carry on the work, and for whom we are actually preparing the way. They are our link with future.

For some years at the Polytechnical School in Zürich, Professor Jung has been conducting a seminar for students. His lectures to them last term were amongst the most important he has ever given. Quite evidently he too senses the response in the youth of today, and feels most deeply the necessity of contacting the young generation.

At the Eranos meetings I personally appreciate the collaboration of young students very greatly. Soon, in years to come, that small group will have grown, and will have become a vital organ in the Eranos organism. To that young man or woman, who may in ten years time be ready to step into my place to take over the task of organizing Eranos work, this talk is dedicated.

Ascona, September 1939

FABIO MERLINI

F abio Merlini is Regional Director of the Swiss Federal Institute for Vocational Education and Training (SFIVET), Lugano, Switzerland, and serves as the President of the Eranos Foundation. In 1998, Merlini was nominated *privat-docent* at the Université de Lausanne, Switzerland, where he taught Philosophy of Culture. Subsequently, from 1999 to 2003, he taught Systemic Philosophy and was appointed professor of Epistemology of the Human Sciences at the Université de Lausanne. In 2003, he was nominated adjunct professor of Communication Ethics at the Università degli Studi dell'Insubria in Varese, Italy, where he taught until 2011. From 1996 to 2000, Merlini co-directed the Groupe de Recherche sur l'Ontologie de l'Histoire at the Husserl Archives of the École Normale Supérieure, Paris. His publications include *Après la fin de l'histoire* (1998), *Historicité et spatialité* (2001), *Une histoire de l'avenir* (2004), *La comunicazione interrotta. Etica e politica nel tempo della "rete"* (2004), *L'efficienza insignificante. Saggio sul disorientamento* (2009; translated into French as *L'époque de la performance insignifiante. Réflexions sur la vie désorientée*, 2011), and *Schizotopies. Essai sur l'espace de la mobilisation* (2013). Merlini served as editor of *Nuove tecnologie e nuove sensibilità. Comunicazione, identità, formazione* (2005), *Identità e alterità. Tredici esercizi di comprensione* (co-edited with Elena Boldrini, 2006), and *Per una cultura della formazione al lavoro. Studi e analisi sulla crisi dell'identità professionale* (co-edited with Lorenzo Bonoli, 2010). Merlini is co-author of the *Cahier de l'Herne* dedicated to Friedrich Nietzsche on the 100th anniversary of his death (2000) and of *La philosophie au risque de la promesse* (2004).

Eranos: A Space and a Time for Thought

FABIO MERLINI

Introduction

I do not think I am wrong to say that those of us who have devoted ourselves to Eranos find it very gratifying that our institution has remained prestigious and long-lived, despite financial and other problems encountered over the years, for over eighty years.

Eranos is an extraordinary initiative, whose central purpose has been to provide time and space for *thinking*, a kind of contemplation and discussion that reach beyond disciplinary boundaries and academic strictures. This was no easy task given the date of Eranos' founding— 1933. Considering the political climate and the limited tools available at that time, one can easily imagine the challenges faced by the first conference organizers. Despite the hurdles, Eranos was able to establish itself as a pioneer in interdisciplinary dialogue. Its contributions to the cultural history of the 20th century are widely recognized by leading thinkers around the world and continue to this day.

The kind of thinking supported at the Ascona meetings is not the self-referential and sterile practice so often found in today's institutions charged with upholding "excellence" (a stylish term used more often as a claim rather than any real achievement). In contrast, "Eranos thinking" focuses on creating new approaches to critical questions, drawing from diverse geographies and disciplines. Such new thinking holds the possibility of exceeding the sum of its parts, which include knowledge from a variety of disciplines: psychology, philosophy, anthropology, theology, as well as natural sciences. This interdisciplinary lens has brought fresh perspectives to questions at hand far more readily than could a single discipline. There are several reasons for this advantage.

While terminology and concepts shared among colleagues within a discipline facilitates communication and exchange, there is a risk that taking shortcuts will overlook key, problematic connections, for which there is not yet, nor ever will be, total clarity. Such familiarity promotes taking assumptions for granted and circumventing details that might ought to be focal topics. Within the comfort of one's discipline, it is easy to revert to the commonplace book of a branch of research. On the other hand, when seeking to communicate and exchange meaningfully with colleagues from other disciplines, one is forced to abandon conceptual and linguistic shortcuts, informalities, and other tricks of the trade.

Interdisciplinary communication requires clarity of mind and meaning, for thoughts and ideas must be understandable beyond the idiolect of one's own scientific community. Even before articulation, the relevance of an issue outside one's own discipline requires an evaluation that entails a sorting out of "research questions." Often a topic is pressing in one field, yet completely irrelevant in another. Academia is full of such questions, which is not to say that they do not have their place. Many discipline-bound questions lead to great advancements in science and technology. Specialization is necessary and, today, inevitable, along with the scientific profiles that specialization fleshes out. Nevertheless, there are quite a few cases where the excessively unilateral nature of a theory or idea hinders objectivity and the establishment of sound theory. When routinized, this practice can engender disciplinary insularity that allows these issues to proliferate with no external scrutiny. Absent some sort of intellectual proctoring, specialization can become disconnected from the broader academic community. In so doing, we risk losing grounding in the "world of life," the *Lebenswelt*, as Husserl put it. Specialized knowledge is most productive and lasting when set in the context of a larger epistemic body. In this respect, the medical field is paradigmatic. The push toward increased specialization decreases the capacity to understand how the total organism functions, how its physical and psychic complexity is articulated, and how it relates to environment and society. In many cases, research ends up spinning its wheels, making little progress and consuming huge financial resources.

But returning to the first point, namely, the need to make ourselves understood by people who do not share the idiolect of our particular discipline: by making this effort, our reflections become more pertinent, because they are held up for evaluation by a community different from our own. We open ourselves up to face others and thereby can take advantage of new perspectives and hence, new links to other topics in other disciplines. This happened regularly during the Eranos Conferences.

The first president of the Eranos Foundation, Adolf Portmann (1897–1982), spoke about the need for biology to open itself to a "broader horizon" in his genial book on the morphology of animals (1960).[1] Portmann was a Professor of Biology and Zoology and, later, Chancellor at the University of Basel. In 1976, he was awarded the prestigious Humboldt Gesellschaft gold medal. This interdisciplinary perspective was exactly what Portmann strove to cultivate in his own studies, although he was fully aware of the risks he was taking. Much of academia is quite comfortable to stay within disciplinary bounds and is often hostile to those who venture outside. There are consequences to straying from the fold. It is an excellent, and I would argue, essential exercise to never stop questioning ourselves about our assumptions and to continue searching for the "new" in dialogue with other disciplines. The important questions are those that shed new light on a given field of study and simultaneously extend its reach. This is where time and space enter the scene.

In their original form, the Eranos Conferences offered ideal conditions for in-depth conversation. Unfortunately, this model is now almost extinct. Although there is wonderful historical documentation, it is nonetheless not easy today to imagine the full meaning of being immersed in such extended discourse. The conferences lasted up to ten days. Everything was planned to stimulate conversations that were sensitive and that galvanized the attention, perceptions, and deeper reflections of participants. The meetings were held in a place of great beauty and designed to minimize distractions and foster continuity, all to facilitate thorough examination of conference themes. Participants included those with impeccable scholarship and reputations, individuals who were ready to listen, learn, and engage, enhanced by these interactions and exchanges. Above all, the participants were happy to give time to each other. They held back from obsessive habits of giving immediate feedback, showing over-concern for tidiness of intellectual output, and media success. In short, they refrained from the very modes of activity that rule the world of knowledge these days.

I would like to add something else about space. Eranos exemplifies what it means to cherish a shared context and a *caring* relationship with the environment. We modern humans tend to neglect the space, the *where*, that we occupy alongside nature, cities, and public resources. In failing to do so, we unwittingly neglect ourselves too, even when convinced, as we are wont to claim loudly, that we are living at the height of our skills and mastery. I would like to take this opportunity to thank, together with the members of the Foundation Board, Gisela Binda, the real pillar of the Foundation space, and Riccardo Bernardini, for his exceptional historical and archival reconstruction of Eranos' history and its leading figures. Both were responsible for cultivating this kind of care and sensitivity to space.

There is something magical that flows out of Eranos where the lake is such a vivid presence. Participants and the public confirm this year after year. Eranos offers a special opening of space and a time for reflection, introspection, and the labor of thinking. You can understand why creation is always a chronotopical issue for writers and thinkers. The quality of the time and the quality of the space, the *where* and the *when*, are critical. As Flaubert teaches, the little rituals that each of us performs before writing illustrates why we need to set up an appropriate space and time.

There is a challenge to maintain this original model of Eranos. It depends not only on financial concerns, but also in addressing changes in how space and time are currently organized for maximizing knowledge production. We are all aware how the pressure to secure funding today influences the ways in which knowledge develops. Financial pressure is one reason we are seeing a re-formulation of the *libido sciendi* ("urge to know") that is increasingly fixated on immediate, tangible results. It is critical to be fully aware of this. Even though it thrived at a different time under different cultural conditions, the Eranos tradition provides a way to acknowledge the value of thinking and the importance of its freedom from other kinds of influences. Thinking as deep reflection plays an irreplaceable role in the development of authentic knowledge, one that can never be replaced by simple methods or techniques.

1. HISTORICAL REFERENCES

Eranos was a project of Olga-Fröbe Kapteyn (1881–1962) that came into being on the banks of Lake Maggiore at Ascona-Moscia. As its name reflects, Eranos (Gr. "banquet") was a place and occasion where contributions were liberally offered at the table by attendees. Its goals were to create a "place of encounter and experience" and a "free space for the spirit," where Eastern and Western thought could meet. Eranos modeled the annual international interdisciplinary Conference (*Tagung*) with traces of Italian Renaissance style, the intellectual circles of German Romanticism, and the great salons of Europe in the 1800's.

The name, "Eranos," was suggested by Rudolf Otto (1869–1937). He was an eminent historian of religion and author of several important studies of the phenomenological analysis of the religious experience. Richard Wilhelm (1873–1930), a German Sinologist whose work made a significant change in the academic interpretation of the religious experiences of non-European cultures, was another important influence. Of course, Swiss psychologist, Carl Gustav Jung (1875–1961) was decisive. Thanks to Jung, the Eranos Conferences provided considerable insights into the study of archetypes, a central feature of the psychic life, whose "archaic" and "primitive" aspects retained their features despite the evolutionary processes that have taken place.

Eranos began with an ambitious program of annual conferences held at Casa Eranos. Each conference lasted about ten days, typically during the second half of August. In the 1940s, the "formal" part of the conference was complemented by "informal" discussions, reserved for a smaller group of speakers and a few other guests, on the terrace of Casa Gabriella, the second building that is still owned by the Foundation. Every day, the group gathered around a large Round Table under two tall cedar trees facing the Lake Maggiore. A stone sculpture with the inscription, *genio loci ignoto* ("to the unknown genius of the place"), stood in the background.

Parallel with the development of conferences was the creation of an Archive for Research in Symbolism and an Institute. The Institute for Research in Symbolism took shape through a series of seminars and specialized publications. The Archive was intended to hold the countless photographic reproductions of images derived from Eastern and Western iconographic traditions: alchemy, folklore, mythology, and contemporary archetypal representations. The Eranos Archive served as an indispensable iconographic base for important studies, such as C. G. Jung's *Psychology and Alchemy* (1944), Mircea Eliade's *The Forge and the Crucible—The Origins and Structure of Alchemy* (1956), and Erich Neumann's *The Origins and History of Consciousness* (1954) and *The Great Mother—An Analysis of the Archetype* (1955). This unique and extraordinary material is now preserved at the Warburg Institute (University of London).

Riccardo Bernardini, to whom I owe these historical notes, traced the history of the Eranos Conferences in his book, *Jung at Eranos— The Complex Psychology Project*.[2] Based on this work, seven phases are identifiable, each having a different focus. The conferences of the first phase (1933–37) are characterized by a comparative phenomenological approach to Eastern and Western spiritual traditions, featuring topics such as *Yoga and Meditation in East and West*, *Eastern-Western Symbolism and Soul-Guidance*, and *The Shaping of the Redemption Idea in East and West*. The conferences of the second phase (1938–46) were increasingly influenced by Jung's work. These meetings brought the perspective of comparative phenomenology to individual archetypal topics, once again in Eastern and Western spiritual traditions. The proceedings coming out of those conferences comprise authentic thematic dossiers (e.g., *The Form and Cult of the Great Mother*, *The Symbolism of Rebirth*, *The Hermetic Principle*, *The Spirit*). The conferences of the third phase (1947–62) revolved around an ambitious program of cultural anthropology focused on the basis of the "inner man" (*inner Mensch*) later developed by Erich Neumann. These meetings featured topics such as *The Human Being and Rite*, *The Human Being and Time*, and *The Human Being and Energy*. Conferences of the fourth phase (1963–71) explored cultural anthropology more deeply through examination of the phases and transformations of life with topics such as *The Polarity of Life*, *Sense and the Changes in the Image of Man*, and *The Stages of Life in the Creative Process*. Conferences of the fifth phase (1972–88) discussed symbolic hermeneutics and featured topics such as *Thought and Mythic Images*, *The Play of Gods and Men*, and *Material and Imaginal Bodies*. The sixth phase conferences (1989–2002) drew from diverse perspectives with the purpose of bringing archetypal psychology and the ancient Chinese oral text, the *I Ching*, onto the common ground of the Imaginal (e.g., *The Shadow of Perfection, Gateways to Identity, Chroniclers and Shamans*, and *The Magic of the Tortoise*). Seventh phase conferences (2006 to the present) have explored the relationship between the individual and society and sought to create a dialogue surrounding great issues that human cultures face, the problematic obstacles that thread contemporary cultures, and the knotty problems that grip the world today (e.g., *The Modernities of East and West, Perspectives on Violence and Aggression, About Fragility in the Contemporary World, On the Threshold—Disorientation and New Forms of Space, Money—Symbol, Enchantment, and Disenchantment, Care of the World and Care of the Self*, and *The Roots of Evil—Figures and Issues from the Abysses of Human Condition*).

Eranos has brought together some of the most influential cultural scholars of the 20th century. Besides C. G. Jung, the following scholars have met and held discussions with each other in houses of the Foundation: the psychologists, Gustav-Richard Heyer, Joseph Bernhard Lang, Erich Neumann, Frederik Buytendijk, Marie-Louise von Franz, Ira Progoff, James Hillman, Hayao Kawai, and Wolfgang Giegerich; the historians of religion, Raffaele Pettazzoni, Gerardus van der Leeuw, Friedrich Heiler, Joseph Campbell, Mircea Eliade, and Ernst Benz; the historians of Christianity, Ernesto Buonaiuti, Jean Daniélou, and Ulrich Mann; the scholars of Gnosis, Henri-Charles Puech and Gilles Quispel; the historians of the religions of the classical world, Walter Friedrich Otto and Károly Kerényi; the orientalists, Caroline Augusta Foley Rhys Davids, Jakob Wilhelm Hauer, Paul Masson-Oursel, Heinrich Zimmer, Erwin Rousselle, Giuseppe Tucci, Dariush Shayegan, and Detlef-Ingo Lauf; the Hebraists, Leo Baeck, Martin Buber, Erwin R. Goodenough, and Gershom Scholem; the scholars of Islam, Louis Massignon, Fritz Meier, Henry Corbin, and Toshihiko Izutsu; the Egyptologists, Georges Hermann Nagel, Charles Robert Cecil Augustine Allberry, and Erik Hornung; the Sinologists, Paul Pelliot and Hellmut Wilhelm; the scholar of Zen Buddhism, Daisetsu Teitarō Suzuki; the theologians, Paul Tillich, Louis Beirnaert, Martin Cyril D'Arcy, Hugo Rahner, Pierre-Jean de Menasce, Victor White, Heinz Westman, and David L. Miller; the anthropologists, Paul Radin, Edwin Oliver James, John Layard, Laurens van der Post, and Gilbert Durand; the ethnologists,

Theodor-Wilhelm Danzel, Wilhelm Koppers, Richard Thurnwald, and Jean Servier; the archeologists, Charles Virolleaud, Vera Christina Chute Collum, and Charles Picard; the philosophers, Helmuth Plessner, Karl Löwith, Chang Chung-yuan, Jean Brun, Pierre Hadot, and Jean-Jacques Wunenburger; the physicists, Erwin Schrödinger, Friedrich Dessauer, Hans Leisegang, Gerald Holton, Shmuel Sambursky, and Herbert Pietschmann; the electronic engineer, Max Knoll; the mathematicians, Andreas Speiser and Hermann Klaus Hugo Weyl; the art historians, Rudolf Bernoulli, Julius Baum, Carl Moritz von Cammerloher, and René Huyghe; the literary critics, Sir Herbert Edward Read, Kathleen Raine, and Graham Hough; the musicologists, Victor Zuckerkandl and Hildemarie Streich; the historians of esotericism, Antoine Faivre and Françoise Bonardel; the scholar of Chinese medicine, Manfred Porkert; and many other scholars along with them.

In 1952, Daniel Brody, the courageous first publisher of the *Eranos Yearbooks* (*Eranos-Jahrbücher*), hung a map of the world on the wall of the Rhein-Verlag publishing house in Zürich to mark the 20th anniversary of the editorial series. The map was marked with multicolor lines, each representing the place of origin of participants, and all converging at an almost invisible point—Ascona. The greatness of Eranos is encapsulated in this image: the convergence at the physical and conceptual summit of Eranos of unique personalities with vastly broad knowledge who engaged in face-to-face dialogue free from any academic or dogmatic agenda.

For a long time, Eranos was the sole venue for gathering experts and lay people who were inspired by different cultural and spiritual interests and unfettered by their fields of specialization. (This length of time alone is exceptional, considering today's hit-and-run cadence of conferences). At Eranos, people were free to discuss the results of their research. As the only European conference center to remain active during World War II, Eranos has made an extraordinary contribution to European intellectual history.

2. The Eranos Foundation, Yesterday and Today

At its founding, Eranos' activities were planned and coordinated by Olga Fröbe-Kapteyn. For the first twenty years, she was accompanied by the "Eranos Circle" (*Eranos-Kreis*) or "Eranos Community" (*Eranos-*

Gemeinschaft), a small group of scholars "of variable geometry," who were attracted by C. G. Jung. These individuals were responsible for suggesting names of potential conference speakers to Olga Fröbe-Kapteyn. The tradition (which continues today) was that successive conference topics were not dictated, but rather emerged organically at the end of the ongoing conference. The given topic was one that made the strongest points in the most significant arguments during the work sessions. At a certain point, a particular issue would be raised and would call out as a candidate for the following year's conference.

In the Spring of 1943, Olga Fröbe-Kapteyn transformed Eranos into a legally recognized foundation that could qualify for public and private funding. The Board of the first Eranos Foundation, which remained active until 1955, was composed of Adolf Portmann, Tadeus Reichstein (1897–1996; Professor at the Institute of Organic Chemistry, University of Basel and 1950 co-winner of the Nobel Prize in Physiology or Medicine for the discovery of cortisone), Hans Conrad Bänziger (1895–1956; a renowned Zürich psychiatrist), and Walter Keller-Staub (a well-known Zürich lawyer). Thanks to Jung's influence, the new foundation obtained the support of the Swiss Federal Institute of Technology (ETH), Zürich, from 1936 to 1956 and of the Pro Helvetia Foundation, which contributed financally from 1943. Once again, thanks to Jung, the Bollingen Foundation placed Eranos within its Program of Contributions to Institutions (General Humanities) beginning in 1947.

A second Eranos Foundation was established in August 1961. As stipulated in Olga Fröbe-Kapteyn's will, Adolf Portmann was nominated as its first president. When Olga Fröbe-Kapteyn passed away in 1962, the guidance of Eranos was inherited by Portmann, who was assisted by Rudolf Ritsema (1918–2006), a scholar of the *I Ching*. Alwine von Keller was a student of Jung's who lived at Eranos from 1937 to the early 1960s. The Alwine von Keller Foundation was established in her memory (1878–1965) by Emma Hélène von Pelet-Narbonne (1892–1967) shortly before her death. In March 1980, the Eranos Foundation and the Alwine von Keller Foundation merged, to become the Eranos and Alwine von Keller Foundation. After Ritsema stepped down, there were several successive presidents: Christa Robinson (1994 to 2001; analytical psychologist), Wanda Luban (2001 to 2002; psychotherapist), Maria Danioth (2002 to 2005; analytical psychologist), and John van Praag (2005 to 2009; classicist and businessman). In January 2008, the Foundation reverted to its original name, Eranos Foundation. The Board of the Eranos Foundation now includes representatives of the Government of the Canton of Ticino and of the Municipality of Ascona as well.

3. PRESENT ACTIVITIES AND FUTURE CHALLENGES

The goals of the current Foundation Board are to consolidate the international reach of the initiatives that it promotes; emphasize dialogue among scholars of different disciplines; open up attendance to a public that includes non-specialists as much as possible; and offer regular opportunities for the local community to meet and discuss various topics with eminent figures.

The Eranos Foundation activities center around three main events. The first is the traditional late-summer Eranos Conference whose specific purpose is to foster dialogue among a select group of scholars from diverse disciplines about a topic that is chosen from year to year. The second activity consists of the Eranos-Jung Lectures, a cycle of monthly lectures named in memory of the important role that Jung played during his twenty-year participation at Eranos. The third activity consists of the Eranos School seminars. These are one- or two-day residential encounters where a limited number of participants are given the chance to discuss psychological, philosophical, and historical issues. In so doing, the Eranos School seeks to provide a workshop for reflection and interaction. Additionally, the workshops are a place and space where knowledge that extends beyond special interests of sectors and disciplines intersects with experience. The aim is to deepen self-knowledge, without which there is no real educational growth. This is why we refer to this activity as a "school."

Increasingly, the Foundation's programs have become part of a network of international collaboration with universities, institutes, and other foundations, whose interests intersect with Eranos either in spirit or by sharing common authors and topics engaged at Ascona during the last century. Two collaborations deserve special mention. Pacifica Graduate Institute, Carpenteria, California, U.S.A., has been working with Eranos for the past ten years. The collaboration with Pacifica, in particular, has helped refine the Eranos School model. The Fetzer Institute, Kalamazoo, Michigan, U.S.A., is a second collaborating institution, which has generously contributed to the support of various Foundation activities. Joint academic programs are now also being developed with the University of Bergamo, the University of Florence, and the University of Pisa, Italy.

In addition to the Eranos events, the Foundation hosts other activities. For decades, Foundation buildings have provided lodging for encounters, events, specialized seminars, and retreat opportunities for people to study and conduct research. The historic Casa Gabriella library holds a wide range of books on psychology, history of religions, philosophy, Eastern studies, literature, and art history. The collection is now being expanded as part of an important initiative for restoration, preservation, and enhancement of the Foundation's archival and library heritage. Over the next few years the Foundation will commit itself to building a new building next to Casa Gabriella. This will guarantee an adequate, well-equipped, and bright space to host scholars and researchers interested in its archival holdings.

I would like to make one additional comment in regard to the Foundation's publishing activities. It has long been the custom that each speaker at Eranos donates the text of his or her talk in exchange for the hospitality that the Foundation provided. This has resulted in the collection of over seven hundred articles published in over seventy *Eranos Yearbooks*. This provides evidence of exceptional research work in the most diverse fields of knowledge, and the custom continues to this day.[3] Eranos has also inaugurated a series of books in Italian, the *Saggi di Eranos*, which collect, in the form of monographs, texts presented at Eranos as well as other studies that reflect originality and excellence of the work undertaken by the Foundation.[4] Moreover, there is a editorial series in English, the *Eranos Series*, where some contributions presented at Eranos also will be published.[5]

In addition to publications that relate to current cultural activities, the Eranos Foundation is supporting a program of specialized studies of its own history. For example, the recent publication of C. G. Jung's *The Solar Myths and Opicinus de Canistris—Notes of the Seminar given at Eranos in 1943* is the result of the successful synergy between the Eranos Foundation and the Foundation of the Works of C. G. Jung. The Eranos Foundation archives were essential in helping to retrieve records of the seminar using notes from Alwine von Keller. In addition, the Foundation made available to the editors substantial numbers of documents. Without this resource, it would not have been possible to reconstruct the historical context of Jung's seminar in its entirety.[6]

The publication of this book is part of a broader program of archival and cultural heritage enhancement. Several publications have already been issued: the catalogue, *Carl Gustav Jung at Eranos 1933–1952* (the testimony of a photographic exhibition of the same name curated and edited by Gian Piero Quaglino, Augusto Romano, and Riccardo Bernardini in 2007, marking the tenth anniversary of the Turin University Faculty of Psychology);[7] the book, *Jung at Eranos—The Complex Psychology Project* (published in Italian by Riccardo Bernardini in 2011, representing the first work dealing with Jung's involvement in the Eranos project and based on a systematic study of the Eranos archives);[8] and a critical edition of the brief correspondence between C. G. Jung and Henry Corbin (published in 2013).[9]

Three outstanding critical editions are among those currently being prepared: an edition of Olga Fröbe-Kapteyn's *Visions*; an edition of Emma von Pelet's *Analytic Diaries*, which includes the unpublished correspondence between Carl Gustav Jung and Emma von Pelet; and an edition of Alwine von Keller's *Pictures of the Unconscious*, which includes the unpublished correspondence between Jung and Alwine von Keller. Further studies have been published in various international journals, such as *The Journal of Analytical Psychology* and, above all, *Spring: A Journal of Archetype and Culture*, with which the Eranos Foundation is fruitfully collaborating. In recognition of this wonderful work, I would like to express my deepest gratitude to Nancy Cater for her trust and support. This ninety-second issue of *Spring Journal* is precious evidence of this cooperation.

CONCLUSIONS

I would like to emphasize what the Eranos Foundation has inherited from its history and, above all, what it means to go down the path blazed by the experiences of this kind of thought and endeavor. However, it is important not to give in to the temptation to turn this vital space into a museum limited to the past. Rather, this inheritance should be managed with good judgment. When the lessons, the styles of thought, and the means of knowledge production are at stake, judgment takes on a specific meaning: recognition that the present's claim on the past is just as legitimate as the past's claim on the present. There is a delicate balance between drawing from the lessons of the past and respecting present-day needs. We should not, therefore, fear that we are not *au courant*. Yet neither should we be unafraid that we are betraying our original model. In the first case, we should refrain from an arrogance that marginalizes "those who came later." In the second case, we should acknowledge that the present has a legitimacy that should absolutely not be sacrificed to some sort of monolithic past. The young Nietzsche wrote unequalled pages on this topic. Forgetfulness and simple repetition are gestures of equal sterility.

Two questions should be clear: to what urgent issues did the work at Eranos respond beginning in 1933, and what pressing needs of today should our current work be directed toward? Retaining respect for the spirit of an institution does not mean that we can freeze it for eventual thawing so it can be experienced as its former self. As the great Hegel taught in his masterpiece, spirit has a phenomenology. It is movement in itself. So, with respect to Eranos, we can apply the same. In other words, a history as glorious as that of Eranos cannot be cast in plaster. We must keep it moving. This is the only way that a "spirit of Eranos" can keep on living and bearing fruit. A present that cannot meet the past without humiliating or idealizing it is a present that is dead because it has no chance to open up to the future.

Eranos has been a wide-ranging attempt to understand the cultural and spiritual manifestations of human beings and their mysteries, quite conscious of the fact that, in the face of everything we know, human beings are still mysteries at their highest as well as their lowest points. In an inspired passage from his *Animal Forms and Patterns*, Adolf Portmann commented that people should find out what is within their grasp and how far their grasp extends. Only by finding this out can they foresee how great things hidden are.[10] Today this preoccupation with the mystery is still with us. It is rooted in the background of civilization's so-called crisis. In this crisis when people question their values, there is a tendency to feel disoriented, weak, and cut-off from social ties. This involves people in their relationship to themselves, the social world, and, equally, the natural world. These concerns increasingly justify our task at hand, the one that we have been striving to execute for the past eighty years. We have tried to confront the roots of the question of sense and its multiple manifestations inside and outside Western culture. We have endeavored to do this, summoning and gathering together various kinds of knowledge in an open and non-dogmatic dialogue among disciplines. Kant's famous three questions have been formative in the background of our dialogue: "What can I know?" "What can I do?" and "What may I hope?"

Even independent of the system to which Kant aspired, I think these three questions perfectly sum up our concern for a kind of knowledge that can bind together ethical-spiritual, anthropological, and theoretical perspectives. This is a potential that cannot be built *solo*, by one person. This is the very reason that the Eranos model still seems to be essential. Firstly, it is based on maintaining a conversation among multiple branches of knowledge wherein we are aware that there is always something that resists scientific hubris. Second, there is a coming together of knowledge of the world with care of the self. This is a remarkable lesson that comes down to us from Stoic thought.

For this reason, in light of the present crisis of civilization (that I alluded to as *toti se inserens mundi*, a "plunging yourself into the whole world"), I would like to entrust my conclusion to the lesson of the Stoics and the words of Seneca. Without this intersection between the inside and the outside—between the individual and the world—knowledge, even the most sophisticated knowledge, loses its meaning. As we see all too clearly today, this way of considering knowledge as power sooner or later turns into its opposite. It turns into a lack of power that, in spite of all the science and technology available, exposes us to forces over which we have no control. This is the real lesson that Eranos has tried to convey from its beginning, as relevant now as it was then.

NOTES

1. Adolf Portmann, *Die Tiergestalt* (Basel: F. Reinhardt, 1960).

2. Riccardo Bernardini, *Jung a Eranos. Il progetto della psicologia complessa* (Milan: FrancoAngeli, 2011).

3. The *Eranos Yearbooks* are now published by Daimon Verlag (Einsiedeln, Switzerland).

4. The *Saggi di Eranos* series is published by Rosenberg & Sellier (Turin, Italy). The books published or planned are the following: Maurizio Ferraris, *Realismo positivo* (2013), and Pietro Barcellona, *L'anima smarrita. La questione antropologica oggi* (2015).

5. The *Eranos Series* will be published by Spring Journal, Inc. (New Orleans, LA).

6. Carl Gustav Jung, *The Solar Myths and Opicinus de Canistris— Notes of the Seminar given at Eranos in 1943*, eds. R. Bernardini, G. P. Quaglino, and A. Romano (Einsiedeln: Daimon, 2015). The Italian edition: *I miti solari e Opicino de Canistris. Appunti del Seminario tenuto a Eranos nel 1943* (Bergamo: Moretti&Vitali, 2014).

7. Gian Piero Quaglino, Augusto Romano, and Riccardo Bernardini, eds., *Carl Gustav Jung a Eranos 1933-1952* (Turin: Antigone, 2007).

8. Bernardini, *Jung a Eranos.*

9. Riccardo Bernardini, "La corrispondenza Carl Gustav Jung-Henry Corbin," *Historia religionum* 5 (2013): 93–108.

10. Adolf Portmann, *Animal Forms and Patterns* (New York, NY: Schocken, 1963).

HANS THOMAS HAKL

Hans Thomas Hakl was born in Graz, Austria in 1947. He earned his J.D. degree in 1970. Hakl founded an international import-export company with an emphasis in the Far East, and was a partner in a Swiss esoteric publishing firm. Since 1990, he has focused exclusively on researching, writing, and publishing. In 1996, he founded *Gnostika*, a German academic-esoteric magazine where he now serves as co-editor. He has edited works by Julius Evola, Eliphas Lévi, Gérard Encausse ("Papus"), Maria De Naglowska, Hans Freimark, and others. He is also a contributor to the *Dictionary of Gnosis and Western Esotericism* (2003) and to the new edition of the *Encyclopedia of Religions* (2005). Hakl attended a series of conferences organized by the Associazione Amici di Eranos in Ascona between 1995 and 2000 and by the Verein zur Förderung der wissenschaftlichen Tagungen von Eranos in 2001 and 2002. His main work, *Der verborgene Geist von Eranos. Unbekannte Begegnungen von Wissenschaft und Esoterik. Eine alternative Geistesgeschichte des 20. Jahrhunderts* (2001), was dedicated to the Eranos phenomenon. The book was subsequently republished in English in a revised and expanded edition as *Eranos—An Alternative Intellectual History of the Twentieth Century* (2012). Among his other writings on Eranos are "Der verborgene Geist von Eranos," in *Gnostika* (2001), "Eranos im Spiegel der Geistesgeschichte des 20. Jahrhunderts," in *Archaeus* (2002), "Plauderei über C.G. Jung und die Eranos-Tagungen," in *Jahresbericht*, published by the Psychologischer Club (2002/2003), "Eranos im Spiegel der Geistesgeschichte des 20. Jahrhunderts," in *Zeitschrift für Ganzheitsforschung* (2004). He also prefaced Riccardo Bernardini's *Jung a Eranos. Il progetto della psicologia complessa* (2011).

Eranos: A Counter Current to the Common Intellectual History of the 20ᵀᴴ Century?

HANS THOMAS HAKL

To sufficiently explain in just a few pages a phenomenon like Eranos, would require a genius. Alas, a genius I am not. I can only give a modest overview of its more than eighty years of history and discuss some of the Conferences' formative ideas along with some of the best known participants. In so doing, I hope to outline some broad intellectual currents that have emerged since the inception of Eranos.

The idea of the Eranos Conferences could have only come alive at the time when it did. By the first part of the twentieth century, modern technical and scientific thinking was universally acknowledged to the point that it overshadowed other ways of perceiving the world. The perceptual and conceptual imbalance engendered a longing, *saudade,* for "deeper" religious, psychological, philosophical, metaphysical, and esoteric wisdom. Including these approaches and fields into scholarship was deemed necessary to even out what many intellectuals felt was a biased and inaccurate view of life. This division coincided geopolitically.

Historically, the East was associated with religion and metaphysics while the West was synonymous with modern analytic and scientific thought. This framing became a metaphor for two conflicting or, in some eyes, complementary worldviews. The flourishing pro-Oriental mood in Germany is described in rather hysterical terms by C. G. Jung in May, 1930: "The spirit of the East penetrates through all pores and reaches the most vulnerable places of Europe. It could be a dangerous infection, but it might be also a remedy."[1]

The tendency among certain intellectuals to look to the Orient in search of meaning is also reflected in contemporary literature of the time. One example is Hermann Hesse who saw the East as the epitome of religion in much the same way that the West represented reason and technology. Jung argued that Occultism had experienced an unparalleled renaissance and that people had become weary of scientific specialization and rational intellectualism. "They want to hear of a truth that does not restrict but expands, that does not obscure but illuminates, that does not flow over us and off us like water but rather penetrates into the very marrow of our bones."[2]

This twentieth-century quest for meaning is part of a much older tradition, the search for the so-called "new man" who can, it is hoped, be "created" given the right circumstances. In the Eranos circle, this was refered to as "New Humanism." The concept of the "new man" seems to have arisen in response to the ever-widening gap between human beings and the modern culture, which they themselves had created. This left essentially two possible solutions: either humans could "free" themselves by forsaking traditional emotional and religious ties for scientific achievements, or they could embrace their "true" emotional and spiritual needs and let go of science. The first way was viewed as "progressive," whereas the second was regarded as "reactionary."

A quote from biologist Adolf Portmann suggests how the Eranos Conferences were conceieved and what they sought to cultivate:

> The Eranos meetings have always aimed to serve the life that exists within the mesocosm [i.e., the intermediary spiritual world between the macrocosm and the microcosm]. Their exploration of archaic traditions of thought has not been for the sake of irrationality per se nor because of any fundamental opposition to the existence of rational attitudes. The reason for cultivating this archaic world view was because it offered a domain where a richer and purer form of harmony exists between rational and irrational experience, and because here the creative powers can bear forceful witness to the vastness of the inner, spiritual realms and to things that have the power to make us whole, things that we are in danger of losing—indeed which many people in the West have already lost sight of to an alarming extent ... Eranos is a grand, earnest game, which is played repeatedly. Each time the game resembles that of the previous year, yet every year the old form is filled with new content, giving us a glimpse of what a re-sanctification of life and the cosmos can

bestow on us and how it can bring us a sense of comforting shelter and vital well-being.[3]

However, to go further without first discussing Eranos' founder, Olga Fröbe-Kapteyn, is unthinkable. Even someone as skeptical as Gershom Scholem wrote in 1979, after three decades of participation at Eranos:

> When we, Adolf Portmann, Erich Neumann, Henry Corbin, Ernst Benz, Mircea Eliade, Karl Kerényi and many others—scholars of religion, psychologists, philosophers, physicists and biologists—were trying to play our part in Eranos, the figure of Olga Fröbe was crucial—she whom we always referred to among ourselves as "the Great Mother."[4]

Olga Kapteyn was born in London in 1881 of Dutch parents, Truus Muysken and Albertus Kapteyn. Nine years later, the family moved to Zürich, Switzerland. From 1906 to 1909, Olga was a student at the School of Applied Arts, Zürich University, where she attended lectures on art history. Already fluent in Dutch and English, she then learned German, French, and Italian. In 1909, she married Iwan Fröbe, a Croatian orchestra conductor of Austrian parentage, with whom she went to live in Germany. They had twin daughters. However, her married life was short, as her husband was killed in an air crash in 1915.

From 1915 to 1920, during and immediately after World War I, Olga returned to live in Zürich. There, she applied her artistic talents, but also became a daring equestrian and a successful skier. However, her main interest was in literature and arts. By the post-war period in Zürich, she had already formed a salon where people gathered and readings took place.

Prior to 1920, Olga and her father had taken a health cure at the Monte Verità Sanatorium above Ascona, which specialized in natural treatment. Olga stated that she never wanted to leave this beautiful place again and so took up residence for a time nearby in Porto Ronco. Shortly thereafter, her father decided to buy Villa Gabriella, which lay directly on the shore of Lake Maggiore at Ascona-Moscia. Olga moved in there permanently in 1920.

In 1927 her father died and left her a princely legacy. With this inherited wealth, she could now enter fully into the role to which she had long felt called, namely, as a hostess to artists, poets, and people of esoteric interests invited to her home. On this property, she was able to build the lecture room that was to play such a central role at Eranos. There were many artists and writers with whom she mingled, but Ludwig Derleth was probably the one who was most influential and who helped lay the foundation for the path she later took.

Ludwig Derleth was born in 1870 in Bavaria. After enrolling in a multi-faceted course of studies in Munich, Germany, he came into contact with the literary circle of Stefan George. Later in life, Derleth travelled to Rome and finally settled in the Tessin district of Switzerland where he died in 1948. Derleth professed an ascetic and militant Christianity in which Christ and Caesar were merged into the single figure of Christus Imperator. For decades, Derleth worked on his magnum opus, *Der fränkische Koran* (*The Franconian Koran*). Unfortunately, he did not live to see it printed in its entirety. Derleth was responsible for introducing Olga Fröbe to the mythology and mystery teachings of classical antiquity that were later to play such an important role at Eranos. All of Olga Fröbe's surviving letters to Derleth revolve around a single theme: physical, mental, and spiritual redemption from Derleth.

Among those in search of the "new man" were some of the inhabitants of Monte Verità in Ascona who had settled there at the turn of the last century. As early as 1889, the Locarno philosopher, Alfredo Pioda, along with the well-known Theosophists Constance Wachtmeister and Franz Hartmann, planned to establish a kind of international lay monastery on the hill above Ascona, which they were to name Monte Verità. Yet, it was only in the second decade of the twentieth century that anything resembling a true reformist colony was founded. It was there that the world-famous dancer, Rudolf von Laban, organized his multi-faceted "School for the Arts." A sanatorium was also built that served vegetarian food and provided arrangements for air- and sun-bathing. Guests included Theosophists, political revolutionaries, and others simply interested in spiritual renewal. Important visitors included Prince Kropotkin, Erich Mühsam, Otto Gross, August Bebel, and the *völkisch* painter, Fidus. Eventually, however, the colony's search for the "new man" brought offense to neighboring communities because of its practice of nudism and a liberal approach to romantic relationships.

Looking back at the various spiritual and intellectual influences that contributed to Eranos, it is clear that while Monte Verità was situated geographically closer, Darmstadt's Keyserling's School of Wisdom was much more important. It was most likely here that Olga Fröbe came to appreciate the kind of discussion forum that was later to characterize Eranos, one with an elevated, yet private and intimate atmosphere. It was no coincidence that some of the same themes and lecturers from the School of Wisdom were to be found at Eranos a decade later.

In the 1920s, Count Hermann Keyserling was known as a widely-travelled philosopher. At the opening ceremony of the School, Keyserling gave two lectures, one on the Indian and Chinese legacy, and the other on the wisdom of the classical and the modern world. These were themes destined to play a central role at Eranos.

By 1930, ten meetings or seminars had been held at the School. Lecturers included Leo Baeck, C. G. Jung, Gerardus van der Leeuw, and Erwin Rousselle, all of whom would reappear at Eranos. Other participants included prominent figures such as Thomas Mann, Alfred Adler, Leo Frobenius, and Rabindranath Tagore. It was at Darmstadt that Jung first met sinologist Richard Wilhelm who had been responsible for bringing the *I Ching* to the attention of the wider public. In all probability, it was at one of the School's meetings in 1930 that Olga Fröbe first met Jung.

During the 1920s, Olga Fröbe lived an extremely reclusive life, spending the majority of her time preoccupied with the study of Indian spiritual paths. But such a life was not congruent with her rather extroverted nature and at the close of the decade, she started seeking friendships with people who shared common interests. In 1928, she built the large conference room where the Eranos meetings would take place.

Beginnings

It was most likely that Olga Fröbe had contacts with members of the Ramakrishna movement and the Theosophical Society. She was said to have even been close to then-president of the Theosophical Society, Annie Besant. Certainly, one can discern a Theosophical influence on Olga Fröbe, but the question is this: to what extent did Theosophical ideas influence the concept of Eranos?

On August 3, 1930, Olga Fröbe co-organized with another esoteric teacher, Alice Bailey, a "School of Spiritual Research." Olga Fröbe gave the opening speech, describing the aims of the teaching, themes which would come to be reflected in the Eranos initiative:

> We represent no society, order or fraternity, no special creed or faith. Our purpose is to create a meeting point where those of every group and faith may gather for discussion and synthetic work along spiritual lines ... The paths of men diverge, according to race, temperament, mentality and tradition, but the goal is the same for all.[5]

She went on to speak of the need to create

> a meeting place for East and West ... If a spirit of synthesis could replace the spirit of competition, the world culture would be greatly heightened, wars would cease, and all problems of a political and social nature would be greatly simplified.

By this time, Olga Fröbe had been exposed to many different influences, but she still could not articulate the object of her innermost yearnings. She kept busy, sketching and painting pictures, probably hundreds of them, and wrote copiously. With the same spirit in which she had undertaken her summer school project, Olga Fröbe was determined to put her lecture room to good use by bringing together people engaged in some form of spiritual endeavor.

Olga Fröbe acknowledged that the name, "Eranos," had been suggested by religious scholar Rudolf Otto, whom she had visited in Marburg an der Lahn in November, 1932. With her characteristically credulous enthusiasm, Olga Fröbe perceived this first meeting with Otto as having been brought about by higher powers. In 1933, after an initial failure to include esoteric themes like theosophical topics, a decision was made to give the meetings an academic character. Despite the academic slant and the implicit analytical and scientific flavor that was certainly suggested by Jung, the theme of the first Conference was "Yoga and Meditation in East and West." Indologist Heinrich Zimmer from the University of Heidelberg, Germany, was the first scholar contacted. Zimmer quickly and enthusiastically accepted the invitation. Olga Fröbe also sent a letter of invitation to Jung, who initially declined, ostensibly because of her close connection to the Theosophical movement. However, after Olga Fröbe told him that she had received acceptances from various of his acquaintances and colleagues, Jung appears to have quickly agreed to attend and give a lecture.

Jung and Olga Fröbe actually possessed quite antagonistic personalities. Jung himself is reported to have been rather hard on her in the early years. However, Olga Fröbe always felt a deep connection to him. In any case, Jung became the "guiding spirit" of Eranos in the first decades of its existence. Every year, proposed speakers and the themes were discussed and approved by Jung. Eranos became a venue to present his ideas to a wider public that included not only Europe, but also the U.S. and Asia. Some of Jung's seminal ideas were introduced through Eranos lectures.

The first Eranos meeting took place in August of 1933 and lasted two weeks. There were more than two hundred participants. Typically, a speaker lectured for the entire morning, interrupted only by brief intermissions. During these breaks, the members of the audience strolled about in front of the house, seeking to speak with the various Conference celebrities. Lectures were delivered in three different languages—English, French, and German—and the audience was expected to listen without interuption. Questions from the audience were strictly forbidden. The Conference's official program ended at about midday when the lecturers and a few of Olga Fröbe's special guests adjourned for lunch at the celebrated round table.

That first year, Heinrich Zimmer opened the round of talks with an address on "The Meaning of Indian Tantric Yoga," a theme still very exotic at the time. Zimmer wanted to re-formulate Eastern wisdom so that it could be understood in terms of one's own experience and way of thinking. For him, this meant a process of mutual transmutation and adaptation since spiritual nourishment assimilates the person who has received it. The process forms and changes his or her substance. Zimmer considered that this was the only possible approach to esoteric wisdom and philosophy, one that sharply contrasted with the distanced and critical attitude of most modern thought. This also distinguished Eranos from purely academic conferences. Zimmer was not alone in his views, as most of the other well-known speakers were in agreement. The Conference's lively style was greatly appealing to the audience and guaranteed the success of subsequent Conferences.

In her welcoming speech at the second conference in 1934, Olga Fröbe emphasized that there had always been a Western "tradition of yoga" in parallel with the Eastern: "One only needs to think of the Hermetic and Pythagorean schools or, later on, the alchemical and Rosicrucian traditions."[6] Similarly, she detected "the beginnings of a modern and Western yoga ... a method of spiritual orientation, guidance and discipline" in Jung's analytical psychology. In addition to speakers from the previous year, Martin Buber was one of the outstanding newcomers at this Conference. Among the lecturers in 1933 were the famous theologians Friedrich Heiler and Ernesto Buonaiuti. A more controversial speaker that first year was the forerunner of psychosomatic medicine, psychiatrist Gustav Richard Heyer. He was a long-standing friend of Jung with some leanings toward National Socialism. But, as in the case of the more outspoken National Socialist, Jakob Wilhelm Hauer, who, as a specialist of Tantrism, made his appearance at Eranos a year later, it is impossible to do him justice in a few words. The subject of Eranos and National Socialism is complex, requiring more than a simple black and white treatment.

With regard to political issues that had already cropped up, Olga Fröbe declared quite openly in her foreword to the 1935 meeting, "hence there are no barriers here between different faiths and different races. Eranos is therefore a real meeting place, it is a 'tent of encounter.'"[7] In 1936, the speakers included a small French delegation from the École Pratique des Hautes Études in Paris, which would send subsequent generations of its staff to Ascona. This included the indologist, Paul Masson-Oursel, and the expert on Gnosticism, Henri-Charles Puech. In an interview by a local newspaper, the *Tessiner Illustrierte*, Olga Fröbe made the point that Switzerland was an island of synthesis in a chaotic Europe.

PROBLEMS AND CHANGES

As time went on, financial problems became increasingly urgent. Olga Fröbe had used up almost her entire fortune for the Eranos organization and for her associated travels. Thankfully, her "talisman," Jung, made a meeting possible with Mary and Paul Mellon. Paul Mellon, who came from a wealthy family, and his wife Mary, underwent Jungian analysis with Ann Moyer and her husband, Erlo van Waveren, who had been Alice Bailey's business manager. Through this connection, the Mellons were introduced to Jung's teaching and came to value him and his work highly. During one of his seminars in New York in which Mary and Paul Mellon also participated, Jung quickly won the couple over with his easy, nonchalant manner. They first participated in an Eranos Conference in 1939. As Olga Fröbe nearly always invited them to join the lecturers at mealtimes, the Mellons had the opportunity to meet not only with Jung, but also Heinrich Zimmer and the islamicist Louis Massignon who was, like Zimmer, a very talented speaker. Eventually, Jung invited the Mellons to his famous tower at Bollingen on Lake Zürich. This place made such a strong impression on Mary Mellon that she chose the name Bollingen as the imprint for her book publishing project that was dedicated to topics similar to those at Eranos.

In 1941, yet another eminent, gifted speaker was invited: Károly Kerényi, the specialist on ancient mythology and religion. This was to be Kerényi's first of many visits to Ascona. Jung regarded Kerényi highly and envisioned him as successor to Richard Wilhelm and Heinrich Zimmer. Kerényi provided many insights regarding the relationship between Jung's theory of archetypes and ancient Greek myths. What distinguished him from other experts on antiquity was that he searched the past not for the historically unusual, but for timeless validity. For Kerényi, history was more than narratives about various ancient gods and goddesses. Rather, he saw there a teaching that still has relevance today.

Although the war years were difficult for Eranos, the Mellons continued to help their friends in Switzerland by sending regular food packages and money. However, even a simple correspondence then could be very dangerous for Americans. The U.S. Trading with the Enemy Act forbade citizens to trade with hostile foreigners. After all, as Switzerland's neutrality accommodated espionage and transactions by both sides, it was plausible that the Mellons' contacts in Switzerland were agents for the German enemy. The Mellon family lawyers urgently advised the couple to cease all postal contact or financial interchange with everyone in Europe, with the result that, suddenly and without forewarning, all Mellon financial support for Eranos was suspended. Fortunately, the subsidies were resumed after the war.

The year 1946 marked a significant innovation. Under the general theme of "Spirit and Nature," the Conference included for the first time a number of established, mainstream physicists, biologists, and other scientists. The most notable was the physicist and Nobel Prize winner, Erwin Schrödinger, and the well-known and respected biologist, Adolf Portmann, who was to become a key figure in the history of Eranos, and who would give more lectures (thirty) than any other speaker. Portmann always intertwined his knowledge of nature with philosophical, cultural, and religious issues, with the purpose of catalyzing inner renewal and a deepening of human religious experience.

The 1947 meeting was attended by Kerényi, Jung, Massignon, and a number of new lecturers such as the rabbi and humanist, Leo Baeck, and the Gnosticism expert, Gilles Quispel. At the 1947 Conference, the year after his wife Mary had died unexpectedly, Paul Mellon pledged to continue his support via his Bollingen Foundation. For more than fifteen years, this gesture provided basic financing for Eranos as well as other forms of support. A long succession of Eranos speakers were awarded fellowships, which covered their living costs while they carried out their research, the results of which were published by Bollingen. Generous subsidies from Paul Mellon also supported the publication of Eranos lectures in English.

Joseph Campbell, who later became a celebrity through his lively television broadcasts and radio interviews, was chosen as editor for this publication project. At the end of 1949, Campbell proposed making the Eranos lectures more accessible to an English-speaking audience. However, Olga Fröbe strongly opposed Campbell, seeing the proposal as a fundamental betrayal to her vision of Eranos as metaphysical, not scientific. After years of quarreling, six volumes were finally published between 1954 and 1968, some of which were consistent with the order and underlying principles of the *Yearbooks*, others less so.

Celebrities

Eranos' real heyday began in 1949 with the attendance of Gershom Scholem and Henry Corbin. Scholem's presence at Eranos has astounded some people. His well-known academic distancing from the Kabbalah was in striking contrast with Olga Fröbe's wish to personally identify with the subject. Scholem acknowledged this problem, but apparently found his stays in Ascona worthwhile as he continued to return, year after year, for nearly three decades.

Henry Corbin attended Eranos every year between 1949 and 1978. His influence on Eranos cannot be overestimated. He was involved with many of the participants, including Mircea Eliade, whom he first brought to Eranos as a speaker, Gilbert Durand, Antoine Faivre, David Miller, and the archetypal psychologist and pupil of Jung, James Hillman. Corbin's central concept is the so-called *mundus imaginalis*, the "imaginal" world. According to Corbin, this realm mediates the absolutely unknowable God and the material world in which we live. As such, it forms the "intermediate realm," which in antiquity was the medium through which divine powers operate on earth. It is regarded as the abode of the soul, the sphere where angels mediate, and the place where sacred events transpire.

Corbin famously stated that even a historian, using critical methods alone, would never be able to grasp the essence of Eranos. Without fail, the historian would completely misunderstand the phenomenon, which concerned neither schools, influences, nor themes, but rather inner meaning. Upon hearing of Corbin's death, Gershom Scholem wrote to his widow, Stella:

> He … was a man who had devoted his life to understanding and researching a world that was as close as I could imagine to the one to which I have devoted my own life. We were, in the truest sense, honest, and possibly we were the first academics to excavate the world of the esoteric imagination, as manifested in Islamic and Jewish Gnosticism. Of all the Eranos speakers, it was he to whom I felt the closest kinship.[8]

This assessment of the arguably most esoteric lecturer by possibly the least esoteric is both astounding and impressive.

Mircea Eliade participated for the first time in 1950. Even though he spoke of the atmosphere being "semimundane, semitheosophical," Eliade was very taken by Eranos.[9] Not long before this, he had become convinced that myths, symbols, and god forms were not merely products of fantasy, but represented fundamental and existential human situations. Eliade soon became a confidant of Olga Fröbe and she spoke to him in a very open way. Eliade attracted criticism not only because of his earlier political involvement, but because of the essentialist phenomenological methods he applied to the study of religion. This approach played down cultural and historical differences between religions, and emphasized their essential commonalities. For Eliade, what mattered was the ahistorical core within shared religious experience.

Jung gave his last Eranos lecture in 1951 when the Conference theme was synchronicity. It was also the year when Olga Fröbe finally gained recognition from her ancestral homeland, the Netherlands. This must have given her great satisfaction. Dutch Queen Juliana invited Olga Fröbe for a two-hour conversation held in her study where the bookshelves were full of *Eranos Yearbooks*. Queen Juliana had pursued religious studies herself and retained this interest in religious phenomenology.

While Jung attended the 1952 Conference, he did not lecture. In the following year, there were several new and well-known speakers including Giuseppe Tucci, probably Italy's most prominent orientalist; the theologian and later cardinal, Jean Daniélou, who had been invited through Mircea Eliade; and the Japanese Zen expert, Daisetz Teitaro Suzuki. Although Paul Tillich spoke only twice at Eranos, he deserves mention. Along with Karl Barth, Tillich was probably the most important Protestant theologian of the twentieth century. Laurens van der Post, an African specialist, gifted writer, and filmmaker, was another who only spoke once, in 1956.

The following years brought a major financial setback for Eranos. Olga Fröbe wanted to collaborate with Walter Robert Corti whom she had known for many years and who planned to create a Platonic Academy in Switzerland. Naturally, such an undertaking would interest Olga Fröbe, particularly when the project was combined with Corti's enthusiasm. Believing that Eranos would not survive her death, Olga Fröbe considered the possibility of collaboration and an eventual fusion with the academy. Subsequently, the merging of Eranos and the Academy was decided upon at the 1959 Conference. But then, Olga Fröbe suddenly changed her mind. By the end of 1959, she had become convinced that the academy would never continue Eranos in her and its original spirit. She felt compelled to dissolve the agreement without delay and at whatever the cost. After lengthy legal wrangling, Olga Fröbe was obliged to donate two plots of land.

TRANSITION

For Olga Fröbe, Eranos involved much than organizing interesting events—it was her life. In a letter dated September 17, 1951, she wrote:

> Eranos is my way of individuation. It was so in its beginnings, in
> its entire development and it is so today in its greatest intensity.
> It happens to be my destiny to have had to work out my way of
> individuation in this way. And I have had to do it alone. Everyone
> is alone on his or her inner way. There is no alternative.[10]

In March 1962, Olga Fröbe suffered a minor stroke, with the
realization that she would have to relinquish her Eranos activities. To
guarantee continuity in Conference administration, overall authority
of Eranos was transferred to the hands of her Dutch fellow countryman,
Rudolf Ritsema, who primary interest was the *I Ching*. Adolf Portmann
agreed with this step. Just one month later, on April 25, 1962, Olga
Fröbe died in her eighty-first year. The ashes of Eranos' founder were
placed in her garden. In her will, she specified that an Eranos Foundation
be established under the leadership of Adolf Portmann, and that Casa
Eranos and the garden pass on to the Foundation.

By 1949, Jung and Dutch theologian and phenomenologist of
religion, Gerardus van der Leeuw, came to a shared conclusion that
something more than a habitual process lay behind the Eranos
phenomenon. To them, this "more" seemed to be an unknown "spirit,"
a personification of an archetype that animated the setting of the
meetings. With this understanding, sculptor Paul Speck created a stele
which was installed in the garden of Casa Gabriella and bore the
inscription, *Genio loci ignoto* ("To the unknown spirit of the place").

The year 1963 saw Ira Progoff standing for the first time at the
Eranos lectern, to which he would return frequently. Progroff's overall
agenda was to create a new concept of the totality and greatness of the
human being. To this end, he collected and combined data from
biology, existential philosophy, and the study of religion. His idea was
that, in this way, human beings could develop the capacity and stature
to react adequately to the problems of the modern world.

Despite being a relative late-comer, James Hillman was a key figure
in Eranos history. For one thing, albeit at irregular intervals, he spoke
there fifteen times between 1965 and 1990. Furthermore, Hillman's
"archetypal psychology" is one of the main schools of thought which
for decades has strongly influenced Eranos. Several representatives of
this school have spoken at Eranos, including David Miller, Alfred
Ziegler, and Wolfgang Giegerich. Because of his "polytheistic"

perspective, Hillman instilled a certain controversy. Understandably, the polytheistic approach had provoked protest, if only, as Hillman says, because the monotheistic heritage makes it very difficult for us even to understand what a polytheistic soul is! This controversy is connected with the age-old conflict between the unambiguous word and the polymorphous image. This tension was bound to intensify in the modern age because, in comparison to those used in ancient times, words were becoming increasingly one-dimensional in meaning. What had been gained in terms of precision and clarity had been lost in depth and symbolic power. Consequently, the gap between word and image had widened.

Unnoticed by most of the audience, the year 1967 brought a significant *caesura* in Eranos's history when Paul Mellon decided to dissolve the Bollingen Foundation. John Barrett, then president and editor of its book series, retired, and Paul Mellon did not wish to continue. Since the creation of the foundation in 1945, Mellon alone had provided financial support. Although the books often sold well, the Foundation remained dependent on Mellon's support. Now, the Conferences were faced with the difficult task of being self-supporting.

It is important to mention a remarkable woman in association with the 1971 Eranos meeting, namely Aniela Jaffé. From 1955 until his death, she had been secretary and colleague to Jung. Jaffé performed a great service as the true author of Jung's "autobiography," *Memories, Dreams, Reflections*. Jaffé was born in Berlin and studied in Hamburg, Germany. Jewish by birth, she had to flee to Switzerland during the National Socialist era. In 1937, she embarked on analysis with Jung. Much of what we know about Jung's last years may be credited to her observations. Encouraged by Laurens van der Post, Jaffé wrote a much-quoted essay on Jung and National Socialism, in which she exonerated him from accusations of anti-Semitism. In 1975, she spoke again at Eranos on the subject of "C. G. Jung and the Eranos Conferences."

The year 1972 saw the liquidation of the Rhein-Verlag, which had published the Eranos Conference volumes from the beginning. Published regularly and with considerable sacrifice, even during the war years, the firm always ensured prompt dissemination of the lectures. In their absence, many speakers would have had less incentive to come to Ascona, as the volumes enabled lecturers to reach a broad readership with relevant cultural interests.

In 1975, on the 100th anniversary of Jung's birth, David Miller visited and lectured for the first time at Eranos. Altogether, between 1975 and 1988, he would speak there nine times. This clearly reflects the influence of archetypal psychology at Eranos. However, his success at the Conferences can also be attributed to his great rhetorical talent, which turned his lectures into veritable sermons.

HIATUS

The year 1988 brought another *caesura*, this time of a much more serious nature. Rudolf Ritsema, who was solely in charge since Portmann's death six years before, announced that the Eranos Conferences would come to an end and that participants should concern themselves with their own personal individuation. Needless to say, this declaration astonished and dismayed his audience. In a lengthy *Neue Zürcher Zeitung* article on August 17, 1990, the author elaborated on Ritsema's decision. The first and most pressing reason was the lack of funding to support Eranos. Second, he maintained that the traditional lecture format no longer held appeal for the younger generation. Ritsema wanted to shift away from the appearance of a "holiday event" to emphasize "soul guidance" for participants.

The politologist, Tilo Schabert, and the Egyptologist, Erik Hornung, and Gilbert Durand voiced opposition to this plan. David Miller, James Hillman, and Jean Servier were strongly in favor of a continuation of the Conferences, but did not feel able to undertake the organization themselves. Shortly before the Conference speakers departed, Ritsema declared unequivocally that this was the last Conference, something that embittered many of the participants. A breach with Ritsema seemed unavoidable.

In the end, an "Associazione Amici di Eranos" ("Association of the Friends of Eranos") was established. This organization took over responsibility for running the conferences and doing so in a more modernized form. Erik Hornung and Tilo Schabert were chosen as president and vice-president, respectively, with the intent of creating joint leadership. Despite the creation of the Amici di Eranos, no conference took place in 1989 because of insufficient organization.

However, one year later, in 1990, the first conference under the umbrella of the new Associazione was a complete success, with attendance by almost two hundred participants.

In October of the same year, Ritsema resumed public conferences, albeit on a much smaller scale, as required by the statutes of the Eranos Foundation. Between 1990 and 2002, Ritsema's Eranos Foundation regularly organized up to four working conferences per year. Apart from Ritsema and his co-translator of the *I Ching*, Stephen Karcher, better-known participants included Claudio Risé, Eiji Uehiro, Pio Filippani-Ronconi, Benjamin Sells, and Claudio Bonvecchio. At every event, there were five to six speakers who, after lecturing, invited discussion. In contrast to earlier Eranos meetings, there was no hierarchical division between speakers and audience. Congruent with the structure of the *I Ching*, there were always eighteen people seated around the table. Participants were selected from a group of applicants. It was hoped that by limiting the numbers of participants, a more intensive group dynamic would evolve. Using work with the *I Ching*, the organizers emphasized themes that would speak to the heart, in lieu of more academic discourse. Conference sessions lasted three days, and greater importance was placed on collective meals as integral to Eranos conviviality.

There was no lack of qualified speakers at the newly founded Amici di Eranos. Annemarie Schimmel, Ilya Prigogine, Erik Hornung, Moshe Idel, and Jan and Aleida Assmann are just a few of the excellent lecturers. Combined financial support from the Ascona Municipality and the Canton of Tessin made it possible to continue the conferences as they had in the past. Fritz Hugelmann, an Ascona town councilor and owner of a gallery specializing in Greek and Etruscan artifacts, initiated this public support. However, by 1999, the Amici di Eranos was beset with quarrels. Differing opinions concerning issues such as modernization, overseas branches, and speaker and Conference subject selection led Erik Hornung to withdraw his future candidature. Subsequently, Tilo Schabert provisionally took on running Amici di Eranos.

There was no meeting planned for 2000. Up to 2006, conferences were held, but eventually subsidies from the official bodies in the Tessin ceased. On November 12, 2007, the Associazione Amici di Eranos was deleted from the business register. Meanwhile, a new group had formed around Erik Hornung who had disassociated himself from Schabert's initiatives. Annemarie Schimmel and Andreas Schweizer, a Jungian analyst from Zürich, were part of the new group committed to the goal of reactivating the old Eranos tradition. Thanks to their efforts, it continues to operate successfully today.

The group, which now calls itself the "Verein zur Förderung der wissenschaftlichen Tagungen von Eranos" ("Association for Furthering the Scholarly Conferences of Eranos"), has a vision to continue Eranos as faithfully as possible to the original. Because it does not receive subsidies from either the Municipality or the Canton, the new Association is financed solely from conference fees and minor contributions from a few sponsors. This provides greater independence. Bearing in mind that the Casa Serodine in Ascona, where the group now gathers, has no more than sixty places, a core group of regular attendees guarantees the continuity of the events. Apart from the organizers, speakers include Annemarie Schimmel, Jan Assmann, Herbert Pietschmann, Alois M. Haas, and Josef van Ess.

Meanwhile, what became of the Eranos-Moscia Foundation? Their most serious problem was an ever-growing financial deficit that hung over it like a Damoclean sword. Then, a serious prospect of support suddenly materialized when John van Praag, a successful Dutch businessman, took over the presidency. Van Praag deserves credit for having put the Eranos Foundation back on a sound financial footing, in part because of his key contacts with large American institutions such as the Fetzer Institute. In October 2009, Foundation leadership changed hands again with van Praag's resignation, evidently prompted by disagreements with local decision-makers. He was succeeded by Fabio Merlini, Regional Director of the Swiss Federal Institute for Vocational Education and Training (SFIVET) in Lugano and formerly Professor of Philosophy of Culture at the University of Lausanne and of Ethics at the University of Insubria, Varese.

Years before, Merlini had been in contact with Rudolf Ritsema and took part in some of the Conferences. He was also involved with the "rescue" initiatives when Eranos was experiencing financial difficulties. The new president's plan for the intermediate future is to create additional, multi-functional space to accommodate the library as well as offices and reading rooms. This expansion will permit Eranos to better serve the numerous visitors from home and abroad. Merlini is strongly supported by the entire Foundation Board in this undertaking. So, for the time being, there are two groups that continue the Eranos program, albeit in somewhat differing ways.

From the vantage of time, the overall picture of Eranos turns out to be much more consistent than one might expect of such a long-lasting project. This consistency stems from a readiness to extend scientific inquiry beyond boundaries set by reason, areas where myth, imagination, and religious experience have important roles. The history of Eranos can be divided into three phases. The beginning was undoubtedly much tinged by esoteric ideas, as is apparent from the titles of the Conferences. Equally characteristic of this phase was the search for a balance between East and West. It was during this period that the influence of Olga Fröbe and Jung was strongest, though as I see it, Olga Fröbe was the one who pushed the esoteric agenda, whereas Jung attempted to restrain her. From the beginning of the 1940s, the focus of the Conferences was increasingly on the Occident with an emphasis on classical antiquity.

In the mid-1940s, Adolf Portmann joined the group and increasingly took the lead. Like Jung, Portmann was adept at swaying Olga Fröbe toward his own intellectual and spiritual interests. From that point on, esotericism, gnosis, and the mysteries receded into the background and were overshadowed by biological and cultural perspectives of humanity. However, the faction surrounding Eliade, Corbin, and, to some extent, Scholem had an interest in the "inner" aspect of religion, which they managed to retain and which paved the way for the prominent role of the "polytheist" group around James Hillman and David Miller. Their "archetypal psychology" begged an important question: which should have precedence, a clear-cut, one-dimensional rationalism based on words and concepts or a more inward-looking, multi-dimensional approach, involving images and multivalent insights?

The fact that Eranos has survived till now, despite the comings and goings of so many eminent people and difficulties, is sufficient proof that there is something deeper with the strength to hold this complex structure together. It is of secondary importance whether one calls the spirit behind the phenomenon a "daemon" or a "hierophany," as Eliade does. But, even thinking purely pragmatically, I believe that nothing can achieve long life unless it accommodates the co-existence of contradictions, perceiving them as complementarities and opportunities. Eranos has always done this by restoring balance to counter any one-sidedness. At the same pragmatic level, the question arises whether Eranos possesses something enriching that fulfills human beings at an inner level. Here too, I believe, the answer is affirmative. In view of the ever-advancing globalization of the world, which primarily has to do with business and consumerism, some spiritual counterbalance is called for.

At the end of this summary, some words on the "reception" of Eranos are due. Eranos is by no means alone in its quest to illuminate "esoteric," "gnostic," or "mystical" matters with academic methods, and to refine out the "best" from both sides. I will name just three groups. On purely geographical grounds, I would acknowledge an initiative from Lugano, about an hour's travel from Ascona. Litttle has been published on the Istituto Ticinese di Alti Studi (Ticinian Institute for High Studies; ITAS), which held summer seminars there between 1970 and 1973. Under the guidance of Elémire Zolla, there was also an attempt to harmonize mythos with logos, but in this case, unequivocally postulating the supremacy of a sacred dimension in human beings. Among the speakers, such as the well-known Jean Servier, Hans Sedlmayr, Karl Kerényi, Pio Filippani Ronconi, Marius Schneider, and Seyyed Hossein Nasr, there were also some Eranos contributors.

A better known group is the Université Saint Jean de Jérusalem (University of Saint John of Jerusalem), where Henry Corbin championed the idea of a spiritual "knighthood," which would have the task of preserving the spiritual and religious heritage of humanity and defending it against modernism, secularization, and a historicist worldview. Between 1974 and 1987, a total of fourteen colloquia were held here.

Finally, there is another group, the somewhat ironically named Academia Palladiana (Palladian Academy), which is comprised mainly of academics whose discussion group on esoteric themes had no particular academic ambition in the beginning. From this emerged what may be the most important official association for the scholarly investigation of esotericism, the European Society for the Study of

Western Esotericism (ESSWE). The Palladian Academy has its origins in January 1997, when the Anglo-American music professor, Joscelyn Godwin, who is counted among the most important researchers of esotericism, issued the first invitation for a week-long meeting at the Palladian Villa Saraceno near Vicenza. After having assembled once in 2001, in Styria, Austria, the spiritual and material founder of the endowment supporting the Amsterdam Chair for Hermetic Philosophy and Related Currents, Rosalie Bastens, announced her willingness to make her château, the Domaine de Taurenne in Provence, available for future meetings.

NOTES

1. C. G. Jung, "Richard Wilhelm: In Memoriam" (1930), in *The Collected Works of C. G. Jung*, vol. 15, ed. and trans. Gerhard Adler and R. F. C. Hull (Princeton, NJ: Princeton University Press, 1966), § 90.

2. *Ibid.*

3. *Eranos-Jahrbuch* 30 (1961): 25–26.

4. *Eranos-Jahrbuch* 48 (1979): 463.

5. William McGuire, "The Arcane Summer School," *Spring* (1980): 146–56.

6. *Eranos-Jahrbuch* 2 (1934): 8–9.

7. *Eranos-Jahrbuch* 3 (1935): 4.

8. Gershom Scholem, *Briefe III: 1971–1982*, ed. Itta Shedletzky (Munich: C.H. Beck, 1999), p. 193.

9. Mircea Eliade, *Journal I: 1945–1955* (Chicago, IL: University of Chicago Press, 1989), p. 112.

10. Olga Fröbe-Kapteyn, letter to Ximena de Angulo-Roelli, September 17, 1951.

II.

ERANOS AND THE
PSYCHOLOGICAL TRADITION

Möge dem Licht des europaeischen Geistes, das von Eranos in diese Zeit des Dunkels für so viele Jahre ausgegangen ist, noch eine längere Lebensdauer beschieden sein, damit es seine Rolle als Leuchtfeuer einer europaeischen Einigung erfüllen kann.

30 März 1957. C.G. Jung.

A dedication written by the psychologist, Carl Gustav Jung, on the occasion of the 25th anniversary of the Eranos Conferences, in 1957, which reads: "May the light of the European spirit, which has shone out of Eranos for so many years in these times of darkness, still have the gift of a long life, so that it can play its role as the beacon of a European union."

CARL GUSTAV JUNG

The Swiss psychologist, Carl Gustav Jung (1875–1961), joined Eranos at its inception and took part in the Eranos Conferences for twenty years. He gave a total of fourteen talks, from 1933 up to 1951. These were published in the *Eranos Yearbooks*. They were then revised, expanded, and published in the *Psychologische Abhandlungen* ("Psychological Treatises")—except for his last essay, *On Synchronicity* (1951), which was not changed from the original version published in the *Yearbook*—and, later, in his *Collected Works*. Jung's annual talks were looked forward to each year. He also gave an impromptu seminar on "The Solar Myths and Opicinus de Canistris" in 1943. He participated at Eranos for the last time in 1952, but only as a listener. Two commemorative *Yearbooks* were published in his honor on his seventieth birthday (1945) and seventy-fifth birthday (1950). The Eranos Archive for Research in Symbolism also served as an indispensible iconographic base for important studies of his, such as *Psychology and Alchemy* (1944). In her first talk at Eranos, *The Creative Phases in Jung's Life* (1971), Aniela Jaffé read some passages of *The Red Book*, still unpublished at that time. Likewise, she gave her last talk in August 1975, *C. G. Jung and the Eranos Conferences*, on the occasion of the 100ᵗʰ anniversary of his birth. It was at Eranos that the contracts for the American, English, and German editions of Jung's *Collected Works* were drawn up in 1947 and that, in August 1956, the project for his memoirs, *Memories, Dreams, Reflections* (1961), became a reality.

Carl Gustav Jung's "Introduction to Eranos," presented in the following pages, was originally written in English in the form of an Introduction to a proposed miscellaneous volume of lectures that presented Eranos to the American public. In 1938, Olga Fröbe-Kapteyn discussed a possible Eranos miscellaneous volume on the "Great Mother" with Mary Mellon, who showed a great interest and who entrusted the editorial project to Cary Baynes. The volume was to include Jung's lectures on "Some Considerations on the *Visions* of Zosimos" (1937) and "The Psychological Aspect of the Great Mother" (1938). The Table of Contents, prepared by Cary Baynes in January 1939, included writings by Heinrich Zimmer, Jakob Wilhelm Hauer, Caroline Augusta Foley Rhys-Davids, Paul Masson-Oursel, Henri-Charles Puech, Andreas Speiser, Ernesto Buonaiuti, Erwin Rousselle, and Jean Przyluski too. On March 31, 1939, Olga Fröbe-Kapteyn wrote to Jung that the publisher, John Farrar—editorial director of Farrar & Rinehart publishing house in New York, which had already published Jung's *The Integration of the Personality* (a collection of his first Eranos essays) in 1939—wanted her to write a Foreword to the volume; she, however, hoped Jung could write his Introduction first. On April 15, she wrote to Jung to request his paper. One month later, on May 15, 1939, Jung finally wrote his Introduction. However, with the dissolution of the first Bollingen Foundation (1942), the project of the Eranos American volume stopped. No trace can be found of Olga Fröbe-Kapteyn's Foreword. The English typescripts of the lectures were donated to Yale University Press and were never published. Ximena de Angulo-Roelli gave copies of the translations to the Analytical Psychology Club of New York as well. They were later rediscovered and given to the Kristine Mann Library. When the Bollingen Foundation was reconstituted (officially, in 1945), the editorial project of an American Eranos volume was replaced by a wider editorial series—*the Papers from the Eranos Yearbooks* (1954–1968), under the supervision of Joseph Campbell. Jung's Introduction (with some annotations by Olga Fröbe-Kapteyn) was rediscovered by William McGuire at Eranos only in 1976 and therefore was not included in the *Collected Works*. The paper was finally published with the original title, "American Eranos Volume: Introduction," *Spring* (1984): 57–59; a Spanish edition appeared as "Introducción a Eranos," in *Los dioses ocultos. Círculo Eranos II (Cuadernos de Eranos—Cahiers d'Eranos). Selección de textos de "Eranos-Jahrbücher,"* ed. A. Ortiz-Osés (Barcelona: Anthropos, 1997), pp. 15–18.

We thank Dr. Thomas Fischer and the Foundation of the Works of C. G. Jung (Zürich) for granting permission to republish Jung's writing in this issue of *Spring: A Journal of Archetype and Culture*.

American Eranos Volume:
Introduction

C. G. JUNG

This book is an apparently heterogeneous composition, and I imagine that the reader may not find it too easy to get his bearings in this wide-spread maze of philosophical, religious, psychological, and mythological problems. Being a selection of the lectures delivered at the Eranos-Meetings between 1933 and 1938, the book does not claim to be an all-round representation of any one subject. On the contrary, it has been compiled to allude to various spheres of knowledge, which one would hardly ever find placed together in close contact between the covers of one and the same volume. The specialization of our time tends to produce accumulations of specific researches in books and periodicals, widely separated from other departments that guard their treasure of knowledge with equal jealousy. The danger of such specialization, however necessary in other respects, consist of the narrowing of the horizon and in the inbreeding, which inevitably follow mental isolation. No work of serious research can be done in our days without equally serious specialization. The enormous extension of knowledge exceeds the capacity of a single brain, which alone might [not] be able to form a syntheses of the innumerable parts contributed by every department. Even the greatest genius, equipped with a fabulous power of memory, would be forced to remain an incompetent dilettante in quite a few important respects. One ought, however, to bring together all the results and information from every branch of knowledge in order to create a complete picture of our world. Such a desire has been expressed long again. But as it is well-nigh impossible to establish a careful comparison of all the detail and knowledge, one should seek a platform or an idea which is common to several forms of knowledge. It would then be possible to gather the various contributions round a central problem.

The Eranos-Meetings are such an attempt; a number of scholars are brought together annually and certain ideas are selected, which express the philosophical, religious, and psychological interest of present day humanity. These ideas form the nucleus of a sort of symposium of learned contributors. As the reader will see from the titles of the essays, it is a matter of thoughts concerning the spiritual outlook of our times. The aim of the meetings is to give each idea or problem a most comprehensive treatment from different aspects. The ideas of the quest, of redemption, of spiritual development, and so on, are treated from the standpoint of comparative religion, mythology, history, philosophy, and psychology. It is a new and unique enterprise, which came into existence through Mrs. Fröbe-Kapteyn's personal initiative. Each meeting has one topic and the essays in this volume (selected from a far greater number) represent some of these subjects. Rousselle deals with the problem of the first meeting in 1933 when there was a symposium about "Yoga and Meditation in East and West" from the point of view of various civilizations and times. Being a sinologist, he shows us how modern Taoism proceeds in this matter.[1] Three essays (Masson-Oursel, Puech, and Speiser) are concerned with the various aspects of redemption in Hindu religion and philosophy, in Manichaeism, and in Plotinus. Other aspects of Indian religion and Philosophy are represented by three contributors, Mrs. Rhys-Davids, the president of the Pāli Society, Hauer, and Zimmer. Christian thought finds an apt interpretation in Buonaiuti's essay on the *Ecclesia spiritualis*. Three more essays (Zimmer[2] and Jung) deal with psychological questions related to Indian myths, to the visions of the Greek alchemist Zosimos, and to the archetype of the Great Mother, which was the subject of the last Eranos-Meeting.

The Eranos contributions are concerned not only with the ideas of the West but also with the treasures of the Eastern mind, so that many points of contact between eastern and western thought become apparent.[3]

In spite of the great variety of these contributions in the form and in the subject matter, they are all related to central and transcendent ideas—to the ideology and phenomenology of the way of salvation or redemption. The study of these subjects inevitably demands detailed and exact research on the archetypal factors that govern this field.

A good many of the lectures held in the last few years therefore treat of archetypes; the central theme of the Eranos conference of 1938 was that of the archetype known as the "Great Mother."

An archive of iconographic material, collected by Frau Fröbe-Kapetyn, is available during the conference, illustrating the subjects treated.

Since 1933 the conferences have been chiefly concerned with prechristian religions. The conference of 1940 and those following it will attempt a thorough study of the Christian age, beginning in 1940 with the "Origins and beginnings of Christianity."

In a time when political unrest and overheated nationalism are destroying international relations, the Eranos-Meeting is a haven of peace, where those, who are trying to maintain and increase the treasures of mind and spirit, can meet and co-operate. The contributors to this Volume belong to no less than five different nations.

Küsnacht-Zürich
May 15th 1939
Edited by William McGuire

This article is © 2007 Foundation of the Works of C. G. Jung.
Used with permission.

EDITOR NOTES

1. Jung refers here not to Rouselle's essay "The Great Mother in China" as in the January 1939 list sent to the Mellons, but to "Spiritual Guidance in Contemporary Taoism," Rousselle's lecture at the first Eranos *Tagung*, 1933. (It appears in Ralph Manheim's translation in *Papers from the Eranos Yearbooks*, vol. 4). Evidently Frau Fröbe had revised the contents further.

2. The January 1939 list gives a paper by Przyluski, not Zimmer. Jung's reference here is apparently to Zimmer's "Indian Myths as Symbols," replacing Przyluski; the other paper by Zimmer must have been "On the Significance of the Indian Tantric Yoga," 1933 (also translated by Manheim in *Papers from the Eranos Yearbooks*, vol. 4). Incidentally, around 1941 Mary Mellon got Zimmer also to write an introductory piece to the ill-fated Eranos volume; it is in the Bollingen Archives at the Library of Congress.

3. The third through seventh paragraphs were probably written by Olga Fröbe-Kapetyn, as they were recognizably typed on her typewriter and pasted onto Jung's typescript. They may be a remnant of her lost foreword.

GIAN PIERO QUAGLINO

G ian Piero Quaglino, Full Professor of Social Psychology, Dynamic Psychology, and Psychology of Adult Education, served as Director of the Department of Psychology (1993–1997), President of the Consorzio Interuniversitario sulla Formazione (COINFO, 1994–1999), and Dean of the Faculty of Psychology (2003–2008) at Turin University (Italy), where he taught from 1977–2010. In 2010, he founded Vivenzia, a school of adult education devoted to "self-cultivation." For the publisher Raffaello Cortina, he directed the "Individuo, Gruppo e Organizzazione" editorial series (1992–2012). He has written over 200 works on organizational psychology and adult education, including *La vita organizzativa. Difese, collusioni e ostilità nelle relazioni di lavoro* (2004), *Fare formazione. I fondamenti della formazione e i nuovi traguardi* (new ed., 2005), *Scritti di formazione 1–5* (1999, 2005, 2006, 2007, and 2010), and more recently, *La scuola della vita. Manifesto della terza formazione* (2011). He also edited *Leadership. Nuovi profili di leader per nuovi scenari organizzativi* (1999), *Autoformazione. Autonomia e responsabilità per la formazione di sé nell'età adulta* (2004), *Scene di leadership. Come il cinema insegna a essere leader*, with Claudia Piccardo (2006), and *Formazione. I metodi* (2014). In Jungian studies, his work includes *A spasso con Jung* (2005), *A colazione da Jung* (2006), and *Nel giardino di Jung* (2010), co-authored with Augusto Romano, *Carl Gustav Jung a Eranos 1933–1952* (2007), co-authored with Augusto Romano and Riccardo Bernardini, *C. G. Jung's Aforismi 1–2* (2012 and 2013), co-edited with Augusto Romano, and *The Solar Myths and Opicinus de Canistris—Notes of the Seminar given at Eranos in 1943* (2014), co-edited with Riccardo Bernardini and Augusto Romano.

CARL GUSTAV JUNG:
HIS LIFE BEFORE HIS WORKS

GIAN PIERO QUAGLINO

As many people know, the conclusion of the Preface to the third English and American Edition of Sigmund Freud's *The Interpretation of Dreams* (1931) is marked by some revealing words:

> This book, with its new contribution to psychology which surprised the world when it was published (1900), remains essentially unaltered. It contains, even to my present-day judgment, the most valuable of all discoveries it has been my good fortune to make. Insight such as this falls to one's lot but once in a lifetime.[1]

Naturally, at a certain point in a person's intellectual journey, one recognizes that a thought has been thought and gathered up at a magical moment. For this reason, this thought is consolidated so solidly that it resists any assault that its author or anyone else might launch. Therefore, Freud's words bear witness to a unique and unrepeatable experience, one that, to a certain extent, is reserved for very few. Its unplanned nature astonished the author himself and transformed what had seemed, not without some worry, to be an entirely autobiographical event in a theoretical project. In fact, Freud expressed a good deal of concern in his Preface to the first edition of *The Interpretation of Dreams*, because he had been almost forced to produce a scientific work wherein his own dreams were submitted as the evidence of a theoretical intuition.[2,3]

In his Preface to successive editions, Freud found a way to justify himself concerning this autobiographical inevitability. He speaks of the hard times he had endured on the level of his personal experiences in the late 1890s when a dream revealed to him his own interpretative potential, namely, heart-rendering events such as only the death of one's father could be. He writes:

> Even the material of this book, even my own dreams ... by
> means of which I have demonstrated the rules of dream-
> interpretation, revealed, when I came to revise these pages, a
> continuity that resisted revision. For me, of course, the book
> has an additional subjective significance, which I did not
> understand until after its completion. It reveals itself to me as
> a piece of self-analysis, as my reaction to the death of my father,
> that is, to the most important event, to the most poignant
> loss in man's life.[4]

Even Cesare Musatti, the general editor of the Italian edition of
Freud's works (*Opere*), felt compelled to wonder, or at least to express
some surprise about this eminently autobiographical element. Forty
years ago, Musatti wrote, with emphatic repetition:

> It is very strange ... that a scientific work of psychology ... is
> part of his autobiography... It is strange that the demonstrative
> material, which this scientific work is based on, is prevalently
> made up of the dreams of its author himself... It is strange that
> the discipline, the science, that has developed on the specific basis
> of this work is in a certain way a personal science—i.e., one bound
> to its author as no other scientific doctrine is. For this reason, it
> seems lacking in that characteristic of impersonality that normally
> constitutes the mark of scientific objectivity.[5]

Now, in my opinion, this contrasts greatly with Carl Gustav
Jung. If there was anything that Jung could ever care less about, it
was the issue of the relationship between the thinker and his
"scientific" work. Jung's worries were very different from those of
both Freud and Musatti. This may lead us to suspect that the famous
break-up between Freud and Jung in 1912–1913 came about not
because they disagreed about any particular concept such as
differing theoretical assumptions, principles, or ideas like the nature
of libido. I suggest that the "falling out" between former teacher
and student derived from Freud, and obviously not Jung, who felt
that he needed to render a body of thought into an irreducibly
"singular" form and, above all, create a corpus of thoughts and ideas
that would become "collective." In so doing, this body of concepts
could be consecrated somehow into a school and become the formal
basis for constructing a complete psychology and, as a result, an
entire psychological society.

Subsequently, I would propose that there are two types of thought by which we can somehow measure psychology. On one hand, there is a mode of thought that we might call, to use Jung's term, *persona*. *Persona-thought* is the process of thinking with the intention of a theoretical project and with a good deal of reverential fear of scientific criteria. In addition, it is a thought that, a moment after formation, risks thinking of nothing but itself and risks not hearing what the thought itself aims to say. Because it is difficult to unhook thinker from thought, *persona-thought* is inclined to believe that what it claims, maintains, and thinks might arise from no one person. This has been referred to as impersonal or scientific objectivity. This kind of thought might be in possession of many people, of 100,000 people, for example. The more, the merrier, given that all evidently are convinced of the good quality of the thought. The *persona-thought* needs people who keep on thinking it, in an imitative, repetitive way. These individuals will confine the thought inside some theoretical cage, which could even become a place for association. It is something definitely established that is offered up as a kind of sacrificial object, as a thought destined for someone other than its originator. In this way, these others will think and naturally maintain some personal identity even though the mask of collective thought will tend to have the upper hand over what would have been their personal thoughts. In this way, *persona-thought* tends to require conformism and allegiance. The worries in *persona-thought* can even lead people to betray their authentic thought in the name of the shared thought. These concerns focus on collective image, acceptance, legitimating, and consensus. Fundamentally, *persona-thought* tends to have an agenda to influence and proselytize, primarily towards itself. *Persona-thought* is vulnerable to becoming a cessation of thinking except in relation to some presumed listener, community, or collectivity.

On the other hand, there is a second type of thought we might call, *anima*. *Anima-thought* is not calculating or opportunistic thought. It is not worried about what others think about it, rather it is concerned about thinking things that are different from those already thought of in the past. *Persona-thought* concerns itself with whether or not others regard the thought in the same or in a different way. In contrast, *anima-thought* is not concerned that others could think in a different way.

Moreover, it is not concerned to think differently later on. To put it another way, *persona-thought* is interested in answers and *anima-thought* is interested in questions. *Persona-thought* takes on the task of supplying answers and *anima-thought* strives to elicit a search or a question, thereby achieving its goal. *Persona-thought* is interested in the fact that others listen to it, see it, and believe it, and *anima-thought* is interested in the fact that others follow it so that, rather than conforming to it, their own thoughts might emerge. In addition, *persona-thought* follows thoughts that are the same, but *anima-thought* looks for thoughts that are different. *Persona-thought* wants a certain standardization and *anima-thought* seeks a certain singularity, an individuation.

Soon after he realized that Freud tended towards *persona-thought* rather than *anima-thought*, Jung decided his own path was leading in an entirely different direction. When we look at Jung's works and, above all, his memoirs, we notice how much Jung is concerned with his own thoughts rather than those of others.[6] Primarily, he may have wanted to show how much his thought was random, accidental, and produced through coincidences and strange passages of existence. Jung wanted to show how his thought had developed as a coming together of images rather than as project that had been shaped *a priori* to conform to some kind of logical coherence or explainable principle. Freud's concern about *The Interpretation of Dreams* could be translated as something like this, "Excuse me, I am not even talking about my patients' dreams, but my own." In contrast, Jung does not worry about this at all in *Memories, Dreams, Reflections* (1961). Nearly all of the content of this "autobiography" consists of Jung's dreams. It is testimony to how much the construction of his thought and work was absolutely inseparable from his existence. His dreams, and his respect of his dreams, illustrate how critical it is to attend to the condition of one's own existence and how little one should heed the collective rules of thought. This is something that Jung's biographers have pointed out. In her famous biography of Jung, Barbara Hannah, his former student, wrote: "Jung's psychology was based throughout on his actual experience... He was his own psychology."[7] She goes on to say,

> Anyone who knew Jung well will have realized that it was just
> this knowing himself that made him what he was. There are no

empty theories in his psychology; everything is founded on rock-bottom experience and it is genuine through and through.[8]

Jung states this clearly in *Memories, Dreams, Reflections*, where the reflections are listed third after the memories and dreams:

> The "autobiography" is my life viewed in the light of the knowledge I have gained from my scientific endeavors. Both are one [his life and his research, obviously]... My life has been in a sense the quintessence of what I have written, not the other way around. The way I am and the way I write are a unity.[9]

In other words, if a person wishes to know what to write, the most important thing for him or her is to know *who he is*. This brings up another concern of the *persona-thought*: what to write about. *Anima-thought* has the opposite worry, mainly, the concern about who is thinking and what is happening to him or her. Thought opens up because of what happens. Every incident, accident, and coincidence has some meaning in it. Thought does not open up because of some set canons. The *anima-thought* conviction is that existence moves thought, and not vice versa. There is no project in thought, but only a walking through it. It is a kind of opening towards what come to us, rather than towards what we want to find at all costs. This is what Freud was concerned with as evidenced by the prefaces of various editions of *The Interpretation of Dreams*. It is also evidenced by the dream he introduced, upon which he built his entire theoretical structure. In this dream, Freud is perhaps a doctor who is not very careful and does not pay close attention to the dictates of a given school, academy, or university. He is someone who must manage the tutelage, custody, maintenance, and preservation of a scientific imperative.

It is somewhat remarkable that Jung's break with Freud took place at the moment Jung left university. He realized that the university was not a place where he could think and listen to his own thoughts. Instead, it was the place where people were led to think thoughts that have already been thought. These individuals did this more or less out of compulsion, flattery, convenience, as a means to something else, or for some other advantage. Jung wrote,

In the midst of this period when I was so preoccupied with the
images of the unconscious, I came to the decision to withdraw
from the university... The material brought to light from the
unconscious had, almost literally, struck me dumb. I could neither
understand it nor give it form. At the university I was in an
exposed position, and felt that in order to go on giving courses
there I would first have to find an entirely new and different
orientation. It would be unfair to continue teaching young
students when my own intellectual situation was nothing but a
mass of doubts.[10]

What Jung wrote represents an attempt to distance himself from
the prison of *persona-thought*. At the same time, he wanted to position
himself to listen. This basically required that he withdraw from the
collective institution and open himself to what existence itself was
leading him towards, to the contents of the thoughts that experience
was offering. During this time, Jung abandoned Zürich, abandoned
his clinic, abandoned the university, and withdrew to Küsnacht, on
the lake of Zürich. As he recalls,

All my works, all my creative activity, has come from those initial
fantasies and dreams which began in 1912, almost fifty years
ago. Everything that I accomplished in later life was already
contained in them, although at first only in the form of emotions
and images.[11]

These were the images that surprised him as he moved from the
academic setting—a place where people could dream only a very little
and have few fantasies—to his place of retreat.

Naturally, the Küsnacht retreat featured a splendid vista of nature
that activated a series of unstoppable visions and dreams—all of which
were to lead him to the writing of *The Red Book*. Jung wrote: "My science
was the only way I had of extricating myself from that chaos."[12]
However, what kind of science does he mean? It was a science anchored
in and bound to that concept of the unconscious, which was his legacy
from the master, Freud, and his own encounter with psychoanalysis:
an unconscious that could be experienced in the same way in which
its founder had experienced it.

This was also the period when Jung wrote his well-known
Symbols of Transformation. It is informative to read a passage from
his foreword to the fourth edition, written more than thirty years

later. It forms a parallel with passages from Freud's prefaces to later editions of his *The Interpretation of Dream*. Notably, Jung's tone is very different:

> I have never felt happy about this book, much less satisfied with it: it was written at top speed, amid the rush and press of my medical practice, without regard to time or method. I had to fling my material hastily together, just as I found it. There was no opportunity to let my thought mature. The whole thing came upon me like a landslide that cannot be stopped. The urgency that lay behind it became clear to me only later: it was the explosion of all those psychic contents which could find no room, no breathing space, in the constricting environment of Freudian psychology and its narrow outlook.[13]

Obviously, we can call this "constricting environment" the *persona-thought*. In contrast, Jung's thought is the progression of thought that originates in an encounter with coincidence, events, and experience as well as with synchronicity. It is the distinctive sign of all the steps and passages that can be recognized as the most meaningful steps in thinking that is Jung's existence itself. As Aniela Jaffé recalled, it is the experience of a man for whom, beyond the outer events of his life and works, "the psyche was a profound reality."[14]

In 1923, Jung moved from Küsnacht to Bollingen, which was situated on a lake shore, from the house where he encountered the personal unconscious to the house where he felt the need to encounter the Self or what would be, in the end, his views about the Self. This transition was a physical expression of the path to individuation. He notes this in his memoirs:

> I had to achieve a kind of representation in stone of my innermost thoughts and of the knowledge I had acquired. Or, to put it in another way, I had to make a confession of faith in stone. That was the beginning of the "tower," the house which I built for myself at Bollingen.[15]

The Tower was primarily understood as "a place where Jung could be 'reborn in stone,' and where he could be entirely himself, a 'place of spiritual contemplation.'"[16]

The Tower at Bollingen served as a refuge to which he withdrew, where he contemplated and, in today's vernacular, "found himself."

We might reflect on what Jung found among the stones at Bollingen. Perhaps it served as the hidden route that mapped out the alchemical path that was to play such a significant role in his life, even before it did in his thought. It became the foundation for his encounters around the Eranos Round Table on the banks of another lake, Lake Maggiore. It also became the meeting point for the myriad of images contained in arcane texts of the fourteenth, fifteenth, and sixteenth centuries, images that were always difficult to express but were founding the thoughts of the ancient masters, Indian philosophy, *Kuṇḍalinī-Yoga*, and the *I Ching,* also known as the "book of transformations." Jung wrote,

> At Bollingen I am in the midst of my true life. I am most deeply myself. Here I am, as it were, the "'age-old son of the mother." This is how alchemy puts it very wisely, for the "old man," "the ancient," whom I had already experienced as a child is personality No. 2, who has always been and always will be. He exists outside time and is the son of the maternal unconscious. In my fantasies he took the form of Philemon, and he comes to life again at Bollingen. At times I feel as if I am spread out over the landscape and inside things and am myself living in every tree, in the splashing of the waves, in the clouds and the animals that come and go, in the procession of the seasons… I have gone without electricity and tend the fireplace and stove myself. Evenings I light the old lamps. There is no running water, and I pump the water from the well. I chop the wood and cook the food. These simple acts make man simple; and how difficult it is to be simple![17]

Jung's move to Bollingen was a purposeful effort to lead a different life, one without modern conveniences. The process helped him *connect his thought to his life* rather than to his works, which he envisioned would emerge as a consequence. He knew intuitively that it was necessary to live a different life in order to evoke a new thought. Only then, would he be able to progress in his works. If he did not move, then his works would become sterile. They would "be made into a *persona.*" They would not individuate. This is perhaps the reason that Jung said, "Luckily, I am Jung and I am not a Jungian!" It was his way of saying the he never wanted his own works to become somebody else's life. One's work can become the reason for an existence, but cannot imprison it.

What Jung found at Eranos is something even more different. Eranos was where he could discover how his own process, though unique, was really everyone's process present in every place. At Küsnacht, he had his relationship with his patients, hence it was the practice of his works. At Bollingen, he had his private relationship with himself. At Eranos, he had his collective relationship with guests and colleagues. This way of interacting and exchange represented by the Round Table provided further stimulus. Eranos was where Jung encountered diverse personifications, incarnations, and manifestations of the same principle. From 1933 on, the Round Table became his third "house," the "house" of his encounter with the collective unconscious.

In a letter written in August 1951, sent in honor of Olga Fröbe-Kapteyn's seventieth birthday, Jung wrote:

> Thanks to the enterprising spirit and devotion of Mrs. Fröbe, Eranos, which I wish a long future for, has become an institution that represents the only chance in Europe for experts and laymen animated by spiritual interests to meet and exchange their own opinions beyond all their specialized limitations. Already 20 years ago, Eranos had thought out today's efforts towards the joining together [*Zusammenfassung*] of all the sciences and thus made a contribution in its unique way to the European intellectual history... What made Eranos so valuable for me personally was the fact that Mrs. Fröbe's hospitable house always provided the opportunity for spontaneous discussions at the Round Table. I recall with pleasure and gratitude countless evenings overflowing with stimulation and information, providing just what I so much needed, that is, personal contact with other fields of knowledge. For all this I am deeply grateful to Mrs. Fröbe.[18]

Aniela Jaffé described dialogue between Jung and the other speakers in this way:

> Conversation between Jung and the other conference speakers took place in a small circle, in pleasant calm, at midday and evenings around the great Round Table in the garden, or in Casa Cabriella. At the very beginning of Eranos, Jung once appeared in Casa Gabriella for dinner, pointed out the Round Table, and said: "This is the true Eranos!"[19]

Yet, as Jaffé continued,

> The lectures, the contact with others, the enjoyment of the
> beautiful landscape and the garden, all explain just one,
> thoroughly personal aspect of Jung's interest in Eranos. There
> was a hidden and impersonal factor which determined his
> relationship to Eranos, in a much deeper sense... This factor lay
> in the archetypal nature of Eranos. Eranos as an archetypal
> phenomenon had a strong fascination for Jung.[20]

Erich Neumann adds: "Eranos, Landscape on lake, garden and house. Inconspicuous and off the beaten track, and yet a navel of the world, a small link in the Golden Chain."[21] Hellmut Wilhelm, son of the well-known sinologist, Richard Wilhelm, drew from the words of Confucius when describing Eranos: "Friends gather at a well-tended place, and together prepare a way for humanity."[22] Eranos provided a place for friendly gathering and the interaction of heaven and earth, themselves contradictory. This "tension of the opposites" was perhaps the aspect holding the greatest attraction for Jung.[23]

The *I Ching*, published by Richard Wilhelm in 1924, played an important role in Jung's life and in the history of Eranos.[24] We cannot help but notice how much the *I Ching* was to compose—Jung would say, "constellate"—an existence where thought flees and that was very well described in the preface to the fourth and last edition to *Symbols of Transformation*: the fury, the impossibility of holding back overwhelming emotion that carries away and captures a person. This is something that cannot be resisted and definitely only asks to be expressed in the most synthetic form through images, in the most immediate form through dreams with the speed in which our dreams take place, and with the same speed at which dream images change. Jung describes the *I Ching* as a book that fits well with meditative and reflective individuals who take time to linger over what they are doing and what is happening to them:

> The *I Ching* does not offer itself with proofs and results; it
> does not vaunt itself, nor is it easy to approach. Like a part of
> nature, it waits until it is discovered. It offers neither facts
> nor power, but for lovers of self-knowledge, of wisdom—if
> there be such—it seems to be the right book ... it does not
> promise anything and therefore it is not forced to keep any
> promise at all. It is never responsible if someone draws the

wrong conclusions. This method must be treated with a
certain intelligence because stupidity is not art.[25]

This is naturally the day-to-day sign of the potential of a kind
of thought, which is deeper than thought that is so careful, so
cautious, so patient, and so worried about the right expression of
the concepts and the coherence of the meanings, postulates, and
assumptions. This thought is deeper than the thought that is so
worried about all those assumptions, which naturally imprison not only
the concept, but the existence of the thinker himself. Such worried
thought may even strip the thinker of the chance to write an
autobiography, because the thinker will worry about whether it will
turn out orthodox or original. But, regardless, it will always end up
being the one or the other of his two masks.

Visions and images are at the center of "scientific" thought. But,
how is the thought being thought? Is it through images, visions,
and through dreams and fantasies? A good deal of psychology has
forgotten this kind of thought. Much of psychology proscribes
thinking in that way, because to do otherwise would lead one to
uncertain, improbable, and impossible ground lacking any firm
principle or rule shared by a collective. Jung's journey through
alchemy revealed that thought through images, signs, and fantasies
provides the only real chance to refresh one's own thoughts at each
moment of existence. There are existences that have produced
thoughts and that have continued through schools, deviating
sometimes in a certain way from their own thinker. There are
thoughts that have been thought and rethought and that have even
become items in admission exams on the basis of some sort of
catechistic form, according to which only those who have learned
the lesson can get in and get out. This too is only one of the
specialties of a certain interpretation of the academic world: that
one gets a grade only if one answers all the questions in the way
that they were written and found in books, which were so important
to read and without which no one could know much.

In the late 1940s Jung wrote, "When I was writing down those
fantasies, I once asked myself, 'What am I really doing? Certainly this
has nothing to do with science. But then what is it?' Whereupon a
voice within me said, 'It is art.'"[26] This is another clue revealing a

connection between science and art. There is an old saying, "Learn art and pack it away," but it might well be used in this way: "Learn science and pack it in the credenza (cupboard)." In fact, even science ends up being exposed to one's credenza (in the sense of belief or superstition) much more than this type of art.

In the concluding paragraphs of *Approaching the Unconscious*, Jung states:

> Our intellect has created a new world that dominates nature, and has populated it with monstrous machines. The latter are so indubitably useful that we cannot see even a possibility of getting rid of them or of our subservience to them. Man is bound to follow the adventurous promptings of his scientific and inventive mind and to admire himself for his spiritual achievements. At the same time, his genius shows the uncanny tendency to invent things that become more and more dangerous, because they represent better and better means for wholesale suicide.[27]

And he goes on:

> The modern standpoint is surely one-sided and unjust. It does not even accord with the known facts. Our actual knowledge of the unconscious shows that it is a natural phenomenon and that, like nature herself, it is at least *neutral*... the study of individual, as well as of collective, symbolism is an enormous task and one that has not yet been mastered. But a beginning has been made at last.[28]

We are encouraged to pursue a kind of thinking that listens to the fury of the emotions, the alarmed rush of events that loom over us, the randomness of encounters that make up part of our existence, and apparent chaos. In short, to be informed by everything that is inside us. In this way, perhaps, psychology may regain some of its authenticity, and at the same time, relinquish some of its alleged objectivity. Perhaps, then, there is a sense that before psychology can become a science, it must first be an art for each of us. A psychology which is the science of scholars is not of interest. What is of interest is a psychology that is an art through which we each cultivate our own existence.

Jung wrote further:

> My life is what I have done, my scientific work; the one is
> inseparable from the other. The work is my expression of my
> inner development; for commitment to the contents of the
> unconscious forms the man and produces his transformations.
> My works can be regarded as stations along my life's way. All my
> writings may be considered tasks imposed from within; their
> source was a fateful compulsion. What I wrote were things that
> assailed me within myself.[29]

Finally, if there is something to write, then let it be something that
assails us from within. For if we write to prevent someone from assailing
us from the outside, we might as well give up the idea of writing it.

NOTES

1. Sigmund Freud, "Preface" to the third English and American
editions of *The Interpretation of Dreams* (1931), in *The Standard Edition
of the Complete Psychological Works of Sigmund Freud*, vol. 4 (London:
Hogarth Press, 1961).

2. Sigmund Freud, *Traumdeutung* (Leipzig/Wien: Franz Deu-
ticke, 1900).

3. Sigmund Freud, "Preface" to the first edition of *The Interpretation
of Dreams* (1899), *Standard Edition*, vol. 4.

4. Sigmund Freud, "Preface" to the second edition of *The
Interpretation of Dreams* (1908), *Standard Edition*, vol. 4.

5. Cesare L. Musatti, "Introduzione," in *L'interpretazione dei sogni.
Opere di Sigmund Freud 1899*, vol. 3, ed. Cesare L. Musatti (Turin:
Paolo Boringhieri, 1966), p. XVII.

6. C. G. Jung, *Memories, Dreams, Reflections* (New York, NY:
Vintage, 1989).

7. Barbara Hannah, *Jung: His Life and his Work* (Wilmette, IL:
Chiron, 1976), p. 31.

8. *Ibid.*, p. 136.

9. Jung, *Memories, Dreams, Reflections*, p. xii.

10. *Ibid.*, p. 193.

11. *Ibid.*, p. 236.

12. *Ibid.*, p. 192.

13. C. G. Jung, Foreword to the Fourth (Swiss) Edition, in *The Collected Works of C. G. Jung*, vol. 5, ed. and trans. Gerhard Adler and R. F. C. Hull (Princeton, NJ: Princeton University Press, 1956; 1990), p. xxiii.

14. Jung, *Memories, Dreams, Reflections*, p. vii.

15. *Ibid.*, p. 223.

16. *Ibid.*, pp. 224–25, quoted in Hannah, *Jung*, p. 153. In his masterful *Temple and Contemplation*, a re-working of three lectures he delivered at Eranos in 1950, 1965, and 1974, Henry Corbin informs us, "It is significant that the Latin word, *templum,* originally meant a vast space, open on all sides, from which one could survey the whole surrounding landscape as far as the horizon. This is what it means to *contemplate:* to 'set one's sights on' Heaven from the *temple* that defines the field of vision. By the same token, the idea of contemplation introduces the idea of *consecration.* The term was actually used above all to designate the field of Heaven, the expanse of the open Heaven where the flight of birds could be observed and interpreted. Perhaps the idea of the cosmic Temple, which we have come across several times in the course of our inquiry, should be viewed in this light. Thus sacralized, the word, *templum,* finally came to mean the sanctuary, the sacred building known as a *temple,* the place of a divine Presence and of the contemplation of this Presence." (Henry Corbin, *Temple and Contemplation* [London: Routledge, 2009], p. 386.)

17. Jung, *Memories, Dreams, Reflections*, p. 225.

18. C. G. Jung, "Dank an Frau Froebe" (1951), quoted in Aniela Jaffé, "C. G. Jung and the Eranos Conferences," *Spring* (1977): 202.

19. *Ibid.*, p. 202.

20. *Ibid.*, p. 204.

21. *Ibid.*

22. *Ibid.*

23. *Ibid.*

24. Richard Wilhelm, ed., *I Ging: Das Buch der Wandlungen* (Jena: Eugen Diederichs, 1924); English edition: *The I Ching or Book of Changes*, trans. Cary F. Baynes (Princeton, NJ: Princeton University Press, 1959).

25. See C. G. Jung, "Vorwort zum *I Ging*" (1948), in *Gesammelte Werke*, vol. 11 (Düsseldorf: Walter, 2006), § 972, and C. G. Jung, "Foreword to the *I Ching*" (1950), in *The Collected Works of C. G. Jung*, vol. 11, ed. and trans. Gerhard Adler and R. F. C. Hull (Princeton, NJ: Princeton University Press, 1969), § 1018.

26. Jung, *Memories, Dreams, Reflections*, p. 185.

27. C. G. Jung, "Approaching the Unconscious," in C. G. Jung and Marie-Louise von Franz, *Man and His Symbols* (New York, NY: Dell-Bantam, 1968), pp. 90–91.

28. *Ibid.*, p. 94.

29. Jung, *Memories, Dreams, Reflections*, p. 222.

ANTONIO VITOLO

B orn in 1945, Antonio Vitolo, Ph.D., is a training analyst of the Associazione Italiana di Psicologia Analitica (AIPA) and a member since 1978 of the International Association for Analytical Psychology (IAAP). In the AIPA he also served as secretary of analytical training (1992–1995) and as president (2006–2010). He taught at Università di Roma "Sapienza" (1990–2006) and at the Seconda Università degli Studi di Napoli (1996–2003). He served as chairman of the Tenth International Congress of Analytical Psychology, held in Berlin in 1986. He also lectured at the IAAP Congresses in Rio de Janeiro (2000) and Montreal (2010), as well as at several other IAAP conferences and seminars. Among his works, are *Un esilio impossibile. Neumann tra Freud e Jung* (1990), "Polythéismes des rêves. Besoin de laïcité et de tolérance: Freud, Jung, Neumann," in *Monothéismes et modernités* (1996), and *Le psicoterapie* (1997). He also edited *Radici della cura laica* (1997), *Nascita, morte, trasformazione. Tra psicologia clinica e psicoterapia* (2002), and *Menti eminenti in sogno* (2007). Together with Luigi Aurigemma, Vitolo edited Carl Gustav Jung's works in Italian for Bollati Boringhieri publishing house from 1977 to 1995. He translated into Italian Jung's *The Concept of the Collective Unconscious* and *Concerning Rebirth* (CW 9–1), Erich Neumann's *The Great Mother—An Analysis of the Archetype*, and Marie-Louise von Franz's *Psyche and Matter*. In 2012 he founded the journal, *Tempo d'analisi. Paradigmi junghiani comparati*, where he is now editor. Vitolo was a research guest at Eranos in 1987, 1989, and 1993. In 1992, at Rudolf Ritsema's invitation, he gave a lecture at Eranos on the topic, "The Ethic of Image." In the same year, he authored a chapter on the Eranos Conferences for the *Trattato di Psicologia Analitica*, edited by Aldo Carotenuto.

THE ANALYTICAL *LEITMOTIF* OF THE ERANOS CONFERENCES

ANTONIO VITOLO

Within the Eranos Conferences, a Jungian analytical *leitmotif* can be outlined, which represents a deep and rich legacy not only for the history of analytical psychology, but also for its current theory and practice.

Carl Gustav Jung was born in in Kesswil, Switzerland, on July 26, 1875, and died in Küsnacht, on June 6, 1961. At least for the first twenty years of Eranos, Jung served as the *spiritus rector* of the Conferences, which began in 1933 and were held at Ascona, on the shores of Lake Maggiore. Jung presented his research at the Eranos Conferences and, over the years, gradually elaborated his reflections on the Eastern and Western cultures and his analyses of the collective unconscious to entail both cultural and clinical aspects. For Jung, Eranos represented a gateway between the making of an individual thinking and the opportunity for a dialogue with a group of creative guests. He was not only a living, enriching resource, but participated as a "guest among other guests." His Eranos lectures became notable essays, which led a process of continuous transformation of thinking.

Jung's fourteen Eranos lectures extend over a twenty-year period, from 1933 to 1951.[1] Starting with the description of a woman's individuation process (Kristine Mann), Jung's work evolved to an advanced level with the culmination of his analytical journey with the concepts of synchronicity and the *coniunctio*.[2] This arc of work entailed a personal and epistemologically paradigmatic growth, which mirrored not only the development of depth and analytical psychology, but also the spirit and events of an evolving century, dubbed by Eric J. Hobsbawm as "The Age of Extremes."[3] Events in the world and those in depth psychology were closely linked. Analytical psychology was born in 1914, the same year that World War I commenced, and Eranos was created in 1933, the same year that Hitler took office in Germany. 1952—the year of Jung's last participation at Eranos, on that occasion only as a listener—marked the onset of Jung's last stage of theoretical development. Subsequent to the publication of *Aion. Beiträge zur Symbolik des Selbst* (*Aion: Researches into the Phenomenology of the Self,* 1951), Jung published *Die Synchronizität als ein Prinzip akausaler Zusammenhänge* (*Synchronicity: An Acausal Connecting Principle,* 1952) and, following this, the *Mysterium Coniunctionis* (1955–1956), which we may be regarded as the *summa* of his work.

The two decades spanning 1912 to 1932 witnessed significant growth of Jung's clinical theory. His ideas generated during this time were rooted in reflections related to his own personal transformation from student of his former teacher, Sigmund Freud, to his full autonomy.[4] The year 1933 represented, in some ways, the "rebirth" of Jungian thought—the beginning of his Eranos lectures and the time of a complex exploration of the forms of totalitarianism, for example, as a dangerous illness that began to surface during the World War I.[5] Furthermore, throughout Eranos, Jung stressed the need for interdisciplinary dialogue on the pressing issues current at the time: analysts needed a cultural "net" as well as other thinkers required a medium for exchange and comparison of intra-disciplinary discoveries encountered in their studies.[6] Jung's entire personal life and Jungian psychology, which he named, *Selbstwirklichung des Unbewußten* ("self-realization of the unconscious"), involved the burgeoning dynamics of archetypical images, which functioned as a mirror of the *Zeitgeist* (spirit of the time).[7] The archetypal nature of psychic life, Jung's approach to religion and to symbols of transformation in the Mass, the connections between Judaism, Christianity, Islam, and Buddhism, and the symbolic bridge between alchemy and Christianity all comprised steps along Jung's creative journey toward the analytical cure of his patients.[8]

Eranos not only facilitated the transformation of Jung's own thinking, but also the blossoming of important contributions to the field of analytical psychology by some of Jung's most eminent patients and pupils, many of whom would later become analysts themselves: Erich Neumann, Marie-Louise von Franz, and Aniela Jaffé. Other analytical psychologists and Jungian psychotherapists who took part in the Conferences were Gustav Richard Heyer, Joseph Bernhard Lang, Ira Progoff, James Hillman, and Wolfgang Giegerich, among others. While these individuals were "Jungian" thinkers, they also opened the door to a post-Jungian psychology. This understanding brings attention to how individuals steeped in the original ideation of Jung's psychology to develop these ideas in the context of Jungian therapy. The Jungian analytical *leitmotif* threaded throughout the Eranos Conferences represents a deep and rich legacy not only for the history of analytical psychology, but also its current theory and practice. There are several examples. One, the hypothesis of a libido not defined by sexuality alone; the primary importance of imagination under normal as well as "pathological" conditions; the concept of dream as an abyssal, dark product of nature; the notion of archetypical determinants; the idea that time is free from causality at the limits of the unconscious psyche; and the postulate that primary religious impulses are connected not with hidden desires, but with the sublime and the spirit. These are core concepts that make up the framework of Jung's theory and, at the same time, provide a *leitmotif* that inspired Jung and his pupils.

From this perspective, we may now discuss the *creatio continua* that succeeded Jung, through some glimpses on the contributions of three analytical psychologists who took part in the Eranos Conferences: Erich Neumann, Marie-Louise von Franz, and Aniela Jaffé.

Erich Neumann

Erich Neumann was born in Berlin, Germany, on January 23, 1905, and died fifty-five years later in Tel Aviv, Palestine, on November 5, 1960. During Jung's lifetime, Neumann was the first and only analytical psychologist to speak at the Eranos Conferences, apart from Jung.[9] He received his Ph.D. in Philosophy in 1927 from the University of Erlangen, Bavaria, Germany. His dissertation focused on the orientalist, philosopher, and linguist, Johann Arnold Kanne, who was close to the eminent Indo-European linguist, Franz Bopp. Neumann also studied Medicine, but when the National Socialists came to power in Germany, Jewish students and teachers were expelled from universities; like many other Jews, Neumann couldn't get his diploma and decided to leave Germany. He underwent analysis with Jung in Zürich for about one year, from 1933 to 1934. In 1934, he moved to

Tel Aviv, Palestine, with his wife, Julie Blumenfeld Neumann, and his oldest child, Micha. Her daughter, Rachel (Ralli), was born in Palestine. After World War II, Neumann received the title of M.D. *honoris causa* from the University of Hamburg, Germany.

As a member of the German Jewish society, Neumann deeply felt the legacy of Jewish thinkers. Among the most important influences on Neumann's inner research were Hermann Cohen, Franz Rosenzweig, Martin Buber, Franz Kafka, Gershom Scholem, Ernst Cassirer, Johann Arnold Kanne, and Carl Abel.[10] The young Neumann was friends with Hannah Arendt, Karl Frankenstein, Erwin Löwenson, and the colleagues of Theodor Ludwig Wiesengrund-Adorno, Max Horkheimer and Herbert Marcuse, in the "Frankfurt School" or Institute for Social Research.[11] Rather than merely reflect a Jewish form of thinking, his goal was to lead a Jewish life and carry out a Jewish clinical practice.

In 1933, before meeting Jung, Neumann wrote an important essay about Franz Kafka's world-famous 1925 novel, *Der Prozess* (*The Trial*). The essay was entitled, *Das Gericht. Eine tiefenpsychologische Deutung* (*"The Trial": An Interpretation through Depth Psychology*, 1933). In the following years, between 1934 and 1948, Neumann's life was dedicated to building and developing analytical psychology in Tel Aviv, Palestine, according to the values of Zionism and Jung's psychological theory. He then published two of his greatest works, *Ursprungsgeschichte des Bewußtseins* (*The Origins and History of Consciousness*, 1949) and *Die grosse Mutter. Eine Phänomenologie der weiblichen Gestaltungen des Unbewussten* (*The Great Mother—An Analysis of the Archetype*, 1955), for which he made use of the iconographical materials collected by Olga Fröbe-Kapteyn in her Eranos Archive for Research in Symbolism.[12,13,14]

Neumann's works on feminine psychology are also very interesting. The most famous of these essays, *Amor und Psyche. Eine tiefenpsychologische Deutung* (*Amor and Psyche. The Psychic Development of the Feminine*, 1952), is based on the psychological interpretation of the short novel by Lucius Apuleius, *Cupid and Psyche*, which belongs to *Metamorphoseon libri XI (Asinus aureus). Tiefenpsychologie und neue Ethik* (*Depth Psychology and a New Ethic*, 1949) is another remarkable work of Neumann's.[15] The themes in this latter publication precipitated intense discussions with Jung. These paralleled earlier exchanges involving key terms, such as "castration" (used by Neumann) and "sacrifice" (first proposed by Jung and later accepted by Neumann in *The Origins and History of Consciousness*). In light of the tragedies of German lagers and Russian gulags, Neumann emphasized the importance of a feminine ethics and the end of patriarchal values. Letters between Neumann and Jung provide the most important documentation of the confrontation between these two pivotal figures in psychology on the relationship between Judaism and Christianity.[16] The letters reveal unquestionable opposites—light and shadow.[17]

Taken together, we can say that Neumann's early monographs represent the systematic part of his thought, whereas the letters embody the core of his subjective and the interpersonal world. Neumann's Eranos lectures can thus be regarded as the structural foundation of a specific post-Jungian theoretical and clinical framework. However, this assertion contains a certain amount of complexity. The entirety of Neumann's writing reveals in fact simultaneously a German and a Jewish soul. This was underscored in 1985 during my stay in Haifa when the well-known patient, analyst, and teacher, Gustav Dreifuss, very kindly allowed me to read Neumann's *Ursprungsgeschichte des jüdischen Bewusstseins* (*On the Origins and History of Jewish Consciousness*, 1930–1940). Neumann considered this work as a "silent book," an "unpublishable work," because he was born in Berlin. This theme of *galut* ("exile") continued throughout his life and work.[18]

Between 1948 and 1960, Neumann lectured at Eranos thirteen times. An additional contribution appeared in a special *Jahrbuch*, which was published on the occasion of Jung's seventieth birthday in 1950. In particular, Neumann's first four Eranos lectures illustrate the author's cultural and clinical attitude. His essays, *Der mystische Mensch. Versuch einer psychologischen Interpretation* (*The Mystical Man. Towards a Psychological Interpretation*, 1948), *Die mythische Welt und der Einzelne* (*The Mythical World and the Individual*, 1949), *Über den Mond und das matriarchale Bewußtseins* (*About the Moon and the Matriarchal Consciousness*, 1950), and *Zur psychologischen Bedeutung des Ritus* (*On the Psychological Meaning of Rite*, 1950), represented cross-cultural gateways to analytical therapy. At the same time, they provided a perspective on the way back from the newly born state of Israel to the European state, Switzerland, where analytical psychology originated and the free analytical and cultural dialogue of Eranos began.

Neumann's first assertion at Eranos is that the unconscious is a source of continuous creativity and this mystic underground works as a completely unconscious basis of archetypical emergence. This process has its roots in the psyche, in the brain, and in the myth where the Self penetrates into the boundaries of the Ego. In this way, the creative process becomes a new enterprise.[19] The core of Neumann's concept of the "mystic man" is the transformation from the ouroboric level to an Ego centered in the Self. Thanks to Jung's interest for the visions of Brother Klaus and to the Kabbalah, as well as his own attention to Theresa of Ávila, Neumann brings the mystical experience at Eranos as a fundamental side of the analyst. According to Jung's theory of the final stage of individuation—or in Neumann's terms, the centroversion—a *geeinte Persönlichkeit* ("unified personality") emerges, a personality in which Horus and Osiris, Ego and Self, coexist. On the basis of the *Talmud*, Neumann highlights that God and man are twins. Kabbalistic material flows through Neumann's studies, Jung's writings and visions (1944), and Scholem's works.[20] Dreifuss described the alchemic and Kabbalistic roots of the *coniunctio* and the Kabbalistic union of opposites in Jung's work.[21]

In his lecture, *Die mythische Welt und der Einzelne* (*The Mythical World and the Individual*, 1949), Neumann focuses on the mythic essence of the archetypes and places the projection into the myth. On the other side, the Ego seems the basic ground of the individual.[22] Neumann credits Johann Jakob Bachofen, Ludwig Klages, and Otto Weininger for conceiving the primary role of the origins of the mother and the images of rhythm of the cosmic life as a dynamic of male and female. From this perspective, he acknowledges Jung's hypothesis of the collective unconscious as a cultural and clinical alternative to Freud's emphasis on myth, tragedy, and dream. According to historian of religions Walter Friedrich Otto, who lectured at Eranos in 1939 and again in 1955, Neumann states that myth is an ontological foundation. Thus, Neumann asserts, the individual effort becomes very important when facing the collective.

In *Zur psychologischen Bedeutung des Ritus* (*On the Psychological Meaning of Rite*, 1950), Neumann deals with the role of rituals in psychic development and the ancient philosophical debate concerning thinking and action. He considers the psychoanalytic value of the ritual as an archetypical ground that contains a dynamic essence. Neumann's background is philosophical. For example, he discusses how Hegel and Cassirer assert that the cult is an eternal process of the individual who is oriented toward his identity not only through the thinking process, but also through action. Ancient and modern forms of ritual are the driving forces of psychic life. Pointing out the deeply transformative level of rituals and the dangers of illusion, Neumann quotes a Chassidic tale reported by Martin Buber, who lectured at Eranos in 1934 and who also participated at the 1947 Eranos Conference as a listener.[23] This discussion also includes clinical examples described by Karl Abraham and Carl Alfred Meier.

A very interesting case concerns Miss Alisa Shavit. As a young patient of Neumann's, she reported dreaming of many worms. Suspecting the risk of a cancer, Neumann wrote Jung in July 1937 to ask for advice. Jung, who was at that time travelling to the U.S.A. and India, replied on April 4, 1938, recommending that Neumann work on the young woman's creative transformation. Jung's suggestion concurred with Neumann's own intention. Over this period, Alisa Shavit created many beautiful paintings and went on to become a very well-regarded painter in Israel. Alisa Shavit recounted this story to me herself on December 22, 1985, in Haifa. This analytical process illustrated the central importance for an individual of the creative process between necessity and freedom. This understanding reflects Neumann's inspired originality.

Neumann emphasizes the sacred nature of individuation and extends this idea beyond individuation to describe the entirety of life's arc as a "rite." Familiar with the legacy of Johann Jakob Bachofen, Leo Frobenius, Ludwig Klages, Émile Durkheim, Johan Huizinga, and Arnold van Gennep, Neumann regards two analytical concepts as significant: the rhythm between projection and introjection, and the experience (e.g., Jung's concept of "psychic reality" and Wilfred Bion's idea of "learning from the experience").[24]

In *Über den Mond und das matriarchale Bewußtsein* (*About the Moon and the Matriarchal Consciousness,* 1950), Neumann lays out the full clinical frame of psyche. This text represents an original development of Jung's theory, although the Moon and the evening are basic concepts in the Jewish calendar initiating year and day. Initial levels of growth of the psyche are contained in the *ouroboros.* Subsequent steps of growth involve the feminine and masculine in the woman and in the man, starting from a common symbol, the Moon. It should be noted that, in German, *der Mond* ("the Moon") and *die Sonne* ("the Sun") represent a *masculine* Moon and a *feminine* Sun. So, in Neumann's view, the Moon is the deepest symbol, one he explores starting from a linguistic point of view. It is interesting to mention here that his emphasis on the etymological roots of the lemma *moon*, which is connected to the Greek, μην, and to the Latin, *mensis*, "month," is also related to the Greek, μενοξ (μενοιναν, μαινομαι, μανία), as well as to the Sanskrit, *mas / manas*, "mind," "spirit," "heart," or "soul." All of these roots converge in the original semantic meaning of "keeping" or "keeping in mind." Neumann asserts that, from a psychic point of view, the Moon not only influences the inner body of women and her menstrual cycle, but the Earth, time, rhythm, music, and art. Astrology is the frame of cosmic order, which determines pregnancies and births. Nevertheless, behind its universal frame, Moon's is an inner law and rules the individual emerging from the collective world. There is also another clear difference: quality is feminine and quantity is masculine. All of Neumann's reflections on feminine psychology distinguish Moon values from Sun values. Further, his original contribution to a post-Jungian clinical approach is based on, as mentioned in a *Midrash*, the essential equivalence between the Moon and the Sun during their perpetual transition from day to night and the utopic idea of an alternating patriarchy/matriarchy.[25]

Neumann's lecture, *Kunst und Zeit* (*Art and Time,* 1951), contains an original theory on the arts, with particular emphasis on literature and painting. He points out the importance of the cultural criterion, which rules the artist's psyche. The creative source emerging from the unconscious abyss has a transformative relationship with the criterion itself. This does not involve a description or a destruction of the past, rather a new interpretation, which represents a breaking point thereby creating new forms and colors for communicating and reintegrating parts of a lost wholeness. Hieronymus Bosch, Edvard Munch, Giorgio de Chirico, Marc Chagall, Rainer Maria Rilke, and Georg Trakl are the interpreters of the earth, the child, and a hopeful attitude that illustrate dissonance in the world.[26] While other eminent thinkers who attended Eranos in 1951 explored the role of time in culture and in Eastern and Western religions, Neumann, as "Jungian," elevates and sublimates time to the highest level of the arts.[27] In so doing, similar to Rabbi Nachman, he reveals the simultaneously terrible and marvelous beauty of the world.

In his 1952 and 1953 Eranos lectures, Neumann shifts his focus to the relationship between psyche and matter. In the first lecture, *Psyche und die Wandlung der Wirklichkeitsebenen. Ein meta-psycologischer Versuch* (*The Psyche and the Transformation of the Reality Planes. A Meta-Psychological Experiment,* 1952), Neumann creatively rebuilds the eminent bridge, elaborated by Jung, between *Naturwissenschaften* (natural sciences) and *Geisteswissenschaften* (human sciences), based on physics and cosmology (Albert Einstein, Erwin Schrödinger, George Gamow). In the second lecture, *Die Bedeutung des Erdarchetyps für die Neuzeit* (*The Importance of Earth Archetypes for Modern Times,* 1953), he explores the dialectic approach to perception, imagination, and knowledge of the two parts of the *Anima Mundi,* earth and the heavens. Using a dream, a vision, and an example of active imagination, he discusses the connection between Adam and *Adamah,* "earth," the role of the *maṇḍala* in the mid-space between sky and earth, and the symbolic nature of objects.

In her *In memoriam Erich Neumann* (1960), Olga Fröbe-Kapteyn quotes a letter by Neumann from 1951 where he clearly acknowledged Eranos as the "earth."[28] Notably, this statement is consistent with his Western birth and Zionism that is intricately related to the choice of waiting for a Messiah and not with the issue concerning the occupation of the territory that would later become Israel. This perspective was also present in *Die Sinnfrage und das Individuum* (*The Question of Meaning and the Individual,* 1957): *der Sinn,* "the meaning," is not eternal, but conceivable as a door opened by archetypes.

Neumann's last lecture, *Die Psyche als Ort der Gestaltung* (*The Psyche as the Place of Creation,* 1960), is the result of Neumann's research and the greatest of all monographs, *The Great Mother,* whose images were named by Neumann, *Gestaltungen des Unbewußten* ("configurations of the unconscious"). The primary role of the form and formation is the basis for an individual's capacity to represent reality in the psyche, a function that develops at a phylogenetic level only late in life. Individuation is the natural living mystery, which illuminates "*im Gegensatz zur Auseinanderfaltung der Massen im Raum und Zeit*" ("in contrast to the mass dissolution in space and in time").[29] Neumann's final message is that the individual is the highest value facing the masses and it is vital to maintain its eminence over totalitarianisms.

Marie-Louise Von Franz

Marie-Louise von Franz was born on January 4, 1915, in Munich, Germany, and died on February 17, 1998, in Küsnacht, Switzerland. She is one of the most prominent Jungian analysts, and her work stands out for its creativity and her ability to delve into vast analytic and cultural issues. Though her presence at Eranos dates from 1937, her work as a teacher, analyst, and essayist limited her contribution at Eranos to just two lectures in 1978 and 1985.

Von Franz studied Philology at the University of Zürich. In 1933, at the age of eighteen and in the same year that the Eranos Conferences began, she met Jung through Toni Wolff 's nephew. The young man had been asked by Jung, who was fifty-eight years old at the time, to invite young people so that he would have contact with generations different from his own.[30] In exchange for analytic sessions, von Franz shared with Jung her humanistic and philological knowledge of alchemy. This research partnership climaxed in the writing of *Mysterium Coniunctionis* (1955–1956), especially as far as the *Aurora Consurgens* was concerned, the book credited to Thomas Aquinas (this subject was later inserted in her book, *Alchemie*). For many years, von Franz collaborated with the fairy tale researcher, Hedwig von Beit, who, in 1952, published the three-volume *Symbolik des Märchens* (*The Symbolism of the Fairy Tale*, 1952). However, von Beit failed to acknowledge the creative contributions by von Franz and she is not mentioned in the book. In the early 1940s, von Franz also contributed in cataloguing the images in the Eranos Archive for Research in Symbolism: she catalogued, for example, the pictures on the Mercurial symbolism, which Jung commented in his 1942 Eranos lecture on that topic. Von Franz also had a remarkable epistolary relationship with the renowned physicist and winner of the 1945 Nobel Prize in Physics, Wolfgang Pauli. He was also her patient for some time. Unfortunately, their letters were destroyed by Pauli's wife after her husband's death.

In addition to her exegesis of myths, legends, and fairy tales, von Franz applied Jung's method to physics and mathematics. She published several important books on numbers, time, and energy such as *Zahl und Zeit* (*Number and Time,* 1977) and *Psyche und Materie* (*Psyche and Matter,* 1988). Her first Eranos presentation, *The Psychological Experience of Time* (1978), was given at the Conference dedicated to the theme, *In Time and Out of Time.* Von Franz's lecture continues Jung's more than three decades of work on this subject and, together with Wolfgang Pauli, David Bohm, Bernard d'Espagnat, Olivier Costa de Beauregard, Ilya Prigogine, and the science historian, Joseph Needham, highlights the link between causality and acausality in the energy-entropy dyad.[31]

Von Franz furthers her theory in the book, *Traum und Tod* (*On Dreams and Death,* 1984). This work effects an analytical treatment of the rhythm of projection and introjection in archetypical passages in *Spiegelungen der Seele* (*Reflections of the Soul,* 1978). In this context, synchronicity is where sense is configured and numbers provide an essential factor to create order. Von Franz's hypothesis on the relationship between quaternity and DNA's base constituents—A, T, C, and G—is also quite original. Her analysis illuminates the profound diversity of the four-base, upon which the 64 hexagrams of the *I Ching* are constructed. In this way, at the crossroads between natural science and human sciences where humanistic interpretation of symbolism, mathematics, physics, and neuroscience are connected, von Franz fully completes the research on these issues first approached by Jung. In this effort, her disciplinary integration perfectly reflects the Eranos spirit.

Von Franz's *Nike und die Gewässer der Styx* (*Nike and the Waters of the Styx,* 1985) contains an illuminating summary of Jung's theoretical and clinical themes. The text refers to hexagram seven of the *I Ching*, "The Army." While it connects mythology, astrology, and analytical psychology at the turn of the twentieth century, her essay also underscores the importance of including anxiety and creativity in the hypothesis of collective unconscious, which Jung had outlined earlier in *Aion* (1951). By positioning her research on the border between the Age of Aquarius and the Age of Pisces and Hell's Styx River that is soaked with masculine and feminine aspects, von Franz reveals the ambivalent nature of Nike, the Goddess of Victory. Through the emblem of the fierce conflict between opposites, she describes a winged force that crucially requires recognition ability: creativity, difficult to repress, lives in a constant circle between individual and collectivity. It is very close to the sudden burst of psychotic status and requires every individual to be delicately open to creativity and to jealously keep the secret of intimacy inside the community.

Von Franz quotes Winston Churchill, the man who defeated Nazism, and his premonitory dream in 1933 of a man (perhaps a father?) on the failure of Nazism; it remembers the archetypical oscillation between the snake and the *lapis*, extreme symbols of both a spirituality made true by Christ and a devouring animality. This warning is consubstantial with the role of Eranos in depth psychology.

In her meticulous style, von Franz implies that individuation that precedes the burgeoning numbers of wars and material and mental poverty at the end of the twentieth century can reveal the relationship between the secret flow of events and the "*Wirken des kollektive Unbewußten im Weltgeschehen*" ("work of the collective unconscious behind the world events," according to Jung). Such a perspective shows the inseparability of light and shadow and the personal and collective dimension. Similarly, the Self and the Ego can be imagined as positioned along an axis.[32] As von Franz told me at a meeting at her house on June 11, 1991, when I was working on the Italian edition of her book, *Psyche and Matter*, what at first may be invisible is nonetheless not unobservable.

ANIELA JAFFÉ

Aniela Jaffé was born on February 20, 1903, in Berlin, Germany, and died on October 30, 1991, in Zürich, Switzerland. She studied Literature and Psychology in Hamburg, Germany. During the Nazi era, she found shelter in Geneva and Zürich. Jaffé was first analyzed by Liliane Frey-Rohn, best known for her 1969 essay, *Von Freud zu Jung* (*From Freud to Jung*). Jaffé began analysis with Jung in 1937.

In the beginning, Jaffé was a guest at Zürich's Psychologischer Club (Psychology Club). However, in 1945, together with the important Jewish analyst, Rivkah Schärf, and thanks to Jung's intercession, she became a regular member of the Club. She worked from 1948 to 1955 as secretary of the newly-formed C. G. Jung Institute (which was located in the Psychology Club building at that time) in Zürich. Subsequently, she became Jung's personal secretary. In that position, she was directly and actively responsible for the publishing of his "autobiography," *Erinnerungen, Träume, Gedanken* (*Memories, Dreams, Reflections*, 1961). This meticulously detailed and accurate work mirrored the complexity of Jung's feelings. I'm very grateful, *in memoriam*, to Jaffé for her letter (April 19, 1985) in answer to my question about Jung's father during my research on the role of father in the relationships between Freud, Jung, Otto Gross, and Sabina Spielrein.[33]

Jaffé's four Eranos essays, presented between 1971 and 1975, are mainly concerned with precognitions, apparitions, creative passages, and other conscious and unconscious states where the experiences of limit and transition dominate.[34] In *Die schöpferischen Phasen im Leben von C.G. Jung* (*The Creative Phases in C. G. Jung's Life,* 1971), Jaffé recalls the important stages in Jung's psychic life: a childhood dream of a shining phallus, his mature years, and finally, his old age. There are many other critical events included. For example, she also describes Jung's fruitful, but tormented, relationship with Freud, his depression, his monumental work, *The Red Book* or *Liber Novus*, his special friendship with Toni Wolff and the work on *Psychologische Typen* (*Psychological Types,* 1921), and the subjective creation and introduction of alterity in Jung's clinical method. There are also details concerning his casual meeting with Sinologist, Richard Wilhelm, the development of a religious and alchemic metapsychology, and his brutal and torn experience with Nazism. All of these are critical themes that relate to and reveal Jung's character, written with attention to detail and with respect by a faithful apprentice analyst who observed the great man every day.[35]

In *C.G. Jung und die Eranos-Tagungen. Zum 100. Geburtstag von C.G. Jung* (*C. G. Jung and the Eranos Conferences. On the Hundredth Anniversary of C. G. Jung's Birth,* 1975), Jaffé explores the roots of Jung's Eranos project. For example, she documents the interactions between Jung and Olga Fröbe-Kapteyn, Rudolf Otto's creative idea for the name "Eranos," the atmosphere of the early meetings and the breaks, Jung's active presence and enthusiasm, his meeting with Rabbi Leo Baeck, and their disagreement that was followed by their eventual reconcilement. At first, Baeck refused (1947), but then accepted the handshake proffered by Jung when the latter admitted his mistake of not having condemned Nazism from the start.[36]

Jaffé's words are crafted with elegant authenticity and fine culture. A prime example is her *Unitary Reality and the Creative (C. G. Jung and E. Neumann)* (1983), where she outlines similarities and differences between the two men in their views on the *unus mundus* and archetype.[37] Pauli's letters to Jaffé as Jung's secretary provide a vital source. Her two precious studies, *Bilder und Symbole aus E.T.A. Hoffmanns Märchen "Der goldene Topf"* (*Images and Symbols in E. T. A. Hoffmann's Tale, "The Golden Pot,"* 1978) and *Hermann Broch: Der Tod des Vergil. Ein Beitrag zum Problem der Individuation* (*Hermann Broch's "The Death of Virgil": A Contribution to the Problem of Individuation,* in *Studien zur Analytischen Psychologie II,* 1955) illustrate her brilliant creativity. Interestingly, the second essay detailed the important Jewish Austrian writer, Broch, who Jung wanted as a collaborator for the magazine, *Weltanschauung,* which never saw the light of day.[38]

The first cultural and analytical period at Eranos brought together tradition and modernity. The analytical *leitmotif* is still evolving as a *creatio continua* (continuous creation). The *numinosum* has rekindled Jung's original ideas with inspired thoughts not only from Erich Neumann, Marie-Louise von Franz, and Aniela Jaffé in Ascona, but also for many more in the whole world's rooms for analysis. Jung's thought, analytical theory, and Eranos have a long life.

NOTES

1. On Jung's Eranos lectures, which were published first in the *Eranos-Jahrbücher* and then in his *Collected Works,* see Riccardo Bernardini, *Jung a Eranos. Il progetto della psicologia complessa* (Milan: FrancoAngeli, 2011), pp. 170–246.

2. Carl Gustav Jung, "Zur Empirie des Individuationsprozesses (Hiezu fünf Bildtafeln)," *Eranos-Jahrbuch* 1 (1933): 201–14.

3. Eric J. Hobsbawm, *The Age of the Extremes—The Short Twentieth Century, 1914–1991* (London: Michael Joseph, 1994).

4. Sigmund Freud and Carl Gustav Jung, *Letters,* ed. William McGuire (Princeton, NJ: Princeton University Press, 1994).

5. Carl Gustav Jung, *Memories, Dreams, Reflections*, ed. Aniela Jaffé (London: Random House, 1961), p. 6.

6. See Bernardini, *Jung a Eranos*, and Hans Thomas Hakl, *Eranos—An Alternative Intellectual History of Twentieth Century* (Montreal: McGill-Queen's University Press, 2013).

7. Carl Gustav Jung, *The Red Book. Liber Novus*, ed. Sonu Shamdasani (New York, NY: W. W. Norton, 2009).

8. See Carl Gustav Jung, "Die verschiedenen Aspekte der Wiedergeburt," *Eranos-Jahrbuch* 7 (1939): 399–447.

9. Antonio Vitolo, *Un esilio impossibile. Neumann tra Freud e Jung* (Roma: Borla, 1990); Antonio Vitolo, "Polythéisme des rêves, besoin de laïcité et de tolerance. Freud, Jung et Neumann," in M. Kerrou, eds., *Monothéismes et modernités* (Tunis: Orient & Occident-Fondation Naumann, 1996), pp. 273–92; Henry Abramovitch, "Erich Neumann, theorist and analyst: a brief introduction," *Harvest* 52 (2, 2006): 9–25; Angelika Löwe, *"Auf Seiten der inneren Stimme…" Erich Neumann-Leben und Werk* (Freiburg im Breisgau: Karl Alber, 2014).

10. See Harold Bloom, *The Strong Light of the Canonical: Freud, Kafka, and Scholem as Revisionists of Jewish Culture and Thought* (copyright by Harold Bloom, 1987).

11. Whose memories on Neumann I personally put together—thanks to G. Dreifuss—in a *nofim* in Jerusalem on December 18, 1985, when I started the final draft of my book, *Un esilio impossibile*.

12. Erich Neumann, *The Origins and History of Consciousness* (Princeton, NJ: Bollingen Series XLII, Princeton University Press, 1954).

13. Erich Neumann, *The Great Mother—An Analysis of the Archetype* (New York, NY: Bollingen Series XLVII, Pantheon Books, Inc., 1955).

14. See Bernardini, *Jung a Eranos*, pp. 247–353.

15. Erich Neumann, *Tiefenpsychologie und neue Ethik* (Zürich: Walter, 1949).

16. See Vitolo, *Un esilio impossibile*; Löwe, *"Auf Seiten der inneren Stimme…"*

17. The letters were only recently published as *Analytical Psychology in Exile: The Correspondence of C. G. Jung and Erich Neumann*, ed. Martin Liebscher (Princeton, NJ: Princeton University Press, 2015).

18. Raphael Jehudah Zwi Werblowsky and Geoffrey Wigoder, eds., *The Oxford Dictionary of the Jewish Religion* (New York, NY: Oxford University Press, 1997).

19. Erich Neumann, *Umkreisung der Mitte I. Kulturentwicklung und Religion* (Zürich: Rascher, 1953), p. 142. Neumann writes:

> *"Das Problem des schöpferischen Unbewußten, ein Zentralproblem der Tiefenpsychologie, ist gleichzeitig das Zentralproblem der Mystik und des mystischen Menschen. Da sich der schöpferische Prozeß außerhalb des Bewußtseins abspielt und deswegen als eine Grenzerfahrung des Ich angesehen werden muß, ist jeder Versuch, sich diesem zentralen Urwirbel zu nähern, ein Unternehmen und ein Unterfangen."*

> [The problem of the creative unconscious, a crucial problem in depth psychology, is also the central problem of mysticism and of the mystic man. Since the creative process takes place outside the individual's consciousness, and therefore has to be considered as a delimitation of the Ego's boundaries, every attempt to approach this "spinal cord" is an enterprise, a beginning.]

See also Erich Neumann, "Der mystische Mensch. Versuch einer psychologyschen Interpretation," *Eranos-Jahrbuch* 16 (1948): 317–74.

20. See Sanford L. Drob, "The Mystical Symbol: Some Comments on Ankori, Giegerich, Scholem, and Jung," *Journal of Jungian Theory and Practice* 7 (1, 2005): 25–29; Sanford L. Drob, *Kabbalistic Visions—C.G. Jung and Jewish Mysticism* (New Orleans, LA: Spring Journal, Inc., 2010).

21. Gustav Dreifuss, "The Union of the Opposites in Kabbalah," *Journal of Jungian Theory and Practice* 13 (1, 2005): 65–71; Gustav Dreifuss, *Studies in Jungian Psychology: Work and Reflection Life Long* (Haifa: privately printed, 2003); and, above all, Gustav Dreifuss, *Erich Neumann's Jewish Consciousness*, in *Papers* (Haifa: privately printed, 2003), pp. 162–69.

22. Neumann, *Umkreisung der Mitte I*, p. 67. Neumann writes:

> *"Die Archetypen sind ... auch 'mythologische Motive' d.h. ihre Projektion konstelliert die mythische Welt. Ebenso scheint das Ich, das in der Mitte unseres Bewußtseins sieht, das Wesen des Einzelnen und seine Individualität auszumachen."*

> [Archetypes are ... also "mythological motifs." This means that their projection constellates the mythical world. In the same way the Ego, that sees at center of our consciousness, seems to produce the individual's essence and his individuality.]

See also Erich Neumann, "Die mythische Welt und der Einzelne," *Eranos-Jahrbuch* 17 (1949): 189–254.

23. Martin Buber, "Sinnbildliche und sakramentale Existenz im Judentum," *Eranos-Jahrbuch* 2 (1934): 339–67. Buber's degree thesis was entitled, *Zur Geschichte des Individuation problems. Nicolaus von Cues und Jakob Böhme* (Wien, 1904). From 1906 to 1963, Buber translated from Hebrew into German *Die Chassidische Bücher,* which could be considered a constant reference source for Neumann, and published in 1923 *Ich und Du* (*I and Thou*), his most famous work. Between July 1933 and 1934 (Hitler became *Kanzler* on January 31, 1933), Buber published *Die Judenfrage*, at first in the form of an open letter to the protestant theologian, Gerhard Kittel, and afterwards in the form of a dialogue with a reply from Kittel. Buber confuted and rejected Kittel's theories as a denial of Judaism. According to Buber, who escaped to Jerusalem in 1938, Neumann felt himself in the Ascona community both a guest, a *ger* (in Hebrew, a "foreigner in transit"), and a citizen (*Insasse*).

24. Neumann, *Umkreisung der Mitte I*, pp. 32–33. Neumann writes:

> "*Das Ritual ist die Bewegung der archetypischen Welt auf den Menschen, die von ihm aufgenommen wird und in seinem Tun beantwortet wird ... Freiheit und Notwendigkeit verbinden sich im Individualritual zu einer schöpferischen Einheit, in der die Persönlichkeit gleichzeitig Subjekt und Obiekt des Geschehens ist.*"

> [The ritual is the movement of the archetypal world towards man, who receives it and puts it in relation to his acts. In the individual ritual, freedom, and necessity are connected in a creative unity, in which personality is, at the same time, subject and object of the event.]

See also Erich Neumann, "Zur psychologischen Bedeutung des Ritus," *Eranos-Jahrbuch* 19 (1950): 65–120.

25. Erich Neumann, "Über den Mond und das matriarchaleBewußtsein," *Eranos-Jahrbuch* 18 (1950): 323–76.

26. See Erich Neumann, *Art and the Creative Unconscious* (Princeton, NJ: Princeton University Press, 1959).

27. These other thinkers include Henri-Charles Puech (*La gnose et le temps*), Gilles Quispel (*Zeit und Geschichte im antiken Christentum*), Louis Massignon (*Le temps dans la pensée islamique*), Henry Corbin (*Le*

temps ciclique dans le Mazdéisme et l'Ismaélisme), Mircea Eliade (*Le temps et l'éternité dans la pensée indienne*), and Hellmut Wilhelm (*Der Zeitbegriff im Buch der Wandlungen*).

28. Olga Fröbe-Kapteyn, "*In memoriam* Erich Neumann," *Eranos-Jahrbuch* 29 (1960): 7–8. Neumann's letter is published in *Zeitschrift für Analytische Psychologie* 11 (3-4, 1980): 187ff.

29. Erich Neumann, "Die Psyche als Ort der Gestaltung," *Eranos-Jahrbuch* 28 (1960): 56.

30. As explained in Nadia Neri, *Oltre l'Ombra. Donne intorno a Jung* (Rome: Borla, 1995). French edition: *Femmes autour de Jung* (Paris: Cahiers jungiens de psychanalyse, 2002).

31. Marie-Louise von Franz, "The Psychological Experience of Time," *Eranos-Jahrbuch* 47 (1978): 173–204.

32. Marie-Louise von Franz, "Nike und die Gewäßer der Styx," *Eranos-Jahrbuch* 54 (1985): 455–583.

33. Antonio Vitolo, "Freud, Gross, Spielrein alle origini del tema paterno in Jung," *Rivista di Psicologia Analitica* 16 (2, 1986): 188–205.

34. See, e.g., Aniela Jaffé, "Synchronizität und Kausalität in der Parapsychologie," *Eranos-Jahrbuch* 42 (1973): 1–42, and Aniela Jaffé, "Auffassung einer Individuation der Menschheit," *Eranos-Jahrbuch* 43 (1974): 329–66.

35. Aniela Jaffé, "Die schöpferischen Phasen im Leben von C.G.Jung," *Eranos-Jahrbuch* 40 (1971): 85–122.

36. Aniela Jaffé, "C.G. Jung und die Eranos-Tagungen: Zum 100. Geburtstag von C. G. Jung," *Eranos-Jahrbuch* 44 (1975): 1–14.

37. Aniela Jaffé, "A Retrospective Paper: Unitary Reality and the Creative," *Harvest* 39 (1983): 9–16.

38. See Bernardini, *Jung a Eranos*, pp. 112–16.

STEPHEN AIZENSTAT

S tephen Aizenstat, Ph.D. in Clinical Psychology, is the Chancellor and Founding President of Pacifica Graduate Institute (Santa Barbara, California, U.S.A.). His book, *Dream Tending* (2009), describes applications of dreamwork in relation to health and healing, nightmares, the World's Dream, relationships, and the creative process. Aizenstat's methodologies extend traditional dream work to the vision of an animated world, where living images in dream are experienced as embodied and originating in the psyche of Nature as well as that of persons. His other recent publications include *Imagination & Medicine—The Future of Healing in an Age of Neuroscience*, co-edited with Robert Bosnak (2009), "Dream Tending and Tending the World," in *Ecotherapy—Healing with Nature in Mind* (2009), and "Soul-Centered Education: An Interview with Stephen Aizenstat," in *Reimagining Education—Essays on Reviving the Soul of Learning*, with Nancy Treadway Galindo (2009). His major work, *Dream Tending*, recently appeared also in Italian as *Vegliare il sogno. Teoria e pratica del Dream Tending* (2013). Inspired by James Hillman, Aizenstat attended an Eranos meeting for the first time in the mid-90's. In 1999, he presented a paper at Eranos on the topic, "Dream Tending: Working the Intersection between Psyche and World." He also lectured at Eranos in recent years on issues such as "Fragility of the World's Dream" (2011), "The Dangers and Opportunity of Cyberspace: A New Vision of Global Dreaming" (2012), and "The Pacifica Story: Money as Psychic Libido" (2013).

ERANOS AS DREAM

STEPHEN AIZENSTAT

E ranos as dream began for me in the way of the dream. I received the call one summer afternoon in the mid-1990s. It originated from a corner room of a small villa in the Swiss Alps, the southern side, the side facing northern Italy. Over the phone came an invitation: "Dr. Aizenstat, I wish to invite you to join us at an Eranos *Tagung*. On behalf of the many that have come before and those present now, we wish to extend to you a 'seat at the Table'."

Dreams visit in just that way: callings from places unfamiliar, unknown, yet to be revealed. Some months later I journeyed from California to Eranos. Upon arriving at the shores of Lake Maggiore, I found myself sitting at what I learned to be the famed "Round Table," the gathering place for many distinguished philosophers, psychologists, poets, spiritual teachers, scientists and others who, over the last eighty years, had also received a call, perhaps even a calling. All were coming together to "take time out of time," to relax, and to engage in free-flowing cross-disciplinary conversation and to dream.

The story keepers of the Eranos Foundation tell us that the name, *Eranos*, was inspired by Rudolf Otto and, shortly thereafter, incarnated through the work of its initial founder Olga Fröbe-Kapteyn in 1933. If we think of Otto's main contribution to depth psychology as naming the *numinous*, then we can imagine the *Tagung*, the Round Table, as a banquet, a feast of imagination, where each guest brings an "other worldly" dish as contribution. Such offerings are not a recapitulation of others' ideas or a rehash of words spoken before, but rather voicing what is presently numinous as it makes itself known, emerging in the company of others through waking vision, synchronicity, as well as spontaneous expressions, and dream.

Even before taking my place at the Table, it was apparent in those first steps onto the beautifully tended grounds that at Eranos the landscape itself opens as a dreamscape. The dreams of so many have been shared here when wandering the verdant gardens as well as around the Table. Here the Elders talk story. Here the community listens to the images of the deep psyche as they make their presence known. Eranos is a place of dreams. It has been said that a dream loves a dream. Eranos loves to be met in the way of dreams and the dreamers who are drawn to these enchanted grounds.

Over the last twenty-five years I have been lured back many times to Ascona, Moscia, home to Eranos. The call of the soul guardians of this *temenos* lure me back repeatedly. The aspirations of the living as well as the voices of the dead make their intentions known, gathering selected travelers worldwide to this seminal gathering place. I have participated at the Round Table, offered formal presentations, conducted workshops in Dream Tending, and most vividly and lovingly experienced the push of the invisibles as I meandered through the gardens and swam in the lake below. Eranos as dream continues to evolve, to individuate, pulled by the calling of the future, informed by soul bodies of the past, and, most elementally, informed by the spirit of the place. As Eranos, the entity itself individuates, as do those of us implicated in her evolution. Her "becoming" pushes our own further development.

In my visits to Eranos, I could palpably feel how the ancestral "shades" of those who came before continue to spark the imagination of place, pushing to be heard at every turn. With the assistance of an old wood-framed two-sectioned chalkboard pulled up and down by frayed ropes, lectures are still offered in the main hall, with seating for about forty-five participants. Fresh wind circulates through the space when the doors are opened to the balcony overlooking the lake below and the mountains above. Before power point and technological communication, exquisite as they can be, the older ways of sharing ideas, informed by embodied empathy and subtle attunement, promoted spirited dialog between guests. This quality of human interaction continues today. At Eranos, though always well kept by the extraordinary stewards of the place, a musty scent of the past adds to the multi-leveled intricacies of a higher order communication. Like an oasis in the wastelands of a manic culture, the gift of slowing down, listening, and imagining are further rich additions to the conversation.

As an invited guest/observer I attended my first Eranos annual *Tagung* in the early 90's. I will never forget two men that I met at that meeting, both in the later stages of life and both contributors to the Eranos dream. Rudolf Ritsema, fire in his eyes, tall in stature, told of the oracular wisdom of the *I Ching*. Charles Boer, deeply introspective, yet exuberant in the ways of living and thinking, talked of Epicureanism. Each man made a deep and lasting impression on my life. Pushed by the hexagram that selected me as well as Rudolf's reading of the ancient symbol, my world shook. I was offered guidance for the challenges I would face in years to come. Charles Boer opened a fully new way of being in the world. Put way too simply (given he was an elite scholar of international note) he suggested rather pointedly, "Be what you enjoy." What a concept! I came away from that first experience at Eranos profoundly affected by both these men as well as the worlds they inhabited, both seen and unseen. Eranos as dream became even more palpable and reached deep inside me, her soul figures touching my own. Later, I would discover that this kind of experience was not unique to me; many leave with more and similar gifts, not all of which are apparent through the senses.

In 1999, I was invited back, this time to assume a new role. I received the somewhat unexpected, though greatly affirming, request to offer a formal presentation at the annual *Tagung*. This time I was invited to the Round Table, not as an observer/participant, but now in the august role of a featured lecturer. By no means did I imagine myself in the company of Carl Gustav Jung, Mircea Eliade, Adolf Portmann, James Hillman, Joseph Campbell as well as so many of the intellectual elite of European and American culture. No, that certainly was not the case. Eranos had changed by the late 90's, and along with it, a loss of many of its intellectual and spiritual champions. Yet, still vibrantly alive and present was the legacy they created and bequeathed to future scholars and seekers, one that still feeds the dream body of Eranos. Their subtle bodies are psychoactive and present, as if their "work," the soul figures of their imagination, were permanent guests of honor at the annual Banquet, holding conversations around the Table and on the terrace. As James Hillman would later say in *Lament of the Dead*, in commenting on Jung's *Red Book*: "He used a rich language. He used the language of the figures of the dead actually."[1]

Hillman goes on to describe by examples from his own work, *The Dream and the Underworld*: "I wanted to study the underworld, where dreams have their home and where they come from."[2] Their language is a kind of "soul speech." Hillman asserted that "I've come to the conclusion that psychological language does do damage, it isn't really language of the soul."[3] At Eranos the soul-bodies of the ancestors continue to be in residence. Now I would enter their house, their gathering-place, as a presenter, adding my ideas to the treasure trove of thoughts and images that pervaded the atmosphere of this enchanted place.

In October of that year, I offered "Dream Tending: Working the Intersection Between Psyche and World." The overarching topic for the gathering was "Synchronicity." I dedicated the presentation to the tradition of Eranos and to the genius of the *I Ching* which had inspired that year's Round Table theme. Particularly potent to the gathering was an acknowledgement that Jung gave his last talk at Eranos on the topic of synchronicity. It is said that this was his last public talk anywhere. The remembrance of the man and his work was palpable. Indeed the bedroom overlooking the lake where he worked and slept while at Eranos was situated above the hall. My life-long work with dreams had brought me to this time and place, and I felt honored to let new ideas come forth to intermingle with those that preceded them.

My work with dreams and the living image engendered sympathetic and respectful responses to the work on the "image" developed by Jung, Corbin, Hillman, and others who opened the conversation and explored the territory while in residence at Eranos. Reflection on their ideas as well as my own contributed to the concept that images of dream (as well as the hexagrams of *I Ching*) are rooted most essentially in the rhythms of nature—in her song, her music, her seasons, and her many creative and destructive expressions. We are born of nature, I was reminded, and we will die back into her web of being. We are image bodies of her dream—of nature dreaming. In service to this oracular way of knowing I presented a number of primary ideas from my own work on "Dream Tending."

I began by first describing the matrix of psychic reality that underpins the dream as it informs other dimensions of consciousness. Synchronicity, complementarity, and oracular knowing, for example, share ground with the imaginal reality of dream. When we work with dreams in an oracular way or work with dreams in conjunction with oracular systems like the *I Ching*, we need approaches to dreamwork that take into account an extended field of what I have come to call the "World Unconscious," an extended field of consciousness, alive in the *anima mundi*. In this dimension of psyche exists a soul spark alive in all things and creatures, in the humanly crafted as well as naturally crafted.

Second, I described an approach to dream work that engages the images of this wider ensouled landscape, asserting that images themselves are accompanied by a reality of their own and are also embodied. Experienced by the dreamer as actual visitants from the wider field of dreaming psyche, living images are understood as originating most essentially in nature's dream. I suggested that the synchronicities here that we experience in waking awareness (the correspondences between psyche in person and psyche in world) occur many times over in the multidimensional landscape of the "dreaming," a realm consisting of the dream, the dreamer, and the dreaming.

Third, when viewed in this way, dream images of person and of world share common ground as they intersect. At these crossings, synchronicity occurs between personal circumstances, individual dream images, and the world's dreaming places and beings. A generative impulse arises in a person's life when an alignment develops between external experience, personal interiority, and the subjective inner natures of the entities of the world psyche. The living dream image, originating from world, and representing the subtlety of world, draws persons to it. Said differently, the moment of synchronicity is the instant when the dreaming of world reveals itself to us. Dream Tending fosters the realization that psychic coexistence forever lives in the broader dimension—the Dreaming—where the dreaming of world intersects the dreaming of persons.

To bring these ideas to life, I told a story. Personal stories seem to touch folks most deeply, and so it was at Eranos that afternoon. I shared a personal story about my first conscious experience of that sense of connection with the voices of the world that occurred when I was 12 years old. Like many of you, I was aware of my dreams as a youngster. Remember, when in dreams trees had faces, and houses could fly? A lot of us remember dreams like that. However, many of us didn't have people to talk with about those occurrences. We were closet "imaginal thinkers," all depth psychologists, each and every one of us. I was in that world as well, attending an American public school, and growing up in a post-World War II family meant that very little of that "inner life" experience was really allowed to be acknowledged—let alone valued. And certainly I wasn't being listened to carefully—except for this one day long ago. And that experience is what came forward.

I was living in the San Fernando Valley, a suburb of Los Angeles. To access the ocean, we had to go over a mountain pass, and what we saw when we came down on the other side was Zuma Beach, one of the most popular along the West Coast. There is a life guard stand every 150 yards or so, and behind the giant parking lot, the first thing that greets you is a big neon sign that screams, FOOD HERE! So you join the other "thousands" of people from the Valley and find a few square inches of sand. Now, the really interesting thing about Zuma Beach is that at the end of the sandy beach, there is a point, an actual peninsula that goes out into the sea. And on the other side of that point, there are no lifeguard stands. Of course, we were told ever since we were little: whatever you do, stay here where you can be watched—don't ever go to the other side. Well, I was twelve years old, so if they wanted to make sure that I *did* go to the other side that was exactly what they should have told me. One adventurous day, I went meandering around to the other side of the point. Once there I started looking at this rock, because there were big rocks and big tide pools, filled with seaweed and different little sea creatures and the wonder of the seascape. I noticed everything, and I just watched. It was all so familiar, like a dream.

As I sat there, the most remarkable thing happened that became one of the most formative experiences of my life. At age twelve, I was visited by the gods. That means a sixteen-year-old boy approached, and said to me as I sat there, "Did you know that rocks can talk?" Unbelievable! I couldn't believe he said that—did you know that rocks can talk? I knew that, but I didn't think that *anybody else* knew. And that was extraordinary for me—rocks could talk. Then he went on his way, and I stayed there for maybe another hour or so, watching the waves grow bigger and coming closer and blocking the way back around the point. Finally I thought, uh-oh, and ran back, with all the folks, and lifeguard stands, food station, and the massive parking lot. And of course, people asked me, where were you? Well, what was I going to say? I was at a place where rocks could talk, and people were swimming without any clothes on? (It was also a clothing optional beach!) No, you don't say that. I simply reported, "I just went on a walk, and it is good to be back." But back on the familiar side of the point, I was aware that life beyond the point was a very different experience altogether, in part because the landscape itself was animated in all its particularity.

And in those moments I was affirmed in a life mystery, one of those mysteries that many of us know about—and in many ways is very much like a dream. This is the knowledge that the things and creatures of our world have voice. That the world over there on the other side of the point, on the other side of the bridge, in "anima country," is alive, vibrant, vital, and always dreaming. Let me restate the "learnings" from that day. They have stayed with me even to today:

- The physical world of the *visible* is also populated with the *invisibles*.
- There are *spirits* and *voices* in the things and creatures of the world.
- On occasion, at certain moments, the *imaginal* reality that I am experiencing *inside* is affirmed by something or somebody *outside* of me.

I have never forgotten that surprising, because so unexpected, experience at Zuma Beach, and to this day it guides the work that I do at Pacifica Graduate Institute, whose motto is, *animae mundi colendae gratia*, "for the sake of tending soul of (and in) the world." That early experience has informed my thinking about a realm of consciousness beyond the Personal Unconscious and the Collective Unconscious, another third dimension of psychic life: the World Unconscious.

Eranos as dream continued to work on me. A number of years later, now steeped in the ways of Dream Tending and the World Unconscious, I found myself back at Ascona-Moscia. However, this time I arrived in a different capacity. I came to offer a workshop on Dream Tending. I arrived several days and, as importantly, "nights" early before the folks from far and wide making pilgrimages to this "mecca" would show up. I slept upstairs in Casa Gabriella, one of the three small villas of Eranos. I was alone on the property, and now actually inhabiting the room where Jung had once slept. Perhaps it was the full moon on the lake or simply jet lag that contributed to what happened over those first forty-eight hours of being in the Casas alone. Of course, the appearance of the place itself evokes memories, associations, fantasies, and spins the imagination. Still, there was more. It is said, "That if walls could talk…" Well, those nights were filled with visitations of every kind: voices, visuals, deep feelings, and a persistent sense of longing for something unnamable. Behind it all I experienced a sensation of deep belonging, a kind of homecoming, a tribal reunion of sorts. Mostly I was simply in an existential state of "not-knowing," yet within a deep reverence. The actuality of the embodied "dream image," the living psychic persons within the act of dreaming were never more apparent. The ancestral elders of our tradition made their presence and knowledge known. I was not at all surprised, then, that the Dream Tending workshop that followed took on another life all together. And, there, in the field of the dreaming, in the rooms over the lake at Eranos, I tended dreams and spoke further of the World Unconscious through the dreams of participants.

Affirmed by what I had experienced over the last days, I talked more fully about the World Unconscious consisting of a deeper and wider dimension of the psyche than that of the personal or collective human experience. In the realm of the world psyche, all creatures and things of the world appear interrelated and interconnected. I went on to suggest that although there are clear differences in orders of complexity, all the phenomena in the world possess intrinsic subjective characteristics. I re-envisioned the term "unconscious" realizing that, for the most part, it is *we* who are unconscious of these impactful inner natures of the world's other inhabitants. These psychic qualities of the world's organic and inorganic phenomena make up an extended field of consciousness that on occasions irrupt into our awareness, particularly in dream.

One would not be surprised, then, to hear that as the workshop went on, and dreams were visited, we all felt we were being captivated by something more than traditional dream interpretation or analysis. Our field had broadened; the ensouled world was revealing herself through living images and Eranos as dream was "quickening" our work and animating our discovery. I remember there was this fellow from the Northern Territories of Australia, who was well steeped in the dreamtime ways of Aboriginal peoples. He felt right at home. At the end of the first day I further described what was occurring and then offered another example from my personal experience.

At the dimension of the World Unconscious, I suggested, the inner subjective natures of the world's beings are experienced as dream images in the human psyche. I offered, again, the idea that dream images are real, have imaginal weight and body, and act in dreams on behalf of themselves and, in fact, are creators of the dream from the beginning (not us). The example I used was that of an elephant that appeared in my dream the night before who was fully engaged in his activity, not mine. In the dream, I watched as he looked intently at me with shiny black eyes and wide flopping ears. He used his trunk to spray dirt and tiny rocks over his fine-haired rump, his tail all the while swatting flies from his sagging hindquarters. After a time he plodded back to join the rest of the herd. This dream elephant, like all dream images, is alive, has body, and moves about according to his own inner nature. I was the recipient of his graceful motion.

Recalling the teachings of Corbin, Jung, and Hillman in particular, I explained this idea that all phenomena in the world possess subjective inner natures and so they must be distinguished from the *ego*centric concepts of: anthropomorphism (attributing human qualities to nonhuman forms of life), animism (humans attributing living soul to inanimate objects and natural phenomena), and personification (attributing personal characteristics to phenomena in the world). Rather, the idea that all beings are ensouled, in and of themselves, locates the life spark *in* the entity—outside of personal human psychic ownership. In this wider view the human experience exists in a field of psychic relationships as one among many. Seen from the perspective of the World Unconscious, the dream image is an independent presence in a broader psychic ecology—a dreamscape where there is room for many beings to "walk around" and be regarded by one another. The elephant that appeared in "my" dream had a life of its own; it visited to interact with me as a fellow creature of the dreamtime—perhaps to heighten my awareness of the plight of elephants in the world. From the perspective of the World Unconscious, the dreamscape is the worldscape. This idea, further formed in those days at Eranos, would impact my work in the world for many years. The art/craft of Dream Tending was flourishing. Yet, as unpleasant as it was to notice, something else was also simultaneously taking place. As I was being pushed forward and supported by the *dream* of Eranos, the *spirit* of Eranos was beginning to dim.

As the Century turned, so too did the fortunes of Eranos. Like a dream, one never knows rationally where the images will lead. Only hints are offered, some louder than others. Eranos at Ascona was in transition. And, like dreams themselves, when the body suffers, the turmoil is picked up in the dreamtime. At Eranos there were changes in leadership, financial hard times, mission ambiguity, and above all, a loss of clear soulful purpose. These afflictions, of course, manifest, at times, in the life cycles of all persons or institutions. When uncertainty befalls and the gods create turmoil, our tradition teaches us to go deeper into the wounding to find the healing knowledge within. Those who sat at the Round Table for three quarters of a century at Eranos knew this path. "Knowledge" of moving forward requires first listening backwards. The rational "fixes" were not working. Opening to the deep psyche and following the pathos of the dream, the community members of Eranos were investing in the time necessary to experience the wounding and to discover the hints of healing that would provide new direction for the years to follow.

The years ahead opened opportunity and a re-vitalization of the community and its sense of destiny, as others in the volume will testify. Let it also be said, a new vision rooted in ideals must also attract community support, regional buy-in, and good banking, which the Swiss are particularly gifted at negotiating! The threads slowly began to weave together and the renaissance of Eranos was under way.

In the years that followed, I was invited back year after year. I offered additional presentations at the Round Table, offered public lectures, served on the Eranos Advisory Board, co-led what we named Legacy Tours originating in Zürich, traveling through Küsnacht, Einsiedeln, and culminating at Ascona, Eranos. The dream body of Eranos over these last fifteen years has been generative and abundant, initiating and furthering a life of its own, with a pulse growing stronger year after year, and as dreams will do, responding to the pull of the future.

As Pacifica Graduate Institute has become increasingly affiliated with Eranos, and as a result, my own engagement grew more involved, I began to notice three primary through-lines emerging as the institution moved into the twenty first century. I was delighted to contribute what I could to this revival. The organizing principles emerging gradually are sympathetic to the originating impulses, the seminal ideas that inspired Eranos from its genesis. Imagination, Evolution, and Revolution were emerging once again to capture the essence of what today is blossoming at this sacred place.

IMAGINATION

Eranos has always sourced and esteemed the role of imagination in human experience and existence. The actuality of the world behind the visible world, or what Henry Corbin named the *mundus imaginalis* in his work and time at Eranos, once again took center stage. Picking up on these ideas I asserted in a paper I presented at the *Tagung* in 2011, "Fragility of the World's Dream," that "the fragility in the contemporary world is rooted most fundamentally in our continuing denial of the pathos active in the *anima mundi*, the soul of the world, as expressed through the images of the world's dream."[4] I underscored the necessity, particularly in today's world, to listen and to engage imaginal reflection as priorities of consciousness. Simply put, I asserted that, "When the imaginal world goes unattended, we live in peril." I cited dreams of teenagers who were suffering mightily as images of ecological devastation, originating in the psyche of the creatures and things in the world, presented themselves in their dream life, which in turn created emotional and psychical havoc.

Having listened to hundreds of dreams of folks growing up in the information age, I shared at the Round Table the importance of differentiating between the "indigenous image," rooted in an authentic impulse deep-seated in the psyche of Nature, and what I have come to call the "counterfeit image," concocted from the advertising industry to sell consumer products. Counterfeit images are a result, I asserted, of too much screen time in the modern world. These commercial images are not organic, do not individuate on their own, and so do not help us grow, deepen, or develop. They are like a genetically engineered plant with a terminator gene. They exist to sell a product and then simply disappear, to appear at some future moment with another product.

I made a plea for the recovery of the indigenous imagination, in all of her capacities, a way of knowing that informs life, creates new opportunities, and opens to what Eranos holds most dear: the beauty and abundance alive in the wellspring of human expression. I truly believe the on-going dream of Eranos is one that sources and, in turn, is sourced by an animated imagination. Imagination opens the way for the second seed idea moving forward at Eranos, that of Evolution.

EVOLUTION

Dreams are not static. The pull of the future makes itself known in virtually every dream. Eranos as dream pushes the evolution of those who interact with her as well as the culture at large. Like an enzyme catalyzing transformation, the *telos* of Eranos is an evolutionary impulse. Historically, new works of every kind were incubated in the fertile fields of the Eranos psyche, then incarnated in the visible world. Now, as the evolutionary impetus moves through the next generations of participants, the fire that fuels the future grows ever more necessary and bright, a kind of alchemical blue fire. In September 2012, Eranos sent out the call once again, this year seeking to explore evolution in the context of "Threshold." I offered a paper and presentation on "The Dangers and Opportunity of Cyberspace: A New Vision of Global Dreaming."[5] In sum, I asserted that the organicity and intelligence of dreamspace is being threatened by cyberspace; that the exponential expansion of cyberspace dissolves thresholds of privacy and may then result in severe physiological and psychological afflictions. Conversely, at this time of planetary turbulence, when used constructively, technology, particularly newer forms of social networking, can create a forum for listening to the world's dream in ways we have just begun to imagine. The world is evolving by the ways in which we communicate with one another; how we communicate has the capacity to open some doors and close others.

Eranos as dream confronted this topic head-on, not only the evolution taking place in the world psyche, but also the individuation of Eranos herself, her development, her mode of being, as well as her emerging relevance in contemporary culture. Her calling evoked our own sense of becoming. Her evolution was shaping, forging, and informing the work of those of us participating in her activities. It was becoming more and more apparent that Eranos as a generative dream image was once again active in today's world, transcending the presentations, the annual *Yearbook*, the gifted papers and research. Her advocacy and intentionality extended beyond the place itself. Eranos was evolving and joining like-minded institutions such as Pacifica

Graduate Institute and the Fetzer Institute. Today, her evolving vitality and reach is giving voice to an increasingly vital advocacy: a creative soul-centered response to the conditions of modern times. Eranos embodies evolution as her most vital force.

REVOLUTION

Evolution is inevitably followed by revolution. Not reform, not protest, but a revolution of heart, mind, and soul. Betwixt and between, on the lines and between the lines, what occurs in the cauldron of psychoactive interaction at Eranos moves us all beyond the comfortable. Neither afraid nor careful, the new generation of leadership listened to the wounded psyche, the primary affliction confronting modern people, and traveled with intense focus directly to the center point of the distress, "Money." Realizing the need to think "outside the box," to dream, to meander into new considerations beyond the avalanche of external explanations and schemes about the manipulation of money, we needed to break free of the mind sets prevalent in Universities of great stature, boasting esteemed schools of business hell-bent on describing new financial formulas as well as producing the next investment products.

To challenge the dominate paradigm of our times, the tribe of Eranos gathered. Mobilized to channel the intelligence of a waking dream to bring forth a mode of perception that sees through the veil of the familiar, we were asked to conceptually and psychologically deconstruct the intricate and sophisticated monetary theories and marketplace devices that remain captive to the zeitgeist of our times: victims of the omnipresent un-imaginative influence of Wall Street's self-interests with its mandate to increase short term financial profit.

Revolution does not come easily, nor for that matter does it come cheaply. Inspired by the spirit of the Eranos intention, my contribution to this bold undertaking was personal and therefore complicated for me. In 2013, I told "The Pacifica Story: Money as Psychic Libido."[6] I talked about our institution, Pacifica, now entering its 40th year, evolving from a not-for-profit institution, to a privately owned organization, then to its present status as an employee-owned corporation. Through all the phases I described its encounters and entanglements with money. I began by reminding the audience that first and foremost money is generated in the places of underworld transactions. At Pacifica, similar to all businesses, our interactions with money constellated business structures and finance models as secondary processes, giving form to our institutional life, but shadowed by her soul figures, the pull of psyche herself. More often than not, these unconscious entities led to unknown territories and multifarious complexes, some more complicated and problematic than others.

In relation to money, what Pacifica accomplished in developing an employee-owned corporation anchored in its core values and rooted in the principle and practice of shared stewardship, is what some refer to as conscious capitalism, or the actualization of the triple bottom line model of business. This is not business as usual, and certainly not the status quo. Other presenters evoked additional considerations of money's profound and elemental impact on societal order, challenging assumptions and revolting against the status quo. Topics included money as muse, money as demon, money as historically new to human transactions, and money as a flawed, artificial construct. Money, the common denominator, the bottom line of the material world's structural fabric, was being challenged at Eranos.

The revolutionary spirit that took on the topic of money also moves through Eranos, the institution herself. Particularized through monetary considerations, more generally the muse is pushing us into new deliberations and relationships with self, value, and worth. Eranos now pulses with the originating zeal and promise bestowed upon her by her founding members, the women and men who through the years were inspired by her spirit and in turn contributed to the life force running through her veins. Eranos is a revolution of soul, upturned and in-turned by the very figures that constitute her dream body, the visibles and invisibles interacting in a banquet, enjoying a feast of imaginal play and significant purpose.

To this day, Eranos continues to take on topics outside the traditional, even non-traditional cultural dialogue. Dreams operate that way, bringing the surprise, the unknowable, surfacing the muses, the insights from dimensions beyond the rational mind, outside the familiar, emerging from an underworld consciousness, and only available to those who have the ears to listen, to hear the call of the deep psyche and her inhabitants, the embodied dream figures who frequent here with an intelligence of their own. Eranos as dream is alive and well, animating imagination, pushing evolution, and igniting revolution. Eranos as dream brings soul to culture, creativity to human expression, and the incarnation of the "new" to the world. Eranos as dream is a friend. May this friendship endure for a very long time.

NOTES

1. James Hillman and Sonu Shamdasani, *Lament of the Dead—Psychology after Jung's Red Book* (New York, NY: W. W. Norton & Company, Inc.), p. 86.

2. *Ibid.*

3. *Ibid.*, p. 87.

4. Stephen Aizenstat, "Fragility of the World's Dream," *Eranos Yearbook* 70 (2009–2010–2011): 178.

5. Stephen Aizenstat, "The Dangers and Opportunity of Cyberspace: A New Vision of Global Dreaming," *Eranos Yearbook* 71 (2012): 218–35.

6. Stephen Aizenstat, "The Pacifica Story—Money as Psychic Libido," *Eranos Yearbook* 72 (2013–2014) (forthcoming).

III.

ERANOS AND THE IDEA OF SACRED

Chicago, le 6 Avril

L'Eranos d'Ascona compte aujourd'hui parmi les phéno-mènes culturels les plus impor-tants de l'Europe. Je suis fier d'y participer !..

Mircea Eliade

A dedication written by the historian of religions, Mircea Eliade, on the occasion of the 25th anniversary of the Eranos Conferences, in 1957, which reads: "The Eranos of Ascona represents today one of the most important cultural phenomenons in Europe. I am proud to take part in it!"

MIRCEA ELIADE

T he Romanian historian of religions, Mircea Eliade (1907–1986), joined Eranos in 1950, on Henry Corbin's invitation. He gave a total of thirteen talks, from 1950 up to 1967. The Eranos Archive for Research in Symbolism served as an iconographic base for important studies of his, such as *The Forge and the Crucible—The Origins and Structure of Alchemy* (1956). He recollected memories of the Eranos gatherings in his autobiographical works, *Mémoire II. Les moissons du solstice* (1937–1960), *Fragments d'un journal II* (1945–1969), and *L'épreuve du labyrinth* (1978). He also published some articles about Eranos, such as "Eranos" (1954), "Les danseurs passent, la danse reste" (1955), and "Encounters at Ascona" (1960).

Mircea Eliade's "Encounters at Ascona," presented in the following pages, was originally written in French in October 1960. It was first translated into English by Willard R. Trask and published in *Spiritual Disciplines: Papers from the Eranos Yearbooks. Selected and translated from the Eranos-Jahrbücher edited by Olga Fröbe-Kapteyn*, Bollingen Series XXX:4, ed. Joseph Campbell (London: Routledge & Kegan Paul, Ltd., 1960), pp. xvii–xxi. Another English edition appeared in Mircea Eliade and Ira Progoff, *About the Eranos Conferences* (Ascona: Tip. Bettini & Co., 1968), pp. 1–8; it was also published in French with the original title, "Rencontres à Ascona," in Henry Corbin and Mircea Eliade, *A propos des Conférences Eranos* (Ascona: Tip. Bettini & Co., 1968), pp. 16–23; in Italian it appeared as "Incontri ad Ascona," in *Il sentimento del colore. L'esperienza cromatica come simbolo, cultura e scienza. Quaderni di Eranos II*, ed. C. Risé (Como: Red, 1990), pp. 9–14.

We thank Prof. Sorin Alexandrescu for granting permission to republish Eliade's writing in this issue of *Spring: A Journal of Archetype and Culture*.

ENCOUNTERS
AT ASCONA

MIRCEA ELIADE

It is characteristic of Eranos at Ascona that the speakers do not address themselves to an audience of specialists. Yet neither do they engage in any form of "popularization"; there is no expounding the latest results gained in various departments of knowledge. The originality of Eranos lies primarily in the fact that the speakers there are able to shed both their timidities and their superiority complexes. Although they are "specialists" in some particular field of study, they are aware that they have every reason to familiarize themselves with the methods used and the results achieved in other areas of research. Nor does this spring from mere curiosity or a desire for a naïve encyclopedism. It is because Eranos at Ascona is one of the privileged places where one is made conscious of the true dimensions of culture. Sooner or later every scholar has to face this problem and learn, from his own experience, the meaning of being "culturally creative." Now, no culture is possible without a sustained effort to integrate, in one embracing perspective, the progress made in all the various fields of study. Indeed, there is no true culture if, finally, the creations that constitute it are not related to man and his destiny.

All this seems so obvious at this date that one almost hesitates to say it for fear of repeating a truism. Yet for many years certain disciplines that studied the deepest experiences of the human psyche and their cultural expressions developed side by side without their results being integrated and articulated toward a more exact and complete knowledge of man. The disciplines of the history of religions, ethnology, paleoethnology, and orientalism have seldom been regarded as *separate but interrelated* phases of a single study. It is only very recently that these disciplines have come to be thought capable of revealing human existential situations worthy of interesting not only the psychologist and sociologist but also the philosopher and theologian.

It is perhaps the greatest contribution of Eranos to stimulate and encourage meetings and dialogues among representatives of the various sciences and disciplines whose field is the human mind and spirit. For it is through such encounters that a culture can renew itself, in a bold widening of its horizon. Depth psychologists, orientalists, and ethnologists interested in the history of religions are those who have most successfully achieved rapprochement and even collaboration. This is perhaps due to the fact that, in the last analyses, each of these disciplines implies encountering and confronting an unknown, strange, even "dangerous" world— dangerous because able to threaten the spiritual equilibrium of the modern West. Certainly, confronting these "strange worlds" does not always entail the same degree of danger; some of them have long been known. Thus, for example, the researches of orientalists had gradually familiarized the West with the eccentric and fabulous nature of the societies and cultures of Asia. But the ethnologists discovered obscure and mysterious spiritual worlds, universes that, even if they were not the product of a prelogical mentality (as Lévy-Bruhl believed), were nonetheless strangely different from the cultural landscape with which Western man had been familiar.

Obviously, it was depth psychology that revealed the greatest number of *terrae ignotae* and thus brought about the most dramatic confrontations. The discovery of the unconscious could be compared to the maritime discoveries of the Renaissance and the astronomical discoveries made possible by the invention of the telescope. For each of these discoveries revealed worlds whose very existence had been previously unsuspected. Each of them effected a sort of "breakthrough in plane," in the sense that it shattered the traditional image of the Cosmos and revealed the structures of a Universe previously unimaginable. Such "breakthroughs" have not been without consequences. The astronomical and geographical discoveries of the Renaissance radically altered the image of the universe and the concepts of space; in addition, for at least three centuries, they assured the scientific, economic, and political supremacy of the West, at the same time that they opened the road that inevitably leads to a united world.

Freud's discoveries likewise represent an "opening," but this time it is an "opening" into the submerged worlds of the unconscious. Psychoanalytical technique inaugurated a new type of *descensus ad infernos.* When Jung revealed the existence of the collective unconscious, the exploration of those immemorial treasures, the myths, symbols, and images of archaic humanity, began to resemble the techniques of oceanography and speleology. Just as descents into the depths of the sea or expeditions to the bottoms of caves had revealed elementary organisms long vanished from the surface of the earth, so analysis retrieved forms of deep psychic life previously inaccessible to study. Speleology presented biologists with Tertiary and even Mesozoic organisms, primitive zoomorphic forms not susceptible to fossilization—in other words, forms that had vanished from the surface of the earth without leaving a trace. By discovering "living fossils," speleology markedly advanced our knowledge of archaic modes of life. Similarly, archaic modes of psychic life, "living fossils" buried in the darkness of the unconscious, now become accessible to study, through the techniques developed by depth psychologists.

This explains why the meetings at Ascona are so stimulating, Specialists in various "strange," "exotic," or "unique" worlds can converse together at leisure on the efficacy of their methods, the value of their discoveries, and the meaning of their cultural adventures. Each of these specialists has devoted his life to the study of an unfamiliar world, and what he has learned during this long frequentation of the "others" obliges him to make drastic changes in the accepted clichés concerning man, religion, reason, beauty. Then too, these discoveries and confrontations form part of the *Zeitgeist.* The rise of Eranos coincided with the political and cultural awakening of Asia and, above all, with the entrance of exotic and primitive peoples into History. Encountering these "others"—which is, as it were, the sign under which Eranos has developed—has, after the second World War, become an ineluctable decree of History.

At a certain moment, the members of Eranos felt that a new humanism could well develop out of such encounters. Then, too, similar phenomena were beginning to appear elsewhere. It would be impossible in these few lines to depict an extremely complex cultural process, which in addition, is extremely difficult to grasp since it is still *in statu nascendi.* We will only say that at Ascona each speaker feels that his scientific creation acquires a new and deeper meaning in the degree to which he undertakes to present it as a contribution to the knowledge of man. It is realized, too, that the new humanism that is here coming to birth could not be a replica of the old-humanism. Eranos has more than sufficiently demonstrated the need to integrate the researches of orientalists, ethnologists, and historians of religion in order to attain an integral knowledge of man.

But there is something yet further, and perhaps yet more important. The researches of depth psychologists, ethnologists, orientalists, and historians of religions have constantly brought out the human interest, the psychological "truth," and the spiritual value of countless symbols, myths, divine figures, and mystical techniques attested not only among Europeans and Asians but also among "primitives." Such human documents had previously been studied with the detachment and indifference with which nineteenth-century naturalists considered it proper to study insects. It now began to be realized that these documents express existential situations; that consequently, they form part of the history of the human spirit. But the proper procedure for grasping the meaning of an existential situation is not the naturalist's "objectivity," but the intelligent sympathy of the hermeneut. *It was the procedure itself that had to be changed.* For even the strangest or the most aberrant form of behavior must be regarded as a human phenomenon; it cannot be understood by being taken as a zoological phenomenon or an instance of teratology.

To approach a symbol, a myth, an archaic mode of behavior as an expression of an existential situation is in itself to give it human dignity and philosophical meaning. This would have seemed the height of absurdity to a nineteenth-century scholar. For him, "savagery" or "primordial stupidity" could represent only an embryonic, and hence non-cultural, phase of humanity.

If the simplest archaic myth deserves to be considered an integral part of the history of the spirit, the mystics and contemplatives of all religions can not but be given a large place. Interest in spiritual disciplines and mystical techniques—especially those of the Orient and the primitive world, hitherto little studies—has from the first been one of the characteristic aspects of Eranos. To be sure, this interest was sometimes subject to misinterpretation by uninformed outsiders, and was in danger of being confused with the suspect fascination with the "occult" that is typical of modern pseudomorphoses and the countless movements of cheaply won "spirituality." But of course no subject has not been "compromised" or "compromising" at some moment in history.

For those members of Eranos, this exceptional interest in spiritual disciplines and mystical techniques arises from the fact that they are documents capable of revealing a dimension of human existence that has been almost forgotten, or completely distorted, in modern societies. All these spiritual disciplines and mystical techniques are of inestimable value because they represent conquests of the human spirit that have been neglected or denied in the course of recent Western history, but that have lost neither their greatness nor their usefulness.

The problem that now arises—and that will present itself with even more dramatic urgency to scholars of the coming generation—is this: How are means to be found to recover all that is still recoverable in the spiritual history of humanity? And this for two reasons: (1) Western man cannot continue to live on for an indefinite period in separation from an important part of himself, the part constituted by the fragments of a spiritual history of which he cannot decipher the meaning and message. (2) Sooner or later, our dialogue with the "others"—the representatives of traditional, Asiatic, and "primitive" cultures—must begin to take place not in today's empirical and utilitarian language (which can approach only realities classifiable as social, economic, political, sanitary, etc.) but in a cultural language capable of expressing human realities and spiritual values. Such a dialogue is inevitable; it is part of the ineluctable course of History. It would be tragically naïve to suppose that it can continue indefinitely on the mental level on which it is conducted today.

One purpose of the Conferences has been, and still is, to develop further this integrating dialogue with "others" through which Eranos makes its own modest though significant contribution to the shaping of the modern psyche in its historical process.

DAVID L. MILLER

David L. Miller, Ph.D., is the Watson-Ledden Professor of Religion, Emeritus, at Syracuse University, New York, and a Core Faculty Member in Mythological Studies (now retired) at Pacifica Graduate Institute, Santa Barbara, California. In 2002, he was made an affiliate member of the Inter-Regional Society of Jungian Analysts (IRSJA) and in 2004 he was elected to be an honorary member of the International Association for Analytical Psychology (IAAP). He is the author of five books and more than one hundred articles and book chapters. His books include *Gods and Games—Toward a Theology of Play* (1970 and 2014) and *The New Polytheism—Rebirth of the Gods and Goddesses* (1974). Miller first attended the Eranos Conferences in 1969 and was a member of the Eranos Circle from 1975 until 1988. He was present at Eranos fifteen times during this period and he lectured at the Conferences nine times. His presentations explored the intersections of classical mythology, depth psychology, history of religions, and postmodern literary theory (*Eranos Yearbooks* 44, 46, 47, 49, 50, 51, 52, 55, and 57). His particular conversation partners at Eranos were Henry Corbin, James Hillman, and Wolfgang Giegerich. Three of Miller's books grew out of his lectures at Eranos: *Christs—Meditations on Archetypal Images in Christian Theology* (1981 and 2005), *Three Faces of God—Traces of the Trinity in Literature and Life* (1986 and 2005), and *Hells and Holy Ghosts—A Theopoetics of Christian Belief* (1989 and 2004). He presented a paper on Eranos at the Sixteenth International Congress of the IAAP, held in Barcelona in 2004.

ON THE EDGE OF THE ROUND TABLE
ERANOS AND THEOLOGICAL STUDIES[1]

DAVID L. MILLER

From 1933 to 1988, there were 592 presentations at the Eranos Conferences. Almost a quarter of these dealt with theological themes or issues. This enumeration does not include the "theological" content in papers having to do with the religions of India, China, Egypt, Japan, and ancient Greece, which, if counted, would bring the number of presentations in the domain of theology to nearly 40%. The "theological" speakers at Eranos were among the most important religious thinkers of the twentieth century, as were the equally luminous scholars in the history of religions (Table 1). This litany of names alone indicates that Eranos was arguably an alchemical vessel of contemporary theological transformation. This is especially so because presentations by those mentioned by no means met the conventional expectations of "theological" discourse. If anything, these presentations set conventional and traditional "theological" discourse on *edge*, a claim that I shall try to make in what follows. But let me begin with an anecdote having to do with the notion of "edge."

I first attended the Eranos Conferences in 1969. Along with Gilles Quispel and James Hillman, the speakers present were Helmuth Jacobsohn, Gilbert Durand, Toshihiko Izutsu, Shmuel Sambursky, Henry Corbin, Ernst Benz, Gershom Scholem, and Adolf Portmann. Seats for the auditors at Casa Eranos were reserved and I was assigned a seat in the fourth row. The aisle and Lake Maggiore were on my right and an elderly British woman sat on my left. During the intermission of the initial lecture by Scholem, I turned to my seatmate and, in an attempt to make conversation, I asked her whether there would be a question-and-answer time following the lecture. She said to me: "You must be an American." I confessed that I was, whereupon she educated me about the spirit of Eranos. "You see," she said, "the presenters are invited to speak at the very edge of their disciplines. If they manage

Table 1: Selected speakers at Eranos, 1933–1988.

"Theological" Speakers	
Leo Baeck	Helmuth Jacobsohn
Louis Beirnaert	Joseph Bernard Lang
Ernst Benz	Ulrich Mann
Martin Buber	Louis Massignon
Ernesto Buonaiuti	Henri-Charles Puech
Henry Corbin	Max Pulver
Jean Daniélou	Gilles Quispel
Martin Cyril D'Arcy	Hugo Rahner
Bernard Delfgaauw	Karl Ludwig Schmidt
Robert Eisler	Gershom Scholem
Erwin Ramsdell Goodenough	Morton Smith
Friedrich Heiler	Daisetz Teitaro Suzuki
Helmut Hoffmann	Paul Tillich
Stanley Romaine Hopper	Heinz Westmann
History of Religions Scholars	
Chung-yuan Chang	Toshihiko Izutsu
Mircea Eliade	Erwin Rousselle
Pierre Hadot	Shizuteru Ueda
Erik Hornung	Heinrich Zimmer
Michel Hulin	

this edge, they are in no better position than the audience to answer questions. It would be premature. On the other hand," she concluded decisively, "if they do not manage to speak at the edge, then they are not worth questioning in the first place!" I was from the beginning of my experience of Eranos learning about the meaning of *edge*!

Even a cursory glance at the list of names above, names that in my view are indicative of theological studies at Eranos, will demonstrate two senses in which these presentations were at an "edge." In the first place, the perspectives of the speakers, even those who came out of monotheistic traditions, were situated at the edges of the religious traditions of Judaism, Christianity, and Islam. For example, the theological arguments were not those of main-line or orthodox Christian theology, but those of "gnostic" Christianity (Daniélou, Lang, Puech, Pulver, Quispel, Smith); not dogmatic or kerygmatic Christian theology, but apophatic and cultural theologies (Tillich); not Church theology, but mystical theology (Beirnaert, Benz, Buber, Heiler, Rahner); not the theology of conventional piety, but existential and radical theology (Hopper, Tillich); not conventional Jewish theology, but Kabbalah or mystical traditions (Goodenough, Scholem); not Shīʿite or Sunni theology, but Sufism in Islam (Corbin, Massignon); and so on. This is theology at the edges of conventional religious traditions.

In a second sense, Eranos represented an openness to understanding theological studies beyond monotheistic traditions, a fundamental understanding of *theologia* as "talk about gods," which could include an a-theistic tradition such as Zen (Izutsu, Suzuki, Ueda), the hodge-podge of religions from late antiquity (Hadot), the religions of ancient Egypt (Hornung, Jacobsohn), sects of Hinduism, including Yoga (Hulin), Taoism in China (Chan), and comparative mythology (Campbell, Zimmer), and much more that puts popular and traditional notions of "theology" on edge! This is why I said earlier that Eranos functioned as an alchemical vessel of contemporary theological transformation.

This transformation of theological studies and of the notion of theological studies—what Hans Thomas Hakl has called, "an alternative intellectual history of the twentieth century"[2]—was acted out by the shores of Lake Maggiore for fifty-six years (until 1988).[3] However, what was demonstrated there in practice was, in one instance, theorized formally. I am referring to the magisterial lecture in 1965 given by Stanley Romaine Hopper who thematized hermeneutically what other theological speakers before and after him enacted, and whose lecture can stand as a parable of the radicalness of *theologia* at Eranos generally. This is what Rudolf Ritsema at the end of the first cycle of Eranos presentations called, "versatility." Indeed, in the Eranos presentations there was a theological versatility where theological studies tended toward the apophatic rather than the kataphatic, toward the esoteric rather than the exoteric. It was the *reason* for these tendencies that Hopper reflected upon in his presentation. For Hopper, the clue to *theologia* today is poetry and the poets. From Hölderlin and Yeats to Eliot and Stevens, the testimony is the same. We are, Hopper discerned in the poetry, "in an age of disbelief, in which the range of disbelief is radical, the gods of rationalistic detachment are quite as much in abeyance as the gods of conventional religion and metaphysics."[4]

Hopper cites testimony from a panoply of poets: "What then is the nature of poetry in a time of disbelief?" (Stevens);[5] "*Wozu Dichter in dürftiger Zeit?*" (Where is the poet in a time of dearth?) (Hölderlin);[6] Things fall apart; the center cannot hold; / Mere anarchy is loosed upon the world" (Yeats).[7] The situation is that of "a heap of broken images, where the sun beats, / And the dead tree gives no shelter, the cricket no relief, / And the dry stone no sound of water" (Eliot)[8] and "The steeples are empty and so are the people" (Stevens).[9] As Stevens puts it in an essay:

> To see the gods dispelled in mid-air and dissolve like clouds is one of the great human experiences. It is not as if they had gone over the horizon to disappear for a time; nor as if they had been overcome by other gods of greater power and profounder knowledge. It is simply that they came to nothing.[10]

Hopper explains the cultural situation carefully, writing:

> The "death of God" is not a metaphysical statement or speculation; but [it] is dramatizing the death of symbol structures of Christendom together with the full panoply of theological, philosophical, aesthetic and cultural elaboration of those symbols which was effected in the medieval period and extended into the modern world.[11]

It represents "a time of the effectual demise of the classical modes for representing and understanding the human."[12] As Hopper puts it: "One has only to mention the names of Kierkegaard, Feuerbach, Nietzsche, Dostoevskij, Marx, Freud, Kafka, and Camus to sense the extent and depth of the cultural revolution that has been going on."[13]

At several points during his presentation in 1965, Hopper referred to another Eranos contribution, namely, that of Joseph Campbell eight years earlier in 1957. It was as if Hopper were continuing theologically the argument that Campbell had made ethnologically and anthropologically. Campbell's lecture was entitled, "The Symbol without Meaning," a title that indeed carried "aptly," as Hopper said, the force of Campbell's argument and his perspective.[14] "The world," Hopper quoted Campbell as saying, "the entire universe, its god and all has become a symbol—signifying nothing, a symbol without meaning."[15] Hopper explains:

> When Joseph Campbell speaks of the symbol without meaning he is referring to something ... radical. It is not merely that figurations, local to our Western way of seeing things have abdicated the regions of the numinous ... but rather that "the place of deity seems to be taken by the wholeness of man."[16]

The last phrase of the citation from Campbell, which both Campbell and Hopper put inside quotation marks, is taken from the writings of C. G. Jung.[17] Jung is speaking explicitly about what Nietzsche called, "the death of God."[18] Jung's phrase, quoted by Campbell and Hopper, is also echoed much later in 2004 by Wolfgang Giegerich who spoke at Eranos five times in the years between 1982 and 1988. Giegerich's title is much in keeping with the perspectives of Jung, Campbell, and Hopper, and is strikingly like Jung's phrase, "The End of Meaning and the Birth of Man," even though the force of Giegerich's argument is critical and follows through with the psychological implications of the perspective more radically than do the earlier writers.[19]

But Hopper is not concerned with the psychological implications, but with the theological implications of the historical and cultural situation indicated by the contemporary poets that he cites. Only four years after Hopper's lecture in 1965, the poet Donald Barthelme wrote an amusing one-page essay for *The New Yorker*, entitled, "On Angels." The opening sentence tells the whole tale: "The death of God left the angels in a strange position." Barthelme's closing is as telling as its opening: "A famous angel appeared on TV and said that the angels had tried adoring each other, as we do, but had found it unsatisfactory. He said that they are continuing to search for a new principle."[20] At Eranos, Hopper implied that, like angels, theologians today are in an awkward position, and seriously so, not humorously.

Hopper's theological language and perspective were philosophically similar to those of Martin Heidegger who, like Hopper, drew upon insights from the logic and language of poetry where *theologia* becomes *theopoiesis*.[21] With a nod to Nietzsche, Hopper writes, "the entire recognition of the 'death of God' in philosophical and theological discussion ... [is the sense that] the old God hath died and as yet no new God lieth in cradles and swaddling clothes."[22] This implies a contemporary situation "of being 'in between'—between the god that has died and the god that has not yet come to be."[23] The notion of "between" is from Heidegger's reflections on the poet Hölderlin. The poet, Heidegger notes, stands "between the gods and the people" in a situation of a double-lack: the no-more of the gods that have fled and the not-yet of the god that is coming."[24] Theologically, Hopper notes, "we have moved into that abyss of the in-between, there to await the new name of God … lest in our eagerness to act we reinstate the patterns which have led us into our impasses."[25]

To be sure, the Eranos of the twentieth century stands *between* the Wars, *between* an industrial-technological civilization and a global media culture, and *between* Romanticism and postmodernism. On the notion of the "between," Hopper cites an earlier Eranos presenter, Erich Neumann, who had written that we live today psychologically "in a world *between* chaos and archetype."[26] But Hopper mainly references the poets rather than socio-political matters. For example, T. S. Eliot had offered a striking metaphor of the modern and postmodern condition:

> As, in a theater,
> The lights are extinguished, for the scene to
>   be changed
> With a hollow rumble of wings, with a movement
>   of darkness on darkness,
> And we know that the hills and the trees, the
>   distant panorama
> And the bold imposing façade are all being
>   rolled away.[27]

Concerning this conceit, Hopper comments: "We are here, between the acts, so to speak, waiting for the lights to come on and action to be resumed within another framework."[28]

In another source, Hopper petitions Matthew Arnold. The poet's "Dover Beach" likened the contemporary human situation to the moment on the English Channel just after one wave has ebbed and before the next wave has come in:

> The Sea of Faith
> Was once, too, at the full, and round earth's shore
> Lay like the folds of a bright girdle furl'd.
> But now I only hear
> Its melancholy, long, withdrawing roar.[29]

Concerning this "between" moment, Arnold writes in "Grande Chartreuse":

> Wandering between two worlds, one dead,
> The other powerless to be born,
> With nowhere yet to rest my head,
> Like these, on earth I wait forlorn.[30]

In "Dover Beach," Arnold speaks of this situation as being in or on "edges drear."[31]

I mentioned above that the presentations at Eranos concerning theology were on an "edge." I also noted that Stanley Hopper's presentation in 1965 was a kind of parable of all of the others; that is, Hopper attempted to explain the reason for the radical theological versatility of Eranos *theologia*. Philosopher Edward Casey recently made the argument that there is a connection between what Heidegger and Hopper call the "between" and the notion of "edge." Casey writes:

> The between itself ... is very much a function of edges... When we are in the midst of any activity we are *in-between* edges... Edges and the in-between are active presences for one another: take away the edges and the domain in-between is undermined by being rendered wholly amorphous. Without edges, there is no in-between; without an in-between edges would not be able to distinguish one object or event from another... Edges supply ... *boundaries* [to the in-between] ... i.e., porous edges that take in as well as give out.[32]

If one follows Casey's argument, notions of "between" and "edge" would seem to be interchangeable, or at least correlative, in Hopper's theological argument.[33]

However, Wolfgang Giegerich has been critical of the logic of "between," in a way that may imply that Hopper might question Heidegger's notion of the "between" and opt instead for a notion of "edge," the "edge" of Edward Casey and my British seatmate. In his book, *The Soul's Logical Life*, Giegerich writes:

> The image of the "middle ground" and the "third" sets up two positive *realms* (matters or senses vs. mind or spirit), with the soul as the in-between. But the soul is the logical (not temporal) *movement as such* from here to there and back. "In-between" and "middle ground" tend to freeze what would actually be sheer

movement into a third realm as a kind of bridge, thereby
fixating it in between and never allowing it to *arrive* yonder
and to *return* hither. The soul does not want to be and stay
locked "between." It wants to be, nay, it is at both "banks" at
once, as well as both on the peaks of spirit and down to earth
(and even in the underworld beneath the earth), which it can
be since it is logical, dialectical (not literal, spatial or temporal)
movement to and fro.[34]

Giegerich is calling attention to a possible syntactical problem with
the notion of "the between," namely, that it defines itself by reference
to two things that it is "between," thus re-inscribing what it announces
is both past (passed) and not-yet. It both fails to take into account the
dialectical nature of being here and there synchronically, and it defines
itself by what it posits (positivizes, objectivizes) being between. In so
doing, it does not allow the present to presence itself as itself. An edge,
like the razor's edge of Asian theology, is not "between" any two things.
When one hones a razor to sharpen it, one puts an "edge" on it. During
the process of honing, the knife becomes sharper and sharper as the
edge has less and less mass, as it approaches nothingness. The closer
one gets to no-thing, the "better" the edge will be. This "nothing"
(including the nothing-ing of the nothing) is the "edge" characterized
by the sort of esoteric and apophatic *theologia* that was a typical mode
of Eranos' theological speakers.

To at least one contemporary theologian, the theological "edge" of
Eranos that I am attempting to identify is particularly relevant to a
proper understanding of *theologia*. Paul van Buren was never a speaker
at Eranos, but his book, *The Edges of Language*, petitions two scholars
for intellectual support: Rudolf Otto, who suggested the name,
"Eranos," to Olga Fröbe-Kapteyn, and Paul Tillich, who lectured in
1936 and in 1954, both of whom were highly significant to Eranos.
Van Buren was attempting to call attention to the fact that "every seeing
is seeing as," and so he emphasized "imaginative vision," parabolic
utterance, dreams, and poetry as typical linguistic models for a
philosophy of religion.[35] This is similar to Hopper's theopoetic
perspective. It is also the manner in which van Buren stresses Rudolf
Otto's definition of religion as *mysterium tremendum et fascinosum* (a
"fearful and fascinating mystery"). Religion is being on the "edge." Van
Buren lists four instances of language lived at the edge: the language

of jokes and puns, the language of lovers, the language of metaphysics, and the language of religion. Here are some of van Buren's examples:

- The language of jokes and puns—"A door is not a door when it is a-jar!"
- The language of lovers—"Even though all the stones of Baalbek split into exact quarters, and the rooks of Repton utter dire prophecies in Greek ... I will love you whatever happens, even though you put on twenty pounds and become afflicted with a moustache!"
- The language of metaphysics—"In the labyrinth of metaphysics are the same whispers as one hears when climbing Kafka's staircases to the tribunal which is always one floor further Up."
- The language of religion—"God is One and Three!"

Van Buren also mentions the parables of Jesus and the *kōans* of Zen as putting one on edge.[36]

Between literal and metaphoric, between Otto's *fascinosum* (identity) and *tremendum* (difference), there is a threshold, which is the edge of language. On this "edge" is the philosophical "logic" of language about ultimate reality, *theologia*. The name that Paul Tillich chose for this edge was *Grenzsituation*, often translated "boundary situation," but which easily could be rendered "edge-situation."[37]

This kind of thinking theologically should not seem strange to the religious imagination. Edge-talk is not uncommon in *theologia*. In Zoroastrianism, the Çinvat Bridge on the road to the next life is a knife-edge that discriminates the paths to heaven and to hell. It is not unlike a similar figure in Islam, and it is analogous to that dangerous edge traversed by the Altaic shaman in the spirit-journey to the underworld realm of Erlik Khan. In the tradition of Zen Buddhism, there is also the metaphor of the "diamond sword," the discriminating religious consciousness whose spiritual essence is that of enduring brilliance, dignity, and strength. More significantly, this Buddhist sword signifies the Diamond Sūtra and its teaching of the Diamond Sword of Discriminating Wisdom, which cuts away all doubts.

In the *Kaṭha–Upaniṣad*, the Hindu version of this religious insight has to do with a razor's edge, which lent its name to the title of W. Somerset Maugham's novel, *The Razor's Edge*. The Hindu text says: "Sages say the path is narrow and difficult to tread, narrow as the edge of a razor."[38] A Hebrew scripture, in which the prophet Jeremiah expatiates against developmental psychology, says: "In those days, they shall no longer say: 'The fathers have eaten sour grapes and the children's teeth are set on edge.' But every one shall die for his own sin; each man who eats sour grapes, his teeth shall be set on edge" (Jer. 31:29–30; cf. Deut. 24:16 and Ezek. 18:2). And in his massive study of Haida religious myths, Robert Bringhurst reports a Northwestern American Native proverb first recorded by Franz Boas: "The world is narrow and sharp as a knife."[39] The reader will think of many more instances.

However, these are material instances of "edge" language in religion. What I am trying to point to here is something formal. It is the edge-nature, not of the religious talk about edges, but that of theological talk *about* religion by the speakers at Eranos whom I have named at the beginning. Their perspectives not only come from the edges of religious traditions materially (Kabbalah, Christian mysticism, Zen, Sufism), but the ways in which they speak *about* such edges is in an edgy, often controversial, manner and style and form. Theirs is a remaking (*poiēsis*) of theology from the edge. Indeed, it is a remaking (poetizing) of theology as an edge—theology on edge. This is what I have tried to demonstrate with what I take to be Hopper's parabolic presentation concerning the nature of the discourse and logic of his fellow theologues.

Hopper worries that "theological language of an objectivizing kind" contains the "inadvertence" of "idolatrous fictions" by "ignoring its parabolic forms." He believes that theology "must learn a new way of speaking, perhaps from the poet's sense of symbolic forms."[40] Theological studies at Eranos had a radical edge in the difficult times of the twentieth century. They seem to have reflected the sentiment of the poet Theodore Roethke:

> In a dark time, the eye begins to see,
> I meet my shadow in the deepening shade;
> … The edge is what I have.[41]

NOTES

1. A somewhat different version of this argument previously appeared as a portion of the following: David L. Miller, "At the Edges of the Round Table: Jung, Religion, and Eranos," in L. Cowan, ed., *Barcelona 2004: Edges of Experience: Memory and Emergence. Proceedings of the Sixteenth International Congress for Analytical Psychology* (Einsiedeln: Daimon, 2006), pp. 129–44. The present version is published here with the knowledge and permission of Robert Hinshaw, the editor of Daimon Verlag.

2. Hans Thomas Hakl, *Eranos—An Alternative Intellectual History of the Twentieth Century* (Montreal/Kingston: McGill-Queen's University Press, 2013); Hans Thomas Hakl, *Der verborgene Geist von Eranos. Unbekannte Begegnungen von Wissenschaft und Esoterik. Eine alternative Geistesgeschichte des 20. Jahrhunderts* (Bretten: Scientia nova-Neue Wissenschaft, 2001).

3. I am writing here only of the first cycle of Eranos presentations, inasmuch as I am not competent to comment on what has happened after 1988, nor on what the future holds for the Eranos project.

4. Stanley Romaine Hopper, "Symbolic Reality and the Poet's Task," *Eranos-Jahrbuch 34* (1965): 170.

5. Wallace Stevens, *Opus Posthumous* (New York, NY: Knopf, 1977), p. 211; Hopper, "Symbolic Reality and the Poet's Task," p. 170.

6. Friedrich Hölderlin, *Selected Verse*, trans. M. Hamburger (Baltimore, MD: Peguin, 1961), p. 111; Hopper, "Symbolic Reality and the Poet's Task," p. 170.

7. William Butler Yeats, *Selected Poems*, ed. M. L. Rosenthal (New York, NY: Collier, 1962), p. 91; Hopper, "Symbolic Reality and the Poet's Task," p. 181.

8. Thomas Stearns Eliot, *The Complete Poems and Plays* (New York, NY: Harcourt, Brace and Company, 1958), p. 38; Hopper, "Symbolic Reality and the Poet's Task," p. 182.

9. Wallace Stevens, *The Collected Poems* (New York, NY: Knopf, 1975), p. 210; Hopper, "Symbolic Reality and the Poet's Task," p. 171.

10. Stevens, *Opus Posthumous*, p. 206; Hopper, "Symbolic Reality and the Poet's Task," p. 172.

11. *Ibid.*, p. 184.

12. *Ibid.*, p. 175.

13. *Ibid.*, p. 177.

14. *Ibid.*, p. 195.

15. Joseph Campbell, "The Symbol without Meaning," in *The Flight of the Wild Gander* (Novato, CA: New World Library, 2002), p. 143; Hopper, "Symbolic Reality and the Poet's Task," p. 202.

16. *Ibid.*

17. C. G. Jung, "Psychology and Religion" (1937), in *The Collected Works of C. G. Jung,* vol. 11, ed. and trans. Gerhard Adler and R. F. C. Hull (Princeton, NJ: Princeton University Press, 1969), § 139.

18. *Ibid.*, §§ 144–45, 148, and 149. ("I only know—and here I am expressing what countless other people know—that the present is a time of God's death and disappearance.")

19. Wolfgang Giegerich, "The End of Meaning and the Birth of Man: An Essay about the State Reached in the History of Consciousness and an Analysis of C. G. Jung's Psychology Project," *Journal of Jungian Theory and Practice* 6 (1, 2004): 1–66.

20. Donald Barthelme, "On Angels," *The New Yorker,* August 9, 1969, p. 29.

21. David L. Miller, "Theopoiesis," in: Stanley Romaine Hopper, *Why Persimmons and Other Poems: Transformations of Theology in Poetry* (Atlanta, GA: Scholars, 1987), pp. 1–12.

22. Hopper, "Symbolic Reality and the Poet's Task," p. 183.

23. *Ibid.*, p. 184.

24. *Ibid.*, p. 174; the Heideggerian allusion is to "Hölderlin and the Essence of Poetry," *Existence and Being* (London: Vision, 1949), pp. 312–13.

25. Hopper, "Symbolic Reality and the Poet's Task," p. 201. Hopper also invokes the "abyss" of Pascal, i.e., a mean "between" the Infinite and the Nothing (*ibid.*, p. 205).

26. Hopper, "Symbolic Reality and the Poet's Task," p. 187.

27. Eliot, *The Complete Poems and Plays*, p. 126.

28. Hopper, "Symbolic Reality and the Poet's Task," p. 200.

29. Matthew Arnold, "Dover Beach," in *The Viking Book of Poetry of the English-Speaking World* (New York, NY: Viking, 1959), vol. II, p. 972.

30. Mathew Arnold, "Grande Chartreuse," *The Viking Book of Poetry,* p. 971; see Stanley Romaine Hopper, *The Crisis of Faith* (Nashville, TN: Abingdon, 1944), pp. 34 and 111.

31. Arnold, "Dover Beach," p. 972.

32. Edward S. Casey, "Edges and the In-Between," accessed March 6, 2015 at http://www.scribd.com/doc/253719040/Casey-EdgesAndTheInBetween.

33. For further amplification of the notion of the "between," see David L. Miller, "Between God and the Gods—Trinity," *Eranos-Jahrbuch* 49 (1980): 81–148; and David L. Miller, *Three Faces of God—Traces of the Trinity in Literature and Life* (New Orleans, LA: Spring Journal, Inc., 2005), pp. 75–92.

34. Wolfgang Giegerich, *The Soul's Logical Life—Towards a Rigorous Notion of Psychology* (Frankfurt am Main: Peter Lang, 1998), p. 190.

35. Paul van Buren, *Theological Explorations* (New York, NY: Macmillan, 1968), pp. 178–80.

36. Paul van Buren, *The Edges of Language—An Essay in the Logic of a Religion* (New York, NY: Macmillan, 1972), p. 110.

37. Paul Tillich, *The Protestant Era* (Chicago, IL: University of Chicago Press, 1948), pp. 195–205.

38. *Kaṭha–Upaniṣad*, in *The Upanishads*, trans. J. Mascaro (Baltimore, MD: Penguin, 1965), p. 61.

39. Robert Bringhurst, *A Story as Sharp as a Knife—The Classical Haida Mythtellers and Their World* (Lincoln, NE: Nebraska University Press, 2000).

40. Stanley Romaine Hopper, "Symbolic Reality and the Poet's Task," pp. 213–14.

41. Theodore Roethke, *The Collected Poems* (Garden City, NY: Doubleday/Anchor, 1975), p. 231.

BERNARDO NANTE

B ernardo Nante was born in 1955 in Buenos Aires, Argentina, where he lives today with his spouse and two sons. He received his Ph.D. in Philosophy and Higher Studies in Psychology, Oriental Studies, Mathematics, and Economics. Nante is Full Professor of Philosophy of Religion at the Faculty of Philosophy and Literature and of General and Compared Mythology at the School of Oriental Studies, Universidad del Salvador, Buenos Aires, Argentina. He has served as visiting professor at various national and international universities and institutions, including the UNESCO Mobile Chair Edgar Morin in Complex Thought (Universidad del Salvador). Currently, Nante serves as the Dean of the Faculty of Philosophy and Literature, Universidad del Salvador, Buenos Aires, and as the President of the Fundación Vocación Humana and its Institute of Jungian Studies. He is the author of numerous works on the correlation between philosophy, anthropology, religion, and, in particular, the alchemical sources of C. G. Jung. He has been involved in the publication of the Spanish editions of Jung's *Collected Works* and *The Red Book: Liber Novus* (2010). He published *El Libro Rojo de Jung. Claves para la comprensión de una obra inexplicable* (2010), the first major analysis of *The Red Book*. Nante's work was recently translated into Italian by Bollati Boringhieri as *Guida dalla lettura del Libro Rosso di C.G. Jung* (2011).

SPRING VOL 92

ERANOS ①

42 Husserl : Lebenswelt : world of life

45 ERANOS : GR = BANQUET

49 scholars "of variable geometries"

96 man as "the age-old son of
    the mother"

117 von FRANZ : the constituents of an
     DNA, A, T, C G in Relationship to
     a QUARTERNITY

125 STEPHEN Aizenstat BOOK:
     DREAM TENDING L12

183 "... on the same side of an
     invisible front..."

246 cultural comparativism ?

265 Santis to theory of cognition
     (look at this)

297 "a place of intellectual excellence &
     relaxed conviviality"

322 I am, because NATURE is, and because she
     is, I am. (Zulu professor)

     check availability

ERANOS: THE STUDY OF RELIGION
AS A RELIGIOUS PHENOMENON

BERNARDO NANTE

In a renowned article written in Tehran in late 1956, Henry Corbin envisioned, not without a certain sadness, a young researcher in the future dedicated to the study of that twentieth-century phenomenon, Eranos. According to Corbin, this hypothetical researcher would be all too ready to identify "causes" and explain "influences," "schools," and "currents of thought" using scientific methods drawn from historicism. Certainly, it is possible the researcher might be able to "explain" something of Eranos. However, as Corbin maintained, the young scholar would fail to comprehend the depth and breadth of the phenomenon. Indeed, this researcher

> will not have divined that the real problem would have been to discover not what explains Eranos, but what Eranos explains by virtue of what it implies: for example, the idea of a true community, bringing together speakers and listeners, a community so paradoxical that it displays none of the characteristics that are of concern to statistics and sociology.[1]

Corbin's discussion raises the very important, essential point at hand, namely how to describe and understand Eranos appropriately. There are polar opposite approaches. On one side, the singularity and complexity of the Eranos phenomenon, and on the other, a merely "historical" perspective which Corbin warns against.

We could, of course, compile an exhaustive catalogue of the prominent religion scholars who participated in Eranos, and even suggest how, in some instances, their presentations anticipated future development of their work, and which in turn became seminal contributions to the study of religion. Such a catalogue would be even richer if it were coupled with research that elucidated mutual influences that might have occurred among scholars and fields. Yet, however much we might encourage such a commendable and useful endeavor, it would not be viable. Not only is there limited space for such a volume of information, but a venture of this type risks leading us astray from the real nature of the Ascona phenomenon: Eranos is not just a place where religion historians and scholars gathered; Eranos is, above all, *a contemporary "religious phenomenon"* and a candidate for study in the history of religion.[2] This conclusion raises an unavoidable epistemological issue, one with which researchers of religion have been grappling since its inception: which methodological criteria guarantee scientific validity of research on religion?

Current methodological trends lean towards favoring data collection via a "historical-descriptive" approach. Although this type of reductionism is common in countless psychological, sociological, and even historical treatments, it implies a certain mistrust of any *a priori* reasoning regarding religion, and even more so of phenomenology. As Ugo Bianchi points out:

> It is no solution to counter historical reductionism with an appeal
> to the irreducible character of religion as perceived by the
> subjective, experiential sensitivity of the phenomenologist as well
> as that of the historicist, there is an illegitimate appeal to an *a
> priori*, preconceived conception of religion.[3]

In the case of Eranos, analysis becomes much more complex if one includes consideration of the diversity of participating authors and views. However, if we put forward the hypothesis that Eranos was "religious" in nature, it allows for a single, or at least summarized, discussion, the boundaries of which may be shaped by the intent of its founder, Olga Fröbe-Kapteyn. In a certain sense, her own symbolic process was "religious." It was inspired by and originated in the first three decades of Eranos' history, from 1933 to 1962. Included in this process is the thorough and passionate work of scholars who are representative of Eranos: Heinrich Zimmer, Mircea Eliade, Gershom Scholem, Henry Corbin, and others. All were part of the same process and all used scientific texts in an attempt to capture and reflect what was ultimately a shared spiritual endeavor.[4] Undoubtedly, C. G. Jung's leadership played a major role for several reasons: his key position at the inception of Eranos, his influence on Olga Fröbe-Kapteyn's symbolic development, and his own theories that allow the religious phenomenon to be recaptured.[5]

Naturally, all of this depends on how Jung's work is interpreted. For example, it may be seen as a psychological contribution to the study of religion that enriches our understanding of religious phenomena. Alternately, it may be seen as merely the psychologizing of religion. The latter tends to be disparaged both from a scientific and, its counterpoint, a theological or metaphysical approach. Even among thinkers closest to Jung, such as Eliade and Corbin, who strove to distance themselves from Jung's psychological approach, it is clear that the recovery of the sacred from the *esse in anima* constitutes the *tópos*.[6] The seminal psychic experiences that took place at Eranos have shed light on new paths to guide other disciplines and methodologies. Thus, Eranos comprises a chapter in the history of religion for the reason that it is a *"religious phenomenon" that deals with the study of religions*.

From this vantage, the goal here is to lay a foundation for the aforementioned hypothesis and suggest possible guidelines for future research that may bring even greater insights and more grounded understanding. Included in and consonant with this exploration is previously unpublished material, Olga Fröbe-Kapteyn's *Visions*.[7]

THE STUDY OF RELIGION AND RELIGIONS IN ERANOS

The vast and diverse material produced from Eranos cannot be easily pigeonholed. But, one can say that its mission and approach were, on the whole, directed towards the fundamental issue of the "soul." This subject was largely tackled through an exploration of symbolic mediations that link humans to the sacred. It is no coincidence that the first *Tagung* (Conference) in 1933 was entitled, *Yoga und Meditation in Osten und im Westen* (Yoga and Meditation in East and West). The Conference initially focused on the various methods employed by different traditions in the treatment and care of the soul. Today, the *Tagung* revisits the subject, but with a different tone.[8] One shouldn't forget that early Roman etymology of the term, "*religio*," is *relego* (*relegere*), meaning "to re-read," "to reunite," or "to revisit." This is something that Cicero clearly associated with religious people, those who carefully and thoroughly reflect and re-examine everything related to the cult of the gods.[9]

From this perspective, generalizations in the study of religions are much more acceptable because there is no special focus given to a particular theology or theological topic as is sometimes the case when understanding *"religio"* as *"religare,"* an interpretation favored mostly by Lactantius, 400 B.C. In this instance, the meaning is taken to be "re-tying," the maintaining of a firm bond between humans, God, and the revelation of the divine will.[10] This has been a rationalist, biased view, deriving from precedence of a certain theological appropriation of religion. However, this upsets the process completely. Instead of aiming for a non-reductive, respectful, rational systematization, the approach becomes a coercive dogmatic instrument that predetermines authenticity of given religious phenomena. On the other hand, the history of ancient Roman beliefs links the term, *"religio,"* with the meaning of "hay knots." Hay knots allude to the knots used by priests in ancient Rome to tie beams of a bridge together in order to strengthen the structure.[11] It would appear that the meaning of "pontiff" and "pontooner" in post-archaic Rome are similarly related.[12] A parallel idea can be found in Jainism, where the term, *tirthâ-ânkara,* means the "ford-maker," or the one who makes the journey easier.

Despite the fact that participants drew from different theoretical frameworks, almost every contribution at Eranos concerns religion and religious phenomena. Critically, this suggests that the understanding of *religio* was *relegere.* Epistemologically, this is translated as a psychology of the religious phenomenon, pointing to the psychic reality behaving religiously and engaged in a critical dialogue with the different theoretical approximations to religion.[13] To better grasp this process, we will take a few moments to visit the vast canvas that comprises Eranos and its contributions.

Among Eranos participants, there were a considerable number of religious studies generalists who can be considered "historians" or "phenomenologists." There were also theologians and scholars of diverse religious traditions including Classical World, Christianity, Gnosticism, Judaism, Islam, Hinduism, Buddhism, Taoism, and Eastern traditions. The latter category included Indologists, Buddhologists, Sinologists, and other scholars of Eastern traditions. There were also philosophers, art historians, anthropologists, archaeologists, and scholars hailing from the natural sciences, such as physicists and biologists.[14] Almost to a person, and with varying degrees of clarity, each worked on how symbols form a gateway to the sacred.[15]

Due to space limitations, we will only offer a synthetic sketch to illustrate their eminently "religious" nature.[16] There is a consistent, intrinsic tension in all the work that is created by the juxtaposition of a Jungian psychological approach (that centers on the *psychic* nature of religious experience) with other views that study the purely "spiritual" nature of such experiences. However, this tension is not irreconcilable. A non-psychological approach underscores the importance of symbolic mediations that express religious experience and in those cases dealing with processes related to the caring of the soul and acquisition of transformative knowledge. This is the case with spiritual hermeneutics.

As Conference records show, the first years (1933–37) were preoccupied mainly with comparisons of spiritual traditions from the East and the West, with study and discussion focusing on praxis and underlying symbolic processes. In the second set of conferences (1938–46), the focus shifted to specific archetypal subjects connected to the mystical experience: the Great Mother, Rebirth, the Trinity, the hermetic principle and mysteries, the soul, and such. Eranos' third stage (1947–62) was comprised of anthropological issues such as those revolving around Erich Neumann's *inner Mensch* ("inner man") concept. Often this theme appears related to rites, time, and energy topics. For instance, the subject of the 1947 *Tagung* was the relationship between humans, Mother Earth, and divine parentage. One can observe the tension between the different perspectives. One "side," as exemplified by Karl Kerényi, views humans from a chthonic, feminine-matriarchal nature. In contrast, as in the case of Quispel, humanity is approached from the perspectives of Gnosticism (in particular, Valentinian Gnostics). This involves a spiritualization that tends to overlook or dismiss the matriarchal dimension of reality. A similar tension emerges from the eighteenth *Yearbook* from 1950, which, in homage to Jung, was dedicated to archetypal images. Kerényi and Neumann focus on the immanentist psycho-energetic aspect, and Corbin on the purely spiritual, metaphysical.[17]

With the passing of Jung in 1961 and Olga Fröbe-Kapteyn in 1962, the question arose: what would be the foundational drive of Eranos, and, critically, its *religious* orientation in subsequent gatherings?

Should a new direction be charted? As mentor until 1978, Henry
Corbin carried on the spiritual, metaphysical, and esoteric framework.
Over time, however, this orientation gradually gave way to a growing
predominance of psychological, and later, secular, perspectives. The
former is evident from Gilbert Durand's 1982 text where he
summarizes Eranos in few strokes, implying that modernity's wretched
consciousness, devoid of meaning, stems from being uprooted from
the unconscious.[18] Although these ideas were present from the
beginning of the Conferences, an increased focus on contemporary
society foretells the growing secularization of Eranos. Indeed, during
the fourth stage (1963–71), the Conferences delve into anthropological
subjects. There is an effort to broaden parochial horizons of Western
conceptions in the examination of human transformation through an
anthropology of the imaginary.

In the fifth stage (1972–88), the Conference undertakes a survey
of various subjects related to "spiritual hermeneutics." In the subsequent
sixth stage (1989–2002) under the direction of Rudolf Ritsema, the
emphasis was on the convergence of archetypal psychology and the *I
Ching*. The current, seventh stage (beginning in 2006) tends to center
on the relationship between humans, society, and their interactions
with contemporary philosophical thinking. This work appears to hark
back to the earliest days at Eranos by its engagement with the symbolic
and religious dimension of reality.[19]

An analysis of religious studies at Eranos is not complete without
discussing how one of its unique aspects came into being. More than
a mere multidisciplinary gathering, the discourse and interactions there
represented a true *inter*disciplinary phenomenon, the key goal being
to integrate different systems of knowledge.[20] Indeed, the very nature
of *religio* as *relegere* and the world of symbols in general provide the
ontic conditions necessary for interdisciplinary work. Religious
phenomena and symbols are, by definition, impossible to reduce or
dissociate from a greater cultural whole. Prior to being rendered into a
scientific method, comparative studies of religions drew from the same
reflections as those of religious traditions. It is difficult to tell what
derives from the founders' own religious experience and what comes
from a need to distance themselves from the phenomenon, be it via
doctrine or praxis. Consciously or unconsciously, the dynamics of
religion are fairly loaded with syncretism that systematizes each

theology.[21] Sometimes there is a more "revelatory" or "inspirational" sense, and at other times a more "regulatory" or "prescriptive" one. Similarly, Jungian psychology, characteristic in the early stages of Eranos, finds commonalities and resonance with scholarship that, in various ways, prioritizes discussion of religious phenomena from "the realm of the middle." This is the symbolic world and concerns processes related to the care of the soul. Without a doubt, the most effective comparativist approach is phenomenological-hermeneutics.[22] It not only accounts for the structure, dynamics, and sense of religious phenomena, but being hermeneutic, facilitates an "empathetic" approach.

Indeed, the sometimes vague use of the term "phenomenology of religion" is quite apt because it describes religious forms.[23] It is not sufficient to articulate a phenomenology—it is also necessary to apply it properly. The vague use of "phenomenology" in religious studies derives in part from a pre-Husserlian use. It is also inspired by a similarly vague use of the Hegelian meaning.[24] This is one reason why the term, "phenomenology of religion," may only be applied to the Eranos religious studies with a proviso. The first general studies text to warrant that label is Gerardus van der Leeuw's *Phenomenology of Religion* published in 1933.[25] We should bear in mind that van der Leeuw participated in Eranos only in 1948 and 1949. His text was succeeded (and criticized) by other phenomenologists such as Geo Widengren and Mircea Eliade.[26,27] In 1933, the religion scholar, William Brede Kristensen, sent a letter to his former disciple, Gerardus van der Leeuw, after having received and read the aforementioned volume. After congratulating van der Leeuw for such commendable work, Kristensen goes on to deplore the use of vague generalizations that convey to the modern reader an acquaintance with such complex matters. Kristensen adds that these studies will encourage an *Einfühlung* typical of "modern sentimentality" thereby linking it to scholars such as Otto Kern and Martin Nilsson. Not without a certain sarcasm, Kristensen writes that whomever thinks he has understood the concept of "power" as "*mana*" (central in van der Leeuw's work) may have fallen under the spell of an illusion.[28]

This kind of methodological agreement among Eranos' key participants helps us understand how the diversity in themes and disciplines fosters, as Giovanni Filoramo points out, "a remarkable uniformity in ideas and issues."[29] But we might grasp this notion more deeply if we understand that the main goal of Eranos' mentors was "religious," that is, "gnostic," and not "scientific." Filoramo discusses how scientific knowledge fostered in Eranos was not seen as an end in itself.[30] The question remains whether the "science of religions" in Eranos' loses relevance because its members' priority was not "scientific."[31] Ultimately, if Eranos was a scientific phenomenon, and in a sense, gnostic-religious, it might be valid to wonder if there was a link between religious knowledge and the scientific discourse that derived from these gatherings. In appreciation of brevity, we state only what current research should attempt: a study of *Eranos as "religious phenomenon,"* its connection to Jungian psychology, and the connection between Jungian psychology and Eranos' comparativist and phenomenological postulates.

Olga Fröbe-Kapteyn maintained that Eranos was an unrestricted group but, nevertheless, had a life, nature, and direction of its own. As a result, there were certain features that distinguished its texts and authors. According to its founder, Eranos' distinctiveness derives from the fact that, though unrestricted, there was an invisible force that gave the Conferences their unique shape and form.[32] One might question the scientific value of that statement, but not its psychic reality or the existence of features characteristic of the "religious phenomenon" we have attempted to outline here.

Undoubtedly, this very statement can be proved by a *reductio ad absurdum*. To name but one example, Pierre Hadot (whose outlook would seem close to the Eranos *ethos*) took part in *Tagungen* on two occasions. However, he appeared alienated from its spirit. As Hadot himself states, Corbin believed that he was excited about Jung's archetypes, archangels, and "the imaginary." Nonetheless, despite the wonderful atmosphere and the charm of Eranos' guests, Hadot admits that he could not adhere to the gathering's orthodox tenets.[33] Eranos proposes a spiritual hermeneutics supported by hermeneutic spirituality. This seems to be the very essence of the Eranos "religious phenomenon."

ERANOS AS A "RELIGIOUS PHENOMENON"

Although there are several texts that touch upon the subject, an exhaustive work has yet to be written about Eranos as a "religious phenomenon." Here, we will point out only several characteristics of the Eranos phenomenon which might deem it, *cum grano salis,* "religious" or, at minimum, provide stepping stones for future research. If we truly apply a phenomenological approach and dispense with sweeping statements of absolute truth so as to "believe the believer," it should be possible to *a priori* rule out some value propositions possibly attributable to interpretations by Eranosians themselves. The epithet "romantic" is often applied to an attitude and theoretical reading about religious phenomenon, thereby falling into a subjectivity devoid of scientific rigor. In the foregoing discussion of van der Leeuw's religious phenomenology, this view was deemed "romantic." It was also charged with reducing the multiplicity and heterogeneity of religious phenomena to universal, often crypto-theological, categories. This diminished their uniqueness. For instance, Arthur McCalla, maintains that romantic phenomenologists considered the religious experience to be an intuition or inner feeling that was irreducible, infinite, and universal.[34] He also claimed that diverse religions were merely manifestations of the same essence, variations, as it were, on a common theme. Ferrer and Sherman point out that, "religion's classic phenomenologists" such as Nathan Söderblom, Rudolf Otto, Friedrich Heiler, Gerardus van der Leeuw, and Mircea Eliade mixed religious fascination and feelings with universal and objectivist assumptions that belong to the Age of Enlightenment.[35,36]

In contrast, from a more balanced and less prejudiced perspective, Filoramo warns that the core of the Eranos project can be found

> in the modern traditions of Christian esoteric beliefs and, in particular, in a certain stream of *Naturphilosophie*, of which Goethe was champion and advocate, as well as early 19th Century romantic philosophy.[37]

It would, therefore, be worth knowing if the Eranos phenomenon itself is susceptible to "religious" characterization. With this goal, the phenomenon of Eranos can only be approached from a historical and religious perspective.

In 1939, Olga Fröbe-Kapteyn wrote that the history of Eranos could be retold in an unwritten book, awash with images. She describes how she often searches to find the connections that will configure a unifying and meaningful whole.[38] Moreover, she adds, the emergent model will be inexorably interwoven with her own life. Today, we realize that her discourse is not merely "metaphorical," but "symbolic." There is an unpublished "book" that Fröbe-Kapteyn put together comprised of painted images, particularly those created between 1934 and 1938, that speak of her own process of visions. This allegedly provides answers to the successive manifestation of "the Eranos archetype."[39] To put it in Jungian terms, these images draw from a process of active imagination. They emerge from a confrontation with the psyche's depth pertaining to Olga Fröbe-Kapteyn herself and to the Eranos *opus*. This symbolic production is quite relevant to our purposes here because it fulfills at least two requirements.

First, the psychic process is accepted as a "religious" and not a merely "subjective" process. Second, the process of the Eranos founder, Olga Fröbe-Kapteyn, is a "religious" process, which is *representative* of Eranos, and not a mere individual (possibly "religious") experience.[40] Notably, however, we should keep in mind that evidence for achieving these criteria will be limited and only indicative of possible future research. In a nutshell, then, we can only state the following:

a) There is a series of "Eranos *maṇḍalas*," which reflect the coming together of opposites and which integrate subjects and participants who comprised some *Tagungen*.[41] The first Eranos *maṇḍala* dates from 1934 and shows the image of a translucent temple with a flower on top.[42] It was created under the frozen lake surface from a peripheral skating dance by Olga Fröbe-Kapteyn and Carl Gustav Jung. Jung maintains that this *maṇḍala* (within which "there are also others" with Shiva and Shakti at its center) concerns the Dance of Creation.[43] According to Olga Fröbe-Kapteyn, it is as if this pre-temporal image of Eranos had taken on life.[44] Successive *maṇḍalas* revisit the founding image. Although a first impression of some of these *maṇḍalas* might suggest that they are merely charts about the topics and lecturers of each *Tagungen*, they actually recount inspiring community symbolic processes. For instance, Olga Fröbe-Kapteyn describes one 1947 *maṇḍala* as embodying several dynamic relationships between the center, the speakers, and the audience. These patterns suggest the nourishing and numinous nature of the center that involves exhibitions and participants involved.[45] Somehow, as if of its own accord, a *sui generis* community of spiritual work is born which puts forward, reworks, and critically assumes an underlying "religious" process.

b) In these *maṇḍalas*, we can see the central role that Jungian psychology takes, not only as integrative knowledge from the epistemological perspective, but, importantly, as knowledge that accounts for the numinous nature of psyche. In other words, "psychology" is revealed as true "religious psychology," not merely a psychology of religion. Jungian theory tackles the link between an empirically limited psychological perspective of psyche and its extension to the sacred opening toward the metaphysical. To this end, the theory takes shape as a phenomenology of human experience that is initially "psychological" in a restricted sense. However, this phenomenology stops short of being solely a "method" to become an ontological orientation. In the order of discovery, Jungian theory emerges as a myth, as a mouthpiece of that which is deemed "supreme-sense" or "supreme meaning" (*Übersinn*) in *The Red Book*. For epistemological justification, it is defined in a restrictive sense as science, an expression of "sense" clothed in the spirit of the time, the "collective consciousness." However, it remains aware of its origin and goal. All that emerges from psyche manifestation derives from imaginative activity, whose synthetic, creative, and ultimate quality spontaneously correlates with *consensus omnium*, "religious experience." This is ultimately linked to the Jungian principle of *esse in anima*, which is both a point of convergence and of controversy among Eranos participants.

c) In Olga Fröbe-Kapteyn's images, and in the stories that accompany them, there are several references to the active, inspirational presence of the "forebears" (*Ahnen*) in Eranos. There is a tale written by Olga Fröbe-Kapteyn associated with a *maṇḍala* dating back to an experience on Pentecost Eve, 1947. The writer describes how, at the time of the Holy Spirit's descent, there was a connection with all the alchemists of the past, and that they were the "ancestors" of Eranos.[46]

d) In a process of active imagination, symbols appear, are renewed, and transformed in the depths of psyche. Christian, Pagan, Hindi, Buddhist, Taoist, and other religious traditions and myths comprise the mosaic and the manifestation of that which the psyche strives to process. This is a *topos* where Eranos subjects were developed *in statu nascens*, and centered in Eastern and Western traditions. We may, therefore, speak of a "syncretism of the psyche."

This accounts for its vitality. It forms the empirical foundation of every comparativist method.[47]

e) Without a doubt, the visions in Olga Fröbe-Kapteyn's stories contain a symbology. This is related to what may be described as "esoteric traditions" or "broad hermetism."[48]

f) The reason that Gnosis prevails is that the psychic-religious process is in some way "gnostic." It is a knowledge that saves. For example, Olga Fröbe-Kapteyn links one of her visionary images with a sort of gnostic-hermetic baptism experience. This insight prompts her to quote a well-known passage from the *Corpus Hermeticum*:

> Baptize thyself with this Cup's baptism, what heart can do
> so, thou that hast faith thou canst ascend to Him that hath
> sent down the Cup, thou that dost know for what thou didst
> come into being![49]

g) Eranos was Olga Fröbe-Kapteyn's "*opus*," the materialization of her personal individuation process.[50] This she carried out with a "devoted" attitude that was not always devoid of a certain identification.[51] Since Eranos' "prehistory," Olga Fröbe-Kapteyn considered her work as in service to the "idea," to an archetype. This implies the subordination of her own individual purposes and will to an Impersonal Will.[52]

According to Olga Fröbe-Kapteyn, the "numinous" nature of Eranos has had an impact on the attitude (*Einstellung*) of its participants, even when they might not be fully aware of this influence.[53] This describes the archetypal "seizure" (*Ergriffenheit*) that should continue to be reflected in conferences inspired by the spirit of Eranos.[54,55] One wonders if such "religious" devotion is limited to the subjective perspective of its founder or if it is possible to extend it to the Eranos phenomenon on the whole. Even if a conclusive answer cannot be provided here, we can point out that, even in a limited fashion, the most representative members of Eranos agreed on the presence of the numinous.[56] The creator of the term "numinous," Rudolf Otto, when proposing the name, "Eranos," to Olga Fröbe-Kapteyn, seems to have realized that the project entailed something greater than a mere academic proposal or group of "romantics" intrigued with the peculiarities of spirit. With a sense of irony, Gershom Scholem considered Olga Fröbe-Kapteyn as a kind of Eranos "Great Mother."

Near the end of his life, in a short piece honoring Eliade—as Wasserstrom reports—Henry Corbin celebrated their common cause at Eranos, as "brothers in arms ... on the same side of an invisible front."[57] There are more examples, but we might wonder whether the theoretical work somehow "appropriates," reflects, or revisits this purported numinous experience.

A valid question is this: given the "religious" nature of the Eranos phenomenon, does it involve significant and key contributions of the *Tagungen*? The answer requires revisiting ongoing historical research connected with the "religious" or "esoteric" nature of the Eranos *opus*. Such exploration would also require philosophical-epistemological research on what kinds of connections between "religion sciences" and the religious phenomenon are possible. It is clear that questions concerning the convergence between science and religion are sparked by these authors, namely: to what extent is a convergence between science and gnosis possible? Further, to what extent can we talk about a "scientific gnosis," a knowledge that can support scientific discourse?

It is well known that Jung asserted that a *Weltanschauung* did not entail a mere concept of the world, but a "way of being" or an "attitude" (*Einstellung*) before the unstable world. The contribution of analytical psychology is not to put itself forward as a new *Weltanschauung*, but to provide an innovative perspective about the state of human being from which a new *Weltanschauung* could emerge. Riccardo Bernardini illustrates how this concept is convergent with that of Olga Frobe-Kapteyn: in our time of transition, defined by the reformulation of religious conceptions, a time in which psychology will help us to reformulate the old maps of the psychic world in a new configuration in accordance with the spirit of the times. In light of everything that has been said before, one could say that the Eranos *Weltanschauung* may be defined not only by the adoption and application of a psychology that reconfigures "old maps," but by a "spiritual" praxis, by careful attention to the symbolic processes.

As psychic-religious, and to a certain extent, "gnostic experiences," Olga Fröbe-Kapteyn's visions stem from a *relegere*, a "care of the soul." This ties in with Jungian theory and its praxis. Research into these visions promise to shed light on the possibility of linking subjective experience with objective work. Furthermore, it is the foundation for more comprehensive study, because it requires re-visiting the links between descriptions of experiences by the most representative members at Eranos and their theoretical contributions.

In conclusion, we not only have to justify whether or not Eranos may be understood as "religious phenomenon," but also whether this phenomenon can involve a "scientific" study of religiosity. A narrowly scientistic perspective would dismiss any attempt of this kind, deeming it too "romantic." However, it cannot by itself ultimately account for its presuppositions. Perhaps our spiritual indulgence and lack of "care of the soul" do not allow us to exercise hermeneutics that are spiritual, not only because of its object, but because of the fact that the spiritual experience is anagogic and conducive. It would suffice to cultivate a method that can appropriate the experience of the numinous. At minimum, it would suffice to lay the foundations of a method that can establish what Henry Corbin himself pointed out: "In every case, the revealing light has preceded the revealed light, and phenomenology does no more than uncover later the already accomplished fact."[58]

NOTES

1. Henry Corbin, "The Time of Eranos," trans. Willard R. Trask, in Joseph Campbell, ed., *Man and Time: Papers from the Eranos Yearbooks* (London: Routledge and Kegan Paul, 1959), p. xiii.

2. The seventy-two volumes of the *Eranos Yearbooks* contain the 1933–2014 proceedings.

3. Ugo Bianchi, "History of Religion," in Lindsay Jones, ed., *Encyclopedia of Religions*, vol. 6 (Detroit, MI: Thomson Gale, 2005), p. 4061. See also Ugo Bianchi, Alessandro Bausani, and C. Jouco Bleeker, eds., *Problems and Methods of the History of Religions* (Leiden: E.J. Brill, 1972), and Joseph M. Kitagawa, ed., *The History of Religions: Retrospect and Prospect* (New York, NY: Macmillan, 1985). For more recent discussions, see Gregory D. Alles, ed., *Religious Studies: A Global View* (New York, NY: Routledge, 2008).

4. We cannot linger on the fundamental matter as to what took place beyond 1962. In a sense, Henry Corbin was the inspirational reference almost until his death in 1978.

5. See Riccardo Bernardini, *Jung a Eranos. Il progetto della psicología complessa* (Milan: FrancoAngeli, 2011). The bibliography regarding Jung and religion is overwhelming. See, for example, James W. Heisig, *Imago Dei. A Study of C. G. Jung's Psychology of Religion* (Lewisburg, PA: Bucknell University Press, 1978), and Murray Stein and Robert L. Moore, eds., *Jung's Challenge to Contemporary Religion* (Wilmette, IL: Chiron, 1987).

6. C. G. Jung, *Psychological Types,* vol. 6, *The Collected Works of C. G. Jung,* eds. Gerhard Adler and R. F. C. Hull, trans. H. G. Baynes (Princeton, NJ: Princeton University Press, 1976), § 45–46.

7. Olga Fröbe-Kapteyn, *Visions* (Ascona-Moscia: Eranos Foundation Archives, 1934–1938).

8. The contributors to the first *Tagung* of 1933 were three orientalists (two specialists in India, Heinrich Zimmer and Caroline Augusta Foley Rhys Davids, and a specialist in China, Erwin Rousselle); two psychologists (C. G. Jung and Gustav-Richard Heyer); and two theologians (Friedrich Heiler and Ernesto Buonaiuti). Olga Fröbe-Kapteyn herself assigns them the labels of "orientalists," "theologians," and "psychologists" in her "Vorwort" to the *Eranos-Jahrbuch* 1 (1933): 6.

9. Cicero, *De natura deorum*, II, 28, 72.

10. Cf. Lactantius, *Institutiones divinae*, IV, 28, 3. See Concetta Aloe Spada, "L'uso di *religio* e *religiones* nella polemica antipagana di Lattanzio," in U. Bianchi, ed., *The Notion of "Religion" in Comparative Research: Selected Proceedings of the XVI IAHR Congress* (Roma: L'Erma di Bretschneider, 1994). A. Ernout and A. Meillet, *Dictionnaire étymologique de la langue latine. Histoire des mots* (Paris: Klincksieck, 1959), p. 859, prefers *"religare"* contrary to Jouon, who follows Cicero. However, the issue is not merely philological. Nevertheless, the Neo-Pythagorean, Nigidius Figulus, and the historian, Titus Livius, derive *religiosus* from *religare* and taught that the believer is "firmly tied up" to the ritual practice. See, on this subject, J. Imscher, "Der Terminus *Religio* und seine antiken Entsprechung im philologischen und religionsgeschichtlichen Vergleich," in Bianchi, *The Notion of "Religion,"* and Maurice Sachot, *"Religio/superstitio.* Histoire d'une subversion et d'un retournement," *Revue de l'Histoire des Religions* 208 (4, 1991): 355–94.

11. Cf. Michel Clévenot, *L'état des religions dans le monde* (Paris: La Découverte/Le Cerf, 1987), pp. 376–77.

12. In Latin, *pontem-facere*.

13. Jung favored the "*relegere*" etymology, although in every edition I know it is wrongly written "*religere*." See also, for example, Carl Gustav Jung, "Theoretische Überlegungen zum Wesen des Psychischen," in *Gesammelte Werke*, vol. 8 (Solothurn und Düsseldorf: Walter-Verlag, 1995), § 427.

14. See Bernardini, *Jung a Eranos*, pp. 51–52.

15. See, for example, the "symbolic ecumenism" of Eranos in Andrés Ortiz-Osés, *Hermenéutica de Eranos. Las estructuras simbólicas del mundo* (Barcelona: Anthropos, 2011), pp. 15–27.

16. See Bernardini, *Jung a Eranos,* pp. 50–51, and Ortiz-Osés, *Hermenéutica de Eranos,* pp. 64–126.

17. We follow here Ortiz-Osés, *Hermenéutica de Eranos*. It should be noted that analogy does not equate to identity, for this is not a case of a difference between traditions being studied, as the first case, but between the researchers' theoretical outlook, as the second one.

18. Gilbert Durand, "Le genie du lieu et les heures propices. Pour le doublé jubilé d'Eranos," *Eranos Jahrbuch* 51 (1982): 243–77.

19. The subject in 2011 was "About Fragility in the Contemporary World," in 2012, "On the Threshold: Disorientation and New Forms of Space," in 2013, "Money: Symbol, Enchantment, and Disenchantment," and in 2014, "Care of the World and Care of the Self."

20. Philosophy, science, art, religion, craftsmanship, and any common knowledge should be included in a truly integrated model. The matter goes far beyond "epistemology," although a broad theory of knowledge or Gnoseology is usually reduced to a theory of *scientific* knowledge. A linguistic vagueness can be noticed in the use of the German words *Erkenntnistheorie* or *Erkenntniskritik*; in the English word *Epistemology*, in the French *théorie de la connaissance*, in the Italian *epistemologia* or the Spanish *epistemología*, etc. See, among others, Nicholas Rescher, *The Limits of Science* (Pittsburgh, PA: University of Pittsburgh Press, 1999).

21. See "Le tradizione religiose nel *Liber Novus*: Il peculiare 'sincretismo' della psyche," in Bernardo Nante, *Guida alla lettura del Libro Rosso di C.G. Jung* (Turin: Bollati Boringhieri, 2010). The term, "syncretism," was associated to what could be deemed, in the words of

Carsten Cope, "metasyncretisms" or "second-level syncretisms." It is mostly applied to mysteries of the late ancient world that are based on a syncretic background typical of ancient mystery religions. A clear example is Mithra's mysteries, which do not presuppose an ancient Iranian mystery, but only the god Mithra itself, a Mithra on a par with The Sun and Helios. However, perhaps the most remarkable example of second-level syncretism is Manicheism. Manicheism can be described as truly Christian, Zoroastrian, Shamanic, Buddhist, and even Taoist. The missionary efforts of Manicheism brought about new syncretic forms. The discussion is if in this case the initial syncretism is repeated (for example, Buddhism in the emergence of Manicheism) or if we're dealing with third-level syncretisms. Manicheism was, in other words, the supreme form of syncretism. We could cite, among others, Western gnosticism, Valentinians, and Setians.

22. See Bernardo Nante, "Notas para una reformulación de la epistemología junguiana," *Revista de Psicología UCA* 3 (3, 2006): 73–100 and 3 (4, 2006): 31–56.

23. Although there is no major survey of the phenomenology of religion, maybe the best general introduction is Jacques Waardenburg, *Classical Approaches to the Study of Religion: Aim, Methods, and Theories of Research* (The Hague: Mouton, 1973–1974).

24. Hegel, in *Vorlesungen über die Philosophie der Religion* (1821–1831), without a doubt, pioneered the concept of "philosophy of religion," which is to say, a discipline that, as opposed to the traditional natural theology (or in Leibniz's words, "Theodicy"), does not concern itself with demonstrating the existence of God or the Divine and determining its essence or justification, but with understanding how the subject appropriates the object ("God" or the "Divine"). But Hegel does it in the context of a previously founded philosophical system, mediated by interpretations of the religious traditions that generally lack historical foundations. "Religion phenomenology" has become only a byword for the application of any comparative method in the study of religions. On the other hand, good phenomenology is not about seeking identities, but seeking what is common within what is different.

25. Gerardus van der Leeuw, *Phänomenologie der Religion* (Tübingen: J.C.B. Mohr, 1933). In English: *Religion in Essence and Manifestation: A Study in Phenomenology*, trans. J. E. Turner (New York, NY: Harper and Row, 1963).

26. For Widengren, phenomenology of religion provides "the systematic synthesis" and the history of religions approach focuses on the analysis of separate religions; see Geo Widengren, *Religionsphänomenologie* (Berlin: Walter de Gruyter, 1969), p. 9, a translation of the Swedish original *Religionens Värld*, dated 1945.

27. See Mircea Eliade and Joseph Kitagawa, *The History of Religions: Essays in Methodology* (Chicago, IL: University of Chicago Press, 1959).

28. See Willem Hofstee, "Phenomenology of Religion versus Anthropology of Religion? The 'Groningen School', 1920–1990," in S. Hjelde, ed., *Man, Meaning and Mystery: 100 Years of History of Religion in Norway. The Heritage of W. Brede Kristensen* (Leiden: Brill, 2000), pp. 173–90.

29. Giovanni Filoramo, "Picnic ad Ascona: La 'gnosi filosófica' di Eranos," in *Il risveglio della gnosi ovvero diventare dio* (Roma-Bari: Laterza, 1990), p. 23.

30. Filoramo, "Picnic ad Ascona," p. 14.

31. Also a valid question is if it is possible to talk about "scientific gnosis." See *Les yeux de chair et les yeux de feu. La science et la gnose. Cahiers de l'Université Saint Jean de Jerusalem* (Paris: Berg International, 1979).

32. See O. Fröbe-Kapteyn, "Eranos. A Survey of its History since 1933," quoted in Bernardini, *Jung a Eranos*, p. 355.

33. Cf. Pierre Hadot, *La filosofía como forma de vida. Conversaciones con Jeannie Carlier y Arnold L. Davidson* (Barcelona: Alpha Decay, 2009), p. 64. Pierre Hadot participated in the 1968 and 1972 *Tagungen* and, as he himself points out, although the atmosphere was friendly, his papers were not very well-received, especially the first presentation.

34. Arthur McCalla, "Romanticism," in *Guide to the Study of Religion*, eds. Willi Bran and Russell T. Mc Cutchen (London: Cassell, 2000), p. 378.

35. The very classification of "classical phenomenologists" could be objected.

36. Jorge N. Ferrer and Jacob H. Sherman, *The Participatory Turn. Espiritualidad, misticismo y estudio de las religiones* (Barcelona: Kairós, 2011), p. 70.

37. Filoramo, "Picnic ad Ascona," p. 26.

38. Olga Fröbe-Kapteyn, "The Psychological Background of Eranos," quoted in Bernardini, *Jung a Eranos*, p. 247.

39. Giovanni Sorge, "Love as Devotion. Olga Fröbe-Kapteyn's Relationship with Eranos and Jung Psychology," *Eranos-Jahrbuch* 69 (2009–2010–2011): 416–21.

40. Olga Fröbe-Kapteyn asserted that, "the same archetypal idea is activating both C. G. Jung's teaching of individuation as well as the Eranos work." (Quoted in Sorge, "Love as Devotion," p. 415).

41. On this subject, see, Bernardini, *Jung a Eranos*, pp. 101–05, 165–66, 255, 258, 321.

42. There is an earlier *maṇḍala*, from the "Theosophical" stage, that dates back to 1927.

43. With it, the message seems to be "other participants in Eranos."

44. See Bernardini, *Jung a Eranos*, p. 102.

45. See *ibid.*, p. 104 and Ortiz-Osés, *Hermenéutica de Eranos*, pp. 73–74.

46. See Bernardini, *Jung a Eranos*, p. 103.

47. As John P. Burns points out: "The comparative-historical method is very much at the heart of the academic discipline of religion. The process of comparative religion proper, taking its place beside traditional biblical theology around 1870, marks the inauguration of the academic study of religion … Comparison is a primary rather than a secondary process within analytical enquiry." John P. Burns, "Comparative-Historical Method [Further Considerations]," in Lindsay Jones, ed., *Encyclopedia of Religions*, vol. 3 (Detroit, MI: Thomson Gale, 2005), p. 1871. For current perspectives and discussions on comparative religion methodology, see the articles in *Numen* 48 (2001).

48. Olga Fröbe-Kapteyn mentions the "hermetic function" of Eranos in "Eranos—A Survey… ," p. 12 (cited in Bernardini, *Jung a Eranos*, p. 152). Many scholars agree that the word "Hermetism" can be understood analogically. For example, according to Antoine Faivre, although "Hernetism" designates the pagan corpus of the so-called *Hermetica* attributed to Hermes Trismegistos, "Hermetism" also designates the various adaptations and developments which that *corpus* gives rise to. See "Hermetism," in Lindsay Jones, ed., *Encyclopedia of Religions*, vol. 6 (Detroit: Thomson Gale, 2005), p. 3944.

49. *Corpus Hermeticum*, IV. Olga Fröbe-Kapteyn quotes the G. R. S. Mead translation. According to this peculiar baptism, redemption comes from the knowledge obtained by being immersed in Spirit.

50. In the words of Olga Fröbe: "*Eranos ist meine Individuation.*" (quoted in Hans Thomas Hakl, *Der verborgene Geist von Eranos. Unbekannte Begegnungen von Wissenschaft und Esoterik. Eine alternative Geistesgeschichte des 20. Jahrhunderts* (Bretten: Scientia nova-Neue Wissenschaft, 2001), p. 33.

51. Cf. Sorge, "Love as Devotion," pp. 390–91.

52. Olga Fröbe-Kapteyn, "The Psychological Background of Eranos," p. 8 (quoted in Sorge, "Love as Devotion," p. 404). Sorge further writes: "Olga Fröbe really experienced Eranos as an archetype." (*ibid.*, p. 416).

53. See Olga Fröbe-Kapteyn, "Eranos—A Survey… ," p. 12. Cf. comments to this excerpt in Bernardini, *Jung a Eranos*, pp. 151–52. See also Sorge, "Love as Devotion," p. 423.

54. See Bernardini, *Jung a Eranos*, p. 152; Sorge, "Love as Devotion," p. 402.

55. "Gershom Scholem remembers … her desire for '*ergriffene*' lectures at the *Tagungen*" (*ibid.*, p. 408).

56. In addition, we know the story and the aura of the lecture room, on which it is not necessary to dwell here. Suffice it to say that it was Jung and van der Leeuw who proposed the erection of a monument "to the unknown 'genius' of the place."

57. Steven M. Wasserstrom, *Religion after Religion—Gershom Scholem, Mircea Eliade, and Henry Corbin at Eranos* (Princenton, NJ: Princeton University Press, 1999), p. 16.

58. Wasserstrom, *Religion after Religion*, p. 27.

MOSHE IDEL

M oshe Idel is the Max Cooper Professor of Jewish Thought, Emeritus at The Hebrew University and Senior Researcher at the Hartman Institute, Jerusalem. He has been a member of the Israeli Academy of Sciences and Humanities since 2006 and was recipient of the Bialik Prize (1994), the Gershom Scholem Prize (1995), the Israel Prize for Jewish Thought (1999), and the Rothschild Prize (2012). Currently, he serves as President of the World Union of Jewish Studies. His areas of interest include the history and phenomenology of Jewish mysticism, Renaissance thought, and the history of scholarship in religion. His writings include *The Mystical Experience of Abraham Abulafia* (1987), *Studies in Ecstatic Kabbalah* (1988), *Language, Torah, and Hermeneutics in Abraham Abulafia* (1989), *Golem—Jewish Magical and Mystical Traditions on the Artificial Anthropoid* (1990), *English Kabbalah—New Perspectives* (1990), *Hasidism between Ecstasy and Magic* (1995), *Messianic Mystics* (2000), *Absorbing Perfections: Kabbalah and Interpretation* (2002), *Kabbalah and Eros* (2005), *Ben: Sonship and Jewish Mysticism* (2008), *Kabbalah in Italy 1280–1510* (2011), *Saturn's Jews: On Witches' Sabbat and Sabbateanism* (2011), and *Mircea Eliade—From Magic to Myth* (2014). In the years 1993 to 2013, Idel lectured at a series of conferences organized by the Associazione Amici di Eranos. In 2008, he gave a lecture at Eranos entitled, "Eros: Paths of Unity and Polarity in Kabbalah."

ARCHETYPES AND ANDROGYNES AT ERANOS

MOSHE IDEL

INTRODUCTION

In the view of Olga Fröbe-Kapteyn, a significant source of inspiration for the Eranos Conferences derived from C. G. Jung's *maṇḍala* archetype, a unifying symbol that "seized" the circle of scholars who gathered each year at Ascona. Her vision was a Romantic one, seeking to merge spiritual intentions of scholars of different ages from a variety of fields.[1]

It is true that the mystique surrounding important academic events can be over interpreted. However, the concept of archetype is inarguably foundational to Eranos, being shared by many key Eranos participants. That being said, some who attended the first Conferences were less interested in the *maṇḍala* than in what might be called the *androgyne*. No Eranos *Tagung* has been dedicated to this topic, but the theme is found throughout the writings of Jung (who favored the term "hermaphrodite"), Erich Neumann, Mircea Eliade, Heinrich Zimmer, and Henry Corbin, as well as younger participants such as Elémire Zolla and Antoine Faivre.[2,3,4,5] The subjects of archetypes and androgyny also attracted the attention of Gershom Scholem, who nonetheless, in keeping with his attitude towards Jung's psychoanalysis, was reticent to address the topic at the Eranos lectures.

References to "archetype" became much more common among Eranos participants after World War II, yet this should not, in my opinion, obscure the existence of other attitudes.[6] For this reason, I examine what participating scholars thought about the nature of the androgyne. This is entirely appropriate because it illustrates how diverse viewpoints on a single topic existed and so illustrates the spirit of Eranos thereby obviating any assumption that a dictatorship of unifying ideas prevailed.[7] The fascination for the androgyne archetype is reflected in the Eranos ethos: the exploration of multiple religions to uncover a spirituality that transcends historical religions.[8]

The androgyne is considered a symbol of the transcendence of ordinary existence governed by division and separation toward a more overarching agenda.[9] Though the aforementioned scholars had their own definitions, there was a general consensus that exemplified a trans-personal, trans-cultural, and trans-religious value, similar to the theory of Platonic ideas. Subsequently, androgyne is significant because it transcends any particular religion or literary writing in which it is embedded. Differences in detail did not create discord between the participants, although Jung expressed uneasiness with Eliade's use of the term "archetype." As we shall see, Eliade articulated it independently, and quite early in his career.

As a trans-cultural concept, androgyne is relatively unencumbered by particular linguistic, cultural, and religious contexts. Such contextual independence made it possible to render a more "objective" or scientific approach to its analysis. This had great appeal to whom I would call, "representatives of the interwar generation of discontents." Though implicitly Eranos strove toward universalism, there was still an effort to maintain fidelity to the original texts and not overlook any hidden messages.

CARL GUSTAV JUNG AND ERICH NEUMANN: ANDROGYNE AS ARCHETYPE

The major intellectual figure at the Eranos encounters, Carl Gustav Jung, understood the androgyne as an archetype of wholeness, as did Erich Neumann and Mircea Eliade, though in a more pronounced way.[10] Each extended their studies beyond the classical Judeo-Christian tradition to include literature and modes of thought hitherto marginal in European culture. Jung continued to develop his theory of archetypes, and, as part of it, the androgyne or the hermaphrodite, that refers to the union of the opposites, or what he called "conjunction."[11] His understanding of wholeness as the union between the contraries draws substantively from Chinese philosophy and alchemical and Kabbalistic texts.

For Jung, hermaphroditic expressions are reflections of inner development and expressions of spiritual progress, rather than symbolic of any behavior. For example, the original totality, or the alchemical *prima materia* of the androgyne Adam, is disintegrated and when reunited by the uniting symbol of the hermaphrodite, fulfills the "transcendent function."[12,13,14] Similar to Jung's image of the sphere as the symbol of the integrated self, the vision of the hermaphrodite as perfection is obviously also of Platonic origins where the initial androgyny is recuperated by the union between the divided sphere.

> The self wants to be made manifest in the work, and for this reason the opus is a process of individuation, a becoming of the self. The self is the total, timeless man and as such corresponds to the original spherical, bisexual being.[15]

When dealing with earlier stages of the spiritual process, Jung maintains: "Our pictures of the *coniunctio* are to be understood in this sense: union on the biological level is a symbol of the *unio oppositorum* at its highest."[16] Further, "The hermaphrodite means nothing less than a union of the strongest and most striking opposites."[17] Jung's reference to the "timeless man" relates to his understanding of androgyny as univeral and is indicative of an ahistorical approach. In general, Jung's theory was presented as a "science."[18,19]

Jung's student Erich Neumann was a second key participant in these studies and discussions on archetypes. This interest is evident in his massive work, *The Great Mother—An Analysis of the Archetype.*[20] Here, Neumann proposes that "Man's original hermaphroditic disposition is still largely conserved in the child" and discusses what he calls "congenital contrasexuality," the innate potential for attraction to both sexes.[21,22] However, after spiritual development, the hermaphroditic symbol reappears as a reflection of "the new unity of opposites."[23] These two stages of development, the primordial state of the infant and its final perfection, are represented by hermaphroditic symbols—*uroboric* or *maṇḍala*-like images.

While Neumann generally followed Jung, his work entails a major modification. Unlike Jung's ahistorical approach, Neumann claims the existence of two main and distinct types of androgyne-archetypes: the female androgyne and the male androgyne. The female androgyne represents the matriarchate period, while the latter, male androgyne reflects the patriarchate.[24] Neumann's developmental approach does not elaborate significantly on an historical trajectory, but it does distinguish between diverse representations of what is labeled the "hermaphrodite archetype."

MIRCEA ELIADE: THE IDEALIZATION OF THE ANDROGYNE

Few scholars of religion exhibit a greater fascination for the androgyne than Mircea Eliade. His interest in the subject began perhaps as early as secondary school and remained constant throughout his academic career.[25] The concept of archetype can be found in the 1937 Romanian publication, *Cosmology and Babylonian Alchemy*:

> In a *Weltanschauung* grounded in the perfect homology between heaven and earth, and in magic, all the things participate in the archetypes, all have certain magical virtues, by themselves or by participation. It suffices that a soulless object will have a certain form or a certain color—that innumerable latencies with magical virtues will arouse in it.[26]

It is obvious that Eliade was not concerned with the Jungian use of archetype as a part of the collective unconscious, but as an objective type of correspondence between various levels of reality. Such correspondence was conceived as having magical implications. This connection between the archetype and the "magical virtues" lingered and continued after Eliade was invited to the Eranos Conferences.[27]

His understanding of the archetype is more cosmic than psychological, emphasizing archaic religiosity rather than a search to resolve psychological issues of individuals in the present. Two years later, Eliade published, again in Romanian, a collection of essays entitled the *Myth of Reintegration*. It was a precursor to *Myth of the Eternal Return* where he speaks at length about the androgyne archetype.[28] However, it seems that it was only a few years later in Portugal, around 1943, that he became acquainted with Jung's views on the archetype as it relates to the collective unconscious—something with which he agreed.[29] Six years later, in 1949, Eliade began participating in the Eranos Conferences.

While some of the same topics are discussed in the *Myth of Reintegration,* Eliade's core treatment of the androgyne is found in his Eranos Conference lecture, *La Coincidentia Oppositorum et le Mystère de la Totalité*, printed in the 1958 *Yearbook*.[30] In 1962, the original text and footnotes were expanded and the lecture re-published in the French collection, *Méphistophélès et l'Androgyne*.[31] This French edition was later translated into English and published in 1965 in *The Two and the One*.[32] It is this version that is best known, forming the basis of many of Eliade's views on the androgyne. However, the 1958 version reflects Eliade's intellectual development in the early fifties which, importantly, includes in addition to Jung, references to shaman and Yogin androgyny. Congruent with studies by Georges Dumézil, Eliade is concerned with older, more ancient theories that he translates in terms of androgyny and conceives as a kind of pre-philosophical form of reflection.[33]

Eliade's theories about the androgyne are quite similar to those of Jung's as articulated in *Myths, Dreams, and Mysteries,* where he describes androgyny as

> an archaic and universal formula for the expression of wholeness, the co-existence of the contraries, or *coincidentia oppositorum* ... symboliz[ing] ... perfection ... [and] ultimate being.[34]

The basic assumption is that androgyny points to an integrated human being as an achievement in perfection. The mythical Adam of Genesis before bisection, or Plato's spherical androgyne, are conceived as ideals where differences between the sexes are blurred through spiritual development that annihilates separation.

Crucial to understanding the present analysis is Eliade's use of the term "universal." The existence of a certain stability in human nature relates to and relies upon the universality of nature. This assumption, however, draws from the archaic where figurines or "texts" rarely contain any reflective account. Thus, the archetype is universal only if we adopt its meaning as found in the Platonic myth that explains the manner in which androgyne was envisioned. Such meaning is projected on innumerable pictures, sculptures, and literary compositions thereby creating the illusion of a consensus not yet proven by a sustained scholarly effort to interrogate the various expressions related to androgyny, in themselves.

GERSHOM SCHOLEM, ARCHETYPES, AND DU-PARTZUFIN

Long before his participation at Eranos, Gershom Scholem frequently discussed the term "archetype" in his 1941 survey of Jewish mysticism.[35] Scholem describes the counterpart of the human person on high (Hebrew *Demuth*) as an "archetype." This, too, is reminiscent of Platonic ideals. They are not, however, identical particularly given their visual nature. According to a medieval thinker, Scholem writes, "The archetype is the deepest source of the soul's hidden activity."[36] These discussions are based largely on esoteric literature written in the early 13th century by R. Eleazar of Worms in the Rhineland, Southern Germany.

Elsewhere in the book, in his discussions of the *Zohar* and when referring to the recurrence of certain themes in the economy of this literature, Scholem also refers to archetype.[37] He refers to the concept of the supernal *Knesset Yisrael*, the Assembly of Israel, identical to the last *sefirah* of *Malkhut*, as the "mystical archetype" of the Jewish community.[38] He goes on to describe Zoharic understanding of creation:

> The seven Sefiroth which flow from the maternal womb of the *Binah* are the seven primeval days of creation. What appears in time as the epoch of actual and external creation is nothing but the projection of the archetypes of the seven lower Sefiroth, which, in timeless existence, are enshrined in God's inwardness.[39]

The concept of archetype also surfaces in association with the cosmology of R. Isaac Luria and the personality of Sabbatai Sevi as the holy sinner.[40,41] In a later work, Scholem uses archetype in discussion of the *Book of Bahir*, what he considers to be the first Kabbalistic document. Here, he also describes an "archetype of the feminine" on high and that of the three forefathers.[42,43,44] More generally,

> It is difficult to say whether we should consider this process as the breakthrough of ancient, mythical images, and 'archetypes' into a world where they had been mere metaphors or as a renewed historic contact with a gnostic tradition that had never ceased to make use of these images.[45]

The passage is ambiguous, and there are two possible interpretations. One is historic, namely that the Kabbalah emerged as the result of a contact with the Gnostic tradition. This serves as Scholem's major explanation for the emergence of Kabbalah during the Middle Ages. This is not the place to delve into details concerning the problems associated with this explanation.[46] More interesting and germane to the present discussion is the second, proffered explanation, which assumes ancient archetypes were in fact "renewed" in the Middle Ages.

Such an interpretation needs to be understood primarily in a psychological manner wherein past themes and images that have been suppressed for centuries suddenly surface with renewed freshness and expanded dimensions. This explanation is also historical since it assumes three temporal stages: the ancient (or mythical), the metaphorical, and then a return to myths. However, it is distinguished from a purely historical interpretation by its Hegelian description of the three stages of religious development culminating with the emergences of mysticism as Scholem previously articulates in *Major Trends*.[47] Here, however, the breakthrough is the institutionalization of religion as the second stage following the more animistic initial stage.[48] In contrast, the 1962 "breakthrough" concerns those elements that were suppressed by the emergence by religion."[49] In 1941, early on in his writing, Scholem expressly denies the need for the breakthrough described in his 1962 treatment, namely, the third, mystical phase of religious development.[50]

In my own eyes, the major difference between the two schemes of 1941 and 1962, derives from the appearance of archetype in the latter publication. I believe the shift reflects the influence of the Eranos Conferences in which Scholem had been participating. This is also apparent in the first lecture he delivered at Eranos in 1949: "Foreign mythical worlds are at work in the great archetypal images of the Kabbalists, even though they sprang from the depths of an authentic and productive Jewish religious feeling."[51]

The Jungian connotation of the psychological in archetype is obvious and provides evidence in argument against those who have maintained that Scholem was in no way influenced by Jung.[52] Granted, it is true that Scholem's use of archetype is not consistent with and, in most of instances, hardly fits Jungian theory. Nonetheless, while he might not have been overly fond of the term, he was not averse to using it from time to time.

A year before his invitation to Eranos, Scholem printed a short text derived from two manuscripts that was attributed to an early Kabbalist and dealing with the Kabbalistic meaning of the Rabbinic phrase, *du-partzufin*. *Du-partzufin* refers to Adam as a two-faced entity.[53] Although he returned to this idea later in a substantively expanded 1962 German edition published many years after his regular summer visits to Ascona, Scholem never interpreted the passage in Jungian terms.[54] In fact, he resorted to the more precise terms *zweigeschlechtig* and *Doppelgesicht*. In contrast, the English translation of the first term is "androgynous," but in no case does he use archetype.[55]

This passage is seminal in the history of Kabbalah and in Kabbalistic literature on *du-partzufin*. Scholem's reluctance to address it in his Ascona lectures constitutes not just a silence or a sign of indifference, but a reticence to engage in dialogue with the prevailing inclination to speculate on the meaning of what could be called the "archetype of androgyne."

Fortunately, we do not have to guess at Scholem's views on the androgyne as distinct from those of Jung. Scholem himself states: "The conjunction of the two principles is certainly not the same as overcoming them in the reestablishment of an original androgynous state."[56] I see this assertion as an echo of his long-standing polemic against Jung's view of conjunction as total union, which can be found in the very same book where he draws on a Jungian concept of archetype.

Scholem's juxtaposition of "conjunction" with "androgyny" differs from Jung's conceptualization, because it is much less strong. His reading also differs from Eliade's strong emphasis on the androgyne as the *coincidentia oppositorum*.[57] For Scholem, "conjunction" is not the same "union." Jung expresses appreciation of this:

> But in mysticism one must remember that no 'symbolic' object has only one meaning: it is several things at once. Sexuality does not exclude spirituality nor spirituality sexuality, for in God all opposites are abolished. One has only to think of the *unio mystica* of Simeon ben Yohai in *Zohar* III, which Scholem (see n. 290) barely mentions.[58]

Scholem's reticence to regard the androgyne as an archetype is even more evident when, as pointed out by Wasserstrom, he interprets an aspect of Walter Benjamin's reference to an androgynous angel that reveals itself to him.[59] In contrast, none of the other Eranos scholars addressed the numerous discussions found in Kabbalah on the special nature of Adam as a bisexual being, nor the text published by Scholem and translated into German.

SOME CONCLUSIONS

Like psychoanalysis, the science of religion *à la Eliade* embodies aspirations to evolve into a kind of science, capable of making strong inferences for a much broader spectrum of human data and, for Eliade, elucidating the structure of the cosmos. This hypothetical uniformity is achieved by de-contextualizing subject matter from its peculiar cultural, linguistic, and historical backgrounds. This material was interpreted in a common framework and compared using what may be described as a matrix. From this vantage, the Platonic androgyne myth is similar to Sigmund Freud's famous "Oedipus Myth." In both instances, we are confronted with a kind of mythical imperialism where the meaning of a given myth is conceived and assumed prior to any "new data" being analyzed. Subsequently, this meaning is imported to or imposed on diverse expressions.

The individual approaches of Jung, Corbin, and Eliade, different as they were, are nevertheless all deeply influenced by a series of occultist sources, in particular, alchemical, Hermetic, and eventually Kabbalistic texts that include terms such as *unio oppositorum, coincidentia oppositorum*, and *coniunctio*. From this perspective, their collective approaches are reminiscent of the Renaissance concept *prisca theologia* where different forms of knowledge are understood as referring to the same message. Just as in the case of the Renaissance figures, Jung and Eliade began with assumptions that were widespread and common in certain earlier phases of Christianity and Gnosticism. These were then enriched and modified by additional sources that were not canonical in the theologies of the Middle Ages. Later, sources from other cultures were added.[60]

The occultist *penchant* so prevalent in Western Europe since the seventeenth century found its expression nearly three hundred years later in the work of the twentieth century thinkers discussed above.[61] Their approaches functioned like powerful filters that shaped the manner in which Kabbalistic material has been selected, interpreted, and in my opinion, misinterpreted. The paramount importance of the psychic, emotional, and intellectual as the main context of the human development is, unlike corporeal, social, or communal dimensions, a filter that reflects the impact of the Platonic and the Pauline attitudes. This has introduced a cultural bias vis-à-vis Hindu, Chinese, and Jewish texts because of a failure to appreciate and investigate their broader contexts. Although influenced to a certain extent by Renaissance understandings of Kabbalah by Christian Kabbalists, Scholem was much less inclined to see a reflection of universal truths in Kabbalistic symbols and therefore did not adopt a theory reminiscent of *prisca theologia*.[62] Though he did not subscribe to the Jungian stance, vestiges of Scholem's understanding of archetype are nonetheless discernible. Today, a more dynamic understanding of cultural issues is developing, one that will likely bring a better understanding of Eranos encounters and of matters of spirit in general.

Though the aforementioned scholars met and discussed these topics in Eranos, it is clear from their writings that their initial convictions did not substantively change. At the time of their first Ascona encounter, all were seasoned and mature scholars (Scholem was fifty, Eliade was forty-two) with well-articulated insights into matters of religion that shaped inquiries for the rest of their lives. As such, cross-pollination among the three scholars was minimal.[63] However, the Eranos Conferences played a significant role in the academic careers of both Scholem and Eliade, particularly the latter. Participation at the conferences in the presence of eminent scholars and before knowledgeable audiences cultivated scholarly excellence. The creativity of their respective studies and writings were further enhanced by the phenomenological propensity of the organizers and the selection of conference topics. The spirit of Eranos left its mark.

In summary, the androgyne myth should be investigated without assuming uniformity or even an archetypal nature as is portrayed in studies by Jung, Neumann, and Eliade. By recognizing the diversity of this theme, one may better understand how it reflects not an unchanging state of consciousness, but different manifestations of a common theme in different cultures.[64] In this context, Neumann's two types of androgyne images are significant, especially when one takes into account that they derive from Jung's closest circle. My own emphasis on the different interpretations of the concept of androgynous is not just a matter of distinguishing the different cultures that host them, but between differing interpretations within a given culture, as evidenced by innumerable discussions found in Kabbalah.[65]

NOTES

1. See Steven Wasserstrom, *Religion after Religion—Gershom Scholem, Mircea Eliade and Henry Corbin at Eranos* (Princeton, NJ: Princeton University Press, 1999), p. 152; Riccardo Bernardini, *Jung a Eranos. Il progetto della psicologia complessa* (Milan: FrancoAngeli, 2011), pp. 90–109; Giovanni Sorge, "Love as Devotion: Olga Fröbe-Kapteyn's Relationship with Eranos and Jungian Psychology," *Eranos Yearbook 70* (2012): 414–18, 422, and 425–28; and Hans Thomas Hakl, *Eranos— An Alternative Intellectual History of the Twentieth Century* (Montreal/ Kingston: McGill-Queen's University Press, 2013), pp. 189, 318.

2. See Heinrich Zimmer, *The King and the Corpse*, ed. J. Campbell (Princeton, NJ: Princeton University Press, 1971), pp. 178–79.

3. See Wasserstrom, *Religion after Religion*, pp. 205–06, 208– 09, and 210–11.

4. Elémire Zolla, *The Androgyne—Reconciliation of Male and Female* (New York, NY: Crossroad, 1981). On the topic of androgyne according to Zolla, Jung, and Eliade, see also Moshe Idel, "Androgynes: Reflections on the Study of Religion," in *Labirinti della mente. Visioni del mondo. Il lascito intellettuale di Elémire Zolla nel XXI secolo*, ed. Grazia Marchianò (Siena: Società Bibliografica Toscana, 2012), pp. 17–48; Elémire Zolla lectured at the 1992 conference of the Associazione Amici di Eranos. See Elémire Zolla, "Die Wanderung," in F. Graf and E. Hornung, eds., *Wanderungen*, Eranos Neue Folge III/1992 (Munich: Wilhelm Fink, 1995).

5. See, for example, Antoine Faivre, *Access to Western Esotericism* (Albany, NY: SUNY Press, 1994); see also his "Sensuous Relations with Sophia in Christian Theosophy," in W. J. Hanegraaff and J. J. Kripal, eds., *Hidden Intercourses—Eros and Sexuality in the History of Western Esotericism* (Leiden-Boston, MA: Brill, 2009), pp. 281–308 and Antoine Faivre, "From Prelapsarian Androgyny to Multipolar Constructs of 'Love' (Aspects of Christian Theosophy in German Naturphilosophie)," *Eranos Yearbook 70* (2012): 274–95; see also Rosemary Radford Ruether, *Goddess and the Divine Feminine—A Western Religious History* (Berkeley, CA: California University Press, 2005), pp. 228–29 and 236–39.

6. See the testimony of Ximena de Angulo as cited in Sorge, "Love as Devotion," p. 410.

7. See Sorge, "Love as Devotion," pp. 416–18.

8. See Wasserstrom, *Religion after Religion*.

9. For the importance of the androgyne at Eranos, see *ibid.*, pp. 203–14.

10. See, especially, Curtis D. Smith, *Jung's Quest for Wholeness—A Religious and Historical Perspective* (Albany, NY: SUNY Press, 1990).

11. See Carl Gustav Jung, "The Archetypes and the Collective Unconscious," in *The Collected Works of C. G. Jung*, vol. 9–1, ed. and trans. Gerhard Adler and R. F. C. Hull (Princeton, NJ: Princeton University Press, 1959), pp. 67–68, 173–75, and 191–92; *Aion: Researches into the Phenomenology of the Self*, vol. 9–2, *The Collected Works of C. G. Jung*, ed. and trans. Gerhard Adler and R. F. C. Hull (Princeton, NJ: Princeton University Press, 1969), pp. 195 and 204; and especially *Mysterium Coniunctionis*, vol. 14, *The Collected Works of C. G. Jung*, ed. and trans. Gerhard Adler and R. F. C. Hull (Princeton, NJ: Princeton University Press, 1970).

12. For a critique of Jung's interpretation of the alchemical material including the androgyne theme, see Lawrence M. Principe and William R. Newman, "Some Problems with the Historiography of Alchemy," in W. R. Newman and A. Grafton, eds., *Secrets of Nature—Astrology and Alchemy in Early Modern Europe* (Cambridge: MIT Press, 2001), pp. 385–434.

13. Jung, CW 14, pp. 438–56.

14. See, for example, Carl Gustav Jung, *Psychological Types*, trans. H. G. Baynes (New York, NY: Pantheon Books, 1953), pp. 159–60 and Jung, CW 9–1, p. 174.

15. Carl Gustav Jung, "The Practice of Psychotherapy," vol. 16, *The Collected Works of C. G. Jung*, ed. and trans. Gerhard Adler and R. F. C. Hull (Princeton, NJ: Princeton University Press, 1966), pp. 308, 313–14 and fn. 17. See also Jung, CW 9–1, pp. 68 and 192.

16. *Ibid.*, p. 250.

17. *Ibid.*, p. 173.

18. Carl Gustav Jung, *The Integration of the Personality*, trans. S. M. Dell (New York, NY: Farrar and Rinehart, 1939), p. 38.

19. Carl Gustav Jung, *Memories, Dreams, Reflections*, ed. Aniela Jaffé, trans. R. and C. Winston (New York, NY: Vintage, 1965), p. 199.

20. Erich Neumann, *The Great Mother—An Analysis of the Archetype*, trans. R. Manheim (New York, NY: Pantheon Books, 1954).

21. Erich Neumann, *The Origins and History of Consciousness*, vol. I, trans. R. F. C. Hull (New York, NY: Harper Torchbooks, 1954), p. 112.

22. *Ibid.*

23. *Ibid.*, vol. II, p. 414.

24. *Ibid.*, vol. I, pp. 46, 75, 95, 157–58, 178–79, and vol. II, p. 405.

25. See Moshe Idel, *Mircea Eliade—From Magic to Myth* (New York, NY: Peter Lang, 2014), pp. 60–103.

26. Author's translation from a reprinted collection of Eliade's earlier Romanian essays in G. Liiceanu and A. Plesu, eds., *Drumul spre centru* (Bucureşti: Univers, 1991), p. 534.

27. See Mircea Eliade, *Cosmos and History—The Myth of Eternal Return* (New York, NY: Harper Torchbooks, 1959), pp. 3–48, and for the participation in the archetype, see *ibid.*, p. 30.

28. Reprinted in Liiceanu and Plesu, *Drumul spre centru*, pp. 369–76.

29. See Eliade's *Commentaries on Master Manole*, reprinted in *ibid.*, p. 445.

30. Mircea Eliade, "La *coincidentia oppositorum* et le mystère de la totalité," *Eranos-Jahrbuch 27* (1958): 195–236.

31. Mircea Eliade, *Méphistophélès et l'androgyne* (Paris: Gallimard, 1962).

32. Mircea Eliade, *The Two and the One*, trans. J. M. Cohen (New York, NY: Harper Torchbooks, 1965), pp. 78–124.

33. See Eliade, "La *coincidentia oppositorum* et le mystère de la totalité," p. 198.

34. Mircea Eliade, *Myths, Dreams, and Mysteries* (New York, NY: Harper & Row, 1975), pp. 174–75; see also Eliade, *The Two and the One*, pp. 78–124.

35. See Gershom Scholem, *Major Trends in Jewish Mysticism* (New York, NY: Schocken, 1960), pp. 117–18; see also Gershom Scholem, *Origins of the Kabbalah*, trans. A. Arkush, ed. R. J. Zwi Werblowsky (Philadelphia, PA/Princeton, NY: Princeton University Press/JPS, 1989), p. 112, fn. 114.

36. Scholem, *Major Trends*, p. 118. See also Wasserstrom, *Religion after Religion*, p. 189.

37. Scholem, *Major Trends*, pp. 172, 233.

38. *Ibid.*, p. 213.

39. *Ibid.*, p. 220. See also several other instances of the use of archetype as referring to the paradigmatic forms of the lower entities, within the supernal world: Gershom Scholem, *On the Kabbalah and its Symbolism*, trans. R. Manheim (New York, NY: Schocken, 1969), pp. 100–01, 103, 112, 124; and Gershom Scholem, *Kabbalah* (Jerusalem: Keter, 1974), pp. 19, 98, 105, 141.

40. *Major Trends*, p. 272.

41. *Ibid.*, p. 293; for other instances dealing with prototypes related to forms of actions, see Scholem, *Kabbalah,* pp. 124, 184.

42. Scholem, *Origins of the Kabbalah*, p. 140.

43. *Ibid.*, pp. 142, 167.

44. *Ibid.*, p. 146.

45. *Ibid.*, p. 162. The German term is *Archetypen.*

46. See Moshe Idel, *Old Worlds, New Mirrors—On Jewish Mysticism and Twentieth-Century Thought* (Philadelphia, PA: University of Pennsylvania Press, 2009), pp. 138–46.

47. See Scholem, *Major Trends*, pp. 7–9. For the Hegelian background of this threefold distinction, see Moshe Idel, *Old Worlds, New Mirrors*, pp. 34–36, 127–28.

48. Scholem, *Major Trends*, p. 7.

49. See also the similar use of "breakthrough" elsewhere in Scholem, *Origins of the Kabbalah*, p. 345.

50. Scholem, *Major Trends*, p. 8.

51. Scholem, *On the Kabbalah and its Symbolism*, p. 98.

52. See Joseph Dan, "Foreword," in Gershom Scholem, *On the Mystical Shape of the Godhead—Basic Concepts in the Kabbalah*, trans. J. Neugroshel, ed. J. Chipman (New York, NY: Schocken, 1991), pp. 6 and 8-9; see also Wasserstrom, *Religion after Religion,* pp. 26 and 188–89 who nevertheless assumes some influence of Corbin's views on Scholem.

53. See Gershom Scholem, *Reshit ha-Qabbalah* (Jerusalem/Tel Aviv: Schocken, 1948), p. 78 (Hebrew). On the scholarly discussions of *du-partzufin* in Kabbalah and in the passage of R. Abraham ben David of Posquieres and some of its reverberations, see Moshe Idel, *Kabbalah: New Perspectives* (New Haven, CT/London: Yale University Press, 1988), pp. 128–36; Moshe Idel, "Androgyny and Equality in the Theosophico-Theurgical Kabbalah," *Diogenes* 52 (4, 2005): 27–38; Moshe Idel, *Kabbalah and Eros* (New Haven, CT/London: Yale

University Press, 2005), pp. 53–103; Charles Mopsik, *Sex of the Soul—The Vicissitudes of Sexual Difference in Kabbalah*, ed. D. Abrams (Los Angeles, CA: Cherub, 2005), pp. 76–82; Elliot R. Wolfson, "Woman: The Feminine as Other in Theosophic Kabbalah: Some Philosophical Observations on the Divine Androgyne," in L. Silberstein and R. Cohn, eds., *The Other in Jewish Thought and History—Constructions of Jewish Cultural Identity* (New York, NY: New York University Press, 1994), pp. 166–204; Elliot R. Wolfson, *Circle in the Square—Studies in the Use of Gender in Kabbalistic Symbolism* (Albany, NY: SUNY Press, 1995), especially pp. 205–06, fn. 53; Eli Hadad, "Du- Partzufin shel 'Ezer ke-Negdo," in N. Ilan, ed., *A Good Eye—Dialogue and Polemic in Jewish Culture* (Tel Aviv: Hakibbutz Hameuchad, 1999), pp. 476–96 (Hebrew); Haviva Pedaya, *Name and Sanctuary in the Teaching of R. Isaac the Blind—A Comparative Study in the Writings of the Earliest Kabbalists* (Jerusalem: The Hebrew University, 2001), pp. 104–05 (Hebrew); and the several discussions in Daniel Abrams, *The Female Body of God in Kabbalistic Literature—Embodied Forms of Love and Sexuality in the Divine Feminine* (Jerusalem: Magnes Press 2004), especially pp. 42–43. (Hebrew).

54. Gershom Scholem, *Ursprung und Anfaenge der Kabbala* (Berlin: de Gruyter, 1962), pp. 191–92; Scholem, *Origins of the Kabbalah*, pp. 217–18.

55. *Ibid.*, p. 217.

56. *Ibid.*, p. 142.

57. Compare also Scholem's reticence to allow the possibility of mystical union in Jewish mysticism, as discussed in Moshe Idel, *Kabbalah: New Perspectives*, pp. 59–72. In my opinion, the cases of mystical union in Jewish mysticism are predicated on the philosophical terminology of Greek origins, while the vast majority of the Kabbalistic discussions of the anthropomorphic *du-partzufin* do not refer to cases I would describe as mystical union.

58. See, however, Jung's views on the alleged lack of *unio mystica* in Judaism in CW 14, pp. 170–71, and my discussion in Moshe Idel, *Enchanted Chains—Techniques and Rituals in Jewish Mysticism* (Los Angeles, CA: Cherub, 2005), pp. 16–17; Jung, CW 14, pp. 442–45; see also *ibid.*, pp. 22–24.

59. Wasserstrom, *Religion after Religion*, pp. 206–09; see also Moshe Idel, *Saturn's Jews: On the Witches' Sabbat and Sabbateanism* (London/New York, NY: Continuum, 2011), pp. 91–95.

60. See Antoine Faivre, "Modern Western Esoteric Currents in the Work of Mircea Eliade: The Extent and Limits of Their Presence," in C. K. Wedemayer and W. Doniger, eds., *Hermeneutics, Politics, and the History of Religions—The Contested Legacies of Joachim Wach and Mircea Eliade* (Oxford-New York, NY: Oxford University Press, 2010), pp. 147–56; and Idel, "Androgynes: Reflections on the Study of Religion."

61. It should be mentioned that a strong proclivity toward occultism is evident in an early piece by Eliade already at the end of his high-school, "Ştiinţă si Ocultism," reprinted in M. Handoca, ed., *Cum am găsit piatra filosofală. Scrieri de tinereţe* (Bucureşti: Humanitas, 1996), pp. 246–47.

62. See, for example, Idel, *Kabbalah*, pp. 1–16 and Moshe Idel, "Johannes Reuchlin: Kabbalah, Pythagorean Philosophy, and Modern Scholarship," *Studia Judaica* 16 (2008): 30–55.

63. For Eliade's neglect of Scholem's studies, see Idel, *Mircea Eliade*, pp. 162–66. Neither did Scholem resort to Eliade and Jung in his studies, though Eliade refers to the latter several times in his later writings.

64. For Zolla's more adequate approach to the topic, see Idel, "Androgynes: Reflections on the Study of Religion."

65. See, for example, *ibid.* and Idel, *Kabbalah and Eros*, pp. 53–103.

IV.

Philosophical Perspectives of Eranos

[Handwritten dedication by Henry Corbin, reproduced as an image, reading:]

ERANOS est beaucoup plus et beaucoup
mieux qu'un phénomène "de son temps";
un signe qui rend présents les uns aux
autres les univers que notre existence de
chercheurs prend en charge,— un signe qui
ne pourra être compris "au passé", car il
s'adresse aux capables de comprendre,
c'est-à-dire d'impliquer eux-mêmes
ce qu'ils expliquent.

Le sens d'Eranos: cette co-présence même

Henry Corbin

A dedication written by the philosopher and scholar of Islam, Henry Corbin, on the occasion of the 25th anniversary of the Eranos Conferences, in 1957, which reads: "ERANOS is much more and much better that a phenomenon 'of its time': a sign, which puts 'in the present' to each other the universe that our existence of researches takes in charge—a sign that couldn't be understood 'to the past,' because it calls upon those who are able to *understand*, i.e., to imply themselves what they explain. The meaning of Eranos: that copresence itself."

HENRY CORBIN

The French philosopher and scholar of Islam, Henry Corbin
(1903–1978), joined Eranos in 1949, on Louis Massignon's
advice. He gave a total of twenty-five talks, from 1949 up to 1976.
Another essay appeared in a commemorative *Eranos Yearbook*, which
was published in honor of Carl Gustav Jung's seventy-fifth birthday
(1950). Among his major works, which were originally presented at
Eranos, are: *Creative Imagination in the Sufism of Ibn al-'Arabī* (1958),
Temple and Contemplation (1981), and *The Paradox of Monotheism*
(1981). Based upon the Eranos model, in 1974 Corbin founded,
together with Gilbert Durand, Antoine Faivre, Richard Stauffer, and
Robert de Chateaubriant, the Université Saint Jean de Jérusalem (USJJ)
in Vaucelles, France. He recollected memories of the Eranos gatherings
in his autobiographical work, *Post-Scriptum biographique à un Entretien
philosophique* (1981). In September 1951, Corbin wrote an esoteric
poem dedicated "To Olga Fröbe-Kapteyn." He also published some
articles about Eranos, "De l'Iran à Eranos" (1955) and "The Time of
Eranos" (1956), as well as an eulogy for Olga Fröbe-Kapteyn and Jung,
"Eranos: Freedom and Spontaneity" (1962).

Henry Corbin's "The Time of Eranos," presented in the
following pages, was originally written in French on December 21,
1956, in Tehran. It was first translated into English by Willard R.
Trask and published English in *Man and Time: Papers from the
Eranos Yearbooks. Selected and translated from the Eranos-Jahrbücher,
edited by Olga Fröbe-Kapteyn*, Bollingen Series XXX:3, ed. Joseph
Campbell (New York, NY: Pantheon Books Inc., 1957), pp. xiii–
xx; another English edition appeared in Adolf Portmann, Rudolf

Ritsema, and Henry Corbin, *Eranos and its Meaning* (Ascona: Tipo Offset Bettini, 1978), pp. 7–17; with a further Preface written in December 1961, it was also published in French, with the original title, "Le temps d'Eranos," and with a further Preface, in *Roger Godel. De l'humanisme à l'humain* (Paris: Les Belles-Lettres, 1963), pp. 177–86; other French editions appeared in Henry Corbin and Mircea Eliade, *A propos des Conférences Eranos* (Ascona: Tip. Bettini & Co., 1968), pp. 1–15, and in Christian Jambet, ed., *Henry Corbin. L'Herne* (Paris: L'Herne, 1981), pp. 256–60; German editions were published as "Eranos-Zeit," in *Geist und Werk. Aus der Werkstatt unserer Autoren-Zum 75. Geburtstag von Dr. Daniel Brody* (Zürich: Rhein-Verlag, 1958), pp. 197–208, and in Adolf Portmann, Rudolf Ritsema, and Henry Corbin, *Vom Sinn der Eranos Tagungen* (Ascona: Tipo Offset Bettini, 1978), pp. 7–17; a Spanish edition was published as "El tiempo de Eranos," *Anthropos. Boletín de información y documentación* 153 (1994): pp. 28–30; in Italian it appeared as "Il tempo di Eranos," in *Le stagioni della vita. Sviluppo biologico, fasi creative e spirito del tempo nel ciclo dell'esistenza umana. Quaderni di Eranos IV*, ed. C. Risé (Como: Red, 1992), pp. 9–19.

We thank Dr. Daniel Gastambide and the Association des Amis de Henry et Stella Corbin (Paris) for granting permission for republishing Corbin's writing in this issue of *Spring: A Journal of Archetype and Culture*.

THE TIME OF ERANOS

HENRY CORBIN

In mentioning the name of Eranos one usually encounters such questions as "What is Eranos?" "How is the Eranos 'Circle' constituted?" "What is the nature of its work, and what are the sources of its inspiration?"

This is an attempt to render something of our common experience—not merely the experience of those who have been intimately associated with the group over the years and are its mainstays, but also of the many persons who, at one time or another and to various degrees, have opened their mind to the spiritual adventures that may come to pass in and about the Eranos meetings. If some passages seem over vigorously bowed in the following piece, it is hoped that the reader will consider the underlying motives.

It should not be thought that it is merely the site of the annual rendezvous, Ascona, on the shore of Lake Maggiore, that lends the conferences their unique attraction. It is rather their spirit that moves scholars of such diverse fields to assemble here from the most remote points of the globe.

In order to give an idea of the nature of this spirit it may suffice to say that the dozen-odd yearly conference speakers, each proceeding from his own field, are all basically intent upon helping to uncover the essential features of man's quest to know himself; that is, they strive to verify what is permanent and eternal in human experience. All the conferences are arranged about the same center: man's image of himself as revealed in the universe proper to him. This value-orientation is made possible a complete freedom of the spirit from any doctrinaire preconceptions. In this environment, devoid of any prearranged covenants save the general conference topic set forth a year in advance, there is annually called into being a fortunate moment of convergence, a climax of scientific and humane confrontation between the speakers themselves, and between them and the audience.

All the participants rest in the conviction that the Eranos Yearbook, already constituting an impressive repository of knowledge, will carry their message to future generations. Possibly in a century or two some historian of ideas, if there are any left, or some thesis-writer will find an ideal monograph topic in the phenomenon of Eranos in the twentieth century. And perhaps his monograph will turn out to be like so many others that, ever since the rise of historical criticism, have been devoted to the "schools" and "ideological currents" of the past, demonstrating their "causes," explaining their "influences," the "migrations of themes," and so on.

But it is to be feared that, if he in his turn does no more than apply a scientific method which has all the virtues except the primary one of establishing its object by examining the reasons whereby it has come to be chosen—it is to be feared that our future historians will completely miss the phenomenon of Eranos. He will perhaps believe that he has "explained" it by a profound and ingenuous dialectic of causes. But he will not have divined that the real problem would have been to discover not *what* explains Eranos, but *what* Eranos *ex*-plains by virtue of what it *im*-plies: for example, the idea of a true community, bringing together speakers and listeners, a community so paradoxical that it displays none of the characteristics of concern to statistics and sociology.

That is why our forecast is made from no vanity of an expected fame, but rather in fear that the soul of Eranos may one day be lost in such a venture. While they explain things and beings by their time, historians *per se* are not in the habit of beginning by reflecting on the nature of historical time, so that perhaps Eranos itself contains the best warning against the dubious formula that would try to explain Eranos "by its time."

It would be well to meditate on the possible meaning of these words: *the Time of Eranos*. For it will be no explanation of Eranos to say that it was "very much of its time," that is, of everybody's time, in accordance with the formula that is so soothing to alarmed or hasty conformisms. Nothing indicates that Eranos ever tried to "be of its time." What, on the contrary, it will perhaps have succeeded in doing is *to be its time*, its own time. And it is by being its own time that it will have realized its own *meaning*, willingly accepting the appearance of being untimely. It is not certain things that give meaning to Eranos; rather, it is Eranos that gives meaning to these other things. How, then, are we to conceive that it is not by "being of our time," as so many well-meaning people say, but by ourselves being our own time, that each of us explains and fulfills his own meaning? Can this be suggested in a brief summary?

To return to our hypothetical future historian: why, undertaking to explain Eranos by the circumstances, the "currents" and "influences" of the period, would he miss its meaning and its essence, its "seminal reason"? For the same reason, for example, that the first and last explanation of the various gnostic families is those gnostics themselves. The historian may suppose every kind of favorable circumstances, draw all possible conclusions, but he would be merely reasoning *in vacuo* if there were not the first and signal *fact* of gnostic minds. It is not the "main currents" that evoke them and bring them together; it is they that decree the existence of a particular current and bring about their own meeting.

Probably, then, the word "fact," as used here, does not signify quite what our current speech commonly means by the word; rather, it signifies what current speech gives an apposite meaning to when it distinguishes between persons and facts or men and events. For us, the first and last *fact*, the initial and final event, are precisely these persons, without whom there could never be anything that we call "event." Hence we must reverse the perspectives of the usual optics and substitute the hermeneutics of the human individual for the pseudodialectic of facts, which today is commonly accepted as objective evidence. For it was only by submitting to the "necessity of the facts" that it became possible to imagine in them an autonomous casualty that "explains" them. Now, to explain does not necessarily mean to "understand." Understanding rather involves an "implying." There is no explaining the initial fact of which we are speaking, for it is individual and singular, and the individual can be neither deduced nor explained; *individuum est ineffabile.*

On the contrary, it is the individual who explains very many things to us, namely all the things he *implies*, which would not have existed if he had not begun to be. For him to explain them to us, we must understand him, and to understand is to perceive the meaning of the thing itself, that is, the manner in which its presence determines a certain constellation of things, which hence would have been entirely different if there had not first been this presence. This is a very different matter from deducing the thing from assumed causal relations, that is, from taking it back to something other than itself. And is doubtless here that the reader will most readily mark the contrast with our current modes of thought, those represented by all the attempts toward philosophies of history or toward the socializations of the individual conscience: anonymity, depersonalization, the abdication of the human will to the dialectic web of its own weaving in which it all too easily becomes ensnared.

What concretely exists is will and relations between wills: failing will, imperious or imperialistic will, blind will, will serene and conscious of itself. But these wills are not abstract energies. They designate or rather are, nothing but the willing subjects themselves, the subjects whose real existence postulated recognition of the individual as the first and only concrete reality. I should gladly admit that I am here in affinity with an aspect of Stoic thought;* for is not one of the characteristic symptoms in the history of philosophy in the West precisely the overshadowing of the Stoic premises by the dialectic that derived from Peripateticism? Stoic thought is hermeneutic; it would have resisted all the dialectical constructions that burden our most current representations in history, philosophy, or politics. It would not have surrendered to the fiction of "main currents," the "meaning of history," "collective wills," whatever these may be.

For the fact is that, outside of the first and final reality, the individual, there are only ways of being either in relation to the individual himself or in relation to what surrounds him; and this means *attributes* that have no substantial reality in themselves if they are detached from the individuals who are their agents. What we call "events" are likewise the attributes of acting subjects; they are not beings but ways of being. As actions of a subject, they are expressed in a verb; but a verb acquires meaning and reality only from the acting subject who conjugates it. Events, psychic or physical, do not assume existence or "take shape," except through the reality that realizes them and from which they derive; and this reality is the acting individual subjects, who conjugate them "in their tense," "in their time," who gave them their own tense and time, which is always essentially the present one.

---

* See Victor Goldschmidt's excellent book *Le Système stoicien et du temps* (Paris: Vrin, 1953).

Hence, detached from the real subjects who realizes them, facts or events are merely something *unreal*. This is the order which had to be inverted in order to alienate the real subject. We give, instead, all reality to facts, to speak of the laws, lesson, or materiality of facts, in short, to let ourselves be trapped in the system of unrealities that we have ourselves constructed and whose weight falls on us in the form of history, the only scientific "objectivity" that we can conceive and as the source of a casual determinism which would never have occurred to a humanity that had preserved the sense of the real subject. Detached from the real subject, facts "pass away." There is past, and there is past that has been "passed beyond," "transcended." Hence the resentment against the yoke of the past and the illusions of progressivism, and, conversely, the complexes of reactions.

Yet, *past* and *future* are themselves attributes expressed by verbs; they presuppose the subject who conjugates those verbs, a subject for whom the only existing tense and time is the *present* on each occasion. Thus dimensions of the past and future are also, on each occasion, measured and conditioned by the capacity of the subject who perceives them, by his instant. They are dimensional to that person, for it depends upon him, on the scope of his intelligence and on his largeness of heart, to embrace the whole of life, *totius vitae cursum*, to totalize or imply in himself all worlds, which he does by falling back to the farthest limit of the dimension of his present. This is to *understand*, and it is a totally different matter from constructing a dialectic of things that have ceased to exist in the past. It is "interpreting" the *signs*, explaining not material facts but ways of being, that reveals beings. Hermeneutics as science of the individual stands in opposition to historical dialectics as alienation of the person.

Past and future thus becomes *signs*, because a sign is perceived precisely *in the present*. The past must be "put in the present" to be perceived as "showing a sign." (If the wound, for example, is a sign, it is so because it indicates not that such and such a one has been wounded, in an abstract time, but that he is having-been-wounded.) Genuine transcending of the past can only be "putting it in the present" as *sign*. And I believe it can be said that the entire work of Eranos is, in the sense, a *putting in the present*. None of the present forty-five volumes of the Eranos Jahrbuch offer the character of a simple historical encyclopedia. All the themes treated acquire the value of *signs*. And if it is true that, even at some future date, the act of Eranos, whose initiative has persisted for forty-five years, could not be explained simply by deducing it from the circumstances that would justify the historian's saying that it was "very much of its time," this is because Eranos is itself a sign. It cannot now or in the future be understood unless it is interpreted as a *sign*, that is, as a presence that ceaselessly and on each occasion puts "in the present." It *is* its time because it puts "in the present," just as each acting subject *is* his time, that is, a presence that puts in the present whatever is related to it. An active presence does not fall "into its time," that is, it is not "of its time" in the sense of the oversimplifying theory that thinks it explains a being by situating it in an abstract time which is "everybody's" time and hence no one's.

In short, the whole contrast lies here. With *signs* with hierophanies and theophanies, there is no history-making. Or rather, the subject that is at once the organ and the *place* of history is the concrete psychological individuality. The only "historical causality" is the relations of will between acting subjects. "Facts" are on each occasion a *new creation*; there is discontinuity between them. Hence to perceive their connections is neither to formulate laws nor to deduce causes, but to understand a meaning, interpret signs, and this implies a composite structure. To perceive a causality in "facts" by detaching them from persons doubtless makes a philosophy of history possible; it does so by affirming dogmatically the rational meaning of history on which our contemporaries have built up a whole mythology. But this also means deducing real time to abstract physical time, to the essential *quantitative* time of objectivity and of mundane calendars lacking the *signs* that used to qualify every present in a sacred way.

It remains for us to gain a better awareness of the abdication of the subject who thus alienates himself in objective history. The first step will necessarily have been ceasing to perceive events on the plane of *signs* and putting them on the plane of *data*. It is in this way that signs have been laicized. But our entire theology, by virtue of an unwitting and fateful complicity, must of necessity bring about the laicization of which it is itself the victim. The meaning of history no longer needs a God incarnate to reveal it. The textbook philosophy of our day claims to be in possession of this meaning and imposes it at will since that philosophy after all, is nothing but a lay theology of "incarnation" in social terms.

The caricature of our own Image (Ivan Karamazov seeing himself in the looking glass) fills us with all the more terror because we have nothing to oppose to it except precisely our own features, which are mirrored in caricature. Now, it is impossible to compete with a scientific, materialistic, and atheistic socialization by a conformism of well-meaning people who can find no justification for their being except in their social activity nor any foundation for their knowledge except the "social sciences." The *no* that must be cried aloud proceeds from a different imperative. It draws its energy from the lightning flash whose vertical joins heaven and earth, not from some horizontal line of force that fades into limitlessness devoid of meaning. For what is called "evolution" would have *meaning* only in the cosmic scale; but our philosophers are too serious to take responsibility for the curiosity that is, at most, "excusable" in Gnostics and Orientals.

Perhaps the reader will take a moment to look at the dates affixed to the end of this presentation by the way of signature. Besides a place name it includes a double date incorporating three calendars: a date of the Christian era and an Iranian date in which the official name of the month corresponds to that of the ancient pre-Islamic Persian calendar, while the year is that of the solar Hegira (all the rest of Islam, outside of Persia, reckons in lunar years). This is a mere example. It is to be supposed that putting these eras in correspondence, putting them together "in the present," conjugating them in the present, can result from a simple mathematical equation, with the aid of a table of correspondences? The answer will be *yes*, if one is naïve enough to suppose that all human beings everywhere are of the same age, have the same desires, the same aspirations, and the same sense of responsibility; and to suppose that good will and proper hygiene would suffice to bring them in to accord in the frame of abstract objective time, the uniform mathematical time of universal history.

But the answer will certainly be *no*, if one has an acute awareness of differences and a concern for the rights of pluralism against all monisms, whether it be well-intentioned or brutal or unavowed. What is in question is a relation between *qualitative times*. The Occidental may be much "older" or "younger" than the Oriental, according to the realms in which they meet. But it is perhaps also true that only the Occidental is able to produce the antidote for the spiritual crisis that the impact of the West has provoked in the Oriental, a crisis which has already forever ruined several traditional civilizations.

This simple example suggests the true task of which we have perhaps not even begun to be aware. It is a matter of perceiving the same *signs* together; it is a matter of each of us on each occasion interpreting them according to the meaning of his own being, but it is also a matter of constituting a harmonious hermeneutics of signs, just as the fourfold and sevenfold meanings of the Scriptures were once in harmony. To accomplish this, there must be no more escaping into an abstract time, the time of anonymous collectivities; there must be a rediscovery of concrete time, the time of persons. And this, at bottom, only means opening the living spring of unconditioned *sympathy*, the sympathy existing before our deliberate and conscious purpose, that causes the grouping of human beings and is the only thing that makes them "contemporaries." What we should wish to call the *meaning* of Eranos, which is also the entire secret of Eranos, is this: it is our present being, the time that we act personally, our way of being. This is why we are perhaps not "of our time" but are something better and greater: we are our time. And this is why Eranos does not even have an official denomination nor any collective name. It is neither an academy nor an institute, it is not even something that, in the fashion of the day, can be designated by initials. No, it is really not a phenomenon "of our time." And this is why it is likely to confound the future dialectical and deductive historian. It will not even interest the devotees of statistics and opinion polls.

If curves and graphs are demanded at all cost, I can refer only to the large map of the world that Dr. Daniel Brody, the intrepid publisher of the *Jahrbuch* for more than three decades, had the happy thought of displaying at an exhibition commemorating the twentieth anniversary of this publication's first appearance. It was a planisphere by lines in many colors, all meeting at the same center: an invisible point on the vast map, Ascona on the shore of Lake Maggiore. The uninitiate would have probably taken it to represent airline routes or the like. However it expressed nothing of the kind but simply the journey that each of us had taken from various points in the world to the center that unites us. The lines had no statistical meaning: they were signs—the sign made *to* each of us and *by* each of us.

The result of the response to that sign was the meeting of acting, autonomous individualities, each freely expressing his original and personal way of thinking and being, apart from all dogmatism and academicism; a constellation of those wills and a constellation of the worlds they bring with them, worlds which they have taken in charge by putting them into the present, the present of Eranos. A composite whole, a structure, not a result conditioned by the laws of the period, or by fashionable crazes, but a whole made strong by its single intrinsic norm: a woman's generous, energetic, tenacious will, that of Olga Froebe-Kapteyn. Her successors, Adolf Portmann and Rudolf Ritsema, continue to propose yearly topics in the true spirit of Eranos in order to stimulate scholars toward further creative activity.

And that is why even those who in the sense of current speech "are no more" nevertheless do not cease to be present in the present of Eranos. An immense work has been accomplished: essays and books have seen the light of day, books that perhaps would not have come into being if Eranos had not put them in the present. Its meaning, finally: that of a sym-phony whose performance would each time be repeated in richer sonorities—that of a microcosm, which the world cannot be expected to resemble but whose example, one may hope, will spread throughout the world.

Tehran, 21 December 1956 = 30 Āzar 1335
Moscia, August 1978

MICHEL CAZENAVE

Michel Cazenave was born in 1942 in Toulouse, France, where he worked for more than thirty years at France Culture, France's national cultural radio. He was a Humanities student at the École Normale Supérieure (ULM) and served as president of the Groupe d'Études C.G. Jung in Paris and of the Cercle Francophone de Recherche et d'Information sur L'Oeuvre de C.G. Jung (CEFRI Jung). Cazenave oversaw the French edition of Jung's collected works for Albin Michel publisher. He is author of more than fifty books, five of which focus on C. G. Jung and the remainder inspired by him. Cazenave feels he owes Jung a great debt based on his discovery in early adolescence of the Swiss doctor's work, an experience that literally saved his life. He has dedicated several works to Jung, including *Jung, l'expérience intérieure* (1997), *À la rencontre de... Carl Gustav Jung* (2011), *Jung revisité* (volume one, *La réalité de l'âme*, 2011, and volume two, *Jung et le religieux*, 2012). Among the *Cahiers de l'Herne* series, Cazenave edited the 21st volume, dedicated to Charles de Gaulle (1973 and 1985), the 43rd volume, dedicated to André Malraux (1982), and the 46th volume, dedicated to Jung (1984). Cazenave attended Eranos for the first time at the end of the 1970's. He has studied in depth the work of Gershom Scholem, Henry Corbin, James Hillman, Pierre Hadot, and Gilbert Durand, the last three with whom he cultivated a mutual and uninterrupted friendship. He recently edited Henry Corbin's unpublished manuscript on Jung given to him by Stella Corbin: *Autour de Jung. Le bouddhisme et la Sophia* (2014).

Remembrances
of Eranos

MICHEL CAZENAVE

Here, I share a few remembrances of Eranos and the people who brought this wonderful creation to life over the many years and to whom I owe so very much. I begin with its beginning. In ancient Greek, *eranos* means a "banquet" where guests bring their own contributions. The original vision for the Eranos Circle was a common space where individuals could gather and share intellectual and psycho-spiritual "food."

It is generally known that Eranos was created in 1933 by Olga Fröbe-Kapteyn, but few appreciate the role played by Rudolf Otto. The Marburg professor is best known as the author of the famous book, *The Holy* (1917), where the concept of the *numinosum* ("numinous," from the Latin word, *numen*) was first proposed. Olga Fröbe-Kapteyn initiated the annual event at Eranos, which is now in its eighty-first year, but Otto provided vital encouragement. C. G. Jung presided as the inspiring genius, or *spiritus rector*, of the gatherings for twenty years before he retired in 1952 in his late seventies and was succeeded by Henry Corbin, the specialist of the Muslim mystic gnosis and Iranian *chi 'it* tradition.

There were an astonishing number of international celebrities who consistently attended the event. Though diverse in perspective and background, this impressive list of luminaries was drawn together by a common passion for the mysteries that lie beyond mundane human life. Each approached the theme of each year's event in unique and pioneering ways. For example, Erich Neumann and anthropologist John Layard. The latter revealed underlying structures of thought through the medium of the virgin archetype. Louis Massignon and Toshihiko Isutzu plumbed the depths of Islam; Jean Daniélou, paleo-Christianity; Mircea Eliade, the history of religion; Gershom Scholem, the Qabbalah; Dominique Zahan, sub-Saharan Africa; and Jean Servier, esotericism. Together, Jean Doresse and Henri-Charles Puech translated the manuscripts of *Nag Hammâdi* (also referred to as the *Codex Jung*). Gilles Quispel from the Netherlands accompanied their explorations with his "secret book of the Apocalypse." Károly Kerényi and Sir Herbert Read brought Ancient Greece and broader themes of art and culture to the table and last—but not least—James Hillman, who carried depth psychology forward into the following century.

Eranos participants and studies were not exclusive to the West. Daisetsu Teitarō Suzuki had an essential role in introducing Eastern philosophy and Buddhism to the Western world. Giuseppe Tucci and Heinrich Zimmer also brought insights from the East. Further, many scientists were part of the core group of "Eranians." Marie-Louise von Franz recounted the decisive contributions from mathematician Hermann Weyl. Biologist Adolf Portmann, whose work was inspired by Goethe, was also part of these early meetings. Of course, Jung himself discoursed with physicist Erwin Schrödinger and collaborated with Wolfgang Pauli.

Despite the passage of time, the Eranos Circle retained its original inspiration and a core group of attendees: the "spirit" was literally ever present. In his obituary of Olga Fröbe-Kapteyn in 1962, Henry Corbin recounted Jung saying, standing in front of the empty Round Table around which the meetings took place, "They are all there!" ("*Ils sont tous là!*")[1], meaning that what truly took place was the meeting of an "invisible company" and an "unknown spirit of the place."

These were exciting and rich times. In one of his letters to Olga Fröbe-Kapteyn, Henry Corbin described how, in his first meeting with Jung, the two spent hours in Swiss psychiatrist's library discussing the deeper meaning of alchemy.[2]

Eranos had quite the reputation for being very serious, so much so that it was quite intimidating for many. I will always remember the time when Hermann Landolt, a brilliant professor of Islam at McGill University, Canada, was asked at short notice to substitute for one of the scheduled lecturers. He was so disturbed by this "honor" and by the importance of his duty that, after taking a glass of water to stop stuttering, he promptly fainted before his audience who were then asked to leave.

Amongst ponderous discussions, however, there was also a *joie de vivre*. One time, as Mrs. Corbin told me, it had gotten very late and they could hear music filtering up from the village to the meeting room. Her husband and Jung became very animated and then one of them jumped up and said, "Let's go dancing!" Off they went. She also talked about Jung's *Jungfrauen*, young admirers of the great man who took baths in the lake adjacent to the meeting hall, and, when finished, waltzed up rhapsodizing, "We bathed in the collective unconscious!" Upon hearing this, Jung laughed aloud, and replied immediately: "Are you sure you believe in the collective unconscious?"[3] Then there was the time when, upon her first arrival at Eranos, Stella Corbin stood looking for a luncheon seat around the large Round Table. There was a seat next to Jung, but she did not dare take it. Much to her surprise, Jung boldly joked with her, saying "So you don't want to face the daemon? Is it because you are protestant?"

Given all this history and tales, it was no surprise that I was eager to attend. Soon that opportunity presented itself when Yves Jaigu, Director of France Culture, asked me to organize an international colloquium in Cordoba in remembrance of the famous meeting between Ibn 'Arabī and Averroës, first reported by Henry Corbin. The goal of the colloquium was to recreate a dialogue between current science and psychology with the purpose of exploring how a spiritual vision of the universe might be described. The Corbins, Gilbert Durand, and James Hillman were well able to dialogue across the multiple levels of modern cosmology, quantum physics, neurobiology, complex psychology, metaphysics, and mystical states. I still remember the communication that Gilbert Durand gave at that colloquium on the relevance of the "imaginaire" in society, the variations of David Miller on the polytheism of the soul, and what James Hillman said on the Neo-Platonic tradition in Jung.

One can easily imagine the excitement that my wife and I felt as we traveled overnight by train to Italian Switzerland, hurriedly consumed a fresh croissant at the Bellinzona station, and then continued the journey to Ascona! I will always remember the village in the glow of the beautiful late August light, under the mountains, just above the Lake Maggiore. Ascona was a popular destination, full of tourist and antiques shops and movie theaters, so it was a challenge to find a convenient hotel and a good restaurant where we could comfortably

dine with James Hillman and Stella Corbin. We then took a taxi that
followed a curved road climbing Monte Verità hill. The branches of
the trees along the way flickered between alternating light and beneficent
shadows, to eventually reach the Eranos circle.

Here, next to the road, we saw a few visitors waiting for return
transportation to Ascona. After gathering our luggage from the car, there
was a lengthy walk along the mountainside to reach Casa Gabriella
and other small houses where the participants stayed and took coffee
or tea with the Ritsemas in their free hours. In addition to lectures,
there were study and communication sessions and a library full of
treasures. There stood the same curved table, the surface of which was
almost planar, where Jung saw everyone present, even those who were
notable by their absence.

As we arrived, Gilbert Durand appeared and welcomed us. He had
been told of our arrival and was quite warm and informal, even ignoring
how much I had read (though I had never been told about them during
my studies) of his *The Anthropological Structures of the Imaginary* and
the work of Jung. I cannot forget his enthusiasm in showing us the
abundant vegetation along the path down to the lake, how he explained
to us in detail that the Italian border was only a few kilometers away,
and how he offered to be our guide in this country unknown to us. He
praised the softness of the Borromean Islands in Lake Maggiore that
were to become an important part of psychoanalysis, asking innocently:
"Of course, you already know who St. John Borromean (St. John the
Baptist) is? And the Borromeo family, you have heard of them?" Then,
as we walked along, we came upon James Hillman and David Miller
to whom we were very cordially introduced. The two men welcomed
us warmly. However, upon noticing the absence of the Corbins, Gilbert
told us: "You will see them tomorrow."

The next day we saw Stella Corbin arriving. She had valiantly
driven her Citroën 2CV from France. As I was told, she did that
every year, but this time she was alone! I had recently met with
Henry Corbin at Yves Jaigu's place, but I failed to notice (was it a
lack of intuition or did I succumb to the weakness of young people
who only focus on their own problems?) that he was so ill. He would
die a few short weeks later.

With an admirable reserve, Stella Corbin told us that she was not
willing to miss the Eranos session. She had thus decided to use her

presence to communicate the enthusiasm and deep faith of her husband. And I truly have to say that, for me, Eranos is intimately linked to her memory. She was the one who helped me come to know James Hillman and David Miller well beyond that first introduction by Gilbert Durand by the lake. During a memorable dinner in the restaurant of the hotel where my wife and I were staying, thanks to her natural kindness, Stella forged intimate intellectual links for us with other participants. We naturally formed a deep friendship.

Because of the relationships developed at Eranos, we were able to invite James Hillman to dine with us during his several visits to Paris and meet with the extraordinary Jungian analyst, Pierre Solié. I will always remember the conversation between the two of them, a combination of Eranos and the Cordoba Colloquium (which, if we go back to the roots, is a pure product of Ascona too). It was during this conversation when Solié introduced Hillman to Lacan's famous ternary: R-S-I (the Real, the Symbolic, and the Imaginary) and the "Borromean node" that linked these terms. Hillman immediately answered, in the true spirit of Jung:

> "Only three? But it is more complicated! What about
> the fourth term?"
> "The fourth... ?"
> "Yes! ... The Imaginal!"

The Imaginal... This term was so precious to Henry Corbin. It referred to a reality that he found, as far as I understand it, in the writings of the great philosopher, Ibn ʿArabī, who used the concept to deal with creative imagination. The Imaginal was linked to what Jung called "active imagination," which opens in the course of the "cure" to spiritual kingdoms. But Solié could not fail to understand as he himself was aligned with Corbin's way of thinking.

In retrospect, I realize how much I owe to James Hillman, not least of which was his bringing to my attention *Spring* publications and this very journal! It was the first time I tasted the work of Layard and his *Celtic Quest*.[4] In so doing, I acquired insights into an old text that I often read with the feeling—without understanding it completely—that it contained so many fundamental things. This was how, in a non-canonical fashion, I approached Jung's seminar on the "Spiritual Exercises" of St. Ignatius of Loyola. I shamefully confess that I did not know until then that they existed! How many new findings I must credit to James Hillman and therefore, of course, to Eranos! I can only assume that the spiritual links shared with Hillman reflected a mutual taste, inclination, or a permeability to melancholic states that also underlay our love for the ancient figure of Greek mythology, Dionysos, for "stories" or faces that could have been thought forgotten.

I must admit that I did not always agree with Hillman's ideas. For example, I believe that there must be a dialectic between the polytheism of his "archetypal psychology" and the well-known "Self," which Jung found in the Indian *Upaniṣad*, and even more so pronounced in the verse of the *Chāndogya-Upaniṣad*. Hillman, who had changed my mind so as to better understand Jung's reference to Friedrich Nietzsche's *Zarathustra*, wrote that the only real student is the one who steps away from the teacher because he thinks and builds upon a radically different interior (and subjective) experience.

I also am very grateful to Gilbert Durand. He was very attentive to me during the ensuing years. The first recording I made at Eranos was a treatment of the *I Ching*. Each time I asked him a question and he was ready to answer, the wind would blow down from the mountain creating loud waves upon the lake, making recording almost impossible. After a while, smiling, he said Nature did not like that he unveiled its secrets. Then he asked if I was really willing to continue. I answered affirmatively and we resumed the recorded conversation. Yet the wind blew and there were terrible creaks with each of his words.

Yes! How much I owe to Eranos, to this alert spirit who was always manifesting! Stella Corbin, James Hillman, Gilbert Durand, and the ever-present *manes* of Carl Gustav Jung and Henry Corbin— these are the memories I can never forget, and why I felt so deeply the loss as Eranos was transformed from its former spirit into an *I Ching* study center after the death of Adolf Portmann. But, as Hillman wrote me at that time, "Spirit never dies. Someday…" and in fact that "someday" has finally arrived!

Before closing, I must mention the important role that my wife played in this great discovery. It should not be forgotten that my wife was loved by Mrs. Corbin as well as by Hillman and Durand. Her silent presence, made even more active by her solar presence, sensitized me to what was happening at Eranos. She had the strong feeling that our existence in its eternal dimension essentially was, to paraphrase Henry

Corbin, *Vivor, cogitor*—"I am lived, I am thought of." I hope that in the mysterious, indefinable place that my wife has reached after she disappeared from this world, she will hear these words that honor so beautifully her own approach of the universe, and to the infinite tenderness that she instantly felt for Eranos!

NOTES

1. H. Corbin, "Eranos: à la mémoire de C.G. Jung et Olga Fröbe," *Eranos-Jahrbuch* 31 (1962): 12.

2. Henry Corbin, letter to Olga Fröbe-Kapteyn, September 6, 1949, quoted in Riccardo Bernardini, "La corrispondenza Carl Gustav Jung-Henry Corbin," *Historia religionum* 5 (2013): 100.

3. I can't stop thinking of the words of Marie-Louise von Franz, when she related Jung's answer to the question: "Did you invent individuation?" She reported to me a similar immediate answer: "So do you think Lao-Tse waited for me?"—and I intentionally write Lao-Tse and not the modern version of his name, Lao-Zi.

4. John Layard, *A Celtic Quest: Sexuality and Soul in Individuation: A Depth-Psychology Study of the Mabinogion Legend of Culhwch and Olwen* (Zürich: Spring Publications, 1975).

ROMANO MÀDERA

Romano Màdera is Full Professor of Moral Philosophy and of Philosophical Practices at the Università degli Studi di Milano-Bicocca, Italy. He previously taught at the Università della Calabria and at the Università Ca' Foscari in Venice. He is a member of the Associazione Italiana di Psicologia Analitica (AIPA), of the International Association for Analytical Psychology (IAAP), and of the Laboratorio Analitico delle Immagini (LAI), a professional association of sandplay analysts. He is on the editorial board of the *Rivista di Psicologia Analitica*. He was among the founding members of the Open Seminars of Philosophical Practices at the University of Venice, at the University of Milano-Bicocca, and at other universities, of the Post-Graduate School of Philosophical Practices "Philo," and of the Society for Philosophically Oriented Biographic Analysis (SABOF). His writings include *Identità e feticismo* (1977), *Dio il Mondo* (1989), *L'alchimia ribelle* (1997), *C.G. Jung. Biografia e teoria* (1998), *L'animale visionario* (1999), *La filosofia come stile di vita*, written with L. V. Tarca (2003) and translated into English as *Philosophy as Life Path—Introduction to Philosophical Practices* (2007), *Il nudo piacere di vivere* (2006), *La carta del senso. Psicologia del profondo e vita filosofica* (2012), and *Approaching the Navel of the Darkened Soul—Depth Psychology and Philosophical Practices* (2013). The works of Carl Gustav Jung, Erich Neumann, and Pierre Hadot were seminal not only for his profession as an analyst and as a philosophy professor, but, above all, for his own life.

THE MISSING LINK
FROM JUNG TO HADOT AND VICE VERSA

ROMANO MÀDERA

E
ranos was a melting pot of decisive and significant encounters among great men of culture from different fields of knowledge and diverse religious convictions and worldviews. But it was also a place of encounters that never took place. One such encounter that failed to happen—with consequences that may be felt to this day—was that between Pierre Hadot and the Jungian universe, and more generally, between Hadot and the extraordinary experiment being conducted at Eranos. This is the missing link between analytical psychology (or complex psychology) and philosophy as a way of life.[1] However, I believe that this lost opportunity may be reconstructed from two lectures given by Hadot at Eranos in 1968 and 1974.[2]

It should first be recalled that Eranos was frequented by few "philosophers" in the strict academic and disciplinary sense. Apart from Hadot, we find only three other key philosophers of the twentieth century: Martin Buber, Karl Löwith, and Helmut Plessner. Jung had a dispute with Buber over key philosophical-religious issues, such as the ontological status of the religious phenomenon and Jung's relationship with Gnosticism.[3] "Jungians" did not take Buber's objections very seriously, nor, with the exception of Ernst Bernhard, did they agree with his thinking in general or his program for spiritual life.[4] Distinct from the vast majority of academic philosophers, Buber represents, as Putnam has observed, a Jewish philosophical equivalent of the invitation to practice a spiritual path that grew out of Hadot's study of Greek and Roman philosophy.[5] It is likely that Buber fell victim to the ostracism inevitably reserved for those who contradict the master.

On the other hand, in my view, Löwith and Plessner represented interdisciplinary scholarship of the most traditional kind. Both were great scholars, Löwith in the field of the history of philosophy and the philosophy of history, and Plessner in philosophical anthropology, the field he himself had founded with Arnold Gehlen and Max Scheler. But academic philosophy is particularly innocuous: its concern with conditions of knowability, logical and linguistic structures, or overarching frameworks—or even with metaphysical assumptions or conclusions—makes it a welcome guest at all scientific gatherings, perhaps because it has been relegated to an ornamental function.

Hadot posed a different kind of dilemma because he reinterpreted philosophy as a way of life. In so doing, he challenged all forms of knowledge, including the natural sciences, at the very level of daily existence. He even went so far as to claim that his perspective coincided with the original Greek philosophical experience. Indeed, the science of nature itself had been, and could once more become—in certain cases, it already is, though perhaps without being aware of that—a spiritual exercise. Thus, the presence at Eranos of this polite professor, philologist, and historian of supreme erudition and refinement had an unsettling effect as had been the case in ancient times with Hadot's model philosophical master, Socrates or *átopos*, one who finds no place among conventional mental categories.

Let us turn then to the first of Hadot's lectures at Eranos. What brought him there? Hadot himself recounted that he had been invited by Henry Corbin.[6] It is true that the theme of his first lecture, on the contribution of Neo-Platonism to the Western philosophy of nature, was close to Corbin's area of interest. In 1968, Hadot had not yet written his seminal essay on the spiritual exercises of ancient philosophy, the first edition of which appeared in 1981.[7] Nonetheless, clearly, he was already oriented towards reinterpreting philosophy as way to provide a horizon of meaning and means of personality formation. This orientation was confirmed and further stimulated by his second marriage, in 1966, to Ilsetraut Marten Hadot, who was then researching the theme of spiritual direction in Greek and Roman philosophy.[8]

In this first Eranos lecture, Hadot remarked that the philosophy of nature appeared to be profoundly intertwined with the art of living and that its primary function should be to expand the opportunities available to us to perceive the world differently, to learn to see the world anew.[9] The artificiality of the economic and technical world had cut modern man off from the world of the senses, to the extent of undermining his or her capacity to connect with the natural world.

Hadot spoke of the duty to restore human perceptive capacity as a "moral requirement," which the philosophy of nature could fulfill by reintroduction to the secret of the art of living. Drawing on scholarly sources ranging from Galen to Jakob Böhme to Goethe, the latter reference implicit in his use of the word, "signature," the French philosopher issued an invitation to learn how to decipher the *hieroglyphics* of nature. The word, *hieroglyphics*, is featured in the subtitle of the 1968 *Eranos-Jahrbuch: Wir muessen von neuem lernen, die Hieroglyphen der Verganheit zu lesen, damit sie uns helfen, das Kommende zu verstehen* ("We should learn again to read the hieroglyphics of the past, so that they can help us to understand what is coming"). Hieroglyphics is the sacred scripture of the world and had become an enigma for the "desouled" gaze, to use an expression of Jung's.

Hadot built up to this position by taking Neo-Platonic philosophy as a starting point. The year 1968 was also the year in which he published *Porphyre et Victorinus*, his authorative study on the relationship between the mystic theology of Victorinus, who influenced the thinking of Saint Augustine, and the Neoplatonic tradition. The first edition of Hadot's study on Plotinus had already been published in 1963.[10] In the philosophy of Plotinus and Porphyry, his closest disciple, both nature and the soul were viewed as emanations of a supreme essence who may be rationally postulated, but who remains unknowable beyond the scope of any determination. Nature and psyche are inferior levels of reality that may not be dissociated from one another. Together, they are joined with the soul of the world that itself is differentiated into a part that tends towards multiplicity and a part that tends towards the One. Hadot's interpretation drew on the language of Neo-Platonic metaphysics by adopting its call for the expression of an inner experience. Ontological levels, the structuring of reality, correspond to the levels of the self. Metaphysics is animated by a fundamental and yet ineffable experience. Plotinus developed his thinking on the basis of his own life practice which is why he should be viewed as a master, or "personal advisor."

In his second Eranos lecture on *The Figure of Socrates*, Hadot returned to the theme of his model philosopher, Socrates.[11] Hadot's contributions at Eranos effectively drew a link between the first and the last of the great pre-Christian ancient masters, thereby demonstrating continuity of tradition with regard to a concept and practice of philosophy that focused on transforming the self and its social context. Individual experience may never be separated from participation in the lives of others. The city is reflected in the soul, while the formation of the soul is the key work to be accomplished if the individual is devoted to the good of the city. Such a line of conduct and thought led Socrates to accept his own condemnation to death, thereby bearing witness to the philosopher's commitment to his community, the preeminence of moral intent over private interest, perfect coherence between thinking and living, and, finally, the supreme exercise of death by one who is a philosopher because he is inhabited by Eros. The two dialogues in the *Phaedrus* and the *Symposium* stage the dialectics between Eros and Thanatos, which are two key spiritual exercises: the exercise of death as the essence of philosophy and philosophy itself as an exercise. Socrates is a disciple of Eros, meaning that philosophizing is born of desire. While Eros, or desire, is the child of Penia, or want and poverty, and therefore he is, in turn, born of the drive towards what is a tension in himself. It is an aspiration or movement towards that which he does not possess. All human beings are inhabited by this demon, by this reality that lies between the human and the divine. Although the majority of individuals are driven by passions limited to the coarser and more deceptive facets of desire, wealth, power, and honor, they are unable to see beyond the external appearance of the body.

This is why yearning desire must be joined together with Poros, the expedient, father of Eros. Poros is the only master who can lead us out of the blind alley of *a-poria*. As is frequently the case in the Platonic dialogues, Socrates often brings up aporias. Yet, Socrates says of himself, that when he cannot access the truth of something through discourse, then it is life experience that will bear witness to that truth. What Socrates does is, "to try to persuade all of you to concern yourself less about what he *has* than about what he *is*" (*Apo. 36c*). Expediency, in the context of Hadot's interpretation, is to be understood as the exercise itself, and spiritual exercises as *the* ancient philosophy. Exercises that concern the entire spectrum of psychism: such is the meaning that Hadot explicitly assigns to his use of the term, "spiritual." The exercises involve training one's ability to make judgments and implement behaviors in relation to one's desires and keeping one's passions under control (*ascesis*, in Greek, literally means "exercise"). They also entail engaging in dialogue with others and with oneself, reasoning, imagining one's relationship with nature and perception, habits of daily life, physical exercise, one's relationship with the master and with others practicing philosophy as a way of life. The outcome of all of this is transformation of daily existence: "I have always conceived of philosophy as a transformation of one's perception of the world."[12] Thus, Poros will help Eros, who is driven by the desire born of want. All forms of wisdom, in all historical eras, from Hinduism to the Abrahamic religions to philosophy, and even to psychoanalysis, have been born from the question and the difficulty posed by want, *suffering*, or *sin*. All are functional equivalents for an unsatisfied torment. Socrates is the historic incarnation of the erotic mythologem and his teaching touches us:

> Not merely on the cognitive level, but on that of the self and of being … a progress which causes us to *be* more fully, and makes us better … a conversion which … raises the individual from an inauthentic condition of life, darkened by unconsciousness and harassed by worry, to … inner peace, and freedom.[13]

This implies renunciation of false values of wealth, honors, and pleasures and a turning toward true values of virtue, contemplation, a simple life-style, and the simple happiness of existing.

Eros' love object transcends the literary dimension. The philosopher obtains such by virtue of his love, his *Philia*, for *Sophia*, wisdom-knowledge, which is unattainable within the human condition. The philosopher aspires to become wise, but can never actually achieve this. The philosopher is the living symbol of the wise man. The reality of wisdom is therefore a symbolic reality. The Wise Man is himself an inaccessible figure that has something of the divine. The philosophical life is that which surpasses us and surrounds us on all sides and which eludes our power and possession. In living such a life, we may experience the happiness available to us because we are aware of and accept the limits that inevitably affect our participation in the human community and the natural cosmos. Others, and the world, and the truth of our own being as part of the whole are the areas of transcendence to which the spiritual exercises are ordered. Transcendence is the sense of overcoming our centeredness on our own private and selfish interests. As is hinted in the words of Diotima at the end of the *Symposium,* beauty has to do with the generation of souls, we might say with the formation of souls and with knowing how to assist at the birth of the philosophical life—*maieutics,* from Socrates' midwife mother. The master, in order to be master, must know that he does not know and not know that he knows. He must empty himself out for others.[14]

This is why Hadot considers the exercise of death to be the very essence of ancient philosophy. The key teaching of spiritual exercises is overcoming of self and the transition from *philautia* (love of self) to *philosophia.* Our constant daily awareness of our mortal condition leads us to live the present moment as intensely and perfectly as possible. However, it is not possible to remain in the present and enjoy simply existing (a theme strongly emphasized by the Epicurean school) without breaking away from the part of ourselves that is slave to the passions, binding us to bad infinity, which does not contain in itself its own good. Thus, the exercise of death also involves making the transition to *megalopsychia,* the great soul that inhabits us and the world. The *Phaedrus'* staging of how Socrates coped with his own death (that is, by declaring that philosophy is the art, or the meditation of death and dying) becomes the dramatization of the spiritual exercise of death.[15] The aim is to achieve the suspension of temporality that is possible when we live the present moment. The motto "remember to live!" links the ancient philosophers together in a golden chain with Goethe and Nietzsche.[16] The moment (which is not the instant viewed as a physical-temporal interval) that is experienced as a continuum of action and lived with the maximum possible intensity allows the passing of time to cease. This goes on generally unnoticed. It is taken for granted and therefore frenetically consumed.

If we are to grasp the breadth of Hadot's vision of Greek and Roman philosophy, it then should be emphasized that he did not show preference for one ancient school or the other. On the contrary, despite the fact that many schools disagreed at the theoretical level, Hadot showed what they shared in common:

> What is the practice of philosophy? In this work I have tried to show, amongst other things, that philosophical practice is relatively independent of philosophical discourse. The same spiritual exercise can in fact be justified by extremely diverse philosophical discourses. These latter are nothing but clumsy

attempts, coming after the fact, to describe and justify inner experiences whose existential density is not in the last analysis susceptible of any attempt at theorization or systemization. Stoics and Epicureans—for completely different reasons—urged their disciples to concentrate their attention on the present moment, and on the imminence of death, in order to free themselves of worries about the future as well as the burden of the past. Whoever practices this exercise of concentration, however, sees the universe with new eyes, as if he were seeing it for the first and the last time. In his enjoyment of the present, he discovers the splendor and mystery of existence and of the world's emergence; at the same time he achieves serenity by experiencing how relative are the things which provoke anxiety and worry. Similarly, Stoics, Epicureans and Platonists, each for their own reasons, exhorted their disciples to raise themselves to a cosmic perspective, plunge into the immensity of space and time, and thereby transform their vision of the world. Seen in this way, the practice of philosophy transcends the oppositions of particular philosophies. It is essentially an effort to become aware of ourselves, our being-in-the-world, and our being-with-others. It is also, as Maurice Merleau-Ponty used to say, an effort to "relearn how to see the world" and attain a universal outlook, thanks to which we can put ourselves in the place of others and transcend our own partiality.[17]

This is exactly what Hadot has in mind when he says, "being born again of the world," a "relearning how to see the world," and an "overcoming of our own partiality." In other words, the matter of dying and being reborn is in keeping not only with Merleau-Ponty, but also with C. G. Jung. For Jung, analysis itself is an exercise in the *ars moriendi*: "Man goes through analysis so that he can die. I have analyzed to the end with the end in sight: to accompany the individual in order that he may die."[18]

In a 1934 essay entitled, *The Soul and Death*, Jung remains in the terrain of the soul's natural life.[19] (This is similar to Freud, though their arguments diverge.) The psyche must follow biological development by cultivating the capacity to expire, to "go down," as one might say to echo Nietzsche in his introduction to *Thus Spoke Zarathustra*, upon which, in the same year of its publication, Jung began to comment in his seminar.[20] However, I would emphasize that Jung linked the natural development of the psyche to the different life stages. This is something that is much more accessible for reflection than what is found in Freud's psychological goal of Eros and death. (The latter is suspiciously similar to Schopenhauerian metaphysics, but lacking an adequate speculative commitment.) Further, it is opposite to Nietzsche's emphasis on the Dionysian destruction of any "over-human" sentiment. In Jung's own words:

> From the middle of life onward only he remains vitally alive who is ready to *die with life*. For in the secret hour of life's midday the parabola is reversed, *death is born*. The second half of life does not signify ascent, unfolding, increase or exuberance, but death, given that the end is its goal. The negation of life's fulfillment is synonymous with the refusal to accept its ending. Both mean "not wanting to live" and "not wanting to live" is identical with "not wanting to die."[21]

Here, Jung appears to be quietly summoning Nietzsche back down to earth. This is clear from his references to an inappropriate exuberance and the possible meaning that is different from the over-turning associated with the advent of the super-human, namely, the "wanting to go down." Only a few lines earlier, Jung uses the same expression "suspended in mid-air" to describe those who fail to follow "the natural life," which is "the nourishing soil of the soul." Later, Jung would frequently repeat this phrase in his *Seminar on Nietzsche's Zarathustra*. In the *Red Book* chapter entitled, "The Way of the Cross," Jung refers to Nietzsche as the prophet of the earth left without any earth beneath him.[22] It is surprising to observe the similarity between this key passage in Jung and a statement from Epicure's: "One and the same are the art of meditation of living well and dying well." (*Letter to Menecaeus*, 126.) "One and the same" are the meditation or the art. However, the Greek term is μελέτη, and, for good reason, "meditation" is the translation chosen by Pierre Hadot for living well and dying well. This is well expressed by the Greek word, καλῶς.[23]

Jung's sense of the profound connection between not wanting to live and not wanting to die, and Epicure's meditation of death which is life, clearly have much in common. Of course, Epicure's vision also understands the need to renounce passions based on desires that are neither natural nor necessary and the curtailing of those that are natural but not necessary. This in itself is a form of death through which we may be reborn to a happier life. In any case, Jung's reference to analysis as means of guiding persons towards "knowing how to die" envisions analysis as a spiritual exercise and means of formation is similarly understood in ancient philosophy. Indeed, Jung himself drew a parallel between analytical psychology and ancient philosophy. Without mentioning Hadot, Marco Heleno Barreto draws attention to Jung's claims in this regard.[24] Again, independently of either Barreto or myself, Paul Bishop makes the connection with Hadot:

> From this point of view Jung's *Red Book* follows in the tradition of the spiritual exercises—*exercices spirituels*—as Pierre Hadot calls them, in which focusing on death is an extremely ancient method of cultivating the awareness of meaning or of contemplation.[25]

Bishop corroborates this by citing Sonu Shamdasani's claim that Jung saw analysis as a modern form of *ars moriendi*.[26]

Therefore, theoretical differences do not constitute an insurmountable obstacle. To the contrary, beyond and beneath these boundaries lies the great common ground wherein the transformation of our attitudes towards existence transpires.[27] This was precisely the case of the ancient philosophical schools. Theoretical adversaries such as Platonists and Epicureans who occupied opposite poles of the theoretical spectrum, represented all other intermediate theoretical distinctions, but nevertheless shared the need for spiritual exercises. With regard to the relationship between life and death and the question of the soul's survival after death, the differences between these two schools appear to be irreconcilable. In terms of what conventionally is held to be their concept of the soul, a rapprochement does not appear possible. For Epicureans, there can be no life after death, whereas for the Platonists, life is regenerated and the individual part of the soul will maintain some influence over its future return to earth. However, both schools consider the exercise of death as critical for the purpose of drawing on as much of the eternal, as much of what exceeds the passing of time, as is available to us in this life.

The central point here is that Jung and Hadot—but also other leading scholars in the field, such as Rabbow, Foucault, Horn, and Nussbaum, who were not familiar with Jung's work—distinguished two concepts and two corresponding practices of philosophy. There is the academic type, which is dominated by an intellectualist approach, far removed from any binding implications for life conduct, and there are the ancient schools, which represented, in Jung's view, the perspectives closest to the truest and most profound meaning of his psychology.[28] This is all the more significant because Hadot had tried to show that even though the ancients' philosophical discourse was closely related to the philosophical experience of the exercises, their philosophical life was ultimately irreducible to theories. Even more importantly, he thought it was possible to take up the ancient philosophical exercises again, minus the theoretical elements incompatible with contemporary culture. It is my own view that modern man can practice spiritual exercises of antiquity, at the same time separating them from the philosophical or mythic discourse which accompanied them.[29]

Hadot himself was favorable towards my attempts to incorporate Jungian analytical practice into renewed philosophical practices.[30] But, what is important here is the objective confluence between the two worlds and Jung's intuitive ability to grasp the fact that ancient philosophy acted as a guide for existence. Given the change in cultural conditions, analytical psychology can fulfill a similar function for contemporary Europeans and Americans. Today, many are disoriented because they no longer adhere to the Christian myth, yet at the same time cannot find a replacement. Like Nietzsche, Jung knew that his own inability to continue identifying with the Christian myth as formulated by the various churches was also the great question of the time. How should one live in a desouled, secularized, disenchanted, and apparently meaningless world? It is clear that the entire Eranos project was intended to tackle this question.

According to Jung, the dialectic between therapist and analysand is the primary foundation for the analytical *opus*. This is particularly so in the phase of Jungian transformation that involves integrating and assimilating contents emerging from an encounter with the unconscious psyche. This occurs after the phases of confession, elucidation, and education:

> As the most complex of psychic structures, a man's philosophy of life forms the counterpole to the physiologically conditioned psyche, and, as the highest psychic dominant, it ultimately determines the latter's fate. It guides the life of the therapist and shapes the spirit of his therapy.[31]

This sentence is dense with meaning. It says that, in the end, the decisive element is not only the analyst's exercising of his or her profession, but a view that "guides life." It is this which ultimately constitutes the spirit of therapy. There are clear reasons why I choose to call Jung a forerunner of the renewal of philosophy as a way of life, or as a biographical philosophy. These are the same reasons why I also view Jung as a forerunner of a therapy—for those sufficiently healthy—that utilizes a philosophically oriented biographical analysis.[32] Jung further comments:

> I could hardly draw a veil over the fact that we psychotherapists ought really to be philosophers or philosophic doctors—or rather that we already are so, though we are unwilling to admit it because of the glaring contrast between our work and what passes for philosophy in the universities. We could also call it religion *in statu nascendi.*[33]

Moreover,

> There are not a few patients who, although they have no clinically recognizable neurosis, come to consult the doctor on account of psychic conflicts and various other difficulties in their lives, laying before him problems whose answer inevitably involves a discussion of fundamental questions. Such people often know very well—what the neurotic seldom knows—that their conflicts have to do with the fundamental problem of their own attitude, and that this is bound up with certain principles or general ideas, in a word, with their religious, ethical, or philosophical beliefs. It is precisely because of such cases that psychotherapy has to spread far beyond the confines of somatic medicine and psychiatry into regions that were formerly the province of priests and philosophers. From the degree to which priests and philosophers no longer discharge any duties in this respect or their competence to do so has been denied by the public, we can see what an enormous gap the psychotherapist is sometimes called upon to fill, and how remote religion on the one hand and philosophy on the other have become from the actualities of life. The parson is blamed because one always knows in advance what he is going to say; the philosopher, because he never says anything of the slightest practical value. And the odd thing is that both of them—with few and fewer exceptions— are distinctly unsympathetic towards psychology.[34]

The so-called, "sufficiently healthy" individual, turns to psychotherapy precisely because philosophy has been reduced to a mere discourse and the cure of souls imprisoned in a sterile repetition of dogmas and preconceptions. Thus, neither can dialogue with this need for an orientation, which is today generalized. Although Jung does not adequately examine the cause of civilization's present spiritual and cultural conditions, he asserts in subsequent pages that concepts and interpretations of mythologems that ground religious beliefs and world views have become "obsolete."[35] Such concepts and interpretations no longer speak to us, and the bridges linking consciousness and the unconscious "collapse." The therapist needs to know that this "is due ... to a shifting of the whole psychic situation over many centuries" and that "in the face of such transformations the individual is powerless."[36] This is why it is critical to attend to all possible unconscious compensations.

If Jung had already intuited this conclusion, why is it that a more fertile encounter never took place with Hadot at Eranos? This is surprising given that Corbin, who had invited Hadot, and Hillman (whom Hadot cites in positive terms on Socrates in the chapter entitled, "The Figure of Socrates," in *Philosophy as a Way of Life*) were both present at the 1974 conference.[37] Of course, Hadot had not yet fully developed his position, expressed later in his 1995 work, *What is Ancient Philosophy?* There, he states:

> The choices of life we have described—those of Socrates,
> Phyrro, Epicurus, the Stoics, the Cynics, and the Skeptics—
> correspond to constant, universal models which are found,
> in various forms, in every civilization, throughout the various
> cultural zones of humanity.[38]

This is a statement in complete harmony with the spirit of Eranos. It is all the more significant because it is advanced self-critically by a scholar who had always been somewhat opposed to cultural comparativism. Hadot did not venture into making theoretical hypotheses. Nonetheless, this citation clearly points up the similarities between the human quest for wisdom and its archetypical dimension. In an interview in *The Present Alone is Our Happiness*, Hadot comments somewhat ironically on his relationship with Eranos saying that perhaps he had never been invited back because he had not agreed with Corbin's archetypical angelology. It could have been that the two great scholars were too distant from another, both in terms of psychological attitude and in relation to their theoretical and practical assessments of whether it was plausible to revive Neo-Platonism within contemporary culture. In the book-testament written jointly with Sonu Shamdasani on the destiny of psychology after Jung's *Red Book*, Hillman recounts that towards the end of his lectures, Corbin would raise his eyes to heaven and appear to be having the same kind of visions as Sohravardī.[39]

Despite experiencing an "oceanic sentiment" both for his life and for his concept of philosophy, Hadot's personality and attitude towards mysticism clearly differ.[40] After a month of self-imposed isolation during which he finished writing the earlier-cited book on Plotinus that underpinned his Eranos lecture, Hadot told this anecdote:

> Seeing the ordinary folks all around me in the bakery, I ... had the impression of having lived a month in another world, completely foreign to our world, and worse than this—totally unreal and even unlivable.[41]

It is no coincidence that in the second edition of his 1997 book on Plotinus, Hadot concludes with a striking contradiction. He is of the opinion that in place of Plotinus' counsel to "remove everything," we should instead "welcome everything." Hadot the philosopher seems more interested in the minutiae of daily life than Hillman, Corbin, and Shamdasani. Hillman and Shamdasani's conversations may also be read as a magnificent "exercise of death." In the "Eleventh Conversation," Hillman explicitly cites Socrates in regard to the famous statement in the *Phaedrus* that identifies the art of death and dying as the core of philosophy.

Hillman's final book confirms his stance that the Soul of the World and the exercise of death are necessary passages towards attaining a higher perspective on all of experience and freeing it of any literal interpretations. These are precisely the same two themes discussed by Hadot at Eranos and what would later become fundamental elements of his thinking. Hillman's notion of a "therapy of ideas" also contains a strong critique of the Jungian world that remains trapped in the family romance of psychoanalysis. Herein lies the paradox. His attempt to release the potential contained in Jung's experience from the shackles of a clinical approach based on subjective experience or the individual unconscious becomes a sort of radical shift from biographical themes. Ultimately only myth emerges victorious. However, as I see it, this implies losing the truly novel contribution of analytical psychology as developed out of psychoanalysis into the field of the "humanities." Its method explores the hidden roots of the rejected material of daily life. This means forgoing one of analytical psychology's two key components, the biographical dimension. (Not by chance this approach also de-emphasizes the function of the ego as conceived by Jung.)

It may reasonably be argued that emphasizing the mythical dimension is more fruitful than the limited personalistic approach that characterizes much of psychotherapeutic clinical practice and which is engaged in an unconscious collusion with the collective narcissism of our time. As envisioned by Ernst Bernhard, myth and biography should go hand in hand, becoming "mythobiography." For Hillman, the shift towards the mythical-symbolic dimension and the figurative narrative ends up in twentieth-century thinking, and not just in psychology. In so doing, it becomes a kind of recursive condemnation of any effort to engage in conceptual thinking. Hillman and Shamdasani appear to view Jung's theoretical-conceptual work as a sort of concession to the generalizations demanded by the profession and by "science."

This position effectively renders a reciprocal and fruitful encounter between complex psychology and the ancient and modern philosophical exercises nearly impossible.[42] In my opinion, it also invalidates any discourse on the symbolic dimension itself. For symbolic discourse or discourse about symbolism to even be formulated, it must be made explicit how it departs from logical-conceptual discourse and, whether we like it or not, is a logical operation. It is helpful to envision thought, as Jung set out to do in the second chapter of *Symbols of Transformation*,[43] as taking two main forms—directed and non-directed thinking. But to wholly shift away from and devalue conceptual thinking, and along with it, conscious will and the indispensable role of the self, appears to me as one of the extremist tendencies that marked the culture of the last century. Though perhaps historically necessary, if this break with the past cannot be reconciled with the legacy left to us by conceptual thinkers, it will only lead to a new rupture, but in the opposite direction.

For this reason, I have proposed a neologism. I believe that we now need a "symbologics." This addresses the need to develop a variety of spiritual exercises. In many cases, the exercise of active imagination, which plays such a critical part in rendering the analysand independent of the analyst and bringing the analytical dimension to bear outside of the therapeutic setting, is not suited to the needs of certain individuals. As Jung repeats incessantly in the *The Red Book,* every individual must follow her/his own way. For this, it is necessary to broaden the available forms of spiritual exercise as an extension and refinement of personal analysis. This provides a range of possibilities for use by individuals to explore until they have developed their own personalized modes of practice. The treasures contained in the spiritual exercises, philosophy, religions, and the arts constitute a goldmine of resources that can be exploited following principles and methods of modern individuality, the biographical dimension of each individual to be immersed once more in its mythical origins. The exercises and reason itself should not be considered enemies of mysticism or of symbolical life. Hadot writes about Marcus Aurelius' *Meditations*:

> Such ... exercises ... lead necessarily to incessant repetitions...
> They must somehow become achievements of awareness,
> intuitions, emotions, and moral experiences which have the
> intensity of a mystical experience or a vision.[44]

As mentioned earlier, Hadot often told of having experienced the "oceanic sentiment" from boyhood onwards, adding that it is almost never referred to in the writings of the ancients, with the exception of passing mentions in Lucretius and Seneca. Therefore, the most intense aspect of his philosophical experience exceeded the world he had adopted as his guide!

> I was filled with an anxiety that was both terrifying and delicious,
> provoked by the sentiment of the presence of the world, or of
> the Whole, and of me in that world... This experience dominated
> my entire life. I experienced it many times again—several times,
> for example, in front of Lac Majeur at Ascona.[45]

That is to say, at Eranos! Independent of any conscious intention, something of the *spiritus loci* of Eranos seems to have succeeded in captivating Hadot too. It functioned to restore in an imponderable and mystical way, a link to the *Philia* of *Sophia* that his encounter with the other great scholars of his time had failed to create.

This paper was translated by Clare O'Sullivan.

NOTES

1. For essential background on the key distinction between analytical psychology and complex psychology, see Riccardo Bernardini, *Jung a Eranos. Il progetto della psicologia complessa* (Milan: FrancoAngeli, 2011).

2. Pierre Hadot, "L'Apport du Neoplatonisme à la Philosophie de la Nature en Occident," *Eranos-Jahrbuch* 37 (1968): 91–132; Pierre Hadot, "La Figure de Socrate," *Eranos-Jahrbuch* 43 (1974): 51–90.

3. For discussion of the texts documenting the controversy between Buber and Jung, see Arnaldo Petterlini, "Il contrasto tra Buber e Jung," in *Rivista di Psicologia Analitica* 2 (54, 1996): 45–53; Barbara D. Stephens, "The Martin Buber–Carl Jung disputations: protecting the sacred in the battle for the boundaries of analytical psychology," *Journal of Analytical Psychology* 46 (3, 2001): 455–91.

4. See my essay, "La spiritualità di Ernst Bernhard nel contesto della psicologia analitica," *Rivista di Psicologia Analitica*, 2 (54, 1996): 131–51, rpt. in Romano Màdera, *Una filosofia per l'anima. All'incrocio di psicologia analitica e pratiche filosofiche* (Milan: IPOC, 2013).

5. Hillary Putnam, *Jewish Philosophy as a Guide to Life: Rosenzweig, Buber, Levinas, Wittgenstein* (Bloomington, IN: Indiana University Press, 2008).

6. See Pierre Hadot, *The Present Alone is Our Happiness: Conversations with Jeanine Carlier and Arnold I. Davidson* (Stanford, CA: Stanford University Press, 2009).

7. The English edition is *Philosophy as a Way of Life: Spiritual Exercises from Socrates to Foucault* (Oxford: Blackwell, 1995), while the latest expanded French edition is *Exercices spirituels et philosophie antique* (Paris: Albin Michel, 2002).

8. Ilsetraut Marten Hadot, *Seneca und die griechisch-römische Tradition der Seelenleitung* (Berlin: de Gruyter, 1969).

9. See footnote 2.

10. *Plotinus, or the Simplicity of Vision* (Chicago, IL: Chicago University Press, 1993). The first French edition dates to 1963, while the most recent revised edition in French came out in 1997. In support of the importance of this theme for Hadot, it should be noted that his last book, first published in French in 2004 and based on decades of research, precisely concerned the philosophy of nature: *The Veil of Isis: An Essay on the History of the Idea of Nature* (Cambridge, MA: Harvard University Press, 2006). See also Mohammed Taleb, "Psiché, Cosmos et Ame du monde. Fragments d'histoire de l' ecopsychologie," *L'Art du Comprendre*, 21 (2012): 187–201.

11. Hadot later reworked this Eranos lecture—confirming its importance for the development of his inquiry—both in his earlier cited work on the spiritual exercises, whose first French edition was published in 1981, with the latest expanded edition coming out in 2002, and in his book on ancient philosophy, which originally appeared in French in 1995: *What is Ancient Philosophy?* (Cambridge, MA: The Belknap Press of Harvard University Press, 2002).

12. See the first chapter of Pierre Hadot's *The Present Alone is Our Happiness*, as well as his *Philosophy as a Way of Life*, particularly p. 6 and p. 254.

13. Hadot, *Philosophy as a Way of Life*, p. 83.

14. Plato, *Symposium* 219a. Lacan observed that these passages may inform the inquiry into the philosophical and historical roots of transference. Jacques Lacan, *Le Transfert, Séminaire VIII*, 1960–1961 (Paris: Le Seuil, 2001), translated into English as, *The Seminar of Jacques Lacan VIII, Transference* (London: Karnac Books, 2002). In a work of my own, I have commented on Epicurus' *Letter to Colotes* (cited in Plutarch, *Adversus Colotem* 1107d, cf. Usener 140), which provides an instance of transcendence towards inner teaching and a prototypical example of mastery of the dynamics of transference and countertransference: see Romano Màdera, *La carta del senso. Psicologia del profondo e vita filosofica* (Milan: Cortina Editore, 2012), pp. 61–63.

15. Plato, *Phaedo* 64A–65A.

16. Hadot, *The Present Alone is Our Happiness*.

17. Hadot, *What is Ancient Philosophy*, p. 276.

18. William Mc Guire and R. F. C. Hull, eds., *C. G. Jung Speaking: Interviews and Encounters* (London: Picador, 1980), p. 360.

19. C. G. Jung, "The Soul and Death" (1934), in *The Collected Works of C. G. Jung*, vol. 8, ed. and trans. Gerhard Adler and R. F. C. Hull (Princeton, NJ: Princeton University Press, 1970), §§ 798–803.

20. C. G. Jung, *Nietzsche's Zarathustra. Notes of the Seminar Given in 1934–39*, ed. J. L. Jarrett (Princeton, NJ: Princeton University Press, 1988).

21. Jung, "The Soul and Death," CW 8, § 800.

22. C. G. Jung, *The Red Book. Liber Novus*, ed. S. Shamdasani (New York, NJ: W. W. Norton, 2009).

23. "It was not without great hesitation that I translated μελέτη as *méditation*. In reality, μελέτη and its Latin equivalent, *meditatio*, indicate 'preparatory' exercises, in particular those practiced by rhetoricians. However I eventually chose to adopt the translation *méditation* in any case, because the type of exercise designated by μελέτη corresponds quite closely to what moderns refer to as *méditation*: an effort to assimilate, to bring to life in the soul an idea, a notion, a concept or principle. But we must never lose sight of the ambiguity of the term: *méditation* means "exercise," and exercise *méditation,* or "meditation." For example, the *préméditation* of death is the 'preexercise' of death; the '*cotidiana meditatio*' ... is 'daily exercise.'" (Hadot, *Philosophy as a Way of Life*, f. 38, p. 113.)

24. Marco Heleno Barreto, "'It is something like antique philosophy.' Analytical psychology and philosophical practical wisdom", *Spring* 77 (2007): 69–88. The essay came out in the same year as my second paper on Jung and the philosophical practices, "Carl Gustav Jung come precursore di una filosofia per l'anima", then published in the *Rivista di Psicologia Analitica* and, subsequently, translated into English as, "C. G. Jung: Forerunner of a Philosophy for the Soul," in Romano Màdera, *Approaching the Navel of the Darkened Soul—Depth Psychology and Philosophical Practices* (Milan: IPOC, 2013).

25. Paul Bishop, "Selbst und Gottesvorstellungen im *Roten Buch*," *Recherches germaniques* 8 (2011): 148.

26. Sonu Shamdasani, "'The boundless expanse': Jung's Reflections on Life and Death," *Quadrant: Journal of the C. G. Jung Foundation for Analytical Psychology* 38 (2008): 24.

27. See also Irvin D. Yalom, *The Gift of Therapy* (New York, NY: Harper Collins, 2009).

28. See footnotes 24–26.

29. Hadot, *Philosophy as a Way of Life*, pp. 211–12.

30. I exchanged letters and books with Hadot, including my own work, *Il nudo piacere di vivere* (Milan: Arnoldo Mondadori, 2006), in which I attempted to come up with a unifying framework for biography and theory, the thinking of Epicure, Hadot's interpretation of ancient philosophy and analytical psychology.

31. C. G. Jung, "Psychotherapy and a Philosophy of Life," in *The Collected Works of C. G. Jung*, vol. 16, ed. and trans. Gerhard Adler and R. F. C. Hull (London: Routledge and Kegan Paul, 1966), § 180. [Translator's note: the original publication bore the title, *Psychotherapie und Weltanschauung*. In English, R. F. C. Hull translates *Weltanschauung* as "philosophy of life."]

32. This is the title both of the practice developed and of the association (Association for Philosophically Oriented Biographical Analysis) founded with a view to providing the missing link between the philosophical life and complex psychology, of which the cultural center Philo, in Milan, is a further offshoot.

33. C. G. Jung, "Psychotherapy and a Philosophy of Life," CW 16, § 181.

34. C. G. Jung, "Fundamental Questions of Psychotherapy," CW 16, § 250.

35. I would here direct the reader to some of my own writings, in which I attempt to advance a different line of analysis that goes beyond Jung's examination of the psychic-spiritual conditions only. See, in particular, my "Eleven Hypotheses about the Crisis of Patriarchy and its Resolution," in Màdera, *Approaching the Navel of the Darkened Soul*.

36. Jung, CW 16, § 251.

37. See Hadot, *The Present Alone is Our Happiness*.

38. Hadot, *What is ancient philosophy?*, p. 278.

39. James Hillman and Sonu Shamdasani, *Lament of the Dead: Psychology after Jung's Red Book* (New York, NY: W. W. Norton & Co., 2013).

40. After a number of references to his experience of the "oceanic sentiment," in the earlier cited *The Present Alone is our Happiness*, Hadot concludes with a brief anthology of sayings about the oceanic sentiment drawn from different cultures, literature, philosophy, and art.

41. I cite Michael Chase's translation in the second edition of *The Present Alone is Our Happiness*, published in 2011: the passage had earlier appeared in a passionate and scholarly tribute to Hadot after his death, "Remembering Pierre Hadot–Part I", *Harvard University Press Blog*, last modified April 28, 2010, accessed on March 24, 2015, at http://harvardpress.typepad.com/hup_publicity/2010/04/pierre-hadot-part-1.html.

42. For further background on this point, I would again refer the reader to the following writings of my own: the earlier cited *La carta del senso* and *Una filosofia per l'anima*, as well as the English-language volumes, Romano Màdera, *Philosophy as a Life Path. An Introduction to Philosophical Practices* (Milan: IPOC, 2008) and Màdera, *Approaching the Navel of the Darkened Soul.*

43. C. G. Jung, *Symbols of Transformation*, vol. 5, *The Collected Works of C. G. Jung*, ed. and trans. Gerhard Adler and R. F. C. Hull (Princeton: Princeton University Press, 1967), §§ 4–46.

44. Pierre Hadot, *The Inner Citadel: The Meditations of Marcus Aurelius* (Cambridge, MA: Harvard University Press, 1998), p. 51.

45. Hadot, *The Present Alone is Our Happiness*, pp. 5–6.

GRAZIA SHŌGEN MARCHIANÒ

G razia Shōgen Marchianò is a specialist in East-West aesthetic, philosophic, and religious studies, and former Professor of Comparative Aesthetics and History and Civilizations of Eastern Asia at the University of Siena (Arezzo, Italy). She is author and editor of several scholarly books, as well as a large number of essays, conference papers, and articles in Italian and English on Indian philosophy, Shingon esoteric Buddhism, and transcultural aesthetics. She is recipient of a doctorate *honoris causa* from The Open University, Edinburgh, and Founding President of the Elémire Zolla International Research Society (AIREZ). Marchianò is the editor of Elémire Zolla's *Collected Works* for Marsilio publishing house, Venice, and keeper of his intellectual heritage acknowledged by the UNESCO National Italian Commission as *"bene culturale dell'umanità."* On the tenth anniversary of Zolla's death, she promoted an international conference in Montepulciano, Italy (May 29–31, 2012), on the topic, "Labyrinths of the Mind—Visions of the World," convening scholars from Asia, Europe, and the United States. The trilingual proceedings volume by the same title was published by Società Bibliografica Toscana in 2012. She now leads a group of young researchers engaged in a systematic examination of Zolla's work and thought. She recently promoted the international seminar, "Seeds of Human Ecology in the Holistic Thought of Elémire Zolla," along with the Eranos Foundation, the Fundación Vocación Humana, and the Spineto Abbey (February 28– March 2, 2014). Within the *Spineto. Incontri e Studi* program, Marchianò is in charge of the Spring and Fall interdisciplinary encounters. She is presently working on the entanglement of living nature, human mind, and consciousness viewed from a trans-disciplinary cognitive perspective.

NON-DUALITY

THE DEEP CHALLENGE OF BRINGING TOGETHER ANCIENT AND MODERN WAYS OF KNOWLEDGE IN AN EPISTEMIC WORLD VIEW

GRAZIA SHŌGEN MARCHIANÒ

OPENING NOTE

The title of this article is somewhat ambitious, and I hesitated until the last minute whether to keep it wholly as is, or to limit myself to a reflection on non-duality (Sanskrit, *advaita, advaya*), emptiness, and the non-substantiality of the Self. This undertaking is ambitious itself because all three themes lie at the heart of Buddhist philosophy, and indeed one could say, form its foundation.

Buddhism is a movement of thought, which spread throughout the entire Asian continent beginning in the early centuries of the Christian era. Its origins are rooted in the teachings of the Indian ascetic, Gautama Śākyamuni, who lived in India between the fourth and fifth centuries BCE. Richard Gombrich is correct when he discusses Buddhism as one of the most enthralling intellectual adventures of human thought, an adventure that is clearly also religious, so much so that it has become an institution that has flourished over the centuries, gathering millions of adherents on four continents.[1]

The religious dimension of Buddhism was undoubtedly crucial in giving rise to a monastic clergy and communities of followers in Asia and the West. However, the reason for Buddhism's burgeoning following of scientists and intellectuals today is certainly not a matter of faith, although some quiet converts are to be found amongst them. The main reason derives from the intersection of Buddhist principles with those of post-modern science: the non-duality of matter and mind, the nature of emptiness, the inter-connectedness of physical and psychic processes, and the non-substantiality of phenomena in the living world. Buddhist concepts resonate considerably with the concepts of many scientific disciplines, which are engaged in developing a unifying and holistic theory. This cognitive convergence is of such import that I feel obliged to raise and elaborate on certain key points of Buddhist philosophy and their conceptual alignment with the work of the founder of analytical psychology, Carl Gustav Jung (1875–1961). I begin by shedding some light on some earlier preconceptions that have hindered a correct interpretation of Buddhism.

A GLIMPSE OF A NON-DUAL DUALITY

The systematic development of the thought of Gautama Śākyamuni, commonly referred to as Buddha, took place over many centuries. It derives from the literature of the "three baskets" (Skt. *Tripitaka*), which gathers his discourses (*sūtra*), the rules that comprise disciplines for adherents of the monastic community (*sanga*), and an extensive number of philosophical treatises. They consist of treatises on logic and philosophical epistemology, and religious exegesis. There are no clear demarcations between them, as the conceptual explorations of philosopher-monks engaged in philosophical studies range synoptically in a theoretical perspective reflecting the original view of Gautama, the ascetic.

The threefold path that the Buddha articulated in his teachings to his first five disciples was the outcome of relentless training that involved deep contemplation of the intrinsic inter-connection between material phenomena and mental processes. The Buddha perfected himself in this practice to the best of his physical and mental abilities and was thus an "ascetic," in the literal sense of the Greek word, *áskēsis*. This term is taken from agonistic terminology that denotes anyone strenuously engaged in cultivating thought and deed. In itself, asceticism has no labels. It is useful to also consider the etymology of the term *Buddha* that was given to Gautama in his lifetime. The Sanskrit word defines someone whose mind has been "awakened" to deep perception (*buddhi*) of the way things are in their intrinsic inter-connectedness. Gautama understood that the elements of reality (*dharmas*) are conditioned and tied to a chain of dependent co-origination in the eternal cycle of cause and effect.

Kārma means "action" or "influence." This influence determines the cycle of causations and becomings, the so-called "wheel of life" (*saṁsāra*), involving pain and submission in suffering. Following the "middle way" (*mādhyamika*) is a method to extract oneself from the tyrannical regime of duality that entrains impulses, thoughts, beliefs, and systems of ideas. Another cause of suffering is the belief in the material substantiality of things. In Buddha's view, all beings—human, animal, and inanimate—are selfless, egoless, and unsubstantial. While the waves on the water's surface certainly exist, can it be said that a wave has its own self? This reasoning is extended to all phenomena, including humans. These ideas lead to the Four Noble Truths: life brings about suffering, suffering has causes, causes of suffering can be extinguished, and there exists a way to extinguish the causes of suffering.

The practitioner's path consists of thorough investigation of each principle, namely interdependent co-origination and selflessness, striving effort, concentration, mindfulness, peaceful thought, and equanimity. The practice of mindfulness brings an awareness of the emptiness of reality (*śūnyatā*). This is a term that has been the subject of much debate. Much of the confusion revolves around equating the Buddhist concept with nihilistic nothingness. *Śūnyatā* is a nothingness characterized by fullness brimming with potential, a meaning that is clear from its Indo-European root *śvi*, to swell up. A budding branch, a womb that accommodates the seed of life—these are images that mirror the coming into being of incessant becoming, a becoming devoid of an abiding substance.

The Buddha consistently shunned questions about ontology. He insisted that it is mistaken and futile to investigate "what exists." Instead, one should ask oneself, "In which way, by what means, do we know?" This reflects his understanding that epistemology is far more fecund than ontology. Further, he refuted the existence of a supreme spirit, creator, or cosmic regulator (*Brahman*) which is so central to orthodox Brahmanic thought. As regards to faith (*śraddhā*), which is also a key concept in all the schools of Indian philosophy, Gautama acknowledges it as a *dynamis* of enormous help because of its capacity to sustain and motivate human endeavor. However, he dissociated it from belief in a higher being. No absolute "Truth" looms over the unceasing flow of things; rather it is the karmic process that is in itself its own truth. At the root of *saṁsāra*, there is thirst (*taṇhā*) that gives rise to attachment, suffering, and the inability to accept the law of cause and effect, which regulates the dynamics of the universe.

In contrast, the Middle Way is to see things as they are, to recognize the possibility of determining things from different standpoints, and to recognize that these determinations cannot be regarded as absolute. Just as the truth (*satya*) does not transcend the flow of things, *nirvāṇa* does not transcend *saṁsāra*. If the two appear separate owing to dualistic perception, the application of insight and diligent effort can uproot this misconception. The long-lasting fruits of mindfulness are to achieve unified knowledge, *prajñā*, and to develop compassion, *karuṇā*. Authentic compassion is not "altruism," which is an attitude that remains within dualistic thinking. The Bodhisattva is one who, having cultivated within the aspiration for the "awakening" (*bodhi*) of awareness, and having practiced the methods for a comprehensive regeneration of his or her own being (*sattva*) is thus able to care for and help others who are suffering.

It is important to remember that the principal schools of Indian sub-continent thought had furnished all sorts of solutions—monist, dualistic, realistic, idealistic, empiricist, and materialist—to the question that engaged Gautama. His thesis about emptiness (*śūnyatā*) as the undivided ground giving birth to material phenomena and mental processes could not fail to provoke a scandal in the orthodox circles of the time. His was a radical assertion, that the self (*ātman*), deemed to be at the core of psychic totality, is empty of inherent substance (*anātman*).

On Buddha's death, the First Council of the Elders was held at Rajagriha in 486 BCE. The corpus of the doctrine was developed in three main schools: the *hīnayāna* or "minor vehicle," which took root in south India, Sri Lanka, Burma, and Thailand; the *mahāyāna* or "greater vehicle;" and the *vajrayāna*, which ramified into ten doctrinary branches in Tibet, Mongolia, Korea, China, and Japan. From the first centuries of the Christian era, there was a diaspora of erudite monks from India that gave rise to a wave of formidable creativity and merged with local philosophies. Such was the case of the tantric schools in Tibet and of Taoism and Confucianism in China. There were a number of great works of logic and of thinkers including Nāgārjuna (100–200 AD), Harivarman (250–350 AD), Asaṅga (410–500 AD), Vasubandhu (420–500 AD), and Kumārajīva (476–529AD). Their works were translated into Chinese and commented on by a constant stream of thinkers and meditators. As the teachings evolved in the Ch'an

(China) and Zen (Japan) schools, theories of emptiness, non-self, and the ultimate coincidence of *saṁsāra* and *nirvāṇa*, gradually lost their heavy dialectical tones that were characteristic of the Indian ways of thinking.[2] They were translated into Chinese and commented on by a continuous stream of thinkers and meditators.

In China, the Buddhist theory of emptiness integrated with Taoist theory of the original wind, also referred to as the cosmic breath, *qi*. The primary aim of both Ch'an and Zen is in fact to overcome the barriers of the discriminating mind once all the resources of discursive thought have been exhausted. In meditative training, paradoxical sentences (*kōan*) are used as a means of breaking down dualistic consciousness, which is always consciousness "of" something or someone. The energy shaping consciousness expands in meditation to comprehend the inherent emptiness of the subtle elements (*dharmas*), of which the whole world of both matter and mind consists.

The ten major schools of far-Eastern thought, which are examined by Junijiro Takakusu in *The Essentials of Buddhist Philosophy*, elaborate on markedly different theories on the connections between the dynamics of the natural world and that of the human psyche and mind.[3] Traditionally five sense organs are named: sight, hearing, smell, taste, and touch; however, the Buddhists include a sixth one, mind (*manas*), which acts as the coordinator of sensory activities. Each sense organ has its own sphere of consciousness. Mental consciousness (*ālaya-vijñāna*) functions as a seedbed of all mnestic, ideational, and imaginative processes.[4] In this respect, the seedbed consciousness is reminiscent of the Jungian notion of psychic totality. However the difference between the two lies in Buddhism's radical negation of a Selfhood, both in relation to the individual "person" and to the sphere of organic or inorganic (*sarva dharmas*) physical processes. The Buddhist universe is not anthropocentric. It is a multi-faceted wholeness that the discriminating mind (*vijñāna*) is able to grasp by removing the belief in the substantiality of things and by developing non-dual consciousness (*prajñā*), which constitutes the goal of a self-creating life. One can search at will in Buddhist doctrines without finding a positive idea that affirms the existence of a Self. Any formulation in this regard is irremediably negative, as in the original thesis of the Buddha's *anattā*, non-Self.[5]

Then, if one considers the importance that the anthropological
category of *otherness* has had in the weaving of relations with Asian
cultures, one easily understands the West's resistance to accept
perspectives such as Buddhist selflessness and the non-duality of
matter and mind.[6] Nevertheless, this has not precluded an
encounter between the West and the East. On the contrary, since
the end of the eighteenth century, as the first Indian texts gained
entry to the libraries of Europe and when Leibniz and Schopenhauer
raised the alarm that the non-European world might reason in a
manner quite different, the "dialogue" with Asian thought has
consolidated itself. One of the major actors in the encounter with
Asian and indigenous *otherness* was the protagonist of that
unrepeatable season of European culture from which emerged the
intellectual constellation of Eranos: C. G. Jung. Although not a
specialist in Jungian studies, I have ventured into areas of his vast
opus that touch on Asian thought. For the most part, I have focused
on his writings collected in *Psychology and Religion: West and East*.[7]
There have been a number of authoritative analyses conducted, such
as the work of John J. Clarke, published in the 1990s, and the
extensive comparative study by Harry Oldmeadow on the different
approaches to the Orient taken by Jung and Mircea Eliade.[8,9] Eliade
was a personal friend of Jung's who, until 1962, frequently delivered
talks at the Eranos Conferences.[10]

Clarke was well aware of the unease that Jung confessed to feeling
toward non-European philosophy. This unease was existential rather
than cultural or scientific, and it surfaced every time he travelled
in such places as India, Sri Lanka, Kenya, and New Mexico in the
American Southwest where he met with the Pueblo Indians.[11] Jung
even had this uneasy sense when dialoguing at Eranos with
European historians of religion such as Walter Friedrich Otto, even
Eliade himself, and illustrious exponents of Buddhist thought such
as Daisetsu Teitaro Suzuki. Jung confessed to feeling a risk in the
radical questioning of his western sense of identity. He asserted that
if we wish to understand the "other," and in particular the
psychology of the "other," such exploration can only take place in a
European framework. He was not aware or, as Clarke believes, he
did not want to take into consideration that European ways of
thinking and feeling are as insular as those that are rooted in Asia.

There is no primacy of any kind to which the western mind can ascribe to itself that would subordinate the Eastern intellect to that of the West.[12]

Oldmeadow underscores that despite Jung's sympathetic enquiries into Eastern spirituality, and despite the importance of his excursions into extra-European cultures, he remained anchored in the West. Further, his "turning his back on India" was a self-defensive reflex.[13] And when he approached certain texts of Asian wisdom, he examined them from the perspective of his own theoretical constructs.[14] Jung refused to imagine a "conscious mental state that does not relate to a subject or ego," or to admit the possibility that a higher, selfless form of consciousness could be attained not via hypnotic regression, but through lucid, relentless mental training aimed at transcending the subject-object duality.[15,16] Jung variously toggled between attraction and aversion towards spiritual experiences, which he deemed confined to a pre-rational stage of the mind. In his commentary to the *Secret of the Golden Flower*, Jung writes, ironically, that there are "secret insights of Eastern wise men … which it is well to stay well clear of, for it would be a case of the 'right means in the hands of the wrong man.'"[17]

These are only some fleeting observations on the "shadow" side of Jung's receptivity to the Eastern thought and philosophy and not intended as a formal criticism which would require an in-depth analysis of both sides of the issue. My point is to share some reflections on the change in the "spirit of the times" (*Zeitgeist*) that have occurred between the end of the twentieth and the start of the twenty-first century.

From Mythopoiesis to Autopoiesis

During the 1930s, thanks to Olga Fröbe-Kapteyn (1881–1962), true *deus ex machina* of the Eranos Conferences, the charismatic figure of Jung attracted to Ascona some of the most brilliant minds— psychologists, philosophers, historians of ideas, and specialists in the fields of gnosis, religious art, and symbolism.[18,19] Eranos hosted a period of creative gestation primarily in the humanistic fields that had their counterparts in that of theoretical physics. The emerging theories of general relativity and quantum mechanics were shaking the very foundations of the standard, prevailing cosmological model. In so doing, this perceptual and conceptual shift gave rise to a complete revision of human knowledge of the physical world and of the laws of nature from micro to macro scales. The great conquests of physics of the twentieth century were the discovery of relativity, dark matter, and the radical redefinition of the void from a state free of matter to a field teeming with infinite electrons of negative energy. These discoveries irreversibly changed the attitude of scientific scholarship to the relationship between mind and nature. In particular, when researchers realized that the observer could not be kept apart from the observed, they were forced to "think" beyond substance to process. Natural phenomena were not an assemblage of pieces, but a seamless expression of the interconnection of "inner" and "outer," what the physicist David Bohm has defined as the *unbroken wholeness* of universal reality.[20] The ineluctable consequence of these discoveries has been the relinquishment of an anthropocentric point of view, which, nonetheless, still has tenaciously remained prevalent, albeit understandably so, in the domains of philosophy, psychology, and the human sciences.

Jung's analytical psychology had the enormous merit of unearthing the *cathédrale engloutie* of the unconscious and recognizing the dynamics of the psyche as an uninterrupted process of unfoldment and enfoldment of the conscious and the unconscious, emotions and reason, I and Self. Furthermore, his fertile intellectual association with the physicist, Wolfgang Pauli (1900–1958), directed Jung's exploration to certain subtle areas that were intermediate between consciousness and the unconscious, in which "the horizon of thinkability is amplified, producing new configurations of meaning."[21] However, this grand *mythopoiesis*, has, in my view, remained constrained to a substantialist and anthropocentric model of the relationship between matter and psyche that characterized the special significance of Eranos in the humanistic culture of the time. In *Eranos—An Alternative Intellectual History of the Twentieth Century*, Hans Thomas Hakl emphasizes the courageously alternative approach taken at Eranos conferences that were conducted with a felicitous blend of "orthodox" humanistic erudition, incursions into Asian and indigenous otherness, and esoteric disciplines in which Jung himself was an expert.[22] However, the time was not ripe then, as it is today with the cognitive horizons of the new Eranos leadership, to realize a project in which humanism, science, and spirituality acknowledge each other as allies in fostering the formulation of a unitary systemic conception based on a planetary philosophy of culture.[23]

In his most recent work, *The Systems View of Life—A Unifying Vision*, co-authored with the Italian bio-chemist, Pier Luigi Luisi, Fritjof Capra makes the point that the Santiago Theory of Cognition, formulated by Humberto Maturana and Francisco Varela in the 1970s, ten years after the death of Jung, was the first systematic attempt to supplant the Cartesian division of mind and matter.[24,25] In the same years, Gregory Bateson was making the case that all living beings share a common pattern of organization. The core concept of the Santiago theory and that of Bateson's is that the identification of the process of knowing is identical with the process of life. Cognition, according to Maturana and Varela, is not a representation of an independently existing world, but rather a continual bringing forth of a world through the process of living. It is a process of *autopoiesis*. Two major implications of the shift from *mythopoiesis* in Jungian terms to *autopoiesis* in cognitive terms are: 1) a notion of "Self" as a transient, non-localizable pattern without a center, and 2) an expanded notion of spiritual awareness that obviates the need for any religious creed. It may grow as a spontaneous *autopoietic* process inside the heart of anyone.[26]

In his pioneering work, *The Tao of Physics* (1975), Capra insightfully pointed out that the approaches taken by physicists and mystics share important characteristics:

> The mystic looks within and explores his consciousness at various levels, including the physical phenomena associated with mind's embodiment. The physicist, by contrast, begins his inquiry into the essential nature of things by studying the material world. Exploring ever deeper realms of matter, he becomes aware of the essential unity of all natural phenomena. More than that, he also realizes that he himself and his consciousness are an integral part of this unity. Thus the mystic and the physicist arrive at the same conclusion: one starting from the inner realm, and the other from the outer world.[27]

In *The Systems View of Life*, Capra and Luisi delineate a new "middle way," which is fully integrated into the scenarios of the present age. It is a way of reconciling the physical and mental sciences with ancient spiritual disciplines of Asia, but set in the framework of a vast interdisciplinary network of projects; woven not solely with biology, not just earth science, but also ecology, urban planning, green architecture, education, sociology, economics, and nutrition. At a deep level, the turning point lies in an overall change of metaphor and attitude—from machine to network, from cynical exploitation to solidarity, from arid, abstract, and arrogant philosophizing to the incorporation of thought into "philosophical practices" that are committed to fostering shared inner growth and the realization of humanity's "vocation."[28,29] This entails perceiving the *totally human* beauty of having a heart. It is a responsible, ethical way, if not an enlightened one, to contribute to the budding of wisdom and compassion in the tree of life.

NOTES

1. Richard Gombrich, *What the Buddha Taught* (Oxford: Equinox Publishing, 2009). Sir Richard Gombrich, son of the art historian, Ernst Gombrich, is one of the leading experts on Theravāda Buddhism, the major works of which he has translated and commented upon in an anthropological key.

2. Among the still unsurpassed major studies on the Mādhyamika philosophy and its spread in Far-Eastern Asia, mention is to be given to: Daisetsu Teitarō Suzuki, *Outlines of Mahayana Buddhism* (New York, NY: Schocken, 1963); Edward Conze, ed., *Buddhist Texts through the Ages* (New York, NY: Harper & Row, 1964); Richard H. Robinson, *Early Madhyamika in India and China* (Delhi: Motilal Banarsidass, 1965); Herbert V. Guenther, *Buddhist Philosophy in Theory and Practice* (Berkeley, CA: Shambhala, 1971); K. Venkata Ramanan, *Nagarjuna's Philosophy* (Delhi: Motilal Banarsidass, 1975); Gadjin M. Nagao, *Madhyamika and Yogacara: A Study of Mahayana Philosophies*, trans. S. Kawamura (New York, NY: State University of New York Press, 1991). A precious edition of Chandrakirti's *Sevenfold Reasonings on the Selflesseness of Persons* is edited by John Wilson (Dharamsala: Library of Tibetan Works & Archives, 1980).

3. Junijiro Takakusu, *The Essentials of Buddhist Philosophy*, eds. W.-T. Chan and C. A. Moore (Honolulu: University of Hawaii Press, 1947). This book collects the materials of a series of memorable lectures given by Prof. Takakusu at the University of Hawaii in 1938–1939.

4. Takakusu, *The Essentials of Buddhist Philosophy*, pp. 92–95.

5. *Anattā* (Skt. *Anātman*) is the original term in the Pāli language, which was spoken in the area of North-Western India where Gautama had his homeland.

6. The question of engaging with the "other" in the context of the East-West dialogue was discussed by Richard Bernstein in his paper, "Incommensurability and Otherness—Revisited," presented at the Sixth East-West Philosophers' Conference at the University of Hawaii in 1989. In relation to C. G. Jung, the topic is extensively covered in Part II (Dialogue) of John J. Clarke, *Jung and Eastern Thought—A Dialogue with the Orient* (London-New York, NY: Routledge, 1994), pp. 57–119.

7. See *The Collected Works of C. G. Jung*, vol. 11, ed. and trans. Gerhard Adler and R. F. C. Hull (Princeton, NJ: Princeton University Press, 1969), and specifically: "Psychology Commentary on *The Tibetan Book of the Great Liberation*" (1954), §§ 759–87; C. G. Jung, "Psychological Commentary on *The Tibetan Book of the Dead*" (1935/1953), §§ 831–58; "Yoga and the West" (1936), §§ 859–76; "Foreword to D. T. Suzuki, 'Introduction to Zen Buddhism'" (1939), §§ 877–907; "The Psychology of Eastern Meditation" (1943), §§ 908–49; and "The Holy Men of India" (1944), §§ 950–63.

8. John J. Clarke, *In Search of Jung* (London-New York, NY: Routledge, 1992); Clarke, *Jung and Eastern Thought*. In chapter 4 of *Jung and Eastern Thought*, titled "Jung's Dialogue with the East," ample evidence is given of Jung's extensive readings on Vedic, Buddhist, and Taoist ideas by the time he came to write his two early major works, *Symbols of Transformations* (1912/1952), vol. 5, *The Collected Works of C. G. Jung*, ed. and trans. Gerhard Adler and R. F. C. Hull (Princeton: Princeton University Press, 1967), and *Psychological Types* (1921), vol. 6, *The Collected Works of C. G. Jung*, ed. and trans. Gerhard Adler and R. F. C. Hull (Princeton: Princeton University Press, 1976). Authors covering the subject of Jung's Eastern interests are listed in Note 1 to the Introduction (p. 193). Clarke's *Oriental Enlightenment—The Encounter Between Asian and Western Thought* (London-New York, NY: Routledge, 1997) explores the role of "orientalism" within the broad sweep of the modern Western intellectual tradition, and demonstrates in detail how Eastern ideas have woven their way through debates in such fields as philosophy, religion, and psychology.

9. Harry Oldmeadow, *Mediations—Essays on Religious Pluralism & the Perennial Philosophy* (San Rafael, CA: Sophia Perennis, 2008), pp. 64–93.

10. Eliade was first invited to the annual Eranos Conferences in 1950 and attended annually until 1962, the year of Olga Fröbe-Kapteyn's death. In 1950, Eliade conducted a lengthy interview with Jung for the Parisian magazine, *Combat*, at a time when Jung's recently published *Answer to Job* was provoking a storm of controversy. An edited version of this interview can be found in *C. G. Jung Speaking: Interviews and Encounters*, ed. W. McGuire and R. F. C. Hull (London: Thames & Hudson, 1978), pp. 225–34. The last occasion Eliade and Jung met was in Küsnacht in 1959, when they had a lengthy conversation in the garden, primarily about the nature of mystical experience.

11. In his *Memories, Dreams, Reflections* (London: Fontana, 1983), Jung gives a vivid account of his encounter with the Taos Pueblo Indians (p. 280) and of his visit to the Athi Plains near Nairobi (p. 284). On his travels in the Indian sub-continent and Sri Lanka in 1938 and 1939, see Sulagna Sengupta, *Jung in India* (New Orleans, LA: Spring Journal, Inc., 2013).

12. Clark, *Jung and Eastern Thought*, p. 163.

13. Oldmeadow, *Mediations*, p. 70.

14. The most notable case concerns the translation from the Chinese of the *T'ai-I Chin-hua Tsung-chih*, an esoteric Taoist text first published in China in the eighteenth century. The German translation by Richard Wilhelm received an extensive commentary by Jung, also found in the English translation (from the German) by Cary F. Baynes: *The Secret of the Golden Flower: A Chinese Book of Life. Translated and Explained by Richard Wilhelm, with a Foreword and Commentary by C. G. Jung* (London: Routledge & Kegan Paul, 1931). The Chinese text has been translated anew into English by Thomas Cleary: *The Secret of the Golden Flower, with Introduction, Notes, and Commentary* (New York, NY: HarperCollins, 1991). In the section "Questions and Answers" and Notes (pp. 73–153), Cleary remarks individually on each passage in which Wilhelm misunderstood the original text as well as commenting on his numerous omissions. In the Introduction, Cleary says: "Although Jung credited *The Secret of the Golden Flower* with having clarified his own work on the unconscious, he maintained serious reservations about the practice taught in the book.

What he did not know was that the text he was reading was in fact a garbled translation of a truncated version of a corrupted recension of the original work" (p. 3).

15. Clarke, *Jung and Eastern Thought*, p. 170.

16. *Ibid.*, p. 174.

17. *The Secret of the Golden Flower: A Chinese Book of Life*, translated and explained by Richard Wilhelm, with a Foreword and Commentary by C. G. Jung, English translation by Cary F. Baynes (London: Routledge & Kegan Paul, 1931), p. 113.

18. The original Eranos spirit is vividly conjured up by Olga Fröbe-Kapteyn with these words: "The Eranos Conferences have set themselves the goal of mediating between East and West. The task of this mediation, and the need to create a place for the promotion of such an understanding of the spiritual realm, have become even clearer... It is not the emulation of Eastern methods and teachings that is important, nor the neglecting or replacing of Western knowledge about these things, but the fact that eastern wisdom, symbolism, and methods can help us to rediscover the spiritual values that are most distinctively our own" (Clarke, *Jung and Eastern Thought*, p. 561).

19. Historical and critical reports on the indelible mark left by Jung on the circle of participants in the Eranos gatherings and contributors to the *Eranos Yearbooks* form an extensive literature supported by accurate chronologies and bibliographies in many languages. The most relevant ones are: Riccardo Bernardini, *Jung a Eranos. Il progetto della psicologia complessa* (Milan: FrancoAngeli, 2011); Sonu Shamdasani, "The 'Red Book' of C.G. Jung," in C. G. Jung, *The Red Book: Liber Novus* (New York, NY: W. W. Norton Company, 2009), pp. 193–221; and the vivid portrait by Hans Thomas Hakl, *Eranos— An Alternative Intellectual History of the Twentieth Century* (Montreal/ Kingston: McGill-Queen's University Press, 2013). See also Bernardo Nante's Introduction to his Guide to *El lLibro rojo de C.G. Jung. Claves por la comprension de una obra inexplicable* (Buenos Aires: El hilo de Ariadna/MALBA-Fundación Costantini, 2010).

20. The concept of "unbroken wholeness" is the keystone of the cosmological theory that the physicist and philosopher, David Bohm (1917–1992), formulated in a series of books and articles of capital importance for the history of science of the late twentieth century; see in particular: David Bohm, *Wholeness and the Implicate Order* (London-

New York, NY: Routledge, 1980), thoroughly analyzed and commented on by the Finnish physicist, Paavo Pylkkänen, in *Mind, Matter and the Implicate Order* (Berlin-Heidelberg: Springer, 2007); David Bohm, *The Undivided Universe: An Ontological Interpretation of Quantum Theory* (London-New York, NY: Routledge, 1993); and David Bohm, *Science, Order, and Creativity*, co-authored and edited by F. David Peat (London-New York, NY: Routledge, 2000).

21. The fecund intellectual dialogue between Jung and the physicist Wolfgang Pauli from the early Thirties is accurately examined by the psychiatrist, Angelo Malinconico, and the philosopher of science, Silvano Tagliagambe, in their huge scholarly work: *Pauli e Jung. Un confronto tra materia e psiche* (*Pauli and Jung. A Confrontation between Matter and Psyche*) (Milan: Raffaello Cortina, 2011). The authors shed special light on Jung's insightful explorations of the "intermediate world," the psychic borderland between consciousness and the unconscious realm, which the transcendental function operates on, thereby acting as an "energy mediator" [*ibid.*, p. 161.]). For the rich correspondence between Pauli and Jung that reveals their influence on each other, see Carl Gustav Jung and Wolfgang Pauli, *Atom and Archetype—The Pauli/Jung Letters 1932–1958*, ed. C. A. Meier (Princeton, NJ: Princeton University Press, 2001).

22. Those who treasure Jung's heritage cannot but be most grateful to the Austrian polymath, expert in esoteric studies, and editor of the journal *Gnostika*, Hans Thomas Hakl, for the tremendous undertaking of having made in *Eranos—An Alternative Intellectual History of the Twentieth Century*, a most accurate picture of the peculiar significance of Eranos seen in its multiple facets: as a niche for strengthening the import of Western cultural and spiritual traditions; as an elected place over a period of seventy years for hundreds of the most distinguished scholars from West to East gathered at Villa Gabriella, Moscia, offering their insights in the fields of religion, philosophy, history, art, and science, also and mostly in relation to Jung. Eranos embodied his daring plan "to build up a systematic, *maṇḍala*-like theory of the human soul pivoted on the principles of analytic psychology and its theoretical and empirical investigations" (Bernardini, *Jung a Eranos*, p. 25).

23. Hakl's "Grand Tour of Planet Eranos" at the time of Jung and Olga Fröbe-Kapteyn ends with the emblematic phrase that gives the

title to Chapter 17: "The end of a cycle ... or perhaps not." All those who are aware of the new direction of the Foundation, taken in 2010 under the presidency of the philosopher, Fabio Merlini, and the scientific secretariate of the analytical psychologist, Riccardo Bernardini, assisted by a Board of five authoritative members, are aware that a *renovatio* of Eranos is taking shape. It is a *renovatio* that is fully discernible in the impetus with which Eranos, also through partnerships with research institutes outside Europe, is pursuing cultural and educational policies of excellence in the Canton of Ticino. It is also happening subtly in the minds and hearts of the leaders of the Foundation, alerting them to the fact that the best way to engage in "spaces without thresholds" in a time "beyond masters" (which seems to characterize contemporary society) is to offer the benefit of cultural and human growth not only to an intellectual elite but to all the citizens of the world. The spirit of *renovatio* underway in the new Eranos is amply documented in two recent publications: *Eranos Yearbook* 70 (2009–2010–2011) and *Eranos Yearbook* 71 (2012).

24. In *The Systems of Life—A Unifying Vision* (Cambridge: Cambridge University Press, 2014), Fritjof Capra and Pier Luigi Luisi expound the new cognitive perspectives consequent on the emergence of systems thinking. In Part III, "A New Conception of Life," three major topics are extensively treated in chapters 12, 13, and 14: "Mind and Consciousness," "Science and Spirituality," and "Life, Mind, and Society." It's worth mentioning a passage from chapter 13 where the authors remark: "Spirituality is a much broader and more basic human experience than religion. It has two dimensions: one going inward, or 'upward,' as it were; and the other going outward, embracing the world and our fellow human beings. Either of the two manifestations of spirituality may or may not be accompanied by religion ... and we may talk about 'lay spirituality,' a form of being spiritual without the need of being associated with a particular religion... On the other hand spirituality in this broad sense need not be in conflict with science. Indeed it is fully consistent with the systems view of life" (*ibid.*, p. 276). The growing alliance between science and Buddhist spirituality is also broadly evidenced by the scientist and expert in Buddhist meditation, Alan B. Wallace, in *Choosing Reality—A Buddhist View of Physics and the Mind* (New York, NY: Snow Lion, 1996), *Hidden Dimensions: The Unification of Physics and Consciousness* (New York, NY: Columbia

University Press, 2007), and *Embracing Mind—A Common Ground of Science and Spirituality*, co-authored by Brian Hodel (Boston, MA/ London: Shambhala, 2008).

25. See Humberto Maturana and Francisco Varela, *Autopoiesis and Cognition* [original title: *De maquinas y seres vivos*] (Dordrecht: D. Reidel, 1980); and Humberto Maturana and Francisco Varela, *Tree of Knowledge*, rev. ed. (Boston, MA: Shambhala, 1998).

26. Capra and Luisi, *Systems View*, p. 181.

27. Fritjof Capra, *The Tao of Physics—An exploration of the Parallels Between Modern Physics and Eastern Mysticism* (New York, NY: Bantam, 1975), p. 23.

28. "Philo," a Superior School of Philosophical Practices founded by the philosopher and Jungian analyst, Romano Màdera, of the University of Milan-Bicocca, is part of a network of successful educational projects aimed at retrieving the original maieutic spirit of philosophical enquiry to plunge it into the tissue of practical life and biographical analysis. *Approaching the Navel of the Darkened Soul: Depth Psychology and Philosophical Practices* (Milan: IPOC 2013) is one of Màdera's recent works illustrating his methodology, at the crossroad with analytic psychology.

29. "Vocación Humana" (Human Vocation) is the name given by the Argentinian philosopher and Jungian scholar, Bernardo Nante, Professor of Philosophy of Religion and Mythology at the Universidad del Salvador in Buenos Aires, to a flourishing Foundation established by him in the Argentinian capital. Seminars, courses, and public lectures lead participants to vocational training in fields such as traditional thought, East-West studies, yoga in theory and practice, Jungian psychology, symbology, and the phenomenology of the sacred.

V.

ERANOS AND THE UNITY OF PSYCHE AND MATTER

A dedication written by the biologist, Adolf Portmann, on the occasion of the 25th anniversary of the Eranos Conferences, in 1957, which reads: "In reverence to take the mystery of the spirit, to bring it intelligently to the speakable language, to know the unspeakable present—in this spirit lies the work of Eranos."

ADOLF   RUDOLF
PORTMANN   RITSEMA

The Swiss biologist and zoologist, Adolf Portmann (1897–1982), served as a Member of the Board of the first Eranos Foundation, created by Olga Fröbe-Kapteyn in 1943 and active until 1955, together with Tadeus Reichstein, Hans Conrad Bänziger, and Walter Keller-Staub. When the Eranos Foundation was reestablished in August 1961, Adolf Portmann was nominated its first President, as stipulated by Olga Fröbe-Kapteyn's will. At Olga Fröbe-Kapteyn's death (1962), the guidance of Eranos was thus passed on to Portmann, who was assisted by Rudolf Ritsema. Portmann edited twenty *Eranos Yearbooks* (1962–1981), fifteen of them with Rudolf Ritsema (1967–1981). He gave a total of thirty-three talks, from 1946 to 1977. Another of his essays appeared in a commemorative *Eranos Yearbook*, which was published in honor of Carl Gustav Jung's seventy-fifth birthday (1950). He collected some of his many Eranos essays in three books: *Das Tier als soziales Wesen* (1953), *Biologie und Geist* (1956), and *Aufbruch der Lebensforschung* (1965). He also published some articles about Eranos, such as "Eranos" (1955), "Vom Sinn und Auftrag der Eranos-Tagungen" (1961), "Eranos. Das Werk und die Aufgabe" (1963), "Vom Sinn der Eranos Tagungen," written along with Rudolf Ritsema (1978), and "Um die Erhaltung von Eranos" (undated).

The scholar of the *I Ching*, Rudolf Ritsema (1918–2006), served as the President of the Eranos Foundation from 1982 to 1994. He cooperated with Olga Fröbe-Kapteyn and Adolf Portmann in organizing the Conferences beginning in 1956. Ritsema edited twenty-seven

Eranos Yearbooks, fifteen with Adolf Portmann (1967–1981) and four with Stephen L. Karcher (1989–1996). He gave a total of four talks, from 1987 up to 1997. Among his presentations and writings about Eranos are: "Eranos: Selbstdarstellung einer Idee in der Zeit" (1961), "Vom Sinn der Eranos Tagungen," written with Adolf Portmann (1978), "The Origins and Opus of Eranos: Reflections at the 55th Conference" (1987), "Encompassing Versatility: Keystone of the Eranos Project" (1988), "Esprit et symboles. Le projet Eranos de traduction du *Yi Jing*," written with Stephen L. Karcher (1994), "Images of the Unknown: The Eranos *I Ching* Project 1989–1997," written with Shantena Augusto Sabbadini (1997), and "The Periplus of the Eranos Archetype" (2002, unpublished). Ritsema translated and edited the Eranos *I Ching* (preceded by ten articles published in *Spring: A Journal of Archetype and Culture* between 1970 and 1984), which appeared in different languages: Italian (in collaboration with Shantena Augusto Sabbadini, 1996 and 1997), German (in collaboration with Hansjakob Schneider, 2000), French (in collaboration with Pierre Gaudissart and Imelda Gaudissart, 2003), and English (in collaboration with Stephen L. Karcher, 1990–1991 and 1994, and with Shantena Augusto Sabbadini, 2005).

Adolf Portmann and Rudolf Ritsema's "Eranos and its Meaning," presented in the following pages, was translated into English by Lee B. Jennings and published in Adolf Portmann, Rudolf Ritsema, and Henry Corbin, *Eranos and its Meaning* (Ascona: Tipo Offset Bettini, 1978), pp. 1–6; a German edition appeared as "Vom Sinn der Eranos Tagungen," in Adolf Portmann, Rudolf Ritsema, and Henry Corbin, *Vom Sinn der Eranos Tagungen* (Ascona: Tipo Offset Bettini, 1978), pp. 1–6.

We thank Dr. Elisabeth von Orelli-Schütz and Dr. Shantena Augusto Sabbadini, as representatives, respectively, of Adolf Portmann and Rudolf Ritsema's heirs, for granting permission to republish their writing in this issue of *Spring: A Journal of Archetype and Culture*.

Eranos and
its Meaning

ADOLF PORTMANN
RUDOLF RITSEMA

The fame of the Eranos Conferences has grown since their founding by Olga Fröbe-Kapteyn more than four decades ago. In looking to the future and in surveying the past, we shall attempt to give some idea of the proper domain of these conferences and to establish their sphere of influence amidst the thought of our time. We shall attempt to outline some of the contemporary questions for which answers are sought in these meetings. The general topics and those of the individual lectures sometimes seem at first glance to be far removed from current issues—an impression whose erroneousness we hope to demonstrate.

Life in our time is characterized by an alarming proliferation of technology, and the belief is prevalent that the attendant changes in life-style reflect a subtle but basic change in human nature. It is therefore far from irrelevant to call attention to those human features that tend to retain their character in the midst of change. These features seem to point to a distinct sub-structure of our being that may properly be termed ahistorical. The aspect of human nature that we have sought to uncover has been called archaic, and it is sometimes referred to in psychological and religious studies as archetypal.

There is one term, which, in our opinion, should not be used in our search for the foundation of humanity—the term, "primitive," which, in the usage of some evolutionists has tended to acquire the derogatory connotation of a surpassed stage of development. This is a concept that is quite inadequate to render the compelling and essential sameness of the varieties of humankind; it stems from a way of thinking which once gave rise to the idea of an earlier, prelogical stage of human development as opposed to the present and higher logical one—a view which ethnologists have now wisely abandoned.

Since the founding of Eranos, the phenomenon of central humanness has been the focus of our contemplations. We hope that we have done our part to combat the view that "archaic" is a term applicable only to the remote origins of man that we look back upon at most with sympathy and some respect and study with mere retrospective fascination. Eranos, on the contrary, has always insisted upon the continuing presence of this original humanity. In the meetings at Ascona there have been numerous occasions to stress the vital presence of man's archaic side in all creative and form-giving pursuits. The Eranos Conferences have always been seriously concerned with the archaic side of man and the archetypal factors at work in our coping with the world about us.

When confrontations with Oriental thought and its ancient heritage have been offered, this has been done to stress the permanently human elements contained therein, and the same may be said of ethnological studies involving the world-views of ancient peoples; such as the treatments of creation myths resting on a ritual repetition of the events of a bygone age of greatness. In the light of these presentations, our present concern with the changing face of existence dwindles to a short-term phenomenon, subject to obliteration in the great rites of renewal that usher in a new epoch, a beginning of beginnings.

Despite our concern with archaic forms of experience, it would be a mistake to think that Eranos has given way to disillusionment and has renounced the concept of historical development to embrace a glorified past. The emergence of historical forces and the nature of their efficacy have, on the contrary, been one of our constant concerns. To take an example: it is precisely in the Judeo-Christian cradle of Occidental thought that we see a decisive transition from the archaic cyclical outlook to that of linear evolution; and while we naturally tend to devote more attention to the non-evolutionary world view as a possible repository of lasting values, it is fully in keeping with this concern of ours that we study also the early emergence of that second way of thinking which is now become so ubiquitous and fraught with consequences.

Eranos has never been content to play a role of a seismologist recording earth tremors that have already happened. Our conferences have always engaged in the reexamination of values during the times of greatest endangerment. For this reason, our lectures, whether in the humanities or the natural science, have increasingly focussed on fundamental human traits, on those constants of our nature, which will continue to have meaning and to be cultivated in future times.

As anthropological research penetrates ever deeper into its field of study, the greater is the importance it assigns to those elements present since the origins of man—the recurring feelings, hopes, and fears that determine human happiness and sorrow, even in our age.

Man stands before us—a creature submerged nightly in his private world of dreams, embarking ever anew at birth upon a new conquest of the experienceable world, building and rebuilding cosmic designs— a creature forever destined to correlate the colorful world of imagination with a world subject to his intellectual grasp and reckoning.

The many Eranos lectures contributing to our understanding of life-phenomena are never aimed merely at being "interesting." It has always been our goal to awaken an awareness of the riches inherent in our nature, not the least of which is our built-in equipment for cognitive experience.

The phenomenon of religion and, for that matter, the nature of the psyche appear to us to attest to a hereditary disposition toward experience-structuring that is forcefully manifested within us. Who among us, after all, may say how great a role is played by this hereditary faculty in the making of those world-structures whereby we seek to comprise the total knowledge of any given age? One of the basic purposes of the Eranos Conferences is to discover how primary mind, through its immediate experience, has sought to create cosmic designs and interpretations of existence itself.

Our work seeks to illustrate and comment upon the realm of origins—to show how the fate of the world is determined, to some small extent, in each of us by virtue of this primal vision, as manifested in the life-course of every individual. Even in our day this inner vision propels people on paths that coincide remarkably with the tracings of the distant past.

The conflicts attending the two coexistent life-modes (archaic-cyclical and historic-linear) permeate all present-day life, individual or societal, deliberate or latent. It is not a question of alternate or successive phases in the life of the individual or the history of nations.

It is a question of perpetually warring life-molding factions, whose simultaneous presence lays as great a claim to eternity as does anything within the human realm.

Of these two modes, the first was in the former times the more powerful even in the Occident; but whereas the two could once coexist in relative harmony, a wholly new situation has now come unto being. Occidental technology has prevailed over other forms of thought by virtue of its self-reinforcing power. This victory of science in the western world is a unique historical event, possible only in this particular cultural milieu with its attendant world-view. It is pointless for us to enumerate here the achievements of this mental breakthrough, which is altering the face of the earth, nor should we complain at this point about the so-called "progress," which threatens to annihilate us. In this late hour, we must rather scrutinize wisely the values competing for our favor and make our decisions accordingly.

We have based our remarks on the hypothesis of a still-potent archaic element in human nature and of a primary world-view corresponding to it. There is scarcely a process of our time through which this primal realm has been more deeply affected than the advance of science into zones where intellect may follow but the imaginative and symbolic faculties of the soul cannot keep pace. We are dealing with a trespassing of the boundaries of the world of immediate experience to enter the worlds of molecular, atomic, and subatomic scope and to those measured in terms of lightyears—the microcosm and the macrocosm.

The change in life-style wrought by science and technology upon many peoples still living in accordance with archaic patterns lends greater weight to the voice of the natural science in the Eranos proceedings. This broadening of scope, however, is not simply aimed at filling out the spectrum of knowledge. We can never content ourselves with more or less popularized offerings of the latest funding of science. Rather, we feel obligated in this time of technological imperilment to point to the nature and value of our peculiarly human world, our mediocosm, the better to know what possibly harmful effects the expansion of knowledge into microcosm and macrocosm may have upon us.

Since the first Eranos Conference of 1933, we have sought to portray the primal experience native to the geocentric cosmos as a repository of permanent values, not merely as an interesting object of all historical regard. The attempt to fully portray life in the mediocosm requires the services of the natural sciences in ways other than mere broadening of horizons. Science and technology have helped to create an inflated man-made mediocosm that increasingly perturbs our relation to the original environment. This intermediate realm has been closely bound to human condition since its emergence. All research into the origins of man has had to cope with major problems involving the transition from the natural environment to one partially created by man himself. These are basic problems of anthropogenesis that cannot be solved solely by the examination of the fossil remains of early man. This early self-molded milieu of man survives into our day in the form of religious experience, artistic creativity, and dreams.

The Eranos Conferences aim at enhancing life in the mediocosm. We seek out the archaic heritage not merely because it represents something irrational or counter-rational that we might favor as a matter of principle, but because the harmony of rational and irrational elements is shown here in especially pure and rich form. It is here that the creative forces attest most fully to the primacy of the spirit and thus give evidence of salutary powers that we are in danger of losing, which have indeed already been lost to an alarming degree in the daily lives and general cognizance of many members of our Occidental civilization.

It is with all this in mind that the work of Eranos seeks to complement the variegated history of culture and ideas with the equally abundant findings of biological research. Our purpose is to direct the gaze to those wellsprings from which we are privileged to partake of the true water of life. We shall have failed to grasp the spirit of our time if we heed only the proliferation of research institutes and the frantic search for new scientific findings of immediate practical application.

Our time is also one in which the work of isolated individuals pursues lines of research that stand apart from contemporary trends. It is clear, however, to those who look beneath the surface that much of this seemingly arcane work represents a necessary compliment to the more modern-seeming pathways of the mind. Eranos favors the kind of thought that embraces both "timely" and "untimely" issues. We live, after all, in a secondary mode of existence, and many of us are coming to realize that a life of this kind represents little more than misery.

The Eranos Conferences may perhaps be said to stand for a type of productivity devoid of public acclaim. They often embody the work of individuals who—quietly tilling their own soil—take courage in the idea that others of similar persuasion are doing likewise. The fruits of these labors come to light and are passed on to others in the August meetings, furthered, as they are, by an attitude of open-minded receptivity on the part of speakers and audiences alike.

SIGURD VON BOLETZKY

Sigurd von Boletzky, retired member of the French National Center for Scientific Research (CNRS), is a zoologist and marine biologist, and a former student (1961–1964) and research collaborator (1965–1982) with Adolf Portmann. His work includes *Das Mittelmeer* (co-authored with Felix Karlinger, Hans Kühner, Franca Magnani, and Alfred Pletsch, 1980) and the scientific edition of Georg Pfeffer's *The Cephalopoda of the Plankton Expedition* (1993). In addition to articles on the biology, development, and evolution of cephalopod mollusks, von Boletzky published several contributions on Portmann's biography, work, and teaching in *Grosse Schweizer und Schweizerinnen* (1990), *I Protagonisti* (1995), *Revue Européenne des Sciences Sociales* (1999), and in Adolf Portmann's *Lebensforschung und Tiergestalt* (2006). At present, he is working on unpublished material from the Adolf Portmann Archives, Basel University Library. Von Boletzky is particularly interested in Portmann's scientific legacy prior to 1946. He considers Portmann's early thinking critical to understanding the research landscape of mid-20th century biology, as well as Portmann's reluctance to engage in a fashionable "mainstream biology." He believes that the questions about the mutual influences between Portmann and Eranos beginning in the late 1940s, as well as Portmann's debate with Carl Gustav Jung about the "inheritance" of psychic features, can best be approached if the situation at the outset is clearly recognized. Subsequently, specific sensitive issues, such as epistemological questions regarding Portmann's "critical finalism" and its possible significance to a modern teleonomy, are then amenable to study.

THE ENLIGHTENING ROLE
OF ADOLF PORTMANN

SIGURD VON BOLETZKY

Adolf Portmann (1897–1982) was a Swiss zoologist, biologist, and anthropologist who promoted a comprehensive view of what is known as the Life Sciences. Owing to Portmann's consistent collaboration from 1946 to the late 1970s, Eranos became increasingly engaged with the natural sciences. Portmann can be credited with much of the impetus to expand conference topics and participants from its initial emphasis on "the Arts" to include the "Sciences."[1] This shift was particularly important, because biology and natural sciences on the whole have evolved rapidly in the last century. This evolution in biological research and teaching are largely related to technological advances and complex attendant ethical problems, many of which have critical implications for human nature. Portmann was extremely sensitive to the potential misuse of genetic studies and eugenics.

During his time at Eranos, Portmann focused on basic human concerns rather than the more spectacular achievements of modern biological research. An astute and responsible scientist, he kept current with latest developments. (In fact, it was well known at his Zoology Institute that he reserved an early morning hour for reading incoming issues of journals such as *Nature* and *Science*). Portmann's lectures at Eranos took a very broad view, representing a fine example of complementarity between the Arts and Sciences and the mutual importance of these broad fields in research and intellectual discourse. Portmann's stance is reminiscent of a quote from Harnoncourt (1982): "What would Einstein have thought or discovered had he not played the violin?"[2]

As a zoologist, it is natural that Portmann's work is oriented by the perspective that humans are members of the taxonomic group that includes nonhuman apes. However, he was never one to be content with the obvious state of affairs. Instead, he reached beyond the conventional to explore the human condition in its own right. Portmann insisted on the uniqueness (*Sonderstellung*) of humans, both biologically (in particular, developmentally) and culturally. This point of view infuses his seminal study, *Biological Fragments for a Theory of Man*.[3] In this work, Portmann reviews extant data on human embryonic and post-embryonic development that include quantitative analysis of early brain growth. He then compares these patterns to behavioral characteristics and psychological peculiarities of human children and to those of other, nonhuman primates. It was here that he coined the term, "extra-uterine first-year," the period of development when humans acquire: (1) upright carriage, (2) social behavior, and (3) speech. Three decades later, Portmann still cautioned readers against any reduction of human characteristics to simplistic representations such as the proverbial "naked ape," which he regarded as merely reflective of "a fashionable craze."[4]

His publications on biological anthropology were based on his long experience researching the comparative morphology of vertebrates. This work culminated in a textbook of comparative vertebrate morphology, which was widely read for decades in many German-speaking universities.[5] Recently, the text has been re-edited and continues to be a staple with zoology and pre-medical students.[6] Interestingly, we should not forget that Portmann started out as an invertebrate zoologist in 1921 with a doctoral thesis on dragonfly biological systematics. Thereafter, he specialized in marine mollusks such as cephalopods, opisthobranch gastropods, and marine cnidarians. Who knows, had he received an appropriate job offer, Portmann might have become a marine biologist for the rest of his life!

A LECTURER POSING CRITICAL QUESTIONS

In contrast to many biologists who are reluctant to explore beyond their fields of research, Portmann deliberately ventured beyond his own. He did not ignore disciplinary boundaries, but rather, used a panoramic view to sharpen his own understanding of complex questions and to convey to his students a sense of critical assessment. The preface of his book, *New Ways in Biology*, closes with this reflection:

> The ways we are following in our survey of basic questions in biology lead us to the limits of scientific assertion. Anyone who stops at such a border also looks beyond it into a different land. I hope that this essay, whenever it invites one to cross the border, will deepen the experience that life is always more than what we can declare at a given time with our scientific means.[7]

Although his intended audience was primarily diverse, interested lay readers, Portmann knew that his books also circulated among students, even though the average biology student might bemoan such an invitation! Of course, most students were expected to learn tangible facts and skills, not just epistemic reflections. Portmann never tested zoology students on these more esoteric questions. However, those who wished to become his doctoral students knew that this kind of intellectual background was requisite. Throughout their academic training in science, students were invited to cultivate this sense of inquisitiveness.

When a doctoral student approached Portmann about a possible thesis topic, he or she first would have to prepare a discussion about potential and practical limits of the proposed research. Portmann had his own ideas and expectations, but was always respectful and open to those of his students. For instance, he accepted candidates even if they refused to kill an animal "for the advancement of science." In these cases, he would endeavor to find an appropriate thesis subject for them.

During thesis development, the working plan would be refined. Whenever possible, quantitative methods were chosen to frame the questions and to provide a solid basis for comparisons among other studies. Indeed, Portmann always insisted on the necessity of quantitative research methods. He consistently applied these methods (but not always statistics) in his own morphometric studies. At the same time, he emphasized qualitative methods that facilitate conceptual analysis of complex systems, thereby retaining the ability to view phenomena holistically. Portmann also often used models of technology as analogs of biological and physiological functions.

Students were reminded that any observed natural complexity is the result of long processes of evolutionary development and diversification. However, he explicitly refrained from theorizing about the causal factors of evolution, particularly in regard to mechanisms of genetic change and natural selection. Students profited from Portmann's lectures because they served to actively exercise intellectual facility. They became quite practiced at mentally shuttling back and forth between a comprehensive "top down" and an analytical "bottom up" view in the study of various organisms. However, in contrast to chemists and physicists, as Portmann pointed out, biologists have to remember that they are "embedded" observers, that is, their observations and interpretations are much more difficult to discretize and objectify.

A POPULAR TEACHER

It is perhaps not surprising, then, that Portmann was well-liked and popular among students. He was always eager to share his scientific knowledge with the public at large, young or old, in lectures or publications. His texts were written in an elegant but plain spoken manner that was comprehensible to anyone willing to gain new insights and truly learn. Yet Portmann was openly scornful of willful arrogance and ignorance. During lectures, he used his great artistic talent in his spontaneous blackboard drawings. He considered this way of public instruction his duty. It was, he felt, his responsibility to share knowledge to people who had little or no scientific learning.

Portmann's role as a purveyor of biology to the general public was established when he became a zoology professor at the University of Basel in 1931. Soon thereafter, he began to use the local radio station as a podium for public lectures. These broadcasts inspired some of his early books (e.g., *From My Book of Animals—Zoological Sketches*, 1942).[8] These early essays prepared the ground for what would culminate in Portmann's first encounter with Eranos. Indeed, after listening to his broadcasts, Olga Fröbe-Kapteyn realized that Portmann was a natural science teacher and thinker of the sort she wished to invite to engage with the Arts in the sense of *Geisteswissenschaften* (the history of ideas). When Portmann finally agreed to join Eranos in 1946, he was in his prime. The fact that he continued to participate in Eranos for over three decades and even took on the charge of presidency, bears witness to his deep commitment and congruence with the goals of Eranos.

It was clear to Portmann that only published texts could have the lasting effect he desired. Consequently, many of his contributions to Eranos were published in arenas with wide distribution (e.g., *Biology and Mind*, 1956 and 2000). These volumes complement other books like *Animal Form* (1948), *Animals as Social Beings* (1953), and *Does Nature Reject Humans?* (1970).[9] In later years, Portmann offered an excellent synopsis of his work in a collection of articles titled, *At the Borders of Knowing* (1974).[10] Finally, he allowed Joachim Illies to write a detailed biography: *The Secret of Living—The Life and Work of the Biologist Adolf Portmann* (1976).[11]

IN AWE OF NATURE

So, we might ask, what were the foundations of Portmann's personal philosophy of life? In recollecting his early years, he maintained that his outlook was always marked by a genuine awe of nature.[12] Portmann's subjective experience and contemplation of nature never lured him into any dogmatic stance. Instead, it kindled a genuine worship of nature that remained, in his eyes, a worldly remnant of mystery (*Geheimnisgrund*).

One of his favorite metaphors, which he employs in "Goethe's Science of Nature," is stage performance.[13] Scientists and other observers of natural phenomena are like spectators seated in front of the stage seeking to grasp sense and meaning of the play while maintaining an appreciation for its aesthetics. Meanwhile, those busy behind the stage (the stage-manager, scene-shifters, and technicians) work in a totally different context. Their job is to create props and settings used by the performers to captivate the audience. Both perspectives, one from stage front and the other backstage, are essential for the entire undertaking. Further, they are both subject to scrutiny and evaluation.

His reference to Goethe is enlightening in several respects, not the least being the reference to an inductive approach to natural phenomena and his corresponding reluctance to subscribe to the so-called hypothetico-deductive approach popularized by theorists following philosopher Karl Popper (Adolf Portmann, personal communication, 1980).[14] However, Portmann clearly recognized the limits of Goethe's view "before the scene of action," as is demonstrated in his assertion:

> Goethe's efforts about colors become an absurdity at the very instant when he tries to understand, from his position before the stage, natural processes for which only the methods of experimental natural science can provide the adequate tools.[15]

EXTERNAL APPEARANCE AND SOCIALIZATION

Portmann dedicated much of his thinking and writing to the phenomena of external appearance and socialization in higher organisms.[16] The key concepts in all his studies dealing with these phenomena were "Inwardness" (*Innerlichkeit*) and "Self-Presentation" (*Selbstdarstellung*). He made it clear that he had adopted the term, *Innerlichkeit*, from a text published by Wilhelm Roux (1915), in which the author speaks about the self-adjusting capacities of living beings.[17] However, the term, *Selbstdarstellung*, does not appear in that text. Instead, Portmann suggests that it emerged from his preoccupation with Goethe's *Metamorphosis of the Plants*.[18] Dewitte observes that before the 1950s, Portmann used the term, *Darstellungswert* ("Presentational Value"), more often than *Selbstdarstellung*.[19] Whichever the case, it is not clear where the latter came from. We find a surprisingly similar, purely poetic, expression in an essay on trees by Hermann Hesse (1919):

> *In ihren Wipfeln rauscht die Welt, ihre Wurzeln ruhen im Unendlichen; allein sie verlieren sich nicht darin, sondern erstreben mit aller Kraft ihres Lebens nur das Eine: ihr eigenes, in ihnen wohnendes Gesetz zu erfüllen, ihre eigene Gestalt auszubauen, sich selbst darzustellen.*

> [In their tops the world rustles, their roots rest in endlessness, but they don't abandon themselves to it; with the whole power of their life they strive for one thing: to fulfill their own law, to build up their own form, to present themselves.][20]

Hermann Hesse was one of Portmann's favorite writers during his postdoctoral years of travels.[21] Coincidently, Hesse spent the rest of his life in Montagnola, only twenty some kilometers southeast of Ascona.

THE MAGIC OF A PLACE

The Casa Eranos in Moscia (Ascona) and Lake Maggiore are reminiscent of northern Mediterranean coastal landscapes. This setting was particularly attractive to Portmann because they reminded him of his beloved Banyuls and Villefranche in the south of France that are characterized by a special combination of steep mountain sides dropping into a vast stretch of water. After the Second World War, however, he was not able to return there as regularly as before.

In his later years, before retirement as Professor Emeritus in 1968, Portmann engaged in many debates with the university administration concerning the selection of successors to the zoology department chair. One of the main issues revolved around the possibility of splitting the position into two chairs. Descriptions of, and commentaries on, these debates can be found in the texts of Stettler and Simon.[22] Much of the lack of support for establishing a "New Biology" at the University of Basel stemmed from Portmann's reservations. However, he was not against the formal establishment of new, innovative disciplines. Rather, he preferred to focus on helping to rescue what remained of traditional biology, which he rightly considered endangered. For this reason, and in view of the newly-created *Biozentrum*, he left the task of campaigning for new disciplines to others competent in fields such as molecular biology and developmental genetics.

During these tumultuous years of ongoing conflict, Portmann thoroughly enjoyed the annual breaks with visits to Ascona. By this time, he was in his late sixties and in frail health. Yet his work load at Eranos was considerable, and in addition to preparing his own contributions, he had demanding work before, during and after the meetings. Nonetheless, he found this effort much more satisfying than fractious university committee meetings. When contemplating the "magic" of Moscia, it is easy to overlook the hard work and effort that took place. However, we know from Portmann's own descriptions how much he loved the atmosphere of Moscia, including the pleasure of a swim in the lake before starting work!

GAINS FOR BIOLOGY

There is no need here to summarize how much Eranos profited from Portmann's contributions. Hans Thomas Hakl quotes a longstanding participant who asserted: "After Portmann came, Eranos became something different."[23] Hakl echoes this sentiment, stating: "Eranos appears to have undergone a change, moving away from a somewhat esoteric approach to philosophy and religion towards a *Weltanschauung* that was more modern and scientific, but still spiritually oriented."[24] However, it is useful to provide an overview of Portmann's role in Eranos in order to see its important contribution to the broader field of biology. The "bio-political" tensions at University of Basel of which Portmann played a part before retirement yield some insights.

In a special issue in 1997 of the University of Basel's magazine, *UNI NOVA*, published on the occasion of Portmann's 100th birthday, there is a short commentary entitled, "Reductionism and holistic thinking are not mutually exclusive, but are necessary parts of the scientific approach." The article is authored by Eduard Kellenberger, who is none other than one of the founding fathers of the *Biozentrum* in Basel and an open opponent of Portmann's views.[25] Kellenberger's more temperate attitude, which contrasts sharply with his bellicose statements of the 1960s, is a reflection of Portmann's enduring impact.[26] Another significant result of his enlightening role in modern biology can be seen in the continued republishing and translation of Portmann's books. Who is buying them? We may assume individuals who are inspired by Portmann's ideas. Likely among them are those who bring his insights and perspectives to bear in their own topics, in particular biology teachers. This succession of students and readers has created a kind of snow-ball effect over the decades that continues today.[27]

Portmann also teaches scientists a sense of humility and reminds them of the necessary balance between existing as human beings with a biological burden and having a potential for humanity.[28] In all instances, the "theoretical function" (necessary in "modern" scientific research) must be counter-balanced with an "aesthetic function" (necessary to respect human nature). This balance is requisite for any research committed to human interests.

NOTES

1. Cf. Hans Thomas Hakl, *Der verborgene Geist von Eranos. Unbekannte Begegnungen von Wissenschaft und Esoterik. Eine alternative Geistesgeschichte des 20. Jahrhunderts* (Bretten: Scientia nova-Neue Wissenschaft, 2001); Erik Hornung and Tilo Schabert, "Portmann und Eranos," *UNI NOVA—Wissenschaftsmagazin der Universität Basel* 79/80 (1997): 112–13.

2. Nikolaus Harnoncourt, *Musik als Klangrede. Wege zu einem neuen Musikverständnis* (Salzburg: Residenz, 1982). Cf. Horst Rumpf, *Was hätte Einstein gedacht, wenn er nicht Geige gespielt hätte? Gegen die Vekürzungen des etablierten Lernbegriff* (Weinheim/Munich: Juventa, 2010).

3. Adolf Portmann, *Biologische Fragmente zu einer Lehre vom Menschen* (Basel: Schwabe, 1944).

4. Adolf Portmann, *An den Grenzen des Wissens. Vom Beitrag der Biologie zu einem neuen Weltbild* (Wien/Düsseldorf: Econ, 1974).

5. Adolf Portmann, *Einführung in die vergleichende Morphologie der Wirbeltiere* (Basel: Schwabe, 1948).

6. David G. Senn, *Einführung in die Morphologie der Wirbeltiere. Begründet von Adolf Portmann* (Basel: Schwabe, 2013).

7. Adolf Portmann, *Neue Wege der Biologie* (Munich: Piper, 1960).

8. Adolf Portmann, *Aus meinem Tierbuch. Zoologische Skizzen* (Basel: Friedrich Reinhardt, 1942).

9. Adolf Portmann, *Die Tiergestalt. Studien über die Bedeutung der tierischen Erscheinung* (Basel: Friedrich Reinhardt, 1948); Adolf Portmann, *Das Tier als soziales Wesen* (Zürich: Rhein, 1953); Adolf Portmann, *Entlässt die Natur den Menschen? Gesammelte Aufsätze zur Biologie und Anthropologie* (Munich: Piper, 1970).

10. Portmann, *An den Grenzen des Wissens.*

11. Joachim Illies, *Das Geheimnis des Lebendigen. Leben und Werk des Biologen Adolf Portmann* (Munich: Kindler, 1976). (The book includes a complete list of Portmann's publications.)

12. *Ibid.*

13. Adolf Portmann, *Biologie und Geist* (Zürich: Rhein, 1956). (New edition, Göttingen: Burgdorf/Nereide, 2000).

14. *Ibid.*

15. Portmann, *Biologie und Geist*, pp. 280–81. (New ed.: p. 244.)

16. Portmann, *Das Tier als soziales Wesen.*

17. Wilhelm Roux, "Das Wesen des Lebens," in *Allgemeine Biologie* (1ˢᵗ volume of *Organische Naturwissenschaften—Die Kultur der Gegenwart*) (Leipzig/Berlin: Teubner, 1915), pp. 173–87; Portmann, *An den Grenzen des Wissens.*

18. *Ibid.*

19. Jacques Dewitte, preface to Adolf Portmann, *La Forme Animale* (Paris: La Bibliothèque, 2013).

20. Hermann Hesse, "Bäume," *Norddeutsche Allgemeine Zeitung*, March 10, 1919, rpt. in Hermann Hesse, *Wanderung* (Berlin: S. Fischer, 1920).

21. Illies, *Das Geheimnis des Lebendigen.*

22. Niklaus Stettler, *Natur erforschen. Perspektiven einer Kulturgeschichte der Biowissenschaften an Schweizer Universitäten 1945– 1975* (Zürich: Chronos, 2002); Christian Simon, *Natur-Geschichte. Das Naturhistorische Museum Basel im 19. und 20. Jahrhundert* (Basel: Christoph Merian, 2009).

23. Hans Thomas Hakl, *Eranos—An Alternative Intellectual History of the Twentieth Century,* trans. Christopher MacIntosh (Montreal/ Kingston: McGill-Queen's University Press, 2013), p. 138.

24. *Ibid.*

25. Eduard Kellenberger, "Reduktionismus und ganzheitliches Denken schliessen sich nicht aus, sondern sind notwendige Teile des wissenschaftlichen Vorgehens," *UNI NOVA—Wissenschaftsmagazin der Universität Basel* 79/80 (1997): 91.

26. Simon, *Natur-Geschichte.*

27. Roger Alfred Stamm and Pio Fioroni, "Adolf Portmann, ein Rückblick auf seine Forschungen," *Verhandlungen der Naturforschenden Gesellschaft Basel* 94 (1984): 88–120. (With a complete bibliography and list of Ph.D. dissertations published by students of Portmann.)

28. Portmann, *Biologie und Geist.*

SHANTENA AUGUSTO SABBADINI

S hantena Augusto Sabbadini, born 1943 in Como, Italy, is a physicist, philosopher, teacher, and translator. He worked as a quantum physicist at the University of Milano and, while at the University of California, contributed to the first discovery of a black hole. He is Associate Director of the Pari Center for New Learning (Pari, Tuscany) and Lecturer at the Schumacher College, Devon, United Kingdom. He has interests in issues of mind, matter, and consciousness, and has translated into Italian several Oriental classics such as the *I Ching* (1996 and 2005), the *Upanishad* (1997), and the *Dhammapada* (1995), and particularly, the works of the Taoist masters, such as the *Tao Te Ching* (2009), the *Chuang Tzu* (2012), and the *Lieh Tzu* (2014). He also translated into Italian works by Marie-Louise von Franz (*Le tracce del futuro. Divinazione e tempo*, 1986), Joseph Campbell (*Le figure del mito*, 1991), Elémire Zolla (*Incontro con l'androgino*, 1995), David Bohm (*Universo, Mente, Materia*, 1996), Rabindranath Tagore (*Gitanjali*, 2006), and others. Among his own books are *Tao. I racconti della Via* (1996), *Buchi neri. L'oscura energia del cosmo* (2003), and *Tao Te Ching: A Guide to the Interpretation of the Foundational Book of Taoism* (2013). From 1994 to 2002, he was associated with the Eranos Foundation as a scientific advisor and collaborated with Rudolf Ritsema and Christa Robinson in facilitating the *Eranos Round Table Sessions*. He regularly gave "Introductions to the *I Ching*" and occasionally lectured on topics such as "Dreams and Divination," "In and Out of Time," and others. He coauthored with Rudolf Ritsema two *I Ching* translations: *I Ching. Il libro della versatilità* (1996) and *The Original I Ching Oracle* (2005).

Eranos, Synchronicity, and the *I Ching*: A Personal Journey

SHANTENA AUGUSTO SABBADINI

Eranos Magic

Are places fated to leave a deep imprint on our lives, sending us a message when we first encounter them? I have felt this about the significant places in my life. Such has certainly been the case with Eranos.

What precisely was the signal I received in May 1991 when I first inhaled the fragrance of the Eranos gardens, when I first walked on the squeaky wooden floors of Casa Gabriella, and when I first browsed through those library shelves full of treasures? I wish I could remember all the details of those first moments. But I remember clearly the message that came with them, "You have stepped into a magic circle and you are caught." I am sure that Eranos has had a similar impact on many people on first contact. Its magic was, and, in some sense still is, tangible and palpable.

I would not know how better to describe this magic than as a conjunction of opposites; a place of intellectual excellence and of relaxed conviviality, a place where some of the most stimulating discussions would take place late at night in the kitchen with a bottle of wine. A place nourishing not just to the mind, but to the senses, with natural beauty and human care surrounding the guests.

The physical surroundings are a remarkable interplay of *yin* and *yang*. In the Eranos gardens, the steep wooded mountain in back of the houses plunges straight into the deep Lake Maggiore. Big trees are reflected in the green water of the lake, so that swimming along the shore you are enveloped by a liquid greenness. The coolness of the lake and the shade of the trees temper the strong midday summer sun. In the afternoon, the heat is countered by the *inverna*, a cool southern breeze that ripples the lake. In the winter, the mountains on the other side of the lake are crowned with a shining ribbon of snow. But at Eranos itself, the sun is often warm enough to sit outside, and even, for the most daring (among them, C. G. Jung), to take a quick dip in the chilly waters.

Just as it enjoys a natural balance of *yin* and *yang,* Eranos stands at a crucial junction of north and south. Ascona is only an hour's drive away from the Gotthard, the main north-south pass on the route that connects Germany with Italy. For northern travelers journeying down that route, it is the first taste of the Mediterranean. As soon as one reaches Lake Maggiore, it is immediately apparent that one is in a different climate, with palm trees thriving alongside pine trees. The lake offers a first taste of the luminous softness of Italy.

Ascona's location at this north-south threshold has made it a significant crossroads of existential, social, artistic, and spiritual experimentation in the first decades of the twentieth century. In 1873, the Russian anarchist, Mikhail Bakunin, had already sojourned for a few months in nearby Minusio. In 1900, the influx of northern immigrants settling in the area started the proto-hippy experiment of Monte Verità, the "mountain of truth." This movement lasted almost half a century. In 1919–1920, Olga Fröbe-Kapteyn, future founder of Eranos, visited the Monte Verità colony together with her father.[1] It is possible that her visit then planted a seed of her own great transformational experiment, which began ten years later only a few hundred meters away.

ARRIVING AT ERANOS

When I first arrived at Eranos in 1991, I had been rather lost for a few years. In California in the early 1970's, I had participated in the great collective dream of creating a brave new world. At the same time, I had also earned my Ph.D. in theoretical physics by contributing to the first identification of a black hole. Afterwards, back in Italy in the late 1970's and early 1980's, I had lived my pioneer dream by setting up a farming and meditation community in Tuscany. But, in the middle 1980's, I found myself without a significant project in which to pour my energies. I was not particularly desperate, just living in a sort of limbo. I did handyman jobs for a living, and each day's achievement supported my subsistence for the next day.

Toward the end of the 1980s, I started working as a member of the editorial board and translator for Red, a publishing house in my natal city of Como, an hour away from Ascona. Both jobs paid ludicrously low amounts, but the first would put me in touch with interesting people and the second had the considerable advantage that I could take it with me wherever I went. At that time, I was frequently traveling to the East, and so the ability to work while sitting in the shade of a palm tree in Goa was a cherished privilege.

While I was somewhat familiar with Jung's work at the time, I barely knew about the existence of Eranos. So it came as a surprise when Maurizio Rosenberg, the founder and publisher of Red, dispatched me to an Eranos Round Table Session.[2] The intention was for me to meet Rudolf Ritsema, president of the Eranos Foundation, and to familiarize myself with the special translation of the *I Ching* he had recently completed. Rosenberg and Red were considering publishing Ritsema's work in Italian.

Unbeknownst to me, quite an earthquake had shaken Eranos just three years before. At the Eranos *Tagung* (Conference) of 1988, Rudolf Ritsema had announced that a phase in the work of Eranos, which had begun in 1933 with Olga Fröbe-Kapteyn and Jung, had come to an end and that, in order to fulfill the spiritual function originally envisioned by its founder, Eranos would enter a new phase. Rudolf felt that the old lecture format had become too dry and academic and had lost touch with Olga's original intention that Eranos should be a place of personal and spiritual evolution, not merely a host for intellectual debates. Rudolf announced that the new phase would place the *I Ching* at the center of Eranos' work and introduce the practice of consulting the oracle in Eranos sessions as a tool for transformation.[3]

This news fell like a bombshell among Eranos speakers. A number of them felt that Rudolf, a devout student and practitioner of the Chinese oracle for forty years, was hijacking the Eranos sessions for his own purposes and subordinating all other approaches to his own particular "toy." Most Eranos speakers refused to go along with the new format. A few even started a separate branch of Eranos under the name, "Amici di Eranos" ("Friends of Eranos").[4]

But the roots of the "1988 revolution" go much farther back in time and can be traced to the rapport that Olga Fröbe-Kapteyn and her successor, Rudolf Ritsema, had with the *I Ching*.

Olga Fröbe-Kapteyn

Olga Fröbe *née* Kapteyn was born in 1881 in London to Dutch parents. Her mother, Truus Muysken, was a feminist, an anarchist, and a friend of Prince Kropotkin. Her father, Albertus Kapteyn, was the only one from his side of the family who did not distinguish himself at school. One of his brothers became a famous astronomer and another, a mathematician. Albert was destined to become an apprentice in the village bicycle repair shop. But, he managed to convince his father to send him to the Eidgenössische Technische Hochschule (Swiss Federal Institute of Technology, ETH) in Zürich, Switzerland, and eventually became an engineer and inventor. In fact, he was the only one in the family who became wealthy. Albert patented a braking system for trains and became director of the British Westinghouse Brake & Signal Company.

Olga was a strong and independent woman. She was quite adept at sports in her youth and is said to have been among the first women to climb Mont Blanc. She was intensely interested in Eastern spirituality and in the 1920's joined the circle of remarkable people that had gathered around Count Hermann Keyserling's "School of Wisdom" in Darmstadt, Germany. The "School of Wisdom" promoted a planetary culture beyond nationalism and cultural ethnocentrism, placing equivalent value on non-western cultures and philosophies. It counted among its members C. G. Jung, the sinologist, Richard Wilhelm, Rabindranath Tagore, and Hermann Hesse.

Jung, Wilhelm—who in 1923 presented at the School of Wisdom his German translation of the *I Ching* shortly before publication (1924)—and the theologian, Rudolf Otto, were particularly influential in Olga's development. From Otto, Olga learned to view religion as a universal drive of the human soul, independent from any institutional form and centered on the sense of an invisible order underlying the apparent randomness of life events. In Jung's notion of "archetype" she found a way to articulate her spiritual intuitions in psychological language. In addition, she found in the *I Ching* a bridge connecting the transpersonal archetypal dimension with daily life.[5]

In 1920, Olga's father bought and gave to his daughter Casa Gabriella, an old house surrounded by a garden on the shore of Lake Maggiore.[6] In 1928, following a still rather undefined hunch, Olga had a meeting hall built, later known as the Sala Eranos, at the western end of the Casa Gabriella grounds. Gradually, she conceived the idea of turning her house into a center for the spiritual meeting of East and West. Initially she involved Alice Bailey and her Arcane School, and from 1930 to 1932 three Summer Schools were held in Olga's meeting hall. Among the speakers, in addition to Alice Bailey herself, was the Italian psychologist and founder of psychosynthesis, Roberto Assagioli. Although small at first, these meetings gained success, attracting a considerable number of people, particularly from the nearby colony of Monte Verità. But the collaboration between the two women was not without friction and came to an end in 1932 when, according to Alice Bailey, "Ascona got overrun by German professors … and the teaching shifted from a relatively high spiritual plane to that of academic philosophy."[7] Various motives have been attributed to the break, one obviously being the "two captains, one ship" effect. An additional, but not insignificant source of friction was the lascivious behavior of Alice's three daughters, which Olga described as "utterly disgusting" in a letter to her.[8]

By 1932, disillusioned by her Arcane School experiment, Olga sought Otto's support for her East-West project. He suggested the name, *Eranos*, for the project, a Greek word denoting a feast to which each participant brings a contribution. At the time, Otto was too ill to get personally involved in the project, and Richard Wilhelm had died two years earlier. So of her original three *maestri*, only Jung remained, becoming a crucial formative influence in the East-West project. For two decades, he made great personal and intellectual contributions to Eranos, sojourning there every year and presenting many of his crucial ideas as "works in progress." His notion of archetypes provided an overarching conceptual framework for the interdisciplinary conversations that developed at Eranos among scholars in the fields of science, religion, psychology, esoteric traditions, and symbolism.

Both Jung and Olga were deeply involved in the practice of the *I Ching*. Jung had written the foreword to Wilhelm's translation, which contributed in no small measure to the acceptance of the book in Western intellectual circles. He saw in the *I Ching* "a formidable psychological system that endeavors to organize the play of archetypes, the 'wondrous operations of nature' into a certain pattern, so that a 'reading' becomes possible."[9] He also found there an outstanding example of that meaningful acausal connection between events for which he had coined the name, *synchronicity*.[10]

From the beginning, Olga wished to introduce the experiential dimension of *I Ching* consultation into Eranos sessions. Her vision for Eranos still was, as it had been in the "Arcane School" phase, that of an experiential laboratory for spiritual growth. In her eyes, it was certainly not just an arena for academic debate. The titles of the first Eranos sessions reveal her preoccupation with spiritual practice and personal development: *Yoga and Meditation in East and West* (1933), *Eastern and Western Symbolism and Spiritual Guidance* (1934), *Spiritual Guidance in West and East* (1935). In 1934, she suggested to Jung that the work with the *I Ching* be included in Eranos sessions. But Jung felt that the time was not ripe for such an "unsavory" personal exposure, even within the intimate circle of Eranos. He suggested that it would be much better to focus on the scientific study of archetypal images and of the religious phenomenon in the manner of Rudolf Otto.[11]

It was in this way that the *I Ching* remained an invisible thread throughout the development of Eranos over the next fifty years. It was that shared strong involvement with this thread that sparked an immediate sense of recognition between Olga and Rudolf Ritsema when they first met in 1948.

RUDOLF RITSEMA

Rudolf Ritsema was born in Velp, the Netherlands, in 1918. His mother, Frances Johanna Van der Berg, had a deep and natural religiosity and was involved in theosophy and Indian philosophy. Rudolf inherited from his mother a sense of "being carried by God in life." His father, Ipo Christiaan Ritsema, was a chemist, a lover of nature and the arts, and a very rational man. Rudolf inherited form his father an interest in nature, biology, and history.

The marriage of Ipo and Frances Johanna was not a happy one, and the constant conflicts in the home had a devastating effect on Rudolf, a sensitive, nervous child. On the advice of a psychologist, he was sent at age eleven to the Odenwaldschule, an avant-garde boarding school in Heppenheim, in the German Odenwald, away from the turmoil at home. The Odenwaldschule turned out to be his salvation, and gradually helped him to develop his self-assurance and social skills.

The school had been created in 1910 by a visionary couple, Paul and Edith Geheeb, based on the principles of "progressive education," a pedagogic philosophy emphasizing experiential learning, critical thinking, group cooperation, social responsibility, co-education of the sexes, and curricula tailored to the students' personal goals. In 1934, with the ascent of Nazism, the Geheebs emigrated to Switzerland and re-founded the school with the name, Ecole d'Humanité, first in Versoix, in the Canton Geneva, later in Lac Noir, in the Canton Freiburg. The school still exists and is located in Hasliberg, in the Berner Oberland.

In Versoix, Rudolf met Catherine Gris, a young music teacher from Geneva. After receiving his baccalaureate, he moved to Geneva. A strong bond developed between the two young people and they married in 1945. Catherine remained Rudolf's faithful companion until his death in 2006.

RUDOLF MEETS THE *I CHING*

Catherine and Rudolf shared a strong devotion to the Geheebs, and in March 1944, they rode their bicycles from Geneva to Lac Noir to visit them. There, they re-encountered Alwina von Keller, whom they had met years before as an English literature teacher at the Odenwaldschule. In the intervening years, Alwina von Keller had been in analysis, first with Ernst Bernhard, and then, with Jung. She then had become a Jungian analyst herself.[12]

At the time of Catherine and Rudolf's visit, she was in Lac Noir to do therapy with her friend Edith Geheeb, who was deeply affected by the distressing situation of the school. The financial difficulties brought about by the war had forced the school to downsize to merely a mountain hut, where the students, many of them traumatized Jewish children coming from Gurs and other concentration camps in France, lived in cramped quarters in rough conditions.

When Rudolf and Catherine arrived in Lac Noir, Edith Geheeb told Rudolf: "Go see Alwina, she has something you will find interesting." The "something" was Wilhelm's translation of the *I Ching*. Alwina described to Rudolf the use of the oracle as an introspective tool and as a complement to dream work.[13] At that time, Rudolf was feeling in total darkness about the direction to give to his life. So he asked the oracle a very broad and fundamental question: "Who am I?"

Many years later, while working with the *I Ching* at Eranos, I learned from Rudolf the importance of asking preferably focused, practical, and emotionally significant questions, rather than large, general, philosophical questions. In our teaching, we would frequently use the small monument dedicated "to the unknown spirit of the place" (*Genio loci ignoto*) on the terrace of Casa Gabriella as a metaphor.[14] It is a simple slab with an hourglass shaped symbol. We saw the upper down-pointing triangle as a representation of the process leading to one's question, the process of narrowing down the complexity of one's lived situation into a pointed, precise question. The lower half of the hourglass represented the oracle's answer, which again opens out into a much larger context.

Now, Rudolf's first *I Ching* consultation certainly did not match this criterion. Still, the answer he received was highly significant for him. The answer was hexagram 16, "Enthusiasm" in Wilhelm's translation, with three moving lines, leading to hexagram 46, "Pushing Upward." Rudolf immediately felt a strong resonance with this answer and recognized in it the excitement of the discovery that was happening for him. He was also encouraged by the development into hexagram 46.

Later, other aspects of that first answer gradually fell into place for him when he started studying classical Chinese to obtain a more intimate contact with the oracular texts and after his knowledge of the *I Ching* deepened. For example, he found that the Chinese characters in the second line of hexagram 16 suggest a "cuirass tending towards petrification." In that image, he recognized the defenses and the rigidity he had built up in his young years to protect his sensitivity. The duke of Zhou's commentary on that line, referring to a "correct use of the center," felt to Rudolf like an invitation to rely on a protection more solid than armor that had its source in the contact with the center of his being. But, perhaps the most significant discovery was finding that a key meaning of the term Wilhelm translates as "enthusiasm" is "providing." The *I Ching* provided Rudolf with a way to contact his inner guidance. Providing others with the same opportunity became Rudolf's central mission in life.

At the time of his first encounter with the oracle, his enthusiasm was so fiery that he wanted to immerse himself immediately in the study of the book. Edith Geheeb had a copy of it, and since the *I Ching* was very difficult to find in Switzerland during the war, Rudolf asked her to lend it to him. Edith consulted Alwina, who was a bit frightened by the exuberant enthusiasm of Rudolf. She answered, "This young man must first live." Subsequently, she suggested a compromise: Edith could lend him the first volume for one week only.[15]

Rudolf returned to Geneva with the book and spent the whole week sitting at his typewriter day and night, typing it down. When later Alwina came to know about this, she realized that Rudolf's enthusiasm was not a flash in the pan. She then let him borrow the entire book for a longer time so that he could complete his copying the text. Rudolf's typed copy of the Wilhelm *I Ching* still exists and is kept in the Ritsema Fund room of the Museum of Cultures in Lugano, Italy.

For Rudolf, the meeting at Lac Noir was the beginning of a lifelong love affair with the *I Ching*. He studied classical Chinese and had the good fortune to find in an antique shop the 1874 Samuel Wells Williams' Chinese dictionary.[16] Catherine gave it to him as a New Year's gift in January 1945. At the University of Geneva library, Rudolf could consult the French translation of the *I Ching* by Paul-Louis-Félix Philastre, which reproduces most of the original Chinese text.[17] By studying it with the help of his new dictionary, Rudolf realized that the Chinese text has many more facets than revealed in Wilhelm's neo-Confucian interpretation.

After the Lac Noir encounter, Rudolf and Catherine entered into analysis with Alwina. On May 8, 1945, they got married. No celebration had been planned. During the war, Rudolf had lost all contact with his family in Holland and was very worried about them. Nonetheless, a celebration ensued, and on a large scale. The day of their marriage, the German Instrument of Surrender was signed and the entire city of Geneva descended to the streets, celebrating.

In April 1946, Catherine and Rudolf moved to Holland, where Rudolf found a job in the antiquarian department of the scholarly E.J. Brill bookshop and publishing house in Leyden. The job provided him with the exceptional opportunity to acquire rare sinological texts. In fact, in 1949, a few months before the fall of Beijing to Mao Zedong, he managed to obtain a copy of the canonical edition of the *I Ching*, the precious Palace Edition published by the emperor Kangxi in 1715, which Richard Wilhelm had vainly sought in China for ten years, before finally finding it in a friend's library in Germany.

RUDOLF RITSEMA AT ERANOS

At the end of the summer in 1947, Rudolf was struck by an attack of poliomyelitis that paralyzed him up to the diaphragm, bringing him to the brink of death. Fortunately, his heart was not affected, but for months he was unable to walk. Much smaller and thinner than Rudolf, Catherine had to help and move him around everywhere. A neurologist prescribed a stay in the coldest part of the winter in a milder climate. Subsequently, Rudolf and Catherine decided to use this opportunity to visit Alwina in Switzerland and devote that time to their therapy.

At the time, Alwina lived in Casa Shanti, the third Eranos house that Olga Fröbe-Kapteyn had built at the eastern end of her property. She found Rudolf and Catherine a place to stay in Casa Sasso, a neighbor's house, and introduced the young couple to Olga. During the stay in Ascona, Rudolf gradually recovered the use of his legs and at the end of the month he was able to walk on the road along the lakeshore for quite a distance, making frequent stops to rest.

In Casa Sasso, there was a piano (in fact, Mr. Sasso had been a founder of the international association of piano technicians), and before leaving Ascona, Catherine gave a concert for friends and neighbors. Olga, who was very much a music lover, was invited. At the end of the concert, remarking that the stairs of Casa Sasso were very difficult for Rudolf, Olga said: "Next year, this poor young man, who walks with so much difficulty, can stay in the Casa Eranos apartment." This was an apartment above the Sala Eranos that Olga had built for her guests, and it had been used first by Jung, then by Erich Neumann.

From that year on, every winter Catherine and Rudolf spent a month as Olga's guests at Eranos. Every night they had dinner with Olga, and between the three, a warm intimacy developed. The love of music connected Olga and Catherine and the shared deep interest in the *I Ching* created a strong bond between Olga and Rudolf. In those years, Rudolf kept deepening his *I Ching* studies and started writing commentaries on the *I Ching* texts for Olga, Edith Geheeb and her students, and Alwina and her patients. In this way, he honed his skills in interpreting the oracular images as dreamlike images, bringing to light aspects of a situation that would normally elude most conscious perceptions.

Olga repeatedly invited Rudolf to come to the Eranos meetings. But, it was only in 1957 that he was able to take an additional week off from his job in the summer to go to Eranos. There, he met the biologist Adolf Portmann, one of the pillars of Eranos, and during the *Tagungen* in subsequent years, Olga, Portmann, and Rudolf had the habit of breakfasting together early in the morning to discuss events of the previous day and to plan for the next.

Olga died in the spring of 1962. A few months before, she had nominated Adolf Portmann and the Ritsemas as her successors in carrying on the Eranos work. The Eranos Foundation was created, and Adolf Portmann became its first president. However, he retained his chair at the University of Basel, Switzerland, and continued to reside there. The day-to-day management of Eranos fell entirely on the shoulders of the Ritsemas.

Over the next twenty-five years, Rudolf and Catherine poured a great amount of energy and creativity into Eranos, just as Olga had done, and the Eranos *Tagungen* continued along the lines developed by Olga and Jung. The Conferences centered on fundamental archetypal research, and after the death of Adolf Portmann in 1982, Rudolf assumed the presidency of the Eranos Foundation.

THE ERANOS *I CHING*

Even though his Eranos duties absorbed most of his time, Rudolf never really abandoned his *I Ching* studies. His research reached a turning point around 1970, when he grew dissatisfied with writing critical commentaries on the Wilhelm translation and conceived the idea of an entirely new translation. As much as possible, this new translation would avoid any *a priori* interpretation and would allow the questioner a direct personal contact with the archetypal images.

This turned out to be a vast project that took twenty years to complete.[18] Various people helped in the early stages, particularly James Hillman and Robert Hinshaw. Towards the end of the 1980's, the American writer, Stephen Karcher, joined Rudolf and helped him to carry the job to completion.[19] Together, they produced a first provisional version of what later came to be known as "the Eranos *I Ching*" with the title, *Chou Yi: The Oracle of Encompassing Versatility*.[20]

The Eranos *I Ching* is a very unusual translation, standing out for its several idiosyncratic characteristics. For one, the focus is entirely on the oracular texts. The Confucian commentaries given so much space in the Wilhelm translation are completely ignored. But the real distinguishing feature of the Eranos *I Ching* is that each Chinese character is translated by only one English word throughout the work. In this way, the English word becomes a kind of code for the Chinese character. No words are added or omitted. Each oracular text is accompanied by a section called, "Associated Contexts." This offers for each "code word" appearing in the text the entire range (as much as is practically feasible) of potential meanings embodied in the corresponding Chinese character.

This method has several advantages. First, it allows a unique identification of all the characters in the book, allowing for the first time a concordance to the oracular texts in a Western language. Second, and most important, the Eranos translation returns to the oracular texts their native multi-faceted ambiguity, which is such an outstanding characteristic of classical and archaic Chinese, a characteristic that brings it closer to the imaginal language of the unconscious. As such, it provides a more "open" translation in which the reader is invited to select, among the various possible meanings associated with a given term, the one, or ones, that most strongly resonate with her or his situation and question, much as one might do in dream interpretation.

Third, rather than constructing coherent sentences in English, this approach adheres to the images evoked by the oracular texts, thereby bringing the reader in contact with a layer of meanings closely associated with the shamanic origin of these texts.

Naturally, for every gain, there is a price to pay. By fragmenting the oracular sentences into single word images, this approach to translation risks leaving out meanings associated with certain sequences of Chinese characters. Obviously, restricting one Chinese character to one English word can produce awkward English sentences. But, as the practice in the Eranos Round Table Sessions amply demonstrated, the imaginal language of the Eranos *I Ching* is a powerful introspective tool, and it activates associative processes that would hardly be possible with a more interpretive translation.[21]

As previously described, at the 1988 *Tagung*, Rudolf announced the end of the old style Eranos sessions and the beginning of a new phase, which would put the Eranos *I Ching* Project at the center of the Eranos activities. This caused quite a stir and Eranos lost most of its current speakers. The sessions then took on an entirely new format.

Instead of the traditional large annual event with some 200 attendees, three or four small conferences were to be held per year with a maximum of twenty to thirty participants. The work now took place around a big round table placed in the Eranos Sala (the same Round Table that had been used for meals on the terrace of Casa Gabriella), which gave these meetings the name of Eranos Round Table Sessions. Speakers and participants all sat around the table, even though the lectures were still delivered from a lectern. Mornings were devoted to lectures and discussion (another innovation as the old lecture format did not include discussions) and the afternoons were dedicated to *I Ching* consultations by both lecturers and participants.[22]

The first *I Ching* sessions prompted various improvements to the provisional translation of the *Chou Yi*. Ritsema and Karcher subsequently produced a revised version that was published by Element Books in the United Kingdom in 1994 under the title, *I Ching: The Classic Chinese Oracle of Change*.[23] But the collaboration between the Ritsema and Karcher was thorny, and Karcher left Eranos shortly after the book's completion.

In 1990, wishing to devote himself completely to the further Eranos *I Ching* translations, Rudolf passed the responsibility for operational management of Eranos to Christa Robinson, a Jungian analyst from Zürich whose father had been Jung's personal physician. In 1994, Rudolf asked Christa also to take over the presidency of the Eranos Foundation, a post she occupied until 2001, though he continued to make fundamental decisions. This resulting ambiguity of authority at Eranos made things sometimes quite difficult for Christa.[24]

The Italian publisher, Maurizio Rosenberg, participated in the first Eranos Round Table Session in 1990. As mentioned previously, in May 1991 he obtained an invitation for me to participate in a session for the purpose of evaluating the feasibility of creating an Italian version of the Eranos *I Ching*. Initially, I assumed that my task would be simply to translate the existing Ritsema-Karcher English translation into Italian. But Rudolf promptly disabused me of that idea. He was adamant that all translations of the *I Ching* must be carried out using the original Chinese text. (In fact, in subsequent years, two translations from the Element edition were created without his consent, one, paradoxically, into his native Dutch, and the other, into Spanish. He always disowned those works, considering them "fake.") The Italian translation project obviously took on a much larger dimension, both in terms of my commitment and in terms of the publisher's financial investment. It was only in 1994 that Rosenberg was ready to give the project the go-ahead. In the meantime, I had corresponded with Rudolf and we had made various translation experiments. Through Rudolf's comments, I had started to imbibe the spirit of the archaic language of the *I Ching*.

I felt attracted to the challenge of this translation. However, quite naturally I consulted the *I Ching* about this undertaking. I received hexagram 39, called "Limping" in the Eranos *I Ching* ("Obstruction" in the Wilhelm translation). That verdict sounded terrible. Not to mention the fact that in Italian a "limping translation" is an inadequate translation. I called Rudolf to share with him the bad news, thinking it meant we should cancel the project. But, he was of a radically different opinion.[25] He pointed out that hexagram 39 describes a situation "in which progress is hampered by obstacles and difficulties, and it is possible to proceed only haltingly," but it is still possible to proceed! So proceed we must, in spite of the difficulties. What did I expect, that this translation would be a leisurely stroll? Well, no, we would limp through it. We had our warning, but onward we must go! That was typical of Rudolf. On his desk, he had a quote of William of Orange, also known as William the Taciturn: "*Point n'est besoin d'espérer pour entreprendre, ni de réussir pour persévérer.*"[26] His personal Chinese seal consisted of four characters: "not/fearing/long-term/enterprises."

In the summer of 1994, I moved to Eranos, and Rudolf and I embarked on our "long-term enterprise." For the next couple of years, I spent most of my time there. The Ritsemas lived in the apartment above the Sala Eranos, the same that they had occupied in their winter sojourns at Olga's. I lived on the library floor of Casa Gabriella, above the apartment that was once Olga's and was now occupied by Christa Robinson. I shared most meals with the Ritsemas, and a warm friendship developed with both of them. Gradually, they came to feel much more like family than working associates.

Rudolf and I spent each morning in our "*I Ching* studio" located in the mansard of Casa Gabriella. It was a small space densely packed with books, dictionaries, and stacks of articles and notes. The most important working tool (after the precious Palace Edition of the *I Ching* and the much more modern, but equally fundamental, *Harvard-Yenching Concordance to the I Ching*) was Rudolf's "rolodex," an accordion-like contraption holding a large number of cards. Each card contained all key information about every character that occurred in the book. Remarkably, because Rudolf's painstaking analysis began before the electronic Age of Information, it still carried the imprint of its time.

The rolodex and its accessory card system allowed us to find all recurrences of a Chinese character in the book and its entries in various Chinese-English and Chinese-French dictionaries. Taking into account the definitions of the character in these dictionaries and the contexts in which it recurred, we discussed what would be the most appropriate Italian term to function as a "code word." Once the code word was selected we would create a list of "associated meanings" that enlarged the semantic field of the Italian term to embrace all principal meanings of the Chinese character. It was truly *un laurà cinès*, a Chinese work, as people would say in Milan. But, the work was enlivened by the pleasure that we shared working together. By temperament, Rudolf was a rather formal, old-style gentleman. Yet in the *I Ching* studio we were simply two kids playing together. We delighted in humor and jokes, and the hours flew past.

In 1996, the Italian Eranos *I Ching* was published under the title, *Eranos I Ching. Il libro della versatilità.*[27] In the meantime, I had started my involvement in organizing the Round Table Sessions. Typically, Rudolf, Christa, and I would sit at the vertices of an equilateral triangle at the Round Table. The circle itself was like an alchemical cauldron for transformations catalyzed by the oracle's dreamlike images. It was often very touching to witness an individual's process as they, as the Chinese would say, "rolled the oracle's words in their heart."

Even after the completion of the Italian translation, I stayed on at Eranos. Rudolf and Catherine had become almost foster parents to me. As it usually happens with real parents, after receiving much from them, a time comes when we have to give back. Around the year 2000, Catherine began to develop senile dementia, and Rudolf's health, which had always been fragile, became increasingly so. They had many friends, but no descendants, so I took on the task of helping them in their daily affairs.

In spite of his health problems, Rudolf did not give up his work with the *I Ching*. In 1997 the Swiss linguist, Hansjakob Schneider, joined him to produce a German translation, which was published in 2000 by Barth, Munich, under the title, *Eranos Yi Jing. Das Buch der Wandlungen*.[28] Then, working under Rudolf's direction, Imelda and Pierre Gaudissart completed a French version of the Eranos *I Ching* that was published under the title, *Le Yi Jing Eranos*, in 2003 by Encre, Paris.[29]

The last step in Rudolf's "work of a lifetime" consisted of revising the English translation of 1994. The work we had done together on the Italian translation had brought about many changes with respect to the Element edition, changes that had been incorporated in the German and the French translation. It seemed natural to incorporate those changes, fermented with the experience of a decade of Eranos Round Table Sessions, into a new English version. Most significantly, the spirit itself of the divinatory process had evolved from a future-oriented and more directive attitude to a present-oriented, non-directive, introspective, and psychological one. This was reflected in the title Rudolf and I adopted for our last *I Ching* seminars: *Mirror of the Present*. It was in this spirit that we prepared an English translation, which was published by Watkins, London, in 2005 under the title, *The Original I Ching Oracle*.[30]

Rudolf died on May 8, 2006, the sixty-first anniversary of his wedding with Catherine. He had successfully accomplished the task he had set out to do after obtaining that first hexagram in 1944. A year-and-a-half later, Catherine followed him into death.

THE FALL (AND RESURRECTION) OF ERANOS

No doubt Eranos had its most glorious years with C. G. Jung. It was Jung's prestige and charisma that attracted both outstanding scholars and funding to the Eranos project. Particularly important was the sponsorship of Mary and Paul Mellon through the Bollingen Foundation. After Jung's death, and when the support by the Bollingen

Foundation faded away toward the end of the 1960's, the finances of the Eranos Foundation started to decline. From then on, through various ups and downs, the situation continued to deteriorate, slowly at first, then more rapidly as the weight of interest on borrowed money kept building. Simultaneously, many of those closely involved with Eranos felt that there was spiritual or motivational deterioration. Christa Robinson described it in the following terms:

> [In the 1980's] the still high-caliber lectures became increasingly intellectual… For some participants a tendency grew to market the event [the *Eranos Tagung*] and to exploit it for personal gain. "If you publish my book, I will organize your presentation at an important conference elsewhere, e.g. in Japan." By this time to present a lecture at Eranos held a reward of enviable status, and sometimes even a salary increase at home… As the desire for prestige gained ground, [Olga's] founding values began, it seemed to me, to slip into the background.[31]

In the hope of bringing back the commitment to personal transformation that Olga had originally envisioned for Eranos, Rudolf attempted his 1988 revolution which was met with hostility and rejection—justified or unjustified—by the majority of Eranos speakers. In this light, the Eranos *I Ching* period can be viewed as a final attempt to reconfigure Eranos energies on a smaller scale, to revive the original spirit of Eranos through a specific tool, the *I Ching*. It was an experiment, and, for a few more years, it managed to keep the spirit alive, not as a big flame as it had been before, but as a small candle. Inevitably, the candle was to be extinguished by the oncoming storm.

By the end of the 1990's, the financial situation of the Foundation had become dire, and various entrepreneurial vultures were circling over the valuable lakefront property of Eranos, awaiting its final collapse. In 2001, Christa Robinson, overwhelmed by the difficulties, stepped down from the presidency. In the next few months, Eranos changed presidents twice and the Foundation officially suspended all activities. Rudolf felt that the Eranos archetype had completed its life cycle and it would find new, disembodied ways to continue its work. It was in this spirit that, in November 2002, Rudolf and I ran a final (unofficial) Eranos Round Table Session with the title, *Beyond Consolidated Forms: Emergence of Change.*

As I write now, in May 2014, the Eranos Foundation has managed to "consolidate its form" once again. It has resumed its activities and enjoys the support of two important American institutions, the Fetzer Institute of Kalamazoo, Michigan, and Pacifica Graduate Institute of Santa Barbara, California. The conditions are ripe for an Eranos renaissance. All of us who have loved Eranos and have grown through it look forward with great hope to these new developments.

NOTES

1. See Sybille Rosenbaum-Kroeber, "Eranos e Olga Fröbe-Kapteyn," in H. Szeemann, ed., *Monte Verità. Antropologia locale come contributo alla riscoperta di una topografia sacrale moderna* (Locarno/Milan: Armando Dadò/Electa, 1978), pp. 119–21.

2. A complete list of the Eranos Round Table Sessions, held between 1990 and 2002, is presented at the end of this issue of *Spring*.

3. Rudolf Ritsema, "Encompassing Versatility: Keystone of the Eranos Project / Allumfassende Wendigkeit: Schlußstein des Eranos-Projekts / Versatilité englobante: Clef de voûte du projet Eranos," *Eranos-Jahrbuch* 57 (1988): vii–lvii.

4. See Hans Thomas Hakl, *Eranos—An Alternative Intellectual History of the Twentieth Century* (Montreal/Kingston: McGill-Queen's University Press, 2013), pp. 242–56.

5. Richard Wilhelm, ed., *I Ging: Das Buch der Wandlungen* (Jena: Eugen Diederichs, 1924); English edition: *The I Ching or Book of Changes*, trans. Cary F. Baynes (Princeton, NJ: Princeton University Press, 1959).

6. Initially he invited his daughter to share the house with him, but Olga answered: "I will live there, but not with you." In recounting this anecdote, Rudolf Ritsema commented: "They were two captains, they could not be on the same ship."

7. Alice Bailey's autobiography, quoted in Hakl, *Eranos*, p. 30.

8. See William McGuire, "The Arcane Summer School," *Spring* (1980): 146–56.

9. C. G. Jung, *Mysterium Coniunctionis*, vol. 14, *The Collected Works of C. G. Jung*, ed. and trans. Gerhard Adler and R. F. C. Hull (Princeton, NJ: Princeton University Press, 1963), § 401.

10. That was the topic of his last lecture at Eranos: C. G. Jung, "Über Synchronizität," *Eranos-Jahrbuch* 20 (1951): 271–84; English edition: "On Synchronicity" (1951), in *The Collected Works of C. G. Jung*, vol. 8, ed. and trans. Gerhard Adler and R. F. C. Hull (Princeton, NJ: Princeton University Press, 1970), § 969.

11. Rudolf Ritsema, personal communication.

12. On Alwine von Keller, see Gian Piero Quaglino, Augusto Romano, and Riccardo Bernardini, "Appendix II. Alwine von Keller (1878–1965). A Biographical Memoir," in C. G. Jung, *The Solar Myths and Opicinus de Canistris—Notes of the Seminar given at Eranos in 1943*, eds. R. Bernardini, G. P. Quaglino, and A. Romano (Einsiedeln: Daimon, 2014), pp. 129–39.

13. Rudolf Ritsema and Shantena Augusto Sabbadini, "Images of the Unknown: The Eranos *I Ching* Project 1989–1997," *Eranos-Jahrbuch* 66 (1997): 9.

14. This monument was placed there by Olga in 1949 at the suggestion of Jung and Gerardus van der Leeuw, to pay homage to the "unknown spirit of the place." They always felt that an unknown presence, rooted in the earth of Eranos, was supporting and unfolding the entire enterprise beyond their own personal wills. See Catherine Ritsema, *L'Œuvre d'Eranos et Vie d'Olga Froebe-Kapteyn* (Ascona: unpublished typescript, undated), pp. 23 and 88; Rudolf Ritsema, "The Origins and Opus of Eranos: Reflections at the 55th Conference / Eranos: Ursprünge und Werk. Eine Betrachtung anläßlich der 55. Tagung / L'œuvre d'Eranos et ses origines: Réflexions à l'occasion de la 55me session," *Eranos-Jahrbuch* 5 (1987): vii–xlvii.

15. The Wilhelm *I Ching* comes in two volumes, a first volume containing the fundamental oracular texts, and a second devoted mostly to commentaries.

16. Samuel Wells Williams, *A Syllabic Dictionary of the Chinese Language, Arranged according to the Wu-fang Yuen Yin, with the Pronunciation of the Characters as Heard in Peking, Canton, Amoy and Shanghai* (Shanghai: American Presbyterian Mission Press, 1874).

17. *Le Yi king, ou, Livre des changements de la dynastie des Tsheou*, trans. P.-L.-F. Philastre (Paris: Ernest Leroux, 1885–1893).

18. On the Eranos *I Ching* project, see Ritsema and Sabbadini, "Images of the Unknown," pp. 7–43. Between 1970 and 1984, Ritsema published ten technical contributions on the *I Ching* in *Spring*.

19. Among his contributions on the *I Ching*, see Stephen L. Karcher, "Oracle's Contexts: Gods, Dreams, Shadow, Language," *Spring* (1992): 79–94; Stephen L. Karcher, "Making Spirits Bright: Divination and the Demonic Image," *Eranos-Jahrbuch* 61 (1992): 27–43; Stephen L. Karcher, "The Yi Ching and the Ethic of the Image: Reflections at the 1992 Eranos/Uehiro Round Table Session," *Eranos-Jahrbuch* 61 (1992): 97–101; Rudolf Ritsema and Stephen L. Karcher, "Esprit et symboles. Le projet Eranos de traduction du *Yi Jing*", in M. de Smedt, ed., *Les mutations du Yi King* (Gordes: Albin Michel, 1994), pp. 144–45.

20. Rudolf Ritsema and Stephen L. Karcher, eds., *Chou Yi: The Oracle of Encompassing Versatility. Volume I: Hexagrams 1–30. Provisional Edition for the Use of Participants in the Eranos Round Table Conferences. Eranos Yi Ching Project, Part I,1, Eranos-Jahrbuch* 58 (1989); Rudolf Ritsema and Stephen L. Karcher, eds., *Chou Yi: The Oracle of Encompassing Versatility. Vol. II: Hexagrams 31–64. Provisional Edition for the Use of Participants in the Eranos Round Table Conferences. Eranos Yi Ching Project, Part I,2, Eranos-Jahrbuch 59* (1990); Rudolf Ritsema and Stephen L. Karcher, eds., *Chou Yi: The Oracle of Encompassing Versatility. Vol. III: Supplementary Materials and Concordance. Provisional Edition for the Use of Participants in the Eranos Round Table Conferences– Eranos Yi Ching Project, Part I,3, Eranos-Jahrbuch* 60 (1991).

21. On the Eranos *I Ching*, see, e.g, Shantena Augusto Sabbadini, *I Ching: Oracle and Divination*, Svenska C G Jung Stiftelsens–Småskriftserie, vol. 3 (Solna: Svenska C G Jung Stiftelsens/CJPCentrum för Jungiansk Psykologi AB, 1998); Valery Zalensky, "Юнг, Зранос, И-Цзин, Россия [Jung, Eranos, *I-Ching*, Russia]," *Ноеая беснa* [*New Spring*] 1 (1999): 74–84; and Heyong Shen, "Yi Jing Yu Xin-Li-Fen-Xi, Chong Fang Ai-No-Si [*I Ching* and Analytical Psychology: Re-visiting Eranos]," *Zhou Yi Yanjiu* [*I Ching Studies*] 3 (2001): 75–79.

22. See, e.g., Catherine Lovering, "Eranos proposait pour l'année 1992 trois séminaires autour du I Ching: Images de l'Inconnu. Image et guérison. Dans les rêves commence la responsabilité," *Cahiers Jungiens de Psychanalyse* 76 (1993): 103–04.

23. Rudolf Ritsema and Stephen Karcher, *I Ching: The Classic Chinese Oracle of Change. The First Complete Translation with Concordance* (Shaftesbury, Dorset/Rockport, MA/Brisbane, Quennsland: Element Books, 1994). This publication was preceded by an audio work: Rudolf Ritsema and Stephen Karcher, *The Eranos Yi Ching or Chou Yi: The Oracle of Encompassing Versatility. The Use, History, and Psychology of the Classic Chinese Oracle*, 2 MC (Woodstock, CT: Spring Audio, Inc., 1992).

24. See Christa Robinson and Robert S. Henderson, "Hearing a Similar Voice," in R. S. Henderson and J. Henderson, eds., *Living with Jung. "Enterviews" with Jungian Analysts*, vol. 3 (New Orleans, LA: Spring Journal, Inc., 2010), pp. 139–55; Christa Robinson and Robert S. Henderson, "Images of Archetypal Forces. An Enterview with Christa Robinson about the *I Ching*," *Jung Journal: Culture & Psyche* 4 (2, 2010): 102–09; and Christa Robinson, "Eranos: A Place, an Encounter, a Story," *Spring* 86 (2011): 165–82.

25. Rudolf, although wonderfully intuitive in his perception of people, was sometimes not altogether objective in his interpretation of oracular answers where he was personally involved.

26. "You do not need to hope in order to embark on an enterprise, nor to succeed in order to persevere."

27. Rudolf Ritsema and Shantena Augusto Sabbadini, *Eranos I Ching. Il libro della versatilità. Testi oracolari con concordanze* (Como: Red, 1996; Turin: UTET, 1996). A new edition of this book entitled *I Ching. Il Libro dei Mutamenti*, was published in 2011 by URRA/ Feltrinelli in Milan.

28. Rudolf Ritsema and Hansjakob Schneider, *Eranos Yi Jing. Das Buch der Wandlungen. Die einzige vollständige Ausgabe der altchinesischen Orakeltexte mit Konkordanz* (Munich: O. W. Barth, 2000).

29. Pierre Gaudissart, Imelda Gaudissart, and Rudolf Ritsema, *Le Yi Jing Eranos. Le livre de la versatilité. Textes oraculaires suivis d'une concordance et d'un lexique Français-Chinois* (Paris: Encre, 2003).

30. Rudolf Ritsema and Shantena Sabbadini, *The Original I Ching Oracle. The Pure and Complete Texts with Concordance. Translated under the Auspices of the Eranos Foundation* (London: Watkins, 2005).

31. Robinson, "Eranos: A Place, an Encounter, a Story," p. 177.

HRH Princess Irene of the Netherlands

Born in 1939, HRH Princess Irene of the Netherlands has for many years been involved in the revaluation and the reconnection of the human-nature relationship, as well as in reconnecting people to their inner nature. She is the founder and president of several organizations, including NatuurCollege, NatureWise (which connects Dutch school children with nature), Bergplaas Nature Reserve, and Isis Transcultural Leadership. HRH Princess Irene is an Honourable Member of the Club of Budapest and Patron of the Irish Peatland Conservancy Council. She also is involved in training, lecturing, coaching, publishing, and media activities, and gives lectures and keynote addresses in universities and institutions in The Netherlands and abroad. These include the IUCN World Parks Congress (Durban, 2003), the Raiffeisen lecture (Amsterdam, 2005), the Volkskrant Lecture (Amsterdam, 2005), the Symposium Sustainability Personalised (The Hague, 2008), the Martin Buber Award (Maastricht, 2010), the World Cultural Forum (Taihu, 2013), and the Jungian Institute Nijmegen. Among her books are *Mujer y Sociedad* (1979), *Dialogue with Nature* (1995), *Samen* (1998), *de Natuur zijn wij* (2003), *Science, Soul and the Spirit of Nature—Leading Thinkers on the Restoration of Man and Creation* (2005), *Leven in Verbinding* (2010), and *The Wisdom Factor* (2012). HRH Princess Irene was a lecturer at the 2007 Eranos Conference, representing a long-standing interest by her family. On October 19, 1951, her mother, HM Queen Juliana of the Netherlands (1909–2004), invited Olga Fröbe-Kapteyn to her residence—by chance, on the day of the latter's seventieth birthday. Olga Fröbe-Kapteyn reported that HM Queen Juliana wished to know in depth about Eranos, and that all the *Eranos Yearbooks* were on display in the Queen's private library.

Our Relation to Nature Determines our Worldview—Eranos and Today's Great Cultural Challenge

HRH PRINCESS IRENE OF THE NETHERLANDS

What is the use of running when we are on the wrong path?
—Gandhi

Carl Gustav Jung, the *spiritus rector* of Eranos, wrote in 1946: "What our world lacks is the *psychic connection*. And no clique, no community of interest, no political party, and no State will ever be able to replace this."[1] Now, almost seventy years after Jung wrote these words, we are witnessing a global disruption of the biological foundations of the Earth caused by human impact. And yet we are part of nature. We *are* nature. Do we still remember? Do we still remember our spiritual connection to all of life? I think we don't understand what we are actually doing to ourselves, when disrupting the biological foundations of the Earth, or life itself.

We have lost the enchantment; we have disconnected ourselves from the Spirit that flows through all that is. To feel that we are participants in this world and to be conscious of this interrelationship enables a deep connection with our own inner being. Or the other way around: when connected to our deepest inner being, our spiritual self, we are immediately connected to all that is. That affinity, that connection, that spiritual flow of life many seem to have lost.

As a result of losing our deep inner sense of connection and ease with all that surrounds us on this beautiful planet, our natural environment, our priorities have begun to shift from a deep spiritual harmony with all of life—or the psychic connection Jung mentioned—to a disconnected way of life. We need to be aware how in modern times the "outer" world tends to devour our everyday lives. We hardly take time for silence and inner reflection, or for being out in nature to enjoy and explore, or sit quietly listening to the song of a bird, the rustling of the leaves, or admire the beauty of a flower. Is not the fact that we make a division between ourselves and the rest of nature artificial and unrealistic? The materialistic greed and the unnatural speed of our everyday lives have favored this disconnectedness with nature. I think it is obvious that this has not made people happier worldwide.

The ways we act in this world, including our policy making, are actually always linked to an inner attitude towards life, *a worldview*. We have arrived at a moment in human history where we seriously need to rethink and revalue our role in the Great Ecosystem Earth. Do we think and act from a view that prioritizes humans, or do we consider *all* of life? In other words: do we think and act from a disconnected worldview or a worldview that understands and feels and acts from the interrelation with all life?

The challenge today lies in the journey from want to wholeness, and in this journey totally different and often-conflicting priorities are at stake. These different priorities and interests originate from the diverse inner perspectives or worldviews that lie behind. The conflict of interests often delays what must be done. At the same time I meet many young men and women who can no longer operate in a society based on want, which is driven by competition and greed. They have the courage to step out of excellent jobs, to follow their inner path, reconnecting to their true inner self, to nature, or life itself.

For me, spirituality is living from a conscious connection to all of existence on a physical and non-physical level. And from this emerges a personal worldview of a broad society, which clearly extends beyond the human society. A global interrelated society of all life and all that is, inclusive of and through and beyond Earth's treasures. A worldview of a sustained wellbeing for *all material and spiritual* existence.

As our incarnated selves are part of the material and spiritual reality that we call Earth, the wellbeing of the Earth and our own wellbeing are one and the same. And so: the way we treat the Earth has everything to do with how we perceive ourselves. The wise South African Zulu, professor Koka, once said: "I *am* because nature is, and because she *is* I am."

The diminished connection with our environment has contributed to a deep separation, a split between humans and nature and a split within ourselves. Thus we have locked up and neglected our finely-tuned inner spiritual nature, which is naturally connected to all life. Behind the economic-financial, climate, and ecological crises lies a deep human moral and spiritual crisis that should be considered and explored. A concept to which we still cling—an economic growth based in *wanting*—has overtaken ancient human values of interconnectedness and interrelation with each other and with that which surrounds us. Is it realistic to take active business measures and make policy decisions from the illusory perspective that we are *not* part of nature, of Earth?

What we ought to remember (and many people of all ages are fully aware of this) is that when human culture merges with the fundamental nature of existence, then we are in harmony with Earth. We must understand this, feel this, and then act accordingly from that very starting point. Then we will act and feel as part of the greater whole, with respect for all existence. Then we will work in harmony with inner and outer nature. Then we will think from the worldview of a community of all life, and act as participants of the Great Ecosystem Earth.

Globally I see a significant shift in consciousness and an intention of many to realize what we could call an "ecological civilization." Many are indeed revaluing their role in the web of life. Many are aware that we, humankind, have in fact become a force of nature, possibly more destructive than tsunamis and earthquakes combined. In very large part, the future of all life now rests in our human hands: we can actually make or break life on Earth, our home. Twenty-four centuries ago, the Chinese philosopher Mencius pointed out how the destruction of the forests began when humankind lost its original contact with its inner-nature, or spiritual self. He described how the mountains used to be places of healing, to preserve health and to strengthen people's vitality. Protecting the health of natural places was seen as a priority, in order to protect the health of all.

Everything in nature has an intrinsic value—its own significance or value in itself—while simultaneously being interdependent; this is how ecosystems operate, this is how the Great Ecosystem Earth operates, humans included. This is what many ancient philosophies taught. This is what we desperately need to understand again, feel again, and act upon. What does this require from us humans in the immediate future?

Significantly more than economic growth is needed for the wellbeing of humankind. We need an economy no longer narrowly defined by mere profit, but one that provides a fundament for the wellbeing of all life. The SGD (Sustainable Development Goals) and the Colombian government recently called for an integrated approach to tackle today's great challenges, from poverty reduction, to social wellbeing, to clean water. The vastness and intensity of human suffering on earth is overwhelming, a wakeup call for each and every one of us. We must work towards realizing essential basic needs for all. And we *can* do this without further exhausting the Earth. We now have the means for developing technical tools to accomplish this in an ecological way, in harmony and in collaboration with nature. I am sure that today's economists would have built a totally different economic system had they done so from Mencius' mountain. In this respect green economy, circular economy, and social entrepreneurship are hopeful developments. *Global citizenship* is needed to realize these goals. Indeed, we must tackle this all together, and restore the balance between outer and inner life.

At the same time, this calls for personal leadership from the perspective of our authentic self in all our personal and professional dimensions. What does this mean in our everyday lives? The individual's role is often undervalued and seen as lacking power to make a difference. Indeed, that may seem true when viewed from a disconnected perspective, but not from an interconnected and interrelated perspective. Our personal thoughts and choices make a difference as they have an effect not only on our personal lives, but, like concentric circles, also on our neighbors, our community, nature itself, and the universe. The moment we understand how each and every one of us is like a drop in the ocean of life, we will also understand that it is everyone's responsibility to be a clear droplet that contributes to the clarity of the entire ocean. This is indeed a joyful responsibility as it makes life and all we do worthwhile! Then "I" becomes "we" and we realize that living is *being in relationship*.

This does not imply that it is easy to change from our anthropocentric worldview in which we consider nature as a soulless thing, to a worldview of a harmonious togetherness with all life. This would be a significant change of mentality and attitude towards life, one we should grow towards together. Small individual decisions are a starting point. There are so many hopeful and courageous initiatives worldwide; there are so many beautiful people worldwide. We live in a fascinating moment in history, in which many are responding to the challenge to invent and discover new technical and spiritual ways for a lifestyle in harmony with nature, a lifestyle we could truly call an "ecological civilization, based on a spiritual awareness."

Eranos founder Olga Fröbe-Kapteyn was aware of the significant role that nature played in the extraordinary psychological experience of the Eranos gatherings. She writes:

> Eranos represents the reaction of a group of scholars and of their audiences to a vital and powerful urge, which they all feel, but cannot yet define… Their depths are stirred, both by the archetypal material handled in the lectures, and by the invisible spirit of these meetings—a spirit that is simply abroad, that is present, that is almost a presence, linked to those who speak and to those who listen—linked to the landscape, to the garden, in which the Lecture-hall stands. Nature plays a large role at these meetings, as do the elements—wind, water, sunshine, and an exceptionally fertile earth. No other conference takes place in such a setting.[2]

Our relation to nature determines our worldview. I profoundly believe and know that a conscious interrelationship with all of life is the fulfilment of our human potential, as the Eranos example shows us and as testified in its founder's words. Therefore the foundation for a sustainable future lies within ourselves. By nature all humans are alike, in spite of our cultural differences, just as all flowers are of the same family in spite of their manifold forms and colors. Reflecting on our common future, we must steer in the direction of a new place where it becomes natural to base our decisions on the wellbeing of all life, where it becomes natural to live as part of the whole. In this place we are in harmony with the primordial essence, or life itself. We must do this together, *as a global human society,* as the human culture we make up together. This also means to consciously decide that we are indeed interrelated with and part of the Great Ecosystem Earth. This decision would bring true transformation. Nations, communities, and each and every one of us can be a leader and an example in this transformation.

Our most precious natural resource, our consciousness, will guide us to the right decisions.

I feel indeed that the change is already visible, although primarily on a grassroots level. I am confident this will eventually bring about a shift in all of society, including the world of politics and business, a shift from wanting to oneness. From "I" to "we."

NOTES

1. Carl Gustav Jung, "An Account of the Transference Phenomena Based on the Illustrations of the 'Rosarium Philosophorum' (1946), in *The Collected Works of C. G. Jung*, vol. 16, ed. and trans. Gerhard Adler and R. F. C. Hull (London: Routledge and Kegan Paul, 1966), p. 323.

2. Olga Fröbe-Kapteyn, "The Psychological Background of Eranos" (1939), published in this issue of *Spring*.

VI.
ERANOS: HISTORICAL PHOTOGRAPHS

The Eranos' founder, Olga Fröbe-Kapteyn, in the 1940s.
(Ph. Margarethe Fellerer. Eranos Foundation Archives)

Figure 1. The small port of Casa Gabriella, at Eranos, opening on Lake Maggiore and the Swiss-Italian Alps, in the late 1920s.
(Ph. unknown. Eranos Foundation Archives)

Figure 2. A view of Casa Eranos (on the left), of Casa Gabriella (in the middle), and of Casa Shanti (at that time, still under construction, on the right) from Lake Maggiore in 1929.
(Ph. unknown. Eranos Foundation Archives)

Figure 3. Olga Fröbe-Kapteyn (1881–1962), the Eranos' founder, sitting in front of Casa Eranos in 1929.
(Ph. unknown. Eranos Foundation Archives)

Figure 4. The first Eranos Conference, with participants standing and sitting on the terrace of the Lecture Hall of Casa Eranos, in August 1933.
(Ph. Margarethe Fellerer. Eranos Foundation Archives)

Figure 5. The first Eranos Conference, with participants sitting on the terrace of the Lecture Hall of Casa Eranos, in August 1933.
(Ph. Margarethe Fellerer. Eranos Foundation Archives)

Figure 6. Olga Fröbe-Kapteyn and Carl Gustav Jung (1875–1961) on the terrace of Casa Eranos in August 1933.
(Ph. Margarethe Fellerer. Eranos Foundation Archives)

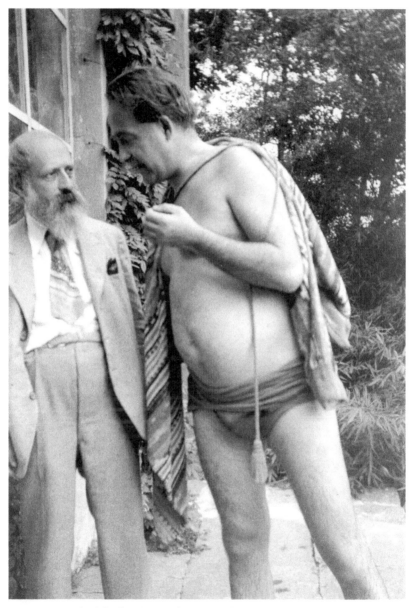

Figure 7. On the left, the philosopher and Hebraist, Martin Buber (1878–1965), and on the right, the Indologist, Heinrich Zimmer (1890–1943), in a break during the second Eranos Conference, in August 1934.
(Ph. Margarethe Fellerer. Eranos Foundation Archives)

Figure 8. A lotus flower blossoming in the Eranos garden in 1934.
(Ph. Margarethe Fellerer. Eranos Foundation Archives)

Figure 9. Olga Fröbe-Kapteyn and the Pāli language scholar, Caroline Augusta Foley
Rhys Davids (1857–1942), at the 1935 Eranos Conference.
(Ph. Margarethe Fellerer. Eranos Foundation Archives)

Figure 10. The historian of Christianity, Ernesto Buonaiuti (1881–1946), at Eranos in August 1935.
(Ph. Margarethe Fellerer. Eranos Foundation Archives)

Figure 11. From the left, Anna Margarethe ("Gret") Baumann-Jung, Barbara Hannah, Emma Jung-Rauschenbach, Carl Gustav Jung, Max Pulver, Jolande Jacobi, Olga Fröbe-Kapteyn, and Toni Wolff attend Paul Masson-Oursel's (1882–1961) lecture on "The Idea of Liberation in India" in the Lecture Hall of Casa Eranos in August 1936.
(Ph. Margarethe Fellerer. Eranos Foundation Archives)

Figure 12. Heinrich Zimmer, on the right, with a series of images belonging to the Eranos Archive for Research in Symbolism in the late 1930s.
(Ph. Margarethe Fellerer. Eranos Foundation Archives)

Figure 13. The historian of religions and scholar of Gnosis, Henri-Charles Puech (1902–1986), at Eranos in August 1936.
(Ph. Margarethe Fellerer. Eranos Foundation Archives)

Figure 14. A night view of the lakeshore of Ascona in the 1930s.
(Ph. Margarethe Fellerer. Eranos Foundation Archives)

The silver reflection of the moonlight upon the lake and the massive shape of the mountains around Ascona are always in my memory. May the contributions made by Eranos be as everlasting as the lake and the mountains there

Chung-yuan Chang
April 15, 1957

Figure 15. A view of Casa Eranos (still without the apartment upstairs, the "Eranos Studio," which was built in 1940) and of Casa Gabriella in (probably) 1937. Above, a dedication written by the philosopher, Chang Chung-yuan (1907–1988), on the occasion of the 25th anniversary of the Eranos Conferences, in 1957. (Ph. Margarethe Fellerer. Eranos Foundation Archives)

Figure 16. William Doge ("Bill") Hutchinson (?–1966) on the small port of Casa Eranos in (probably) 1939. Bill Hutchinson was the husband of the sculptor, Louise Frederike Susanna ("Li") Hutchinson-Wolf (1883–1968), who created the busts of some Eranos lecturers, including Carl Gustav Jung.
(Ph. Margarethe Fellerer. Eranos Foundation Archives)

Figure 17. Olga Fröbe-Kapteyn, with one of her two dogs ("Yin" and "Yang"), at Eranos in 1939.
(Ph. Margarethe Fellerer. Eranos Foundation Archives)

Figure 18. Mary Elizabeth Conover Mellon (1904–1946), the co-founder (along with her husband, Paul Mellon) of the Bollingen Foundation, and the archaeologist, Charles Virolleaud (1879–1968), at Eranos in 1939.
(Ph. Margarethe Fellerer. Eranos Foundation Archives)

Figure 19. Carl Gustav Jung and the philologist and historian of religions of the Classical world, Walter Friedrich Otto (1874–1958), at Eranos in 1939.
(Ph. Margarethe Fellerer. Eranos Foundation Archives)

Figure 20. The philologist and historian of religions of the Classical world, Károly (Karl) Kerényi (1897–1973), on the small port of Casa Eranos in the 1940s. (Ph. Margarethe Fellerer. Eranos Foundation Archives)

Figure 21. Carl Gustav Jung and the physicist and 1933 Nobel Prize winner, Erwin Schrödinger (1887–1961), at the Eranos Round Table in August 1946. (Ph. Margarethe Fellerer. Eranos Foundation Archives)

Figure 22. On the left, the historian of Christianity and scholar of Gnosis, Gilles Quispel (1916–2006), and on the right, the biologist and zoologist, Adolf Portmann (1897–1982), at the Eranos Round Table in August 1947. (Ph. Margarethe Fellerer. Eranos Foundation Archives)

Figure 23. Paul Mellon (1907–1999), the co-founder (along with his wife, Mary Mellon) of the Bollingen Foundation, and Kristin Bühler at the Eranos Round Table in August 1947.
(Ph. Margarethe Fellerer. Eranos Foundation Archives)

Figure 24. Olga Fröbe-Kapteyn and the historian of religions, Gerardus van der Leeuw (1890–1950), at the Eranos Round Table in (probably) 1948. (Ph. Margarethe Fellerer. Eranos Foundation Archives)

Eranos, Landschaft am See, Garten und Haus. Unscheinbar und abseits, und doch ein Nabel der Welt, kleines Glied der Goldenen Kette. Als Sprechende und als Hörende, immer haben wir zu danken.

E. Neumann

Figure 25. Olga Fröbe-Kapteyn in the Eranos garden, in front of Casa Eranos, in 1948. (Ph. Margarethe Fellerer. Eranos Foundation Archives).
Above, a dedication written by the psychologist, Erich Neumann, on the occasion of the 25th anniversary of the Eranos Conferences, in 1957, which reads: "Eranos, Landscape on lake, garden and house. Inconspicuous and off the beaten track, and yet a navel of the world, a small link in the Golden Chain. As lecturers and as listeners, we always have to thank."

Figure 26. The Eranos Round Table in (probably) 1947. Olga Fröbe-Kapteyn gave to this photograph the title, "The Round Table is waiting." When Carl Gustav Jung saw this picture, he said: "The Image is perfect: they are all there."
(Ph. Margarethe Fellerer. Eranos Foundation Archives)

Figure 27. The Hebraist and scholar of Kabbalah, Gershom Scholem (1897–1982), at Eranos in August 1951.
(Ph. Margarethe Fellerer. Eranos Foundation Archives)

Figure 28. Carl Gustav Jung in a "terrace-wall session," on the terrace of Casa Eranos, surrounded by his pupils and other participants at the 1951 Eranos Conference. (Ph. Margarethe Fellerer. Eranos Foundation Archives)

Figure 29. From the left, Emma Jung-Rauschenbach, Erich Neumann, Aniela Jaffé, John David ("Jack") Barrett, Jr. (of the Bollingen Foundation), Carl Gustav Jung, the financier and industrial engineer, Lancelot Law Whyte (1896–1972), and Gilles Quispel at the Eranos Round Table, on the terrace of Casa Gabriella, in August 1952. (Ph. Margarethe Fellerer. Eranos Foundation Archives)

Figure 30. The theologian and Church historian, Ernst Benz (1907–1978) (on the left), the scholar of Zen Buddhism, Daisetsu Teitarō Suzuki (1870–1966) (in the middle), and his secretary, Mi-Ko-Ho Okamura (standing), at the Eranos Round Table in August 1953.
(Ph. Margarethe Fellerer. Eranos Foundation Archives)

Figure 31. From the left, Vaun Gillmor (of the Bollingen Foundation), Károly (Karl) Kerényi, and an unidentified woman at the Eranos Round Table in the late 1940s-early 1950s.
(Ph. Margarethe Fellerer. Eranos Foundation Archives)

Figure 32. From the left, the poet and literary critic, Sir Herbert Edward Read (1893–1968), the historian of religions, Mircea Eliade (1907–1986), the scholar of Zen Buddhism, Daisetsu Teitarō Suzuki, and the philosopher and scholar of Islam, Henry Corbin (1903–1978), at Eranos in 1953.
(Ph. Margarethe Fellerer. Eranos Foundation Archives)

Figure 33. The psychologist, Erich Neumann (1905-1960), on the terrace of Casa Gabriella, at Eranos, in the 1950s.
(Ph. Margarethe Fellerer. Eranos Foundation Archives)

Figure 34. From the left, the historian of religions and scholar of mythology, Joseph Campbell (1904–1987), his wife, Jean Erdman (1916), and Richard Francis Carrington Hull (1913–1974), the translator of Carl Gustav Jung's *Collected Works*, on the lakeshore of Ascona in 1953.
(Ph. Margarethe Fellerer. Eranos Foundation Archives)

Figure 35. Henry Corbin and Olga Fröbe-Kapteyn in the Eranos Lecture Hall in the 1950s.
(Ph. Margarethe Fellerer. Eranos Foundation Archives)

Nowhere in our distracted world
has the human spirit found such
a perfect haven. In Eranos
" we have sheltered under the same
                        portico
listening to the silver voice of
                        wisdom ".

                    Herbert Read .

Figure 36. Daisetsu Teitarō Suzuki (in the middle), the psychotherapist and essayist, Ira Progoff (1921–1998), and other participants gathered at the Eranos Round Table, on the terrace of Casa Gabriella, in (probably) 1953.
(Ph. Margarethe Fellerer. Eranos Foundation Archives)
Above, a dedication written by Sir Herbert Edward Read, on the occasion of the 25th anniversary of the Eranos Conferences, in 1957.

Figure 37. On the left, Mircea Eliade, and on the right, the theologian and scholar of Islam, Louis Massignon (1883–1962), at Eranos in c. 1954–1955. (Ph. Margarethe Fellerer. Eranos Foundation Archives)

Figure 38. The Indian statue donated by Baron Eduard von der Heydt (1882–1964) to Olga Fröbe-Kapteyn in the 1930s—now in the Eranos garden. The Baron was Emperor Wilhelm II's banker and an important collector of primitive, oriental, and contemporary art. In 1926, he acquired the Hotel Monte Verità and regularly hosted lecturers and participants of the Eranos Conferences. He converted its beautiful park into a botanic garden, where he placed exotic plants, Chinese birdcages, and sculptures inspired by Far-Eastern art and the "Great Mother." (Ph. Margarethe Fellerer. Eranos Foundation Archives)

Figure 39. The anthropologist, Laurens van der Post (1906–1996), at Eranos in 1956. (Ph. Margarethe Fellerer. Eranos Foundation Archives)

I am pleased to add my tribute
to Frau Fröbe as the presiding
genius of Eranos, and to all
those colleagues and friends who
have contributed to its blossoming.

John Layard

Figure 40. The monument dedicated "to the unknown spirit of the place" (*genio loci ignoto*), sculpted in 1949 by Paul Speck (1896–1966) and placed on the terrace of Casa Gabriella, in a picture from the mid 1950s. The monument was the fruit of an idea of Carl Gustav Jung and the historian of religions, Gerardus van der Leeuw. (Ph. Tim Gidal. Eranos Foundation Archives)

Above, a dedication written by the anthropologist, John Layard (1891–1974), on the occasion of the 25th anniversary of the Eranos Conferences, in 1957.

Figure 41. Rudolf Ritsema (1918–2006), the scholar of the *I Ching* (first row), Daisy and Daniel Brody, the first publisher of the *Eranos Yearbooks* with Rhein-Verlag (third row, in front of the lecturer), Gershom Scholem (behind Dr. Brody), and Maria Wirth attend Herbert W. Schneider's (1892–1984) lecture on "Peace as Scientific Problem and as Personal Experience" in the Lecture Hall of Casa Eranos in August 1958. (Ph. Tim Gidal. Eranos Foundation Archives)

Figure 42. On the left, Erich Neumann, and on the right, Max Knoll (1897–1969), the electrical engineer and inventor of the electron microscope (1931), in front of the Lecture Hall of Casa Eranos in August 1958. (Ph. Tim Gidal. Eranos Foundation Archives)

Figure 43. The philosopher and scholar of Buddhism and Taoism, Chang Chung-yuan (1907–1988), lecturing on "Self-Realization and the Inner Process of Peace" at Eranos in August 1958.
(Ph. Tim Gidal. Eranos Foundation Archives)

Figure 44. The Lecture Hall of Casa Eranos in 1958.
(Ph. Tim Gidal. Eranos Foundation Archives)

Figure 45. Catherine Ritsema-Gris (1917–2007) (in front), Rudolf Ritsema (second from right), and Olga Fröbe-Kapteyn (first from right) at the Eranos Round Table in the late 1950s.
(Ph. Tim Gidal. Eranos Foundation Archives)

Figure 46. On the left, the anthropologist, Gilbert Durand (1921–2012), and on the right, the philosopher and scholar of Islam, Toshihiko Izutsu (1914–1993), on the small port of Casa Eranos in 1970.
(Ph. Tim Gidal. Eranos Foundation Archives)

Figure 47. The lecturers of the 1975 Eranos Conference gathered at the Round Table. Among them, Gilbert Durand (in front, in the middle) and the philosopher, Jean Brun (1919–1994) (in front, third from right).
(Ph. Luciano Soave. Eranos Foundation Archives)

Figure 48. The psychologist, James Hillman (1926–2011), in Casa Gabriella, at Eranos, in 1980.
(Ph. Luciano Soave. Eranos Foundation Archives)

Figure 49. The theologian, David L. Miller, lecturing on "The Two Sandals of Christ: Descent into History and into Hell," at Eranos in August 1981.
(Ph. Luciano Soave. Eranos Foundation Archives)

Figure 50. From the left, [unidentified], Marie-Jeanne Auzas, Michel Cazenave, Catherine Ritsema-Gris, the ethnolohist and scholar of African cultures, Dominique Zahan (1915–1992), Rudolf Ritsema, Eva Zahan, James Hillman, [unidentified], Gilbert Durand, [unidentified], Jean Brun, [unidentified], David Miller, Jacky Brun, gathered at the Eranos Round Table in August 1981.
(Ph. Luciano Soave. Eranos Foundation Archives)

JUNGIANA

Olga Fröbe-Kapteyn and Carl Gustav Jung among the lotus flowers
of the Eranos garden in August 1936.
(Ph. Margarethe Fellerer. Eranos Foundation Archives)

KRISTINE MANN:
JUNG'S "MISS X" AND A PIONEER IN PSYCHOANALYSIS

BETH DARLINGTON

> [W]e must not forget that only a very few people are artists in
> life; that the art of life is the most distinguished and rarest of
> all the arts.
>
> —C. G. Jung

> From the middle of life onward, only he remains vitally alive
> who is ready to *die with life.*
>
> —C. G. Jung

INTRODUCTION

For many years I have been interested in the history of the earliest Jungians in the United States.[1] All were women living in New York City. The first was Dr. Beatrice Hinkle, who began to practice as a Jungian analyst there just before World War I; the next three were Drs. Kristine Mann, Eleanor Bertine, and Esther Harding, who launched their New York analytic careers in the early 1920s. Different sources disagree slightly on the dates, but, as far as I surmise, Mann and Bertine began in 1921, and Harding in 1924. A fifth woman, Frances Wickes, came to the scene at roughly the same time.

A graduate of the C. G. Jung Institute of New York, Beth Darlington, Ph.D., is a licensed and certified Jungian analyst and has a private practice in Poughkeepsie, NY, where she has been a professor of English at Vassar College for many years. She is a member of the New York Association for Analytical Psychology and the International Association for Analytical Psychology; she serves on the Boards of the C. G. Jung Institute of New York and the Kristine Mann Library, has taught both at the Institute and New York's Jung Foundation, and edits the book review section for the Foundation's journal *Quadrant.* Her books, articles, and lectures include work on the English Romantic poets, mythology, fairy tales, and Jungian psychology.

Each has a unique story, and those stories testify to the courageous lives lived by these wise, strong, and passionate women.

Mann's life especially interests me, as I found out that—like me— before becoming a Jungian analyst she had taught in the English department at Vassar College, where Eleanor Bertine had been her student. I became curious about that Vassar connection and discovered that several distinguished early Jungians were Vassar graduates—Dr. Cary Fink Baynes, who never practiced as an analyst but became a trusted friend of Jung in Zürich and translated some of his work from German as well as *The Secret of the Golden Flower* and the *I Ching*, for both of which he wrote the forewords; Dr. Elizabeth Goodrich Whitney, who was the first Jungian to practice west of the Hudson River and brought analytical psychology to the Bay area of California; Dr. Margaret Doolittle Nordfeldt, another early New York analyst; and Mary Conover Mellon, whose ambitious dream established the Bollingen Foundation to publish all of Jung's work in English. But my focus here is on Kristine Mann.

I would like to introduce Kristine Mann through the eyes of Elizabeth Goodrich Whitney, who was her student at Vassar and then many years later intermittently a patient. Whitney's portrait describes Mann's physical appearance and demeanor, but it goes beyond that to reveal something of her character and inner life as well. Whitney's words suggest the qualities in Mann that all who knew her came to recognize, revere, and love.

> Kristine Mann was the new English Instructor at the College. Fair-skinned, with ash-gold hair, free-moving, self-contained, direct, simple, grave. She taught us the principles of logical thought and language structure. One day she corrected the misleading words, the cloudy non-sequitur of my composition. Suddenly I realized that she was concerned with truth; and truth under her quiet look and concentrated effort was not rules and correctness, but a reality she served, a snowy peak she climbed towards.
>
> This was the first I saw of her journey[,] which was always trail-breaking. She was serving scholarship and culture; a woman pioneering in a man's domain.

When I saw her fifteen years later, she had pioneered still further into that world, into science and medicine. She had to know the truth about the body, about our basic nature. She was teaching men and women students.

But it was not even this mastery which struck me most. She was as simple and direct as before. She enjoyed light-heartedly whatever the moment brought. But in the midst of a mutual friend's crisis she gave sympathy, tenderness, heart. She shared deeply. She was much older [45] and worn. She had entered the domain of woman as well as of mind; of human love, of human values.

Something else she had. What it was I did not know then. Already she planned to study with Dr. Jung. Already she was breaking trail into the world of the psyche. What was she seeking? All I knew was that beyond the single-mindedness and single-heartedness she had won, there was a commitment, a devotion to a further, greater quest.

From that time on, this journey of the soul was her central preoccupation. She gave generously to friends, to her students, to group needs, to analytical studies. She still lived as forthrightly and happily in the moment. But whatever the ebb and flow of circumstances, whether the world was at peace or in the most devastating war of its history, whether she was sick or well, even through [her] long last year of illness, she grew in tenderness and in wisdom; steadily she unfolded and lived the core of her own being.[2]

Whitney's moving tribute evokes the personality of a woman I would like to have known: a vibrant, brave seeker, fearlessly engaged in the process that the poet John Keats called soul-making and that Jung later referred to as the development of personality, or individuation. Whitney saw Mann as a quester, a heroine pursuing her inner Grail. Others who knew her shared that sense of her grounded identity and purpose. But who was Kristine Mann? What is her history? What was her relationship to Jung and the Jungian world? What is the legacy that she left us?

MANN'S PERSONAL HISTORY

Very little is known about Mann's life. She was born in Orange, New Jersey, on August 29, 1873. Her father, Charles Holbrook Mann (1839–1918), was a Swedenborgian minister there and came from an old New England family; Cotton Mather performed the marriage ceremony for Kristine's great- great- great- great-grandfather and his wife Priscilla Grice in Boston in 1711. Kristine's mother, Clausine Borchsenius, emigrated at the age of fourteen from the picturesque medieval town of Rudkøbing in Denmark; she became interested in Emanuel Swedenborg's teachings while working her way through the Northwestern Female College in Evanston, Illinois, which was later incorporated into Northwestern University.[3] Swedenborg's thought influenced Kristine Mann from her early years onward and probably strengthened the affinity that drew her to Jung's work later in her life. We know that from his own early years Jung also felt a strong kinship with Swedenborg's sensibility. "I admire Swedenborg as a great scientist and a great mystic at the same time," Jung affirmed. "His life and work has always been of great interest to me, and I read seven fat volumes of his writings when I was a medical student."[4] Swedenborg's striking ability to hold the tension of opposites, a dual consciousness, helped to shape the vision of both Jung and Mann.

Mann grew up with two older brothers, Horace and Riborg; an elder sister, Clausine; a younger sister, Anna; and a younger brother Holbrook. Kristine began her formal education at the age of four at the Dearborn Morgan School in Orange and graduated from it at eighteen. In 1891, she entered Smith College, graduating with a Bachelor of Arts degree in 1895. She subsequently returned home to work as a private tutor and for her father, in his editing of the weekly *New Church Messenger*, the official publication of the Swedenborgian General Convention. In 1898–1899, she taught Latin and science at the Dearborn Morgan School, but then traveled to Berlin to teach ancient history and English for a year at the Willard School for American girls. While she was there, she continued her education by developing her proficiency in German and attending classes in literature and science at the University of Berlin; she spent vacations in Italy and England. On her return to the United States in 1899–1900, Mann enrolled at the University of Michigan and worked as an assistant in the

Department of English; there she received a Master's degree, and subsequently taught English at Vassar College from 1901 to 1905, specializing in argumentation and debate. But, restlessly, Mann moved on, as if seeking something she had not yet been able to find, or perhaps even define. She next spent several years in New York, first taking graduate courses in education, philosophy, and psychology at Columbia University (studying under John Dewey) and then teaching at the Brearley School.[5] Here a new focus emerged, as Mann's later friend and colleague Dr. Marguerite Block recorded:

> The first important turning point in [Mann's] career was now approaching. From her contacts with girls of school and college age, she had become convinced of the necessity for better health education of women. She had always been fond of athletics, and had been captain of the first basketball team at Smith. She had improved her own physical condition by systematic exercise, and she now felt a strong desire to work for the improvement of women's health. She, therefore, began the study of anatomy at the Women's Medical School in 1907, and two years later, at the age of thirty-six, she entered Cornell Medical School. She received her M.D. in 1913, and went to Wellesley College as a member of the faculty of the Physical Education Training School, having charge of corrective exercises and freshman hygiene.
>
> In 1914 Dr. Mann returned to New York to begin a two-year investigation of the health conditions of saleswomen for the New York Department Store Education Association, and, after our entrance into World War I, she served under the [army's] Ordnance Department, supervising the health of women in munition[s] plants [in Washington, D.C.]. But after the Armistice there came an opportunity for even wider service. The War Work Council of the Y.W.C.A., finding itself at the sudden conclusion of the war with a large amount of war work money, undertook a nation-wide experiment in health education for women. An able corps of women physicians was engaged to lecture and put on health demonstrations in educational institutions all over the country, and Dr. Mann was one of the lecturers on social hygiene.[6]

Eleanor Bertine also participated in this successful, ground-breaking program. The project took Mann to twenty colleges for women; at each she spent a week lecturing and "interviewing hundreds of young women

as a contribution to her intensive study on 'the Psychology of Sex,'"
euphemistically referred to as "social hygiene."[7]

A 1920 article from this period by Ida Clyde Clark in the *Pictorial
Review* contains an interview with Mann, referring to her as "one of
America's most distinguished women physicians."[8] The magazine
boasted a large circulation and supported many reforms in women's
rights, including both suffrage and birth control. In that interview
Mann's radical feminism is apparent as she calls for more social and
political involvement for women. She sharply criticizes the education
of girls and women in the United States, advocating their "mass
education," and urges them to "discard artificialities and aim for greater
simplicity, fearlessness, self-reliance [and] strength." Anticipating
science's later recognition of the strong, significant connection between
mind and body, Mann asserts that those qualities are contingent on
good physical health, which the education of women usually ignored.
While arguing that women and men have the same inherent intellectual
and creative capacities, Mann maintains that in general a woman "uses
her brain differently."

To support her belief in that difference Mann cites her medical
education, which she reports loathing because of the coldly factual,
detached, scientific objectivity of the faculty's attitude toward illness
and suffering and the "atrocious standards" that the training upheld.
She recalls an incident when a mother came into the school's clinic
with a syphilitic baby. The training physician was "one of the greatest
children's specialists in New York" and told his students that the case
was typical. When the mother had left, he instructed the class, "Never
tell the mother what is the matter with the child when you find a
condition like that." Mann "boldly" asked, "Why?" and "he replied
testily, 'Why you always run the risk of causing a misunderstanding
and breaking up a marriage.'" In striking contrast, Mann affirms the
need for empathy and relatedness between doctor and patient, qualities
that the two other women in her medical class at Cornell also recognized
and valued. Their concern was for the baby and the danger of allowing
the woman to produce other diseased children, whereas the twenty
men in the class saw only the facts of a scientific case.[9]

During her early years in New York City a number of Mann's
acquaintances—including Vassar alumnae—were active feminists and
embodied the values of the emancipated New Woman, popularized in

the writing of Ibsen, Shaw, Henry James, and Edith Wharton. Mann's article "Training Women for Marriage," published in the *Smith Alumnae Quarterly* for 1915, articulates her belief in the necessity for women to work to attain confidence in their autonomy.[10] It anticipates a succinct quotation from a 1921 interview that was printed in her obituary in the *New York Times* in 1945:

> I heartily recommend at least a year's business experience for every girl. It is a splendid booster for self-respect. Every woman, whether she expects to marry or not, should possess the feeling of self-reliance which comes with earning a salary. The young wife who knows that, if necessary, she can resume her place in the business world, has a much greater chance of maintaining an equal part in her household than has a young wife who must rely absolutely on the support of someone else.[11]

Dr. Block's account provides more information about Mann's life in the years following World War I:

> Another important project founded at this time under the auspices of the Y.W.C.A. was a Health Center for Business and Industrial Women in New York, of which Dr. Mann became Director in 1920. [The appointment continued, though perhaps part-time, until 1924.]
>
> But it was yet another Y.W.C.A. project, an international convention of women physicians held in New York in 1919 [from September 15 to October 24], which brought Dr. Mann to her second great turning point. One of the major emphases of this convention was on the psychological aspects of individual and social health, and here Dr. Mann came face to face with her true life work. She was greatly attracted to the Jungian system, so ably expounded by Dr. Constance Long, of London, and resolved to enter this new field. She began her preparation under Dr. Beatrice H. Hinkle.[12]

An influential early disciple of Jung and the first woman in England to practice as a psychoanalyst, Constance Long edited and translated a number of his early works, publishing them in England as *Collected Papers on Analytical Psychology* in 1916. Later that year Hinkle's translation of Jung's *Psychology of the Unconscious* was published in the United States. (The work is titled *Symbols of Transformation* in his

Collected Works.) In 1917 Hinkle's volume played a leading role for Mann in an incident, which Eleanor Bertine vividly recalled and described years later as a "curtain raiser." A fierce war was raging in Europe at the time, but that summer she and Mann

> were tramping together in the White Mountains and our ruck-sack contained two warm sweaters, one cake of sweet chocolate, a thermos of water and—Jung's <u>Psychology of the Unconscious</u>! We were just discovering Jung, and the eternal mountains were the perfect setting for that adventure. We were thrilled to recognize the voice of a Master, but we could little guess how deeply it was to influence our lives.[13]

Hearing Constance Long speak in 1919 inspired Mann's determination to become a Jungian analyst herself. Her quest finally had a clear goal. Records from Jung's seminar in Sennen Cove, Cornwall, do not reveal whether Mann joined Beatrice Hinkle and Eleanor Bertine there in 1920, but we do know that Mann studied with Jung the following year.[14] She also began practicing as an analyst part-time in the United States in 1921, and studied abroad with Jung several more times during the 1920s. Early in 1925, she hosted a lecture by him in her New York apartment when he visited the United States, and she saw an American patient, a woman named Sidney Robertson, in Zürich under his supervision during a sojourn there that same year.[15] In 1928, she traveled to Zürich for an intense analysis with him, which began in October.[16] Regarding Mann's new career, Marguerite Block observed,

> In accepting this, her new vocation, Dr. Mann was, consciously or unconsciously, fulfilling one of her father's dearest dreams, for Charles Mann was one of a number of New Church thinkers who were groping toward a system of psychological healing. Swedenborg [1688–1772] himself had stated clearly that the causes of disease are spiritual, though he was too much of a scientist to deny its physical reality, and as early as the 1830's his followers were attempting to formulate a system of healing based on his doctrines. An article in a New Church periodical of 1833 states that "disease always implies a conflict between the internal and external," and Charles Mann, in his remarkable little book *Psychiasis* [1900], writes, "I believe in the healing of the body through the soul. … Every disease corresponds to its own evil

… lusts and passions of the mind, hatreds, jealousies, etc.—The
removal of spiritual causes is the true means of healing—but a
kind of therapeutic method is needed—the clearing of the mind
of all obstructions." It is not surprising that Dr. Mann, in her
paper, "The Self-Analysis of Emanuel Swedenborg," speaks of
him as "a forerunner of Jung." This paper is revealing, not only
of Swedenborg as interpreted in Jungian terms, but also of
Swedenborgianism itself as a matrix for the shaping of a great
Jungian analyst.[17]

That "great Jungian analyst," of course, was Mann herself. And
Block's assessment is on the mark. With several Jungian colleagues Mann
helped to shape the Jungian community in New York. They founded
the Analytical Psychology Club there in 1936, the same year that Mann
and three of those colleagues—Drs. Beatrice Hinkle, Eleanor Bertine,
and Esther Harding—organized Jung's 1936 visit to Bailey Island in
Maine, where the Mann family had summered since 1885 or 1886.
Her father had built a small summer home for his family there in 1887,
which his descendants share to this day. As an adult, Mann bought a
larger vacation home on the island's coast, where Bertine, and later
Harding, joined her for one month each summer and, beginning
in 1926, saw patients who also vacationed on Bailey Island. They
called that house the Trident, perhaps in reference to the friendship
the three women shared. In 1944, they purchased a spacious home
called Inner Ledge, also on Bailey Island's shoreline, where analytic
hours with patients continued. At the Bailey Island Library in 1936,
Jung gave the weeklong seminar, "Dream Symbols of the Individuation
Process," based on the dreams of a brilliant scientist later revealed
to be Wolfgang Pauli.[18] Jung and his wife Emma ate meals at the
Trident, but stayed next door at the home of Mann's sister, Clausine
(Mrs. Perry MacNeille).[19] Jung returned with Emma for a visit in
1937, after giving the Terry Lectures at Yale, and that time stayed at
the home of the three doctors.

Mann died in 1945, before the formal establishment of a training
program in New York. She left her Jungian library to the Analytical
Psychology Club, where it became the nucleus of an outstanding
collection of Jungian materials, and, in its current, expanded form, still
bears her name. It is housed at the Jung Center in mid-Manhattan,

sharing a building with the Jung Foundation, the Jung Institute, the Archive for Research in Archetypal Symbolism (ARAS), and the Analytical Psychology Club.

RECOLLECTIONS OF MANN'S FRIENDS AND COLLEAGUES

The testimonies of others flesh out the picture of Mann's life during her years as an active member of the Jungian community. I have already quoted Elizabeth Whitney's tribute. Statements by her analyst and colleague Beatrice Hinkle, her friend and colleague Esther Harding, as well as her former student, close friend, and colleague Eleanor Bertine bring her to life as a person.

Beatrice Hinkle recalled Mann as "a rare and beautiful woman" and remembered the occasion of their first meeting in 1918, when Mann was helping to organize the world conference of medical women with Y.W.C.A. funds. Hinkle explained,

> At that time I was the only woman analyst in the country and, as there were very few men analysts, I had been working almost alone for nearly ten years. It was therefore a great pleasure to be asked to participate in a conference to which a number of the best known women of Europe were to be invited. … This was the beginning of a long and deep relationship with Dr. Mann.[20]

One result of the conference was Mann's decision to work with Hinkle as her analyst. "As everyone with any experience knows," Hinkle observed,

> the most intimate relationship in the world is that between analyst and analysan[d]. Everything in the character and personality is revealed and here the fine, sensitive, and idealistic quality of Kristine Mann came clearly into view. Her fibre was of a particularly fine substance and coupled with her inquiring and interesting mind created an individual of unique character. … Although Dr. Mann generally preferred a person-to-person relationship, nevertheless she was always an important member of any group with which she was associated and contributed a full share to its activities, its well-being and significance. There was never any aggressiveness in her attitude, but her quiet, unobtrusive spirit carried a strength that hid her shyness and created a sense of power that was reflected in many of her interests.[21]

For many years Esther Harding, like Bertine, came almost every summer to Bailey Island when not working abroad with Jung. Mann, Harding, and Bertine also shared a weekend home in Connecticut farmland near New Milford. Harding sketched the more personal side of Mann's life in a tribute immediately following her death, recalling the times when Mann

> doffed her professional manner with her city clothes, and set off so gaily for Farm or Island home. There the natural zest for life which was so characteristic of her had free play, whether in discussing the latest book she had been reading, or in playing with Baba, who gave her a particular doggie devotion, or going birding in the woods with her field glasses. In each and all she lived fully, with youthful enjoyment of whatever life presented. Even into her sixties she could pull an oar with the best, discounting any praise by saying: "What you have done all your life you do easily"; or she would sit by the hour at her window looking out over the ocean she had known from childhood. It was there that much of her thinking and reading were done, and something of the sea's own blue was reflected in her eyes. But it was as a friend that she was at her best. For she gave of herself freely to her friends. To her, conversation—talk—was an art, deserving of the best one had to give. Discussion of world affairs, about which she was always well informed (she was reading the latest books about the European situation right up to the end of her life), was interspersed with the exchange of news and gossip about the smaller interests of a very human woman. She never grudged the long hours spent in translating articles, and indeed whole books, so that her friends, who did not read German, could share the latest treasures from Zürich without having to wait for the official translations.
>
> She lived, truly and humbly, the truth she had found through her own inner search, which, indeed, she taught, perhaps most effectively, by the reality of her own spiritual achievement.[22]

But we must give the last words to Eleanor Bertine, who knew Mann intimately from Vassar days until her death, and asserted, "A friendship such as this is one of the most precious gifts of life."[23] In mourning, Bertine emphasized the love that Mann inspired.

What can I say in memoriam for my friend, Kristine Mann? Others may speak of her professional achievements, her matured character, her service in the sphere of her life work. None knows better than I how true all that is. But I leave it to those who knew her chiefly through her activities and attainments. To me it was as a friend and companion on the way that her memory will be forever green. We have shared so much in our forty odd years of friendship, and things were always more interesting and exciting for the sharing. Her mind was always questing and inquiring, and from whatever she saw or read, she brought back something of interest to recount and discuss. She could work hard and did. But what a grand loafer she was: She never made the mistake of thinking that time was worthily spent only in busy-ness. Doing nothing, for her, was a fine art, not an empty place on the schedule. After breakfast at Bailey or at the farm, she would light a cigarette, pull up to the fire and begin the day with a good old "talk-fest", for as she used to say, "Spiritual values should come <u>before</u> material." Indeed it became an affectionate little jest in our household to refer to cigarettes as "Kristine's spiritual values!" Such precious times they were, when the talk drifted of its own accord hither and yon. Many a knotty problem of the analytic way was thrashed out together in front of the open fire, and the clarification which resulted could never be attributed to any one of the three of us, for it was truly the fruit of our comradeship in doing nothing in a corner outside of time.

She liked a slow and orderly rhythm of life, with time to heed the inner reverberations of events. Experience for her was always a chord, the melody of the visible interwoven with the deeper notes from the invisible, so the actual moment was never flat or merely obvious. She felt the significant riddle of human fate behind the incidents that make up the facade of daily living.

Relationship to her was not a surface thing to be taken for granted or kept smooth at any price. Rather, in its tides and ripples were revealed the significant movements of the heart, with all its waywardness as well its devotion. This did not make for an easy placidity, which a part of her would have so much liked. Rather the way led at times over stormy seas, but the upshot was always a deeper mutual understanding and trust, in which affection could flower naturally.

She had a genius for friendship. Her amazingly well-stocked mind could always produce something rich or racy to talk about and, in conversation, she gave herself lavishly. The circle was large of those who felt that they had a warmly intimate contact with her. From every period of her long life, devoted friends remained to her. Even when she was stricken with mortal illness, she held court in her bed, and all those who visited there felt the inspiration of her frank and courageous way of facing death.[24]

In 1946, just after the end of another horrific war and after Mann's death, Bertine reflected,

In days like those we are living through, when the human race is showing the depths of evil of which it is capable, it is good to have known a person like Kristine Mann, who in her utterly unostentatious way kept faith to the end with the spirit and with her fellow man. For us her memory will stay alive as one who loved and whom we greatly loved. Her best memorial, and the one she would most have valued, will be built in the hearts of those to whom she has been, and will always be, the beloved friend.[25]

Mann's Analysis with Jung

Without revealing her name, many years earlier Jung had built another memorial to Kristine Mann by presenting a series of *maṇḍalas* that she painted in his well-known essay "A Study in the Process of Individuation." He lectured on her case at the very first Eranos conference in August 1933 and published his paper with five of her paintings the following year in the Eranos-Jahrbuch.[26] In 1939, Stanley Dell produced an expanded translation of that lecture with the same title in an influential collection of Jung's essays: *The Integration of the Personality.*[27] Jung revised, enlarged, and re-published that essay in 1959 in volume 9, Part I, of his *Collected Works.*[28] The revision includes twenty-four of Mann's paintings. Another forty-eight paintings exist in the picture archive of the Jung Institute in Küsnacht, Zürich, three of which were published by Vicente de Moura in 2012 in *The Sacred Round: Mandalas by the Patients of Carl Jung.*[29] All his versions of this paper testify to the respect Jung felt for the extraordinary inner journey that Mann undertook and the inspiration that it provided for Jung himself. In the paper's final form, Jung freights his initially straightforward case study with references to numerous alchemical concepts. His goal appears to be the demonstration of their archetypal nature, power, and universal presence in the psyche. In presenting his work with Mann in 1959, Jung refers to her as "Miss X" and slightly alters the date of her birth.[30] James Webb, nonetheless, was able to claim convincingly in 1976 that Kristine Mann was indeed the woman behind that pseudonym by studying the biographical facts of her life and her astrological chart.[31]

In 2013, the Jungian scholar Jay Sherry discovered two letters from Jung to Esther Harding, dated October 30 and November 19, 1948, in files relating to the Analytical Psychology Club and owned by the Kristine Mann Library. The October letter begins,

> I'm just revising my paper about the Individuation-process of 1933 in which I dealt with Dr. Mann's mandalas up to a certain point. There is going to be a new edition of this paper and at this occasion I have entirely rewritten the whole thing and I have included some of the mandalas which you have brought me recently.[32]

He asks Esther Harding if she and Eleanor Bertine believe that mentioning breast cancer as the cause of Mann's death would seem inappropriate. Apparently the two women saw no indiscretion in this. In the second letter Jung requests the dates of Mann's birth and death and also her astrological chart, if it is available.[33] (A copy of the chart was with the letters in the recently discovered documents.) The letters prove the correctness of Webb's 1976 conjecture and formally establish Mann as the anonymous "Miss X" in Jung's "A Study in the Process of Individuation."

Jung valued Mann's paintings especially highly because of their alchemical implications, their confirmation of the healing power of active imagination, and their *maṇḍala* images. He had become aware of the symbolic power of *maṇḍalas* during his own spiritual crisis documented in *The Red Book,* now familiar to many of us since its publication in 2009. Alchemy became a subject of strong interest to Jung in 1928, the year of Mann's intensive analysis with him and in which Richard Wilhelm sent him the German translation of the Taoist text, *The Secret of the Golden Flower.* Significantly, at the conclusion of the 1939 revision of his Eranos lecture on Mann's case material, Jung baldly states that when she came to him he had no knowledge of alchemy and that "this very case ... led [him] to the study of alchemy."[34] He omitted this statement in the 1959 publication, and James Webb points out that Jung had in fact encountered alchemical concepts much earlier in reading the work of Herbert Silberer.[35] In alchemy Jung recognized a new symbolic system that moved beyond the models of Gnosticism and Christianity, which he felt he had outgrown, but for which he had been unable to find a satisfactory substitute before 1928. In interpreting Mann's paintings he repeatedly insists that the images derived spontaneously from Mann herself, not from any influence that his own intellectual interests might have imposed upon her. How much Jung in fact knew about alchemy at the time remains uncertain, and he claimed Mann's ignorance of the tradition; it is probable, however, that, from her father, Mann had gleaned some knowledge of healing and alchemy that was known to writers on Swedenborg, who had associated his teachings with the Hermetic tradition.

In his writings Jung describes Mann in less personal terms than her New York friends and colleagues did, but he acknowledges that her father was "exceptional" and notes that she herself had "varied interests, was extremely cultured, and possessed a lively turn of mind."[36] He reports that "Miss X" began treatment in 1928 because of "some difficult experiences that could not be avoided" and her realization that she had gotten "stuck."[37] Modern readers have assumed that the difficulties that he alluded to may refer to the complex personal relationships that existed between Mann, Bertine, and Harding. It seems probable that Mann and Bertine had been lovers and that in the early 1920's Harding replaced Mann as Bertine's partner.[38] In his commentary Jung simply refers to Mann's "two women friends who shared her intellectual interests and were joined to her in a lifelong friendship."[39] Impressively, and perhaps because of Mann's work with Jung, the three remained close friends and colleagues for roughly a quarter of a century; acquaintances sometimes referred to them as "the troika."

Jung keeps the nature of the women's relationships confidential but does reveal that "Miss X" had a very positive father complex—she was a "fille à papa"—and "did not have a good relation to her mother."[40] Mann's father had died in 1918 and her mother in 1923. Mann realized that visiting Denmark, her mother's birthplace, might help her connect more positively to her maternal roots, and she made that pilgrimage in 1928, just before coming to Zürich to work with Jung. (He did not name Denmark as that birthplace in his 1939 version of his essay, but did so in his 1933 Eranos lecture.) In Denmark Mann discovered that her most powerful emotional response was to the landscape, and unexpectedly she experienced a desire to paint it. She had never drawn or painted before but at age fifty-five took up watercolors. The resulting "modest landscapes filled her with a strange feeling of contentment," Jung recounts, and "seemed to fill her with new life."[41] In Zürich before her first appointment with him she began painting another landscape from memory, but it transformed into an image of a woman—Mann herself—on a rocky seacoast, the lower half of her body stuck fast and helplessly within a block of stone. She gazes out to the sea on her left. In his *Visions* seminar on May 4, 1932, Jung comments on a vision of Christiana Morgan in which she stood, rather than sitting, by the sea; however, the scene is relevant to what Mann depicted:

> The sea is always the symbol of the collective unconscious, and standing on the seashore is a symbolic situation which occurs often in dreams or visions, meaning that one is on the edge of the conscious world, as it were, looking into the limitless distance, or the uttermost depths of the ocean. The sea, the unconscious, looks like a mirror; one cannot penetrate into it, but one knows that its shining surface covers an immense depth containing all sorts of mysterious forms. And when standing there, she [Morgan, but Mann as well] naturally expects something to happen or to appear; she is looking into the distance, or down into the sea, and that *looking*, psychologically, brings about the activation of the object. It is as if something were emanating from one's spiritual eye that evokes or activates the object of one's vision.[42]

Mann experienced such an activation, for as she painted she had a fantasy image of Jung as a medieval sorcerer releasing her from imprisonment with a magic wand. Jung's continuing commentary on Morgan's vision might well have been a description of Mann's process as she contemplated the image before her.

> The English verb, to look at, does not convey the meaning, but the German *betrachten*, which is an equivalent, means also to make pregnant. *Trächtig* means to carry, to be big with young,

> pregnant, but it is used only for animals, not for human beings; a pregnant cow is a *trächtige Kuh*. So to look at or concentrate upon a thing, *betrachten*, gives the quality of becoming pregnant to the object. And if it is pregnant, then something is due to come out of it; it is alive, it produces, it multiplies. That is the case with any fantasy image; one concentrates upon it, and then finds that one has great difficulty in keeping the thing quiet. It gets restless, it shifts, something is added, or it multiplies itself; one fills it with living power, and it becomes pregnant.[43]

Mann and Jung both recognized the sexual symbolism in her fantasy of the appearance of the wizard with his wand, but both read the image symbolically. To Jung's surprise Mann spontaneously discovered active imagination, which had proved so fruitful to him during the years that *The Red Book* documents. Jung believed that Mann was trapped in the unconsciousness of Mother Earth. In her painting of herself at the coastline, several of the rocks behind her resembled eggs, and he was certain that they presaged a process of transformation for her, although he had no notion of how it might develop; he does not specifically mention that the waves of the sea also imitate ovular shapes, also foretelling a birth. Mann's images of the earth and the sea both contain her undiscovered self. With Jung's encouragement and no knowledge of what the next images might be, Mann continued her spontaneous process, although it sometimes felt very dangerous to her.

In her next painting, labeled Picture 2, and the first *maṇḍala* that we see, lightning strikes one of the stones on the seashore—which Jung had seen as an egg—and a transformation begins. Jung, the sorcerer, becomes a flash of aerial fire, and Mann represents herself as a sphere with a red center containing a seed.[44]

According to Mann, her third painting and the actual moment of painting it represented "the 'climax' of her life."[45] It incorporates two major dreams from her earlier life, and in it she saw the vibrating silver "wings of Mercury" as a band encircling a "planet in the making," with a golden serpent overlooking its movement from above.[46] Liberation comes with this presence of Hermes (the messenger of the gods), himself the god of revelation, and the spirit—Jung explains in his revised text—presiding over alchemical processes. Mann's vibrant images that follow—more snakes, wings, a symbolic coniunctio, quaternities, dualities of exquisitely balanced sun and moon, day and night, then

Manhattan's skyline, rainbows, flowers, plants, trees, animals, hexagrams from the *I Ching*, eyes, and a few human forms— subsequently unfold in exuberant plays of bright, confident colors, which Jung encouraged her to use. In his discussion of these images Jung saw Mann free herself from dominant animus energy, to open receptively, to new feminine energy, as she gave her creative intuition the power to overrule her critical thought processes.[47]

The final painting by Mann that Jung includes is a breath-taking image of what appears to be a prototypical white lotus, cradled in green petals above two golden snakes, with a single golden star above it—all enclosed in a shining golden circle. In her note on the back of the painting Mann reveals that she painted the image in May 1938 on her last trip to Jung, and she calls the flower "night blooming cereus."[48] The identification is significant for several reasons. One is that the blossom is the flower of a tall, tropical American cactus. Mann is not copying a lotus from the mythologies of India or the medieval mystical white rose to which Dante pays homage in *The Divine Comedy* as an image of Paradise with God at its center surrounded by saints. Instead she defines her own American source of inspiration. The word *cereus* derives from the Latin word *candle* and the Greek word meaning *wax*, and the theme of light, which the word implicitly suggests, occurs repeatedly among Mann's metaphors. In her active imaginations and analysis Mann found the light within her own inner darkness and loneliness, her fears, her negative feelings toward her mother, her regret at not having had children, and other issues that Jung does not reveal. The stuck feeling she had experienced before her deep work with him began appears to have transformed into a new serenity.

Mann's Later Work

Mann continued to paint until shortly before her death and left a painting unfinished.[49] She never wrote as much as her colleagues Bertine and Harding did, but three late talks for New York's Analytical Psychology Club show the clarity of her thinking and eloquence of her expression. They also reveal some of her values and outlook. In one lecture, "The Self-Analysis of Emanuel Swedenborg" (1940), Mann traces the process of a life-changing experience that Swedenborg underwent beginning in his fifty-fifth year—her age when she embarked on her intense work with Jung.[50] Mann's father, too, had gone through a spiritual crisis, beginning in his late fifties, after which he elected to leave the Swedenborgian church to found his own, which was more personally focused, psychologically deeper, and more compelling to him. Mann examines Swedenborg's dreams and his surrender to a disorienting process demanding a radical sacrifice of ego that concluded in a profound spiritual transformation and reorientation in his work. His encounter with the unconscious parallels aspects of Jung's description of his own descent in *The Red Book*, which similarly transformed his life and work. Mann demonstrates that Swedenborg recognized the dangers of projection, the limits of rationality, the value of the tension of opposites, and suffering as a guide to life. She sees him as "a forerunner of Jung" and interprets his experience, though incomplete, in Jungian terms.[51] In Swedenborg's dreams Mann also detects a suggestion of *maṇḍala* imagery, another similarity to what Jung had discovered and that to his surprise Mann herself independently discovered in her 1928 analysis with him. Discussing Swedenborg's visions and feelings, Mann affirms the value of recognizing unconscious processes and the importance of moving beyond rationality to honor the symbolic life, to claim a life of the spirit that opens us to deeper mysteries. In writing about Swedenborg's crisis, she appears to be formally re-experiencing both her father's and her own crises, and from a detached, objective perspective acknowledges the absolute necessity of the integration of opposites in individuation.

The strong influence of Swedenborg's integrated vision of human existence appears in Mann's comments on a *maṇḍala* she completed in the autumn of 1943, after an operation for breast cancer, the illness that took her life two years later. The vibrantly colored image contains eight small circles holding pictures of twelve flying geese above, and a frog on a lily pad below; along the right side an old stone church, a scroll bearing the words "Whoever is near to ME is near the Fire," and a dog (perhaps Baba?); and on the left, a bluebird on a branch feeding a fledgling, a crucifixion, and two sheep beside each other in a pasture. Flames radiate out from a star at the center, and four blue fans curve out to mark four corners for the painting. Mann titles the piece—unpublished until 2012—"The Mandala is born," and comments,

> From the black depths of the unconscious it is forced up into
> the light of day. It must breathe. The transition is fraught with
> suffering. The whole weight of evil threatens to overcome one

until one differentiates between body and spirit. The fan-like expansions are like lungs—opening and closing to draw in and absorb from the outer world. The crucifiction [sic] is what my feelings went through when I was operated upon. I shared some of the horror of humanity brought on by the most deadly of all diseases at the present day. I shared in one of the deepest afflictions of humanity. But there might be compensations in the vigor of the spirit. The idea (so prevalent—and particularly so among Swedenborgians) of the all-pervading goodness of life must be crucified—however overwhelming the suffering in the acceptation [that is, reception or approval] of the evil, the dark inscrutable horrors of life.[52]

In her remarks at the Analytical Psychology Club's memorial service for Mann, Esther Harding quotes passages from the Gnostic "Acts of John," which, she says, Mann "asked to have read to her again and again during the last days of her life."[53] Following the Resurrection in that text Christ appears in a dark cave and explains the paradoxical experience of the crucifixion, suffered and yet not suffered, because of the transcendent mystery of the divine spirit within.

In a lecture that Mann read at a meeting of the New York Analytical Psychology Club in 1938, the same year that she last saw Jung in person, she spoke on "The Shadow of Death." I cannot help wondering if she had unconscious premonitions of her own painful death seven years later. In "The Soul and Death," Jung asserts that dying "has its onset long before actual death," and her reflections seem to confirm that.[54] Mann quotes a stirring passage from the "Tibetan Book of the Dead":

O nobly born, when thy body and mind were separating, thou must have experienced a glimpse of Pure Truth, subtle, sparkling, bright, dazzling, glorious and radiantly awesome, in appearance like a mirage moving across a landscape in spring-time in one continuous stream of vibrations. Be not daunted thereby, nor terrified, nor awed. This is the radiance of thine own true nature. Recognize it.

From the midst of that radiance, the natural sound of Reality, reverberating like a thousand thunders simultaneously sounding,

> will come. That is the natural sound of thine own real Self. Be
> not daunted thereby, nor terrified, nor awed.[55]

Mann accepts death here as an opportunity "to come into closer and closer relation to what we really are, through the withdrawal of libido from a life lived almost solely in the conscious." She asks, "Who can say, then, that the later years may not be a time of preparation for a dimly perceived future rather than for the actual process of dying?"[56] In her case it would seem difficult to deny.

Mann's conclusion to this 1938 lecture implicitly circles back to the beautiful flower which she painted in her last analytic sessions with Jung in the same year as her lecture and which he printed in 1959 as the final image in the series of her *maṇḍalas*. She wrote,

> It is as if there had been implanted in each of us at birth a seed,
> "smaller than the small and greater than the great" which is
> nurtured largely in unconsciousness during the passionate
> strivings of early and middle life. But that as the conflicts of the
> ego period abate and the shadows approach there could take place
> within the psyche a complete unfolding of that four-petaled
> flower of eternal life which Jung has called the Self.[57]

Mann's painting of her serene, multi-petaled, white flower symbolically depicts the numinous manifestation of the full energy of that seed.

Mann gave her last talk at the Analytical Psychology Club in the spring of 1943, two and a half years before her death, while another devastating war brought death in Europe and the Pacific. The context was a memorial meeting for the distinguished mythologist Heinrich Zimmer, who had died that year at age fifty-three. She quotes his words from his last lecture to the Analytical Psychology Club on "The Integration of Evil":

> Nothing dies, nothing perishes, nothing meets utter annihilation.
> No Energy, no virtue is lost—neither in physics nor in <u>psychics</u>.
> Death and destruction are an outer mask of transformation—
> for better or for worse, for higher or for lower.[58]

Mann closes, "It is given then to us, the living, to keep fresh in our hearts the inspiration which [his] ... brief stay among us has bequeathed as a lasting heritage."[59]

CONCLUSION

Mann learned to accept life's tides of change, but also to see the
radiance of eternity that shines through them. She was hospitalized
for five months before her death on November 12, 1945, while suffering
agonizing pain from breast cancer. Nine and a half months before that,
and feeling the isolating effects of World War II, Jung wrote her a warm,
personal letter describing his near-death experience following a heart
attack the year before. As far as I am aware, it is his first written account
of that experience. Years later he published an expanded description
in Chapter X of *Memories, Dreams, Reflections*, titled "Visions." I have
quoted Jung's letter in full, below, as it testifies to the strength of the
respect and friendship that he felt for Kristine Mann and demonstrates
a kinship that they shared in facing life's final mystery of death:

> 1 February 1945
>
> My dear Dr. Mann,
>
> Eleanor Bertine has already given me the news of
> your illness in a letter I received a few days ago. I wish
> I could talk to you personally, but one is so far from
> each other and it is such a long time we are separated
> from the rest of the world that one feels quite hopeless
> about a communication. We don't even trust our
> letters to be capable of jumping over the abyss which
> yawns between us and the wide world. Still I hope that
> a good star conveys my letter to you.
>
> As you know, the angel of death has struck me
> down too and almost succeeded in wiping me off the
> slate. I have been practically an invalid ever since,
> recovering very very slowly from all the arrows that
> have pierced me on all sides. Fortunately enough my
> head has not suffered and I could forget myself in my
> scientific work. On the whole my illness proved to be
> a most valuable experience, which gave me the
> inestimable opportunity of a glimpse behind the veil.
> The only difficulty is to get rid of the body, to go quite
> naked and void of the world and the ego-will. When
> you can give up the crazy will to live and when you
> seemingly fall into a bottomless mist, then the truly

real life begins with everything which you were meant to be and never reached. It is something ineffably grand. I was free, completely free and whole, as I never felt before. I found myself 15,000 km. from the earth, and I saw it as an immense globe resplendent in an inexpressibly beautiful blue light. I was on a point exactly above the southern end of India, which shone in a bluish silvery light with Ceylon like a shimmering opal in the deep blue sea. I was in the universe, where there was a big solitary rock containing a temple. I saw its entrance illuminated by a thousand small flames of coconut oil. I knew I was to enter the temple and I would reach full knowledge. But at this moment a messenger from the world (which by then was a very insignificant corner of the universe) arrived and said that I was not allowed to depart and at this moment the whole vision collapsed completely. But from then on for three weeks I slept, and was wakeful each night in the universe and experienced the complete vision. Not I was united with somebody or something—it was united, it was the hierosgamos, the mystic Agnus. It was a silent invisible festival permeated by an incomparable, indescribable feeling of eternal bliss, such as I never could have imagined as being within reach of human experience. Death is the hardest thing from the outside and as long as we are outside of it. But once inside you taste of such completeness and peace and fulfillment that you don't want to return. As a matter of fact, during the first month after my vision I suffered from black depressions because I felt that I was recovering. It was like dying. I did not want to live and to return into this fragmentary, restricted, narrow, almost mechanical life, where you were subject to the laws of gravity and cohesion, imprisoned in a system of 3 dimensions and whirled along with other bodies in the turbulent stream of time. There was fulness, meaning fulfillment, eternal movement (not movement in time).

Although your letter is dated Nov. 27th/44, I hope
that my answer will reach you. Your letter arrived
today and I am writing at once.

Throughout my illness something has carried me.
My feet were not standing on air and I had proof that
I have reached a safe ground. Whatever you do, if you
do it sincerely, will eventually become the bridge to
your wholeness, a good ship that carries you through
the darkness of your second birth, which seems to be
death to the outside. I will not last too long any more.
I am marked. But life has fortunately become
provisional. It has become a transitory prejudice, a
working hypothesis for the time being, but not
existence itself.

Be patient and regard it as another difficult task,
this time the last one.

I greet you, CARL G. JUNG[60]

Jung's farewell reads as a welcome to the other realm that he himself
had visited with such intensity and ecstasy only months before. Again
in Mann's final transition, he could play the role of the wise guide
whom she trusted and who had encouraged her in the past. One
morning three or four months before her death she beheld "an ineffable
light glowing" in her hospital room, which "lasted for about an hour
and a half and left her with a deep sense of peace and joy ... that
remained indelible" even though her health worsened and her mind
deteriorated. Jung later told Eleanor Bertine he believed that at the
time of that experience "her spirit had left her body."[61]

A few years earlier, in "The Shadow of Death," Mann had
speculated,

[P]erhaps there is a light that shines in darkness, and perhaps the
darkness is growing to comprehend it. It is the light that gives
meaning to life and in its brilliance enables us to comprehend in
our own experience the purpose of that which we have lived.

Perhaps it is just our more understanding contact with our
unconscious processes that will enable us more and more to
comprehend this light that shines in darkness so that the later
years of life may help (as people live them with more wisdom) to

> throw light on that greatest of all mysteries—possible life after death, about which even after eons of life on earth we know nothing. Just perhaps even at death the continuity of consciousness will not be broken. By a bare possibility, a deeper level of awareness may arise which demands for its comprehension the withdrawal of the light of life itself.[62]

Mann understood that the soul afraid of dying never learns to live. Her transcendent vision of human existence grounded in her own consciously lived life is her final legacy to us—the supreme gift of an artist in life.

NOTES

1. I am indebted to many scholars, analysts, librarians, and relatives of Kristine Mann for information and assistance in the preparation of this essay. I particularly wish to acknowledge Doris Albrecht, Polly Armstrong, Chris Beach, Peggy Brooks, Robin Brown, Janet Careswell, Vicente L. de Moura, Suzanne Gieser, Gretchen Lieb, Kay Mann, Michele McKee, Ronald Patkus, Lorna Peachin, Phil Richardson, Jay Sherry, and Nanci Young. I presented earlier versions of this paper at the "Celebration of the 75th Anniversary of C. G. Jung's 1936 Visit to Bailey Island and Three Bailey Island Summer Residents Who Hosted Him: Drs. Kristine Mann, Esther Harding & Eleanor Bertine," September 25, 2011, Bailey Island Library Hall, Bailey Island, Maine; at "Founding Mothers: An Event Honoring the Four Women Doctors Who Introduced Jung's Analytical Psychology to the United States—Beatrice Hinkle, Kristine Mann, Esther Harding, and Eleanor Bertine," the C. G. Jung Center, New York, March 31, 2012; and at the XIXth International Congress for Analytical Psychology, "100 Years on: Origins, Innovations and Controversies," sponsored by the International Association for Analytical Psychology, Copenhagen, Denmark, on August 18–23, 2013.

2. Elizabeth Goodrich Whitney, *In Memoriam: Kristine Mann, 1873–1945* (New York, NY: Analytical Psychology Club of New York, 1946), pp. 24–25.

3. Mann family records given to the author.

4. Quoted in Harvey F. Bellin, "Opposition Is True Friendship," in Harvey F. Bellin and Darrell Ruhl, eds., *Blake and Swedenborg:*

Opposition Is True Friendship (NewYork, NY: Swedenborg Foundation, 1985), p. 44.

5. Mann family records.

6. Marguerite Block, *In Memoriam: Kristine Mann, 1873–1945* (New York, NY: Analytical Psychology Club of New York, 1946), pp. 8–9.

7. Ida Clyde Clarke, "Has Woman Any Real Creative Genius?" *Pictorial Review*, April 1920. A xeroxed copy of this article exists in the archives of the Kristine Mann Library. The name of the journal and its date are written in by hand. Despite searches, I have not been able to find the article in its stated context. In addition to its text, the article is valuable in providing a photograph of Mann early in her career as a medical doctor. Her eyes are thoughtful and her forehead high and slightly furrowed between her eyebrows. Seeing the photograph made me understand a remark that Grace Childs, President of the Analytical Psychology Club at the time of Mann's death, made in her introductory words at the club's 1946 memorial service honoring Mann: "I was not one of those fortunate persons who knew Dr. Mann well, but I remember the deep impression her face made upon me the first time I saw her. I was sure I had seen her before—her face haunted me. Sometime later I realized suddenly her face resembled strikingly one of the Sybils [sic] in the ceiling frescoes of "The Creation" in the Vatican, by Michael Angelo—frescoes I had studied long ago. The night she read her paper on "The Shadow of Death" a new vista opened for me. I realized for the first time what a creative old age might mean" (Block, *In Memoriam*, p. 5). In addition to Mann's sibylline appearance, she also might be regarded as a seer in her deep understanding of what human life may be.

8. *Ibid.*

9. *Ibid.*

10. Kristine Mann, "Training Women for Marriage," *Smith Alumnae Quarterly*, vol. 6, April 1915, pp. 158–63.

11. Obituary of Kristine Mann, *New York Times*, Nov. 13, 1945.

12. Block, *In Memoriam*, pp. 9–10.

13. Eleanor Bertine, *In Memoriam: Kristine Mann, 1873–1945* (New York, NY: Analytical Psychology Club of New York, 1946), p. 13.

14. In 1921 Mann accompanied her former student Cary Fink de Angulo (better known as Cary Baynes after her 1927 marriage to H. G. Baynes) and Cary's three-year-old daughter Ximena to Europe, where Mann studied with Jung. [C. G. Jung, *Analytical Psychology: Notes of the Seminar Given in 1925*, ed. William McGuire, (Princeton, NJ: Princeton University Press, 1989), p. xiv].

15. *C. G. Jung Speaking: Interviews and Encounters*, eds. William McGuire and R. F. C. Hull (London: Picador, 1980), p. 48; C. G. Jung, *Analytical Psychology: Notes of the Seminar Given in 1925*, ed. William McGuire (Princeton, NJ: Princeton University Press, 1989), p. xii.

16. Vicente L. de Moura, "Mandalas of the Picture Archives of the C. G. Jung Institute Zürich, Küsnacht: Case 016," in Vanya Nick, ed., *The Sacred Round: Mandalas by The Patients of Carl Jung* (Atlanta, GA: Oglethorpe University Museum of Art, 2012), pp. 25–37.

17. Block, *In Memoriam*, p. 10.

18. The text was expanded and published as "Individual Dream Symbolism in Relation to Alchemy," in *The Collected Works of C. G. Jung*, vol. 12, eds. Herbert Reed, Michael Fordham, and Gerhard Adler, trans. R. F. C. Hull (New York, NY: Pantheon Books, Inc., 1953), §§ 44–331.

19. Henrietta Bancroft, "Bailey Island: The Contribution of a Place to Analytical Psychology," *An Annual of Archetypal Psychology and Jungian Thought* (Dallas, TX: Spring, 1983), p. 195.

20. Beatrice Hinkle, *In Memoriam: Kristine Mann, 1873–1945* (New York, NY: Analytical Psychology Club of New York, 1946), pp. 19–20.

21. *Ibid.*, pp. 20–21.

22. Esther Harding, "In Memoriam: Dr. Kristine Mann," *APC of New York Bulletin* 7 (9, 1945): 2–3.

23. Bertine, *In Memoriam*, pp. 13–14.

24. *Ibid.*, pp. 11–13.

25. *Ibid.*, p. 14.

26. C. G. Jung, "Zur Empirie des Individuationsprozesses," *Eranos-Jahrbuch* 1 (1933): 201–14.

27. C. G. Jung, *The Integration of the Personality*, trans. Stanley M. Dell (New York, NY and Toronto: Farrar & Rinehart, Inc., 1939).

28. C. G. Jung, "A Study in the Process of Individuation," in *The Collected Works of C. G. Jung*, vol. 9–1, eds. William McGuire, Herbert Read, Michael Fordham, and Gerhard Adler, trans. R. F. C. Hull, 2ⁿᵈ ed. (Princeton, NJ: Princeton University Press, 1959/ 1968), §§ 525–626.

29. de Moura, "Mandalas of the Picture Archives," p. 25.

30. Changed from August 29, 1873; see Jung, CW 9–1, § 606.

31. James Webb, *The Occult Establishment* (La Salle, IL: Open Court, 1976), pp. 188–91.

32. C. G. Jung, manuscript letter, Oct. 30, 1948, Archives of the Kristine Mann Library, New York.

33. C. G. Jung, manuscript letter, Nov. 19, 1948, Archives of the Kristine Mann Library, New York.

34. C. G. Jung, "A Study in the Process of Individuation," in *The Integration of the Personality*, p. 51.

35. Webb, *The Occult Establishment*, p. 391.

36. Jung, CW 9–1, § 525.

37. *Ibid.*

38. Bertine's obituary in the *New Milford [Connecticut] Times* from Jan. 4, 1968, mentions Harding as Bertine's "friend and partner."

39. Jung, CW 9–1, § 543.

40. Jung, CW 9–1, § 525.

41. *Ibid.*

42. C. G. Jung, *Visions: Notes of the Seminar Given in 1930–1934*, ed. Claire Douglas, vol. 2 (Princeton, NJ: Princeton University Press, 1997), p. 660.

43. *Ibid.*

44. Jung's revised 1959 text mentions a "glowing red centre" (§ 543), but in the 1939 text he specifies that the red center contains a seed; see Jung, *The Integration of the Personality*, p. 35.

45. Jung, CW 9–1, § 549.

46. Jung, CW 9–1, § 545.

47. Mann discusses the difficulty of overcoming domination of the animus in "Individuation and the Family Problem," a paper that she read at a meeting of the Analytical Psychology Club in New York in March 1942 and subsequently published in *Spring*'s annual journal for 1942, pp. 80–92; without reference to her own history pp. 88–89

appear to reflect her own experience. *Spring* was originally published for its members by New York's Analytical Psychology Club, which remained its sponsor through the 1970s when James Hillman took over its leadership.

48. Jung, CW 9-1, § 615, fn. 172.

49. Vicente L. de Moura, *Individuation: The Case of Mrs. X* (Atlanta, GA: Jung Society of Atlanta, 2012), CD.

50. Kristine Mann, "The Self-Analysis of Emanuel Swedenborg," typescript (New York, NY: Analytical Psychology Club of New York City, 1940); this essay was reprinted by Dr. Anna Richardson, Mann's sister and literary executor, in *The Review of Religion X* (3, 2000): 266–93.

51. *Ibid.*, p. 52.

52. Quoted from Mann's notes on the painting; de Moura, "Mandalas of the Picture Archives," p. 37.

53. Harding, *In Memoriam*, pp. 26–28.

54. C. G. Jung, "The Soul and Death" (1934), in *The Collected Works of C. G. Jung*, vol. 8, ed. and trans. Gerhard Adler and R. F. C. Hull (Princeton, NJ: Princeton University Press, 1970), § 809.

55. Quoted in Kristine Mann, "The Shadow of Death," Typescript (New York, NY: Analytical Psychology Club of New York City, 1938) p. 22.

56. *Ibid.*, p. 23.

57. *Ibid.*

58. Quoted by Gertrude Ingersoll in her tribute to Mann, *In Memoriam: Kristine Mann, 1873–1945* (New York, NY: Analytical Psychology Club of New York, 1946), pp. 18–19.

59. *Ibid.*, p. 19.

60. C. G. Jung, *Letters*, ed. and trans. Gerhard Adler and R. F. C. Hull (Princeton, NJ: Princeton University Press, 1973) pp. 357–59.

61. *Ibid.*, p. 436.

62. Mann, "The Shadow of Death," p. 21.

BOOK REVIEWS

Olga Fröbe-Kapteyn in her library at Casa Gabriella in the 1950s.
(Ph. Margarethe Fellerer. Eranos Foundation Archives)

Book Review

Hans Thomas Hakl, *Eranos: An Alternative Intellectual History of the Twentieth Century*, translated by Christopher McIntosh. London: Equinox, 2013.

REVIEWED BY ROBERT HINSHAW

E ighty years after the initial Eranos Conference in Ascona in 1933 there is at long last an English-language, in-depth treatment of the history of Eranos, filling a gaping void. The original German-language version of this book appeared in 2001 after years of research, but only very recently has this excellent translation made its appearance in English.[1] I am happy to note that the author, Hans Thomas Hakl, has also contributed an essay to this issue of *Spring Journal* (see pp. 57–78).

While there have been numerous publications by and about the oft-renowned protagonists of the Eranos story—or, more accurately, stories—there has never before been such a thoroughly researched publication as this one; it immediately comprises a major source and welcome contribution towards whatever renaissance Eranos might yet be able to achieve. Utilizing the private diary of Eranos founder Olga Fröbe-Kapteyn, an unpublished history of Eranos by Catherine Ritsema, and many other previously inaccessible sources along with his own extensive knowledge, research, and diverse direct contacts, Hakl has succeeded in weaving a fascinating and well-documented history not only of Eranos itself, but also of its significant contributions to interdisciplinary scholarly debate in the intellectual history of the twentieth century.

Robert Hinshaw, Ph.D., a former *Spring* editor, co-founded and is publisher of Daimon Verlag in Einsiedeln, Switzerland, and is a faculty member and training analyst/supervisor at the C. G. Jung Institute of Zürich in Küsnacht.

His relationship with Eranos began as a student in the 70s and has continued to the present day.

This is not an easy read by any means, but it is an informative one. For those interested in learning about how Eranos came to be, the context out of which it arose and the phenomenon it became as the twentieth century unfolded, this book contains a wealth of information interwoven with anecdotes and asides. These illuminate not only the phenomenon of Eranos itself, but also the many cross-currents in play, often out of sight, before, during, and after the heyday of the actual conferences. As this work richly illustrates, the "stories behind the scenes" often prove to be far more fascinating—and, at times, more influential—than what had previously been known or assumed; however, while he endeavors to be scientifically and historically correct in his presentation, the author's own interests also become more evident as the text unfolds.

Hakl was already familiar with much of this background information and he was able to consult with the relevant archives and some of the surviving witnesses to further put together many pieces of the puzzle, sharing his findings in often meticulous detail. The text, including its preface, consists of some 300 pages, followed by ninety-seven pages of footnotes, thirty-five of bibliography, and fourteen of index (small print); it is obviously also conceived as a work of reference, and that is surely its destiny.

For the casual reader, it will likely serve *only* as a reference work; to read it thoroughly from cover to cover would undoubtedly prove tedious, if not overwhelming. For this reviewer, as a long-time *afficionado* of Eranos, it was a pleasure—in particular, the many asides and detailed footnotes with quotations of unpublished material, often from relatively obscure sources.

For those not familiar with the background of these classic conferences, which began in 1933, it may come as a surprise to learn of the abundant "esoteric" influences that were involved. Hakl devotes considerable attention to this aspect in his introduction and in a lengthy early chapter entitled, "An Esoteric Prelude to Eranos," in which he not only provides biographical information about its founder Olga Fröbe-Kapteyn, but also the history of the Ascona region where Eranos is located. The now well-known Monte Verità counter-cultural movement had been taking place just up the road from Frau Fröbe's home since the turn of the century. She was influenced by the spirit of this settlement of innovative people seeking creative cultural alternatives and later invited some of the participants to "parlors" in her lakeside home. From 1930 onward, in the years immediately preceding the actual founding of the Eranos Conference, there were so-called "summer sessions" in her newly constructed lecture hall in the lakeside garden. One of the participants was the theosophist Alice Bailey, with whom tensions developed, as we learn, and she was not to return.

Olga Fröbe did a tremendous amount of searching, consulting, and exploring in the years leading up to her formally founding the first Eranos meeting in the summer of 1933; it was both an inner and an outer process. The author details the great interest among European intellectuals for "Eastern thought" in those times, as embodied in the Monte Verità movement and also present in the "School of Wisdom" gatherings in Darmstadt, among others. Olga Fröbe attended and made contacts at both, and her intuitive plan began to take form, all the more so after meeting C. G. Jung at one of the Darmstadt conferences and a visit with German theologian Rudolf Otto, who provided her with the idea of the name for her new conference: *Eranos,* Greek for a festive meal to which each guest contributes a gift. It seemed a perfect fit for what she had in mind and continued to be an apt description through the decades of lectures and lively discussions at the famous round table in her fruitful garden.

East-West themes dominated the first several conferences, interdisciplinary gatherings, with psychologists Jung and G. R. Heyer sharing the lectern and the round table with theologians and experts on Eastern philosophy, among them Martin Buber, Paul Tillich, and Heinrich Zimmer who later was to mentor Joseph Campbell. Hakl provides detailed background information about each of the speakers, how they came to be invited, and how their careers and their relationships with one another and with Olga Fröbe evolved through the decades.

National Socialism and World War II were major influences on the development of Eranos in the early years and until the end of the war. First, German scholars were forbidden to attend the conference and eventually the Swiss borders were closed to travel of any kind, which severely limited the possibilities on all levels. In this regard as well, the author has painstakingly researched the writings and correspondences of each participant, examining, to the extent possible, their attitudes toward National Socialism and the consequences thereof—in several cases, not only resulting in loss of position and stature, but necessitating exodus to another country. Olga Fröbe was determined to keep the conferences alive even in the darkest of times and proclaimed, as Hakl reveals from her correspondence, that she would continue to hold them, even if she were the only participant! It never went quite that far, but there were years when only a handful were able to attend. Aniela Jaffé has beautifully described what some of those sparsely attended but all the more impressive gatherings during the dark years of the war were like.[2]

Olga Fröbe struggled with financial difficulties throughout the history of Eranos, and Hakl devotes a chapter to "interest from the United States," referring primarily to the role of Mary and Paul Mellon, who developed a personal friendship with her and, beginning in 1939, provided substantial support over extended periods, not only to Eranos itself and Olga Fröbe personally, but also to many of the conference speakers who were engaged in research. Towards the end of the war they established the Bollingen Foundation, named after the location of Jung's tower, and, even after Mary Mellon's untimely death in 1946, life-sustaining support for Eranos continued to flow from this source, including the publication of numerous books by Eranos speakers, and, most famously, Jung's *Collected Works* in English and Richard Wilhelm's translation of the *I Ching* (rendered into English by Cary Baynes). The Bollingen Foundation also funded a series of six volumes of selected Eranos lectures in English (a most controversial undertaking, as we learn), edited by Joseph Campbell, who was himself later to become an Eranos speaker (1957, 1959). It was Campbell's plan to pick out the pearls and issue selective volumes; whereas, Frau Fröbe said she would prefer not publishing in English at all if that were to involve interrupting the continuity and interconnectedness of the context, thus breaking the spirit of each year's event. After considerable conflict, they eventually came to an agreement and the project could move forward. With the information we now have from Hakl, it can be said with certainty that the Eranos conferences would not have been able to survive beyond the 1930s without the support of the Mellons.

Chapter 11, "The Heyday Begins," describes the post-war conferences of the late forties, comprising one of the most fruitful periods of Eranos activity and also marking the approaching end for Jung, who last lectured there in 1951, though several brilliant new participants were joining: Karl Kerényi, Adolf Portmann, Gilles Quispel, Henry Corbin, Erich Neumann, and Gershom Scholem, to name the more prominent ones. As with the earlier generation of speakers, Hakl has done "background checks" on each of them, and consulted not only their works, but also their correspondences and, in some cases, their acquaintances. Detailing the *who's who* of that era of Eranos speakers, the chapter also provides a cross-section of the intellectual leaders during this remarkable period of European history and serves as a kind of guidebook to the conferences and to the historical context in which they took place.

The author's descriptions of transitions—of "the changing of the guard"—are well-crafted. "The Early 1950s" describes when Campbell, Laurens van der Post, Mircea Eliade, Daisetz Suzuki, Paul Tillich, Ernst Benz, Herbert Read, and others joined in. This is followed by "Polytheism Versus Monotheism"—the title, while reflecting a main tenet of the work of James Hillman, is also very apt for the streams of interest, loyalty, and conviction that were flowing and often conflicting in those years at the conferences. Was the approach of Hillman, who became a leading figure in the 1970s and 1980s, at odds with Jung, Corbin, Scholem? For Hillman himself this was clearly not the case—rather the contrary!—but Hakl's analysis leaves the rhetorical question standing: he is a chronicler, not a debater. Many interesting connections between Eranos, the Psychology Club in Zürich, and later the Jung Institute are also detailed.

In lamenting the liquidation in 1972 of Rhein Verlag, the eminent publishing house of the Eranos Yearbook from the beginning, Hakl sings the praises of publisher Daniel Brody, claiming that he "contributed as much as Olga Fröbe and C. G. Jung" to the success of Eranos. This is not inherently obvious, but very likely true. Through the yearbooks, Eranos developed a world-wide reputation and following, though it was anything but a profitable undertaking for the idealistic publisher.

The concluding chapters are for this reviewer somewhat disappointing, which actually is probably appropriate; for what happened at Eranos in 1988, with the sudden and unilaterally declared ending of the interdisciplinary conferences by Director Rudolf Ritsema, was just that. Hakl describes the resulting shock and aftermath, the subsequent years of *Yi Ching* roundtables, the founding of *Amici di*

Eranos and other attempts to keep the spirit alive, as well as the valiant efforts of the current stewards of the Eranos spirit—those in direct contact with the original container, grounds, and organization and some others who claim to more truly be carrying on the Eranos tradition. It is difficult terrain for the participants themselves, for the author, and for the readers of this book. Hakl's chronology ends during the period of 2010/2011, and, of course, further developments have taken place since and will continue; the ensuing chapters of Eranos history have yet to be written.

A late chapter entitled, "Eranos as a Prototype," details some of the many organizations and writings that have been spawned, in one way or another, by Eranos. The Archive for Research in Archetypal Symbolism (ARAS) in New York is perhaps the one best known today, but a considerable influence on the founding of Esalen on the California coast is also disclosed, and we are reminded that the work of numerous Eranos participants has been published in the popular New York quarterly, *Parabola*.[3] Hakl also returns in this section to the topic of underground Gnostic connections that were kept by certain key Eranos participants (Corbin, Puech, Quispel, Faivre, Durand, Raine, and others) maintaining that these ties played an essential role in the flourishing of the conferences. The considerable emphasis and detail devoted to Gnosticism and the role it played for certain individuals at Eranos is obviously a field of particular interest for the author.

In the final chapter, Hakl reflects on "The End of a Cycle... Or Perhaps Not." It is an exercise of the kind that unavoidably all friends of Eranos engage in, and we are much better equipped to do so in an informed manner now that he has provided us with this rich source of historical information.

My overall reaction? I find this only-one-of-its-kind work by Hakl invaluable. Not only are the outer developments of Eranos through the decades laid out in a clear and interesting way, but fascinating and essential background information, previously unknown to the great majority of us, helps us to understand a great deal more about what was behind the history and some of the crucial, and at times controversial, decisions that were made. Hakl goes through admirable effort to remain as objective as possible, but it becomes obvious that there is a subjective author, with deep gnostic and hermetic interests, writing, and we are looking at "the facts" through his lens. Much of what he has written is verified by my own more limited experience and reading from other sources. The author does, however, as he readily admits, occasionally speculate based upon limited information and his conclusions are not always accurate (the case of Laurens van der Post being one example where the mark was unfortunately missed).[4] There is more information about Eranos yet to be uncovered and it will be of great importance to continue the task of historical research.

I was disappointed to discover that many of the sources are listed in the bibliography only in their original other-language editions, i.e., the editors/publisher often did not elect to track down the English-language versions, even of some well-known works, and list them here.

I also regret the surprising absence of any photographs whatsoever in this edition and wonder why they were dropped after having been an impressive and essential part of the German-language version where the visual documentation added greatly by providing images of the people and places being discussed in the text. Fortunately, there are other publications where the interested reader can find visual documentation of Eranos and its participants, but, as with the bibliographical incompleteness mentioned above, this book would be a more inclusive and complete source had the photographs from the German edition been retained.[5]

In addition to the work of Hakl, the rich and little-known history of Eranos continues to be researched under the present administration of Eranos Board President Fabio Merlini, who has contributed the opening essay to this special issue of *Spring Journal* (see pp. 39–55), while Eranos scientific advisers Riccardo Bernardini (Guest Editor and also a contributor to this issue, see pp. 1–26) and Giovanni Sorge both have been preparing works for publication that will bring forth additional documents from past Eranos Conferences.[6] It is to be hoped that ever more of the riches from the archives of this unique gathering will become available to interested readers in the years to come.

NOTES

1. Hans Thomas Hakl, *Der verborgene Geist von Eranos—Unbekannte Begegnungen von Wissenschaft und Esoterik* (Bretten: Scientia Nova-Verlag Neue Wissenschaft, 2001).

2. Aniela Jaffé, "C. G. Jung and the Eranos Conferences," *Spring* (1977): 201–12.

3. The Archive for Archetypal Symbolism (ARAS) in New York contains approximately 17,000 photographic images collected over some sixty years, cross-indexed and accompanied by scholarly commentary. Website: www.aras.org.

4. In his sketch of Laurens van der Post, Hakl mentions a very negative and controversial book written about him, citing numerous assertions made by the author (J. D. F. Jones) claiming that his subject falsified much of his life story. Hakl concludes that because Jones had been granted access to family documents and had received the family's "permission to publish … it therefore seems probable that his account is basically accurate." Having personally known van der Post and his family very well, I can assure Hakl and the reader that this is anything but true; rather, the Jones "biography" contains many "twists of fact" and false "assumptions" made by the author himself in attempting to sully the reputation of his subject. Representatives of the van der Post family immediately protested to the publisher after publication and a list of corrections was prepared for a second edition, should there ever be one; however, to date no further edition has been issued.

5. See, e.g., Aniela Jaffé, ed., *C. G. Jung: Word and Image* (Princeton, NJ: Princeton University Press, 1979), pp. 180–87; Gerhard Wehr, *An Illustrated Biography of C. G. Jung* (Boston and Shaftesbury: Shambhala, 1989), pp. 123–43; Paul Kugler, "Eranos and Jungian Psychology: A History in Images," in L. Cowan, ed., *Barcelona 2004—Edges of Experience: Memory and Emergence—Proceedings of the Sixteenth International Congress for Analytical Psychology* (Einsiedeln: Daimon, 2006), pp. 99–114.

6. C. G. Jung, *The Solar Myths and Opicinus de Canistris—Notes of the Seminar given at Eranos in 1943*, eds. R. Bernardini, G. P. Quaglino, and A. Romano (Einsiedeln: Daimon Verlag, 2015); Giovanni Sorge, "Eranos in the Middle of the 20th Century" (working title of a not-yet-completed manuscript).

BOOK REVIEW

C. G. Jung, *The Solar Myths and Opicinus de Canistris—Notes of the Seminar given at Eranos in 1943*, eds. Riccardo Bernardini, Gian Piero Quaglino, and Augusto Romano. Einsiedeln, Switzerland: Daimon Verlag, 2015.

REVIEWED BY KEIRON LE GRICE

The central focus of this publication is an impromptu lecture given by Jung at Eranos in 1943 in which he provides psychological commentaries on solar myths and on a series of symbolic illustrations by Italian medieval priest Opicinus de Canistris (1296–c. 1352 CE). For anyone with an abiding interest in Jung's work, this book is a real gem, providing numerous fascinating insights on a range of topics such as the dark side of the divine, Christianity, the tension of opposites, mythic symbolism, and the evolution of human consciousness.

As we learn in the foreword (by Thomas Fischer) and the introduction, the genesis of the book was the fortuitous discovery, in 2012, of some handwritten lecture notes in Jung's former house in Küsnacht. These notes comprised "six untitled, small slips of paper" (p. 4) giving a rough outline of the 1943 talk. As it turns out, the discovery—by the book's editors Riccardo Bernardini, Gian Piero Quaglino, and Augusto Romano—was serendipitously aligned with their endeavor, already underway, to bring to publication a transcript of this very lecture. With Jung's own notes to hand, there was even more incentive to publish Jung's lecture in written form for a wider

Keiron Le Grice, Ph.D., is a professor of depth psychology and chair of the Jungian and Archetypal Studies program at Pacifica Graduate Institute, California, and founding editor of *Archai: The Journal of Archetypal Cosmology*. His publications include *The Archetypal Cosmos: Rediscovering the Gods in Myth, Science and Astrology* (2011), *Discovering Eris: The Symbolism and Significance of a New Planetary Archetype* (2012), *The Rebirth of the Hero: Mythology as a Guide to Spiritual Transformation* (2013). His website is www.keironlegrice.com.

audience, especially given that it provides a genuine addition to the existing body of Jung's work.[1]

Jung's speaking notes, which are reproduced in the original German in the appendices and translated in the main section of the book, provide an intriguing glimpse into Jung the man, preparing to give a lecture, as any of us might, listing keywords that would trigger his amplifications on specific topics, and producing different versions of his planned talk as he revised his thoughts. The notes, which were likely "stimulated by the very papers he had listened to during the conference," (p. 36) supplement more detailed transcripts recorded at Eranos by two of Jung's students: Rivkah Schärf Kluger and Alwine von Keller. Both these accounts, although challenging to follow in places, are mutually consistent and complementary, forming the centerpiece of this publication.

The book is helpfully divided into clear sections presented in logical sequence. A sixty-four-page introduction by the editors provides essential background to the Eranos conferences and their significance for the scholarly development and dissemination of Jung's thought. Jung gave fourteen talks at Eranos between 1933 and 1951, and, as one would expect, was very much the dominant presence at the gatherings, which explored a diverse range of topics and viewpoints, fostered by the atmospheric setting and enriched by the contributions of figures such as Neumann, Corbin, and Kerényi—the latter speaking at the 1943 gathering. Jung, we learn, had not originally intended to present at that year's event, but had acceded to popular demand, giving "an exciting and multifaceted impromptu talk" (p. 28) to "about twenty-seven people," (p. 25) which served as "an astounding epilogue" (p. 28) to the conference outside of the regular program of presentations.[2]

As noted, Jung's talk consisted of two components: the first, an exegesis of solar myths, and the second, on which the editors place greater emphasis in their introduction, a psychological commentary on images from the *Codex Palatinus Latinus 1993*, attributed to Opicinus.

Jung had a deep interest in figures of a mystical or visionary disposition—including Goethe, Nietzsche, Hölderlin, Hildegard von Bingen, Niklaus von Flüe ("Brother Klaus"), Paracelsus, Jakob Böhme, Meister Eckhart, and alchemists such as Gerhard Dorn and Michael Maier—who each came face to face with the numinous power of the unconscious, some succumbing to a tragic fate as a result. Jung's psychological analysis of the illustrations of Opicinus provides a further example of this kind, exploring the fate of an individual within a medieval Christian view of the world, struggling to come to terms with the tension of opposites in his psyche, and failing to successfully face and integrate the shadow. Reading *The Solar Myths*, one gets the sense that Opicinus had a visionary revelation of the kind Jung's describes in "Psychology and Literature." Such a revelation, according to Jung, bursts forth

> from the hinterland of man's mind, as if it had emerged from the abyss of prehuman ages, or from a superhuman world of contrasting light and darkness. … Sublime, pregnant with meaning, yet chilling the blood with its strangeness, it arises from the timeless depths: glamorous, daemonic and grotesque, it bursts asunder our human standards of value and aesthetic form, a terrifying tangle of eternal chaos.[3]

The editors' introduction provides essential details of Opicinus's life, based on the priest's autobiographical testimony—a life which appears to have been largely unremarkable until the onset of an illness in 1334, during which he fell into a coma for ten days.

> When he came out of the coma, he had been weakened both physically and psychologically. He could not speak. His right hand was paralysed. He complained of a serious loss of memory. Along with his illness came apparitions and nightmares that tortured him. He recorded a vision that he had in June, when he saw "a vase in the clouds." In his bizarre annotations, the vase has a remarkable role since, by a play on the double meaning of the word, *canistra* ("vase"), it is linked to his own name, Canistris. He also had recurrent visions of the Virgin Mary with her son in her arms. She appeared sorry and was sitting on the ground, stricken with sorrow because of Opicinus' spiritual perdition. Nevertheless, Opicinus tells us, "the weakening of my right hand was transformed into a strengthening of my spiritual potential." (pp. 42–43)

The visions were recorded by Opicinus as fifty-two drawings in the *Codex Palatinus Latinus 1993* on which he is believed to have worked until his death. The drawings, as the editors note, are "full of annotations and correspondences that are theological, symbolic, astrological, historical, and cartographic." (p. 45) Indeed, Opicinus, who was appointed scribe to Apostolic Penitentiary by Pope John XXII, was an astrologer, and thus "tried to superimpose classical astrological symbolism on such features of the Christian calendar as the feast days of the saints" and "produced an interpretation of his city, Pavia, in the light of 'Christian astrology.'" (p. 45)

A peculiar and striking aspect of his illustrations is his projection of anthropomorphic and theriomorphic symbolism upon the geography of Europe and North Africa. Continents and seas take on human or bestial form, and apparently represent the extreme tension of opposites playing itself out in Opicinus's psyche. The editors explain:

> In Opicinus' cartography ... the Mediterranean Sea is actually represented as a demonic world, a dark "anti-world," in contraposition to the luminous world of dry land. In plate 39 of the *Codex Palatinus Latinus 1993* (figures 43 and 43*bis*) in particular, if Europe is represented symbolically as a figure of male gender and Africa as a woman (in other representations by Opicinus, the genders of the two continents may be inverted), the Mediterranean appears as a demonic figure—Jung notes, from Alwine von Keller's account—"with a goat's beard" and the Atlantic as a monstrous animal, probably a fish, which swallows up Europe from the north-western coast of France. (p. 35)

For Opicinus, the world assumed a sexualized character ("a gigantic and geographical copulation," [p. 47] as Claude Gandelman described it) and is thus consistent with Mircea Eliade's understanding of the sexualized hierophany or sacred cosmology behind the origins of alchemy, which was concerned with reconciling the same pairs of conflicting opposites that appear in Opicinus's cartographical art.[4]

Jung's analysis centers on the conflict between the upper realm of the light of God in the form of *sol*, the sun, and the lower realm of "*aries*—ram, horned ram, goat beard, and ... the devil," as depicted in the *Codex*. (p. 98) Identifying with the light side, the "lamb of God," Opicinus, in Jung's judgment, was unable to integrate the dark side of the divine and was caught in an irreconcilable tension of opposites between Christ and the devil, good and evil, light and dark. Jung explains, "He wanted to rule this fearsome conflict out and shut himself off inside the *corpus mysticum* of the Church." (p. 98) Unable to face the conflict within himself, Jung adds, "he did not ... master ... the spitting-in-two in his *unconscious*, which was the problem of the new era. This is a picture of a schizophrenic." (p. 109)

Jung sees in some of Opicinus's drawings the basic structure of a *maṇḍala*, incorporating circles and quaternities, no doubt compensating for the psychological turbulence the Italian priest was experiencing. Alongside this, the editors draw our attention to the wealth of symbolic and allegorical content, such as the Christian image of a "new Jerusalem descending from heaven," the alchemical *coniunctio* of *sponsus* and *sponsa*, astrological symbolism, and juxtapositions of opposites such as sun and moon, East and West, spirit and flesh, and the "bright" inner man and the shadow of the outer man. (pp. 48–49) The age, decaying condition, and fine detail within the Opicinus documents make some of the illustrations of the *Codex* difficult to clearly discern, in electronic format at least, so we can be grateful to the editors for their careful commentary.

While the Opicinus material provides a fascinating and unique case study, perhaps the principal theoretical contribution of the 1943 lecture is to be found in Jung's treatment of the emergence of human ego-consciousness, as symbolized by the development of solar myths over time. Jung notes that "the Sun is basically a living symbol for the illumination of consciousness." (p. 83) Solar creation myths thus refer to the process of "becoming conscious" (p. 83); just as the sun rises out of the darkness at dawn, consciousness emerges daily from the dark ocean of sleep and dream, and ego-consciousness, over the millennia, is progressively differentiated from the dim twilight existence that characterizes the primordial condition of *participation mystique*. Like the sun, the individual human ego, carrier of the light of consciousness, rises up out of the dark primordial mists towards a pinnacle of illumination.

This process ultimately leads, Jung suggests, to the Christian revelation, especially the Gospel of John, and is further developed in the theological speculations of the Scholastics. (p. 86)

> By now we have observed how the Sun god runs through a development in older culture and, in fact, takes on ... a more and more spiritual shape; and, in the end, this light of the Sun becomes the light of John's logos, which shines out in the darkness and undoubtedly means spiritual illumination and the raising of human consciousness. It is the light of the *gnosis theou*. (p. 86)

Although Jung (and others, such as Erich Neumann) has made similar arguments elsewhere, in this lecture Jung more explicitly connects the development of solar symbolism to the emergence of a differentiated ego consciousness. For Jung, the course of development of solar myths reflects a profound transformation in the human psyche by which the conscious ego emerged as an independent and autonomous self-willing agent, bringing a concomitant progressive strengthening of the human will. The fortification of an independent will enabled human beings to move beyond the *heimarmene* of the ancient world—characterized by fatalism, compulsion, crippling superstitions, and subservience to the will of the gods. As Jung puts it, "The dependency of people of the ancient world on *heimarmene* is [due to] this lack of consciousness that one is in the hands of." (p. 88) In the ancient world, human will, to the extent that it existed at all, was secondary in its power and authority to the will of the gods.

If the emergence of the ego and an autonomous human will is a great cultural achievement, as Jung believes, it also brings with it certain attendant dangers, which he proceeds to discuss. With the development of the individual human subject, a subtle but consequential shift occurs, which places singular emphasis upon the willing agent—the "I" principle—utterly disregarding divine will.[5] From the Renaissance and the Reformation on, Jung argues, "the individual no longer said: I *know*, I *will*, but the sound-stress shifted and now he said: *I* know, *I* will. As the human being became conscious of his size and freedom, the undermining of godly authority began." (p. 108)

This psychological transition gave birth to a dualism—between subject and object, God and nature, consciousness and unconscious, light and dark—that so defines the modern era, for better and for worse. It is a dualism that finds primary philosophical articulation in the work of Descartes. As Jung describes it:

> This freedom of human consciousness, the emancipation of the judgment and will from dependency on what is higher, brought one, I would like to say, one problem into the world—*duality*, a problem that really had never been there before. There had never been the sovereignty of the person in this sense. There had always been higher controlling powers at hand, which put a damper on things. So, this duality brought about a foundation of human consciousness, which had never been there before. (p. 89)

For Jung, of course, the light of human consciousness, supported by a differentiated ego, fulfills a singularly important role in the world. He repeats in this lecture his proclamation of the world-constitutive power of consciousness: "Consciousness has a meaning that is entirely extraordinary. ... Without consciousness, nothing exists. The world had really been nothing at all until somebody said: that is the world; that *is*." (p. 86) Similarly, here, as in *Answer to Job*, Jung stresses the critical role of the human in bringing the unconscious divine (the "Dark Father") to consciousness. (p. 104) As we read in von Keller's transcript: "[God] revealed a functioning independent human consciousness. Now, the human being is instrumental; he was invented for that. God wanted consciousness so that he could be expressed." (p. 104)

It is on this note that the two components of Jung's talk come together. The dualism between the light, all-loving God and the dark power of nature, personified in Opicinus's Christian astrological imagination as the goat-devil, is at the heart of the schizophrenic splitting of the Italian priest's psyche, and it is a "prelude," Jung suggests, "of what today we are the shaken witness of." (p. 109) It is a dualism that we ourselves must reckon with if we are to meet the spiritual challenge of our time.

The central content of *The Solar Myths* thus provides us with an illuminating example of the symbolized psychological process of an individual in the wake of a spiritual revelation, failing to come to terms with the deep-rooted transformation impinging on the Christianized psyche. And the book's main theoretical contribution to Jungian psychology is its concise discussion of Jung's view of the collective development of consciousness in the context of solar myths. The inclusion of a wide selection of photographs, mostly from Eranos, including many of Jung himself, and biographical accounts of the two sources of Jung's lecture, Rivkah Schärf Kluger and Alwine von Keller, completes the truly fascinating and eclectic collection of materials within this volume. The publication is successful in bringing to life the spirit and personalities of the Eranos gatherings at that time, giving what feels like intimate access to the seminar, including a rare glimpse of Jung as a lecturer. For all these reasons, we owe Bernardini, Quaglino, and Romano a large debt of gratitude for making this material available to us.

NOTES

1. For a number of reasons, an editorial decision had been made not to include this material in Jung's *Collected Works*.

2. These descriptions are from two sources: (1) the words of Swiss artist Hedy Alma Wyss, from a short summary of the seminar written on August 28–29, 1943 some two weeks after the event; and (2) Olga Fröbe-Kapteyn's letter to Hans Conrad Bänziger on August 13, 1943, written after Jung's seminar on the preceding days: "From 9:30 until noon Jung spoke to about twenty-seven people in the best of moods and they had the feeling that the old days of the seminar had come back to life." (p. 25)

3. C. G. Jung, "Psychology and Literature" (1950) in *The Collected Works of C. G. Jung*, vol. 15, ed. and trans. R. F. C. Hull (Princeton, NJ: Princeton University Press, 1966), § 141.

4. See Mircea Eliade, "The World Sexualized," in *The Forge and the Crucible* (Chicago, IL: The University of Chicago Press, 1978).

5. The position Jung advances in this lecture is broadly consistent with perspectives in recent work such as Charles Taylor, *A Secular Age* (Cambridge, MA: The Belnap Press of Harvard University Press, 2007) and Richard Tarnas, *Cosmos and Psyche: Intimations of a New World View* (New York, NY: Viking, 2006).

BOOK REVIEW

Dick Russell, *The Life and Ideas of James Hillman, Vol. 1, The Making of a Psychologist*. New York, NY: Helios Press, 2013.

REVIEWED BY STANTON MARLAN

W hile the works of James Hillman stand for themselves and on their own, the life, times, and ideas of Hillman are brought to life in this stunning and important biography. At times, the play between biography and autobiography, between a biographer and his subject, produces an alchemical mixture that renders a quintessence, an illuminating and transformative result that could not have been achieved otherwise. The cooperative alchemy between Hillman and Russell forged this major contribution to our understanding of the ideas of this innovative and controversial psychologist and thinker. It has often been said that James Hillman is one of the most original American psychologists of the twentieth century. He is the primary founder of archetypal psychology, considered by some to be a major post-Jungian orientation growing out of Jung's psychology and by others to be a perspective or faction within it. In either case, Hillman's archetypal psychology has had a wide influence both in the United

Stanton Marlan, Ph.D., A.B.P.P., L.P. (clinical psychology), and Ph.D.(philosophy) is a clinical psychologist and Jungian analyst in private practice in Pittsburgh, Pennsylvania and an adjunct Clinical Professor of Psychology and clinical supervisor at Duquesne University Psychology Clinic. A training and supervising analyst with the Inter-Regional Society of Jungian Analysts, Dr. Marlan is also President of the Pittsburgh Society of Jungian Analysts, and is board-certified in both clinical psychology and psychoanalysis from the American Board of Professional Psychology (ABPP). He is a director on The American Board and Academy of Psychoanalysis (ABAPsa) and is now its President-elect. Dr. Marlan has published numerous articles on Jungian psychology and is the editor of four books, including *Archetypal Psychologies: Reflections in Honor of James Hillman*. He was a Fay lecturer at Texas A&M and the author of *The Black Sun: The Alchemy and Art of Darkness*.

States and internationally and has had an impact not only on professional psychology and analysis but also on the wider range of cultural imagination.[1]

James Hillman passed away on October 27, 2011. At a memorial for him in New York City, he was eulogized by many family, friends, and colleagues. Richard Tarnas noted that James Hillman "brought the very word 'soul' back to psychology, he brought psychology out of the consulting room into the world," and contributed to our thoughts a wide-ranging vision with reflections on "ecology, aging, war, destiny, puer and senex, the city and urban design, architecture, economics, the men's movement, racism, pornography, language, philosophy, cosmology, astrology, phenomenology, public education, art, animals, emotion, Shakespeare, the Renaissance, Romanticism, [and] Neoplatonism." Hillman's ideas are well known to the readers of *Spring Journal*, as was his irreverent brilliance and challenging style.

Given the range and depth of Hillman's contribution, it is not surprising that the first half of Russell's biography is 678 pages in length. Helping to create this large tome, Hillman played an active role, pointing the way, filling gaps, supplying details, and, perhaps most importantly, offering perspectives that only one who personally lived this particular life could do. Hillman's contributions were also obviously catalyzed, drawn forth, and shaped by Russell, whose literary talents and passion for the work were essential components of this biography. Hillman often said in his lectures that if you wanted to know more, "press me like a grape." Russell took him up on the offer.

For Russell, the work was a *via longissima*, a seven-year commitment to the process. In a note to this reviewer, he recounted Hillman's saying to him in 2004, "This will take years, you know. I hope you're not looking at this as a fast book." Russell was in for the long haul. In his acknowledgements, he recounts that he was "helped along … by family, friends, colleagues, archivists and more," but primarily he expresses his thanks and gratitude to Hillman who opened himself to many hours of personal discussion about the facts of his life, as well as the meaning behind its various stages and how they related to his work. For Russell, this made the writing "an endlessly fascinating and ever-expanding effort." (p. 637) The experience of his endless fascination captures my experience of reading this work as well. In some ways, the biography reads like a novel or adventure story, and what first appeared as if it might be a tedious read (because of its length) turned out to be a page-turner that grips the imagination and leaves a mark on the soul.

Russell told me that he was "neither a psychologist nor therapist and did not major in psychology in college," yet at the time he started this project, he was already an accomplished and recognized writer, having published "on the Kennedy assassination, the genius of African Americans, following the migration of grey whales," and most recently, "collaborations with wrestler-turned-governor Jesse Ventura." (personal communication) Hillman's best-selling book *The Soul's Code* became for Russell a guiding vision for the work. In his introduction to Hillman's biography called "The Figure in the Carpet," he quotes Hillman's idea that "The great question of biography is what Henry James called the 'figure in the carpet.' How to discern a definite pattern, a comprehensible figure." (xxiii) For Russell, searching for this figure became a modus operandi for understanding Hillman's life, an archetypal approach fitting for the primary architect of archetypal psychology. Russell, using Hillman's insight, traces the important patterns of his life and character, giving us a portrait both personal and archetypal, a description not only of the figure in the carpet, but also of the larger weave, the textures of time, place, persons, and more—all scintilla-like "soul sparks" illuminating the imaginal life at the core of Hillman's psyche.

Russell's story masterfully follows the threads of Hillman's life and weaves them together using revelatory images, chapter after chapter. He describes an outline of its flow from

> his boyhood on the teeming Atlantic City Boardwalk, negotiating the ancestral presences of his forebears … (to) working with disabled and blind veterans in military hospitals … a radio correspondent in post-war Germany, a student at Paris' Sorbonne during the heyday of Existentialism and Left Bank café society, and an editor for an Irish literary magazine working in the midst of J. P. Donleavy and Brendan Behan … journeying into the heart of Africa and settling in Kashmir to work on a novel … [arriving] in Zürich in the 1950s when psychoanalysis was at its peak of popular interest. Enrolling at the C. G. Jung Institute and spending time with Jung … [and becoming] in the 1960s the Institute's first Director of Studies. (xxii-xxiii)

and later, an important speaker at the Eranos Conference which, over the years, "had drawn many of the twentieth century's leading thinkers—philosophers, theologians, anthropologists, mythologists, ethnologists, and others." (p. 559)

In all, Russell's description follows the narrative of Hillman's life, but more it circumscribes and circumambulates a vibrant core of rich imagery that runs through the narrative unfolding Hillman's story, tracing the awakening of his daimon, and exposing the subtle tissue of psychic life in and beyond simple subjectivity.

Right from the beginning chapter, Russell captures one such poignant moment from Hillman's boyhood memories, a recollection that his older brother Joel

> would put him on his shoulders so that [he] could see (and breathe) in the midst of the teeming Boardwalk crowds. Images would embed themselves in streams of consciousness. Midgets, snake charmers, and giants ... Here were taffy pulls, and giveaway pickles from H. K. Heinz, and free nuts from Mr. Peanut, who paraded the Boardwalk. ... Here was the FBI booth with the counterfeit money John Dillinger used. (p. 7)

Russell continues:

> Out at the edge of Million Dollar Pier, every hour a barker would beckon the crowds to gather around what was apparently a trapdoor, to witness the Deep Sea Net Hauls. These especially fascinated young James. "They'd let a gigantic net down to the bottom of the sea, and then drag the net up with pulleys, with the most crazy-looking fish you ever saw—crabs, clams, eels, flat fish, everything."

To Hillman, however, what mattered most was imagining what went on in that dark undersea world. (p. 8)

In these fascinating images of "Deep Sea Net Hauls" and the "crazy looking fish," we get a sense of what gripped and pulled Hillman toward the depths. What was going on around this experience may also give us a clue to the sensate quality that was such an important aspect of Hillman's intellectual and aesthetic life and work.

Russell recounts that "One historian relates that nearby snack vendors would time their preparations so that 'their tempting aromas of fried, steamed, or stewed seafood would waft over the crowd just as the net was dropped back into the briny deep.'" (p. 8) Attention to such details shows that biography for Hillman, and in Russell's hand, is never simply intellectual but also olfactory. Russell refers to *The Soul's Code*, where Hillman noted that "the self starts off amid the smells of a geography." (p. 4) Such "smells" are not simply literal, but reflect the subtle background aromas and complexities of a larger life. Hillman recounts that he grew up in Atlantic City surrounded by a "double-sidedness of American culture. Here was a family resort where everybody could come and bring the children. It was both a Quaker and a Kosher city—so Puritan. ... Yet, the other side, the underbelly of Atlantic City, was filled with corruption." (p. 11)

One might imagine that the double-sidedness of the Atlantic City Boardwalk set the stage for the constellation of the archetypal forces that followed Hillman into the struggles of his later life. Russell reports that Hillman noted, "I came from New Jersey where we have sea gulls who fly right down and get what they want from the oceanside. I am like them, dropping down into the depths of our culture and seizing what I need to understand things and make a point!" (p. 4) Though not noted by Russell, this gull-like scavenging style would be further elaborated in Hillman's master work, *Re-Visioning Psychology*, in the image of "The Knight Errant" and "bricoleur." Hillman describes the Knight Errant as a "scrounging rogue, ... an odd-job man, like Eros the Carpenter who joins this bit with that, a handyman, a *bricoleur* ... psychologizing upon and about what is at hand."[2] As a bricoleur, Hillman opportunistically swoops down gull-like, using bits and pieces, creating an original and provocative tapestry of ideas—like the Knight Errant, an "anarchic, a law breaker, knowing no bounds of proprium. Not criminal—no—but not moral either."[3] Diving in and seeing into the depths and below yields what Hillman calls a "picaresque taste for the psychological."[4] Hillman further notes that "the rogue errant can teach—psychological survival."[5] Opportunism played a role in the story about how Hillman met his first wife Kate, approaching her while she was on a date with another man. What chutzpa, what daring, it took to follow and act on the call of anima. In this case, the action of the romantic rogue led to a significant, soulful relationship and a compelling love story for both of them that exceeded the propriety of convention and collective mores; however, to simply follow one's anima promptings can also lead into treacherous waters and at times, tragic disasters.

Hillman confessed at one point, "I let my state-of-being-as-felt (anima & images) be my guide—or worse <u>have no guide</u> but act, dare I say irresponsibly." (p. 513)

In Hillman's life, such actions also led to deep betrayals of his relationships and analytic practice. Hillman and Russell appear to hold nothing back. In a painful chapter (entitled "Betrayal"), Russell recounts multiple betrayals, some perpetrated by Hillman's analyst Meier who had an affair with his own analysand (Hillman's wife, Kate) and another perpetrated by Hillman who likewise had a liaison with an analysand who was the wife of a student at the Institute. The psychological reflection that opened up around these revelations and others raises psychological, moral, and archetypal issues that go to the core of the still difficult struggle to understand the issues of transference, love, and soul, as well as their interrelationships.

In a letter dated in 1965, Hillman's friend, Bob Stein, appears to attempt to comfort Hillman about his actions. Reflecting on the analytic situation, he wrote,

> I feel betrayal in one form or another is the rule rather than the exception. But I know now that this is not essentially the blame of either of the participants. Rather it is due to the 'promise' of wholeness and healing which Jungian analysis especially seems to offer, and the absolute obstruction to the fulfillment and realization of wholeness, which is contained in the model of the analytical vessel proposed by Jung. In this sense it is Jung who has betrayed us by opening the door to all the ancient and rejuvenating pagan gods, only to turn around and chain us to the destructive and anti-life Christian dogma of the superiority of the spirit over the flesh. (p. 530)

Russell goes on to say,

> Hillman, when asked years later about [his betrayal of a patient], responded that it was "[a] foolish affair ..." "I'm sure I knew that I was tempting fate. When you consider reading life backwards, I think that unconsciously I had to fall, to have something terrible happen. I had to really sin, to be initiated." "It was a kind of violation or rupture with the professional code, [one] that put me among the 'big boys': Meier, Jung, and other Zürich analysts who were my mentors and seniors. It was like a jump from the bridge, all the codes of practice violated. I could become disbarred,

> kicked out, tarred and feathered as they say. Of course in the moment one does not think of any of that. ... But the temptation was much more than her. I think it was the symbolic importance of the 'initiation.'" (pp. 530–31)

Both Stein's and Hillman's explanations for their betrayals sound (to contemporary sensibilities) hollow and defensive. Their conjectures—respectively, that "it was Jung's fault" or it was for "the sake of initiation"—hardly draw our sympathy. Yet there is something that remains haunting in Hillman's recognition that "We are led to an essential truth about both trust and betrayal," that "they contain each other." Russell adds, paraphrasing Hillman, "they entered the world at the same moment." (pp. 509–10) To tie these two moments together is troubling, but perhaps there is an archetypal truth tying them together that is at the core of moral dilemmas; however, even if this is true, it is still the case that for the ego to use such a truth as a path to initiation or as a justification for one's actions is far from satisfactory.

Hillman recognizes this issue in a letter to Stein, noting, "I can no longer justify nor explain what I am up to & aiming at, living for—I seem at times to have lost my moral bearings—not just the outer collective ones, but vis-à-vis myself." Hillman goes on to quote Gabriel Marcel: "Perhaps it is necessary, moreover, to admit that there is in me that which transcends all possible justification. Very important!" (p. 513)

How are we to understand such a statement? Is it offered here still as a justification? As a *fact* of our "archetypal nature," or is it also a call to respond to and take a stance with regard to the complexity of the conflicting quality of archetypal realities? Different philosophical, ethical, and religious responses have been offered to this difficult, perhaps flawed, reality of our human condition. My interest here is not to put forth any easy solution, but simply to appreciate that Hillman and Russell had the integrity to bring forth these highly personal and painful aspects of Hillman's life, so valuable in understanding Hillman, his times—and ours as well.

It has been easy for some to condemn, dismiss, or valorize Hillman's behavior and ideas from opposing points of view, at times with a holier-than-thou attitude. Further insight into Hillman's complex struggle with these issues is revealed in his work on the shadow. Although not noted by Russell, I think the following is worth mentioning here with regard to the complexity of the issue. Hillman argued that a moral stance toward the shadow is essential and cannot be abandoned, but this is not enough: "At one moment something else must break through."[6] Facing the shadow and its cure requires a conjunction of seeming opposites, a confrontation, and a paradoxical union of two incommensurables: "the moral recognition that these parts of me are burdensome and intolerable and *must* change, and the loving laughing acceptance which takes them just as they are. ... [One] both judges and joins gladly." Each position holds "one side of the truth."[7] Hillman gave an example from the Jewish mystical tradition of the Chassidim, where "deep moral piety is coupled with astounding delight in life."[8] To achieve such an attitude requires considerable psychological development. Hillman's struggle with this issue gives us a look at how he/we might engage our guilt and shame. He asks how we can take the broken, ruined, weak, sick, inferior, and socially unacceptable parts of ourselves, and, for him, cure these shadow images requiring love. He asks, "How far can our love extend to these broken and ruined parts of ourselves ... ? How much charity and compassion have we for our own weakness and sickness? How far can we ... allow a place for everyone?"[9] Because the shadow can be socially unacceptable and even *evil*, it is important that it is carried by us, and that we do not project our unacceptable parts on to others or act them out. This is an ethical responsibility.[10]

In this statement, I believe, Hillman attempts to take responsibility for coming to terms with the psychological struggle with personal shame and guilt, as well as with the importance of not imposing our "evils" on others. Perhaps much more must be said about how acting out can violate others and about the importance of developing a sense of compassion for them as well. But while Hillman is not a moralist or ethicist, his insight into questions of psychological complexity is essential to psychological and ethical concerns. Hillman's continuing recognition of the complexity of psychological life and its paradoxes are addressed in his work on alchemy. In "Silver and the White Earth," Hillman considers the recognition of such paradoxes as a kind of illuminated lunacy and, in addition, he sees the work of psyche as a return of the soul to the world, a reality that goes beyond insular subjectivity and *moral passivity*. In "Concerning the Stone," he again reflects on the paradoxical issue of the dual nature of seemingly opposing realities.

Hillman prefers to read alchemy otherwise than as a Christian allegory and to see its goals

> as *images of psychic conditions always available.* Then the pathologized aspects of the grit and the pearl, the lead and the diamond, the hammer and the gold are inseparable. The pain is not prior to the goal, like crucifixion before resurrection, but pain and gold are coterminous, codependent, corelative [sic]. The pearl is also always grit, an irritation as well as a luster, the gilding also a poisoning.[11]

Such insights into the depths of psychological life help us to be less hypocritically identified only with our gilded and lustrous ego, moral and ethical inflations, which so often secretly carry our poisonous shadows of revenge and superiority. With regard to such issues in Hillman's life, Russell quotes Scott Becker's interpretation:

> If Jung, as Stein suggests, opened a door between the pagan and Judeo-Christian worlds, then analysis and psychotherapy could be said to take the place in the doorway, in the liminal space where passionate aesthetics and moral restraint collide. And if, as Jung opened it, that door had been shut for two thousand years, is it any wonder that the vital, 'rejuvenating' energy that was emerging from the pagan side was dangerous when viewed from the Christian side of the door? Perhaps Hillman's indiscretion can be viewed from perspectives other than the moralistic. While acknowledging the destructive or foolish aspects of his actions (and the sexual 'misconduct' of so many of the psychoanalytic old guard), we might find some compassion for those who first met Aphrodite, Eros, and Priapos as they surged through the doorway. More to the point, if the male analysts who failed to see that it was … the goddess and not the patient with whom they sought union, then their literal, patriarchal impulses can perhaps be better understood, if not entirely excused by the goddess herself. (p. 531)

Becker's interpretation suggests a more compassionate appreciation for, and deep ambiguity about, the complexities of the archetypal depths playing themselves out in and behind the erotic scene of analysis. I can only add that if our indiscretions are in fact excused by Aphrodite, we would be cautious not to identify with her wiles as the last word in what continues to be a deeply problematic concern.

All in all, I want to reiterate that this first half of Russell's biography of Hillman is an invaluable tour de force, a labor of love and scholarship, that gives a comprehensive, deep, and fair reading of Hillman's life and ideas. I value it because it is written with an archetypal sensibility that does justice to Hillman's vision of psyche and does not fall prey to psychobiography in the worst sense of that genre by reducing the fullness of life to stereotyped psychological reductions and judgments. In addition, while giving voice to Hillman's own self-assessment, it is not the product of simple compliance, but a careful and scholarly reading that shapes and structures a view of Hillman's life and ideas that creatively emerge from real, open dialogue and engagement. In this regard, Russell pushes the envelope, pressing for more detail, more clarity, more of the collective and personal background that fills out a living image of the soul of his subject. Because of the fullness of the description of Hillman's life, laudatory and otherwise, I'm certain there will be other readers who will use this material to bolster their own ends.

James Hillman's thought can be inspiring and some will begin to or continue to identify with and idolize him, but the challenging nature of his ideas can also destabilize, disrupt, and challenge the ideologies of other people in ways that wound and hurt, causing some to envy or to strike out in revenge in an attempt to defame and scapegoat him, to protect themselves against what has been threatening, and to aggrandize their own ends for personal, professional, and/or emotional profit.

Perhaps this anticipation sees with a jaundiced and dark eye, but I think it is also a response to the power of this biography to touch the depths of its readers. Perhaps I have not given its readers credit enough to come away with an integrated perspective. I believe this biography is balanced, giving credit where credit is due and resisting the extremes of over-idealization or defamation.

In spite of my negative reaction to Hillman's early indiscretions, to let them color our overall evaluation of his revolutionary contribution to the field of psychology and the larger cultural imagination of our times is, to my mind, short-sighted and highly reductive. I continue to greatly value James Hillman and his work as one of the most original and remarkable psychologists of our time. Richard Tarnas, stated at Hillman's Memorial on May 4, 2013,

> How deeply James enriched us with his unending flow of insights, placing so many things in new light—and in shadow. His depth of soul and breadth of knowledge, his sparkling language, his heretic originality, his sharp-edged individuality will be deeply missed, but he left us with so much that we will be integrating for a long, long time to come.

Dick Russell's biography immeasurably adds to this legacy.

NOTES

1. See Stanton Marlan, "Hillman, James and Alchemy," in *Encyclopedia of Psychology and Religion, Vol. 1*, ed. David A. Leeming (New York, NY: Springer, 2014), p. 401.

2. James Hillman, *Re-Visioning Psychology* (New York, NY: Harper & Row, 1975), p. 164.

3. *Ibid.*, p. 162.

4. *Ibid.*, p. 161.

5. *Ibid.*, p. 162.

6. James Hillman, "The Cure of the Shadow," in *Meeting the Shadow: The Hidden Power of the Dark Side of Human Nature*, eds. Connie Zweig and Jeremiah Abrams (New York, NY: G. P. Putnam's Sons, 1991), pp. 242–43.

7. *Ibid.*, p. 243.

8. *Ibid.*

9. *Ibid.*, p. 242.

10. See Stanton Marlan, "Facing the Shadow," in *Jungian Psychoanalysis: Working in the Spirit of C. G. Jung*, ed. Murray Stein (Chicago and LaSalle, IL: Open Court, 2010), p. 8.

11. James Hillman, "Concerning the Stone," in *Alchemical Psychology* (Putman, CT: Spring Publications, 2010), pp. 239–40.

BOOK REVIEW

Erel Shalit, *The Complex: Path of Transformation from Archetype to Ego.* Toronto: Inner City Books, 2002.

Erel Shalit, *The Hero and His Shadow: Psychopolitical Aspects of Myth and Reality in Israel,* Revised. Carmel, CA: Fisher King Press, 2004, 2011.

Erel Shalit, *Enemy, Cripple & Beggar: Shadows in the Hero's Path.* Carmel, CA: Fisher King Press, 2008.

Erel Shalit, *Requiem: A Tale of Exile and Return.* Carmel, CA: Fisher King Press, 2010.

Erel Shalit, *The Cycle of Life: Themes and Tales of the Journey.* Carmel, CA: Fisher King Press, 2011.

REVIEWED BY STEVE ZEMMELMAN

CONTAINING A JUNGIAN LIGHT: THE BOOKS OF EREL SHALIT

Dance me to the children who are asking to be born
Dance me through the curtains that our kisses have out worn
Raise a tent of shelter now, though every thread is torn
Dance me to the end of love
—Leonard Cohen, "Dance Me to the End of Love"
(*Various Positions*, 1984, Columbia Records).

Steve Zemmelman, Ph.D. is an analyst member of the C. G. Jung Institute of San Francisco. He is an Associate Clinical Professor in the Department of Psychiatry at the University of California at San Francisco, adjunct professor at Pacifica Graduate Institute, core faculty member of the Sanville Institute for Clinical Social Work and Psychotherapy, and a former lecturer in the School of Social Welfare at the University of California at Berkeley. Dr. Zemmelman has a private practice of Jungian analysis and psychotherapy in Berkeley and San Francisco, California. Contact: stevezemmelman@comcast.net or www.drstevezemmelman.net.

I was listening to these lyrics by Leonard Cohen during the time I was reading Erel Shalit's books for this review, and it struck me how well these poetic lines capture the essential tensions between past, present, and future, fragmentation and wholeness, coming into being, and passing away. They orient the listener to limitation and suggest a depth of meaning that can only come from facing the inevitability of mortality and the potential for redemption through love. The tune in which the lyrics are embedded is a lamentation with a distinctly Jewish sensibility. It leaves me moved, tearful, despairing, and hopeful, all at once. It is soulful, satisfying, and true. It seemed so fitting a soundtrack for a moment in which Shalit's work was so much pulsing through me.

INTRODUCTION

It has been my great pleasure over the past year to have studied the body of Erel Shalit's written work. While at first it felt like an overwhelming task to creatively review a body of work by a highly regarded and prolific colleague, I approached the task I was invited to take on as an opportunity for learning and creative reflection. The effort was more than amply rewarded. In his six books (I did not include in this review an e-book or his most recent book, *The Dream and Its Amplification* (2013), which he co-edited with Nancy Swift Furlotti, since it had already been reviewed in *Spring*, vol. 90) one encounters a master interpreter of Jung's many contributions to depth psychology illuminating a wide range of topics in ways that present Jung's foundational psychological thinking and amplify his mythopoetic approach to the soul, navigating between the empirical and the imaginal, engaging with each perspective as both an impetus for and a limitation to the other. Shalit's work stands solidly in this territory, taking Jung's original, creative thinking and building upon it, simultaneously enlarging it and nailing it down. While the density of his writing style can be challenging at times, requiring the reader to slow down and ponder complex ideas, more often Shalit's words sing with a poetic, intuitive perspective that grips the reader and leaves him in a state of deep appreciation for the opportunity to contemplate an issue or problem from a new, more enriching, vista. His books should find their way into many courses on Jungian psychology and analytic training programs as they offer both clear explications of basic concepts without falling into the trap of overly concretistic definitions, as well as thoughtful and scholarly interpretations and amplifications that illustrate and deepen the ideas being discussed. In addition, seasoned analysts can also learn much from these books, about themselves and their patients, and can make good use of these books in teaching this material to others.

Shalit brings into Jung's work a wealth of perspectives and stories embedded within Jewish culture and history including biblical exegesis, midrash, Talmud, Zohar, and folklore. One can think of him as writing in the tradition of Sigmund Hurwitz, James Kirsch, Erich Neumann, and Rivka Sharff Kluger—first generation Jungians who expounded on analytical psychology from a specifically Jewish perspective—and more recently writers such as Henry Abromovitch and Sanford Drob. He contributes a sort of corrective to Jung's primarily Christian *weltanschauung,* much as one finds in the recent work of Tom Cheetham, who has done a masterful job of integrating Sufi perspectives into analytical psychology through his explorations of the work of Jung, Henry Corbin, and Ibn Arabi.[1,2] It is most satisfying to see Jung's pioneering work expanded and enriched in ways that are more truly reflective of the diversity among peoples and cultures.

In addition to his integration of Jewish knowledge into analytical psychology, Shalit writes as an Israeli deeply troubled by the polarizations in the Middle East, turning the lens of analytical psychology toward the forces and tensions that have shaped Israel from the time of its socialist pioneers in the early twentieth century to the present. He makes extensive use of the concepts of projection and shadow in their many forms to call for more humane and just relations between Jews and Palestinians that echoes the call for integration of the shadow by his fellow countryman and first generation Jungian analyst, Erich Neumann, which one finds in his classic work, "Depth Psychology and a New Ethic."[3] One sees also in Shalit's work a deep wrestling from the point of view of Joseph Henderson's ideas about the cultural complex as links are drawn between the intrapsychic and social/cultural dimensions of life.[4]

THE BOOKS

The Hero and His Shadow: Psychopolitical Aspects of Myth and Reality in Israel puts Israel's recent history on the analyst's couch with a particular focus on the intertwining development of individual and collective identity in the Jewish state. It traces its vicissitudes from the absorption of the self within the idealism of the Zionist pioneers through a process of social and psychological maturation, eventually achieving what are likened to firm ego boundaries in the relationship between self and other, who, in the politics of the Middle East, is often seen as the enemy. For me, it was a particular challenge and pleasure to read this book since, as an American Jew who is on the quintessentially Jewish path of questioning what it means to be Jewish, there was a great deal here that I found new and challenging. I imagine that others with greater familiarity with the Jewish state and its history will be more familiar with much of the story but perhaps still find fascinating the ways the author is able to make use of a Jungian perspective to deepen the narrative. Shalit offers an anamnesis that highlights the formative influences of image and mythology that infused the Zionist founders, tying them to the redemption of the desert lands in a socialist society passionately embraced along with a vision of a peaceful life with Arab neighbors. *The Hero and His Shadow* offers an intelligent, sensitive, humanized perspective on the trajectory of events that led to the current tragic situation in the Middle East, a sort of depth psychological companion to Ari Shavit's recent book, *My Promised Land.*[5] Unlike Shavit's excellent history that examines in searing honesty the social and political dimensions of Israel's founding and development, particularly in relation to the Arab world, Shalit's analysis reflects a skillful blending of the inner psychological and archetypal dimensions of the problem without collapsing it into a homogeneous whole. He couples this with a particular sensitivity to the human cost and ethical failure of losing contact with the suffering face of the other, a theme which is also taken up in *My Promised Land.* The central theme of Shalit's book, however, is more psychological, focusing on the relation between hubris and nemesis, grandiosity and limitation, the projection of evil and the suffering of one's own imperfection. This is not a book espousing a clear-cut view of the complex problems in the Middle East, a situation in which there is no Archimedean perspective. In fact, if anything, Shalit's analysis complicates those problems in a helpful way that brings to light the confusion and conflicting dimensions of inner (psychological) and outer (historical and social) conditions. For example, while exploring the ways projection onto the enemy can serve both constructively in creating and maintaining ego boundaries as well as destructively in contributing to, or even creating, a state of denial and petrification, Shalit notes that relying on military strength "carries within it the seeds of vulnerability."[6] He then adds what I find to be an example of the kind of honest and grounded, practical observations throughout this book: that giving up force may be the result of a "misreading of the other."[7] In this light I find Shalit's approach to be realistic and even-handed throughout, courageously and truthfully demonstrating the psychological underpinnings of militarization and religious fanaticism on both sides, the impact of the broader social and historical forces on the psychology of individuals and peoples, and the necessity for all sides to withdraw projections and wrestle with their fears and insecurities. There is a loss of relatedness for zealots on both sides of this conflict, each of whom are caught in destructive processes of splitting and projecting shadow onto the perceived enemy. I particularly appreciated the emphasis on the need to transform the masculine warrior hero ideal to a more related, feminized Eros. In one section where he discusses the yearning for a strong leader by Israelis and Palestinians who are gripped by terror and the tendency to see the world in terms of polarized opposites, Shalit comments, "peace … poses a threat to those who identify with the quest for grandiose wholeness and totality, in which there is no room for the *other*."[8] I could not help thinking at the same time about the current situation in American politics where there is so much polarization and such limited capacity on the part of so many to see self and other as part of the civic whole.

Requiem: A Tale of Exile and Return, published six years after *The Hero and His Shadow*, is another exploration of the psychological and political dimensions of the situation in Israel but told in a more personal way that becomes a journey toward the discovery of soul. *Requiem* is unique among Shalit's books in that it is a novella in which the narrator, a professor Eliezer Shimeoni (who shares the same initials as the author) gives voice to a combination of despair and hope that is the legacy of the ideal of the Israeli socialist pioneers eclipsed by mutual shadow projections and the resulting polarization by Palestinians and Jews which created a culture of militarization and terrorist attacks. It is also a story of the alienation of the Western educated Jew from their religious heritage and the potential for finding a way back to a renewed Judaism and humanism through a revitalized understanding of self and other. For Professor Shimeoni it is a fight against denial, a battle for consciousness, and the courage to take a stand against evil that define the integrity one can maintain even in a situation that is seemingly hopeless in so many ways. He writes, "Consciousness will determine the future of Israel, and the preservation of Jewish civilization and its cultural heritage. When denial collaborates with demonization in the collective consciousness of the world, catastrophe lies in wait for its victim."[9] It is through self-scrutiny that essential elements in the often neglected and untold story of loss and despair can be identified and understood. While following this path may be the only way to find ourselves, to do so is to risk becoming lost in the depths of our own suffering. Shalit poses the essential question underlying all forms of depth psychology: "What witness is more trustworthy than the *sitra achra* (the other side, the story which is not told) which holds so many secrets, even secrets that we have forgotten, and secrets that are hidden from ourselves?"[10] *Requiem* is ultimately a story of the possibilities of the spirit and its capacity to transform fate into destiny, for the human capacity to surpass mere repetition or adherence to collective thought and action, and to find the courage and creative intelligence that can lead to a new way in the face of despair. This story is an appeal to the power of the symbolic life as an alternative to the literalism and concretism of fundamentalist and militaristic ideologies that underlie war and terror. This central concern is woven throughout this book that returns over and over to the story of the *akedah*, the binding of Isaac, and the fact that it was sufficient for the sacrifice to occur as a symbolic act that did not need to be acted out. Shalit writes, "By substituting the sacrificial animal for the actual son, the story of the akedah represents the separation of meaning from act, which is essential to culture and civilization."[11] The evolution of consciousness involves a movement from the literal to the symbolic, from action to thought.

As in Shalit's other books, in *Requiem* one finds literary and historical treasures that capture the reader's sense of awe and move the reader's spirit. For example, he reminds us of Elie Wiesel's observation that we may one day have an explanation for the Shoah (Holocaust) on the level of man but how Auschwitz was possible on the level of God will always be a mystery. The narrator then complicates this further, turning Wiesel's comment on its head, when he notes that Abraham substituting the ram for his son passed God's test but questions whether he passed the human test. The patriarch showed his complete devotion to God but how is a parent ever justified in being willing to murder his own child? The reader also finds here the story of a Wickard von Bredow, a county officer in Nazi Germany who was ordered to burn down the synagogue in the Prussian town of Shirwindt on the night that all synagogues in Germany were to be torched. Von Bredow put on his army uniform and stood in front of the synagogue when the Nazis arrived to burn it, loaded his gun, and made it clear that they could only enter over his dead body. This was the only synagogue in that district that was not destroyed that night.

Although I began this essay with two books addressing psychological hero and shadow within a primarily Jewish and Israeli context, I would not want to give the reader of this review the impression that Shalit's work is solely a Jewish perspective on analytical psychology. The work has deep roots in Judaism and Israel but it is truly much more universal in its inspiration and its focus. It is informed also by a deep respect for the esoteric dimensions of the wisdom traditions to be found in Christianity, Islam, Buddhism, and Hinduism, as well as folklore, mythology, etymology, and, of course, psychology where Shalit shows himself to be a master integrator of perspectives from psychoanalysis and Jungian psychology. The other four books included in this review, to which I now turn, reflect this universalist and humanist perspective within analytical psychology.

The Complex: Path of Transformation from Archetype to Ego reads as a primer on the psychology of complexes. Shalit carefully and thoughtfully places Jung's thinking about the complex within its intellectual lineage dating from the pioneering work of Galton, Wundt, Charcot, and Janet. He outlines the specific, creative contributions Jung made through the association experiments he developed while working at the Burgholzli, the psychiatric hospital at the University of Zürich. He then discusses Jung's phenomenological conceptualizations of these psychic phenomena: that they have a particular emotional feel ("feeling tone"), as well as an archetypal core around which can be found a cluster of unique personal ideas and memories. These are dynamic—not static—entities which function between ego and archetype, allowing the impersonal, objective psyche to infuse the personal, subjective psyche of the individual. Throughout the book, Shalit skillfully uses clinical examples, fairy tales, and myth to draw a sharp distinction between complexes in their normative aspect—as necessary, useful, and creative phenomena—and in their pathological aspect when they become autonomous and function unconsciously in the shadow of the psyche. Viewing this critical distinction in developmental terms, where there is "good enough" parenting, or help in containing and translating the archetypal energies, the complex serves as a vehicle—in the mode of a step-down transformer for electrical current—that makes it possible for overwhelming archetypal forces to be humanized and made available for use by the individual. Archetypal energy that is not adequately mediated through a complex will overrun the ego, and so may be defended against through projection, denial, repression, or splitting, thus creating states of dissociation or even psychosis. On the other hand too little contact with archetypal energies leaves the individual emotionally flat, devoid of the *elan vital* needed for a creative, full life.

Following an overview of complex theory, the book illustrates how complexes work through a creative re-examination of the Oedipus myth. Freud was quite taken with the idea of complexes but saw them primarily in sexual terms and eventually rejected the idea of all complexes other than the Oedipal complex which became a cornerstone of his psychological theory. Jung, as noted above, understood the complex to be a functional part of the psyche that served as the path for the transfer of psychic energy from the objective (collective) psyche to the personal (individual) ego. Further, he maintained that complexes were not solely paths for sexual energy but for all other forms of energy, as well. For Freud, the Oedipus drama illustrated a universal psychological truth that the sexualized love for the mother and murderous rivalry with the father had to be relinquished to make the developmental transition from infantile fantasy to the mature capacity for love and work. Shalit applies Jungian ideas of the story of Oedipus in a way that portrays Oedipus in the role of the autonomous complex, his murdered father Laius as the all-too-masculine ego that relies on strict and rigid boundaries and rules, and his mother Jocasta (whose beautiful name means "Shining Moon") as the feminine, related dimension of human consciousness. In Shalit's psychological reworking of the drama, the threat faced by the masculine consciousness of the father precludes suffering the complex as an inner problem and so Laius wounds and abandons his son. Rather than dying off, however, Oedipus, as personification of the autonomous complex, functions independently and surreptitiously in the psyche causing all sorts of mayhem and resulting in the murder of the father (ego) and living out the incestuous fantasy with the mother. Shalit writes,

> If Oedipus had not been in the grip of his own complex, a dialogue could have ensued for him to understand that it is the unconscious, his archetypal parents, the omnipotent parents of early childhood, that paradoxically have to be both slain as well as fused with. Instead, like the autonomous complex he is, he sets forth on his journey of acting out, so typical of someone like Oedipus, whom we know was easily enraged and now also overcome by the horror of his predicted fate.[12]

As we know, it is through Oedipus solving the riddle of the sphinx, by articulating the temporality of the arc of life, that the beast is defeated and Oedipus is awarded Jocasta as a bride. Shalit comments, "So what kills the terrible man eating monster seems to be the awareness of one's existential condition, with a beginning, a peak and an end, where the best one can do is carry the spark of the divine, potentiated and enabled by lameness."[13] It is this keen capacity to appreciate and articulate the woundedness and incompleteness at the true heart of human existence that is one of the great strengths one finds in Shalit's work. In *The Complex* he is able to convincingly show the gift one might receive through a conscious relationship with the problems we encounter and the limitations of our lives.

In *Enemy, Cripple, Beggar: Shadows in the Hero's Path* the reader finds Shalit revisiting, but in a less overtly political context, the phenomenology of the concept of the hero that he addressed previously in *The Hero and his Shadow* and *Requiem*. Within Jungian psychology the hero is not the outer hero or "hero ideal." He or she is not the individual who performs acts of bravery in the world celebrated in collective consciousness such as the brave soldier or the athlete whose determination and skill win the game. Rather, the hero in a Jungian context refers to the capacity of every individual to venture into the unknown, shadow regions of psyche to retrieve the treasure of self-knowledge. Shalit writes,

> The hero is, psychologically, that function within the ego, which has the capacity and the courage to face the awesome unknown in a conscious search for meaning (logos) and relatedness (eros). The hero abandons the known and the typical, the normative and the mediocre, often without knowing what lays ahead.[14]

He goes on to say,

> The task of the hero is to wrestle himself out of collective consciousness, the ingrained norms and prevailing worldview, our neurotic defenses, those rites of the soul and rituals of the spirit that have fallen into the ruins of obsessive litany and compulsive decree.[15]

The encounter with the shadow, an essential part of the heroic function, is often accompanied by anxiety and self-doubt. Facing inner reality, the hero retrieves something of great value for him or herself, and sometimes for the collective, as well.

The book begins by placing the hero within a mythic context. In this light, Shalit offers a clear differentiation between Freud's myth of psychosexual development leading both to genital maturity and the capacity to love and work on the one hand, and Jung's myth of meaning that has at its core the journey of the hero out of the known territory of individual ego and toward the hidden realms of shadow, retrieving through complexes the archetypal energies found in the objective psyche. In Freud's view the ego takes the place of the unconscious as famously explained in his New Introductory Lectures on Psychoanalysis where he wrote "Where id was there ego shall be."[16] While from Jung's perspective, ego and unconscious dynamically interpenetrate in a continual process of conflict and union. The hero in the Jungian myth leaves the comfort and certainty of the known to reach into the uncertain and not as yet related to dimensions of the unconscious. The heroic function develops through the encounter with various forms of projected dimensions of psyche which may take the form of polarized otherness (the enemy), limitation and woundedness (the cripple), and anonymity (the beggar).

The enemy is, psychologically speaking, a part of each individual consciousness that is disavowed in the self but hated when seen in the other. Shalit writes, "The enemy is an archetypal image taking shape by projection; the intentions and the deeds of that other as an external object in living reality, may or may not justify the perception of him as evil."[17] Furthermore, "it is, paradoxically, by recognizing one's evil that one becomes human, rather than by denial and acting out."[18] Shalit argues that this is not simply about perseverance or surrender by the ego to a greater self, but more that the ego finds dignity through the struggle and by recognition of its limitations. The encounter with the cripple is another example of the move from the primitive hubris of the ego to mature acceptance of limitation. It is the result of the normative ascendency of the archetypal wounded child replacing the divine child. In early childhood the divine child archetype is expected and necessary; however, when carried forward into later stages in life it can lead to projection of one's perceived weakness and limitation onto others, thus stultifying acceptance of one's woundedness and foreclosing a psychological process leading away from an idealized and unrealistic perfection to a greater, more mature state of wholeness. In other words while the denial and projection of those wounded aspects of psyche may be motivated by a sense that they are unbearable, their expulsion from consciousness only gives them that much greater a measure of the power to bring harm. On the other hand, acceptance of woundedness can lead to a greater sense of wholeness and authenticity. Shalit likens this as a movement from Mars—those aggressive energies characteristic of the encounter with the enemy—to the relatedness and love of Eros, the ability to experience a living connection with the inferior, suffering side of life. In this light the ego is understood more fully through an encounter with its limitations and the self is seen as offering a path toward healing. It is through acceptance of our woundedness, fear, and imperfection—carried by our complexes—that channels are opened allowing a fluid movement between ego and self. He illustrates this dynamic in a number of ways including the telling of the archetypal story of Hephaestus (whose name means "fire" and who wears the insignia of the wounded god), the wonderful Hans Christian Anderson story "The Cripple," as well as a most interesting clinical example of a therapist lost in the depths of a projected and eroticized countertransference. We learn here about not only the wounded healer but also his counterpart, the wound*ing* healer. The discussion of the psychology of the cripple ends with a focus on death as the ultimate incapacity and limitation, the mortal wound.

The final section of the book is, in my view, the most compelling and original. I found it particularly moving in light of the ever increasing economic and social dislocations in recent decades which have resulted in so many homeless people living on the streets and begging for spare change to be able to eat, find shelter, or just to find some temporary relief from their suffering in a bottle or a needle. Our encounter on the street with their anonymous and heartbreaking requests for help reflects the helpless, weak, raw, limited, and isolated dimensions of our common humanness to which we are so often blind and deaf. Shalit locates the essence of the beggar in the anonymity and universal human nature that is revealed when the persona is stripped away. He writes, "the beggar huddles in the shadows and unmasks those who come his way, that is, everyone who ventures far away from the royal court of unquestioned convictions. Without the protection of a social façade, the image of the beggar expresses the Inner Voice or the Daemon."[19] The beggar "holds something for us to receive … a wisdom free from conventional ethics."[20] The beggar has an attitude of submission which is so permeable that he allows himself to be spoken through. He longs to be heard. Our individuation journey ripens when we listen respectfully to the beggar within. I am reminded of the way that beggars were regarded as serving a useful function in Ancient Greece as they afforded others an opportunity for being charitable. The beggar is an archetypal energy in all of us, an impoverished nature within the psyche that speaks without identity, in hushed tones, asking for help and sustenance.

I particularly loved the way Shalit related the archetypal beggar to the ending of analysis, which can be such a troubling and confusing event. Writing about what he identifies as "the beggar healer," the part of the individual that is left behind after psychotherapy ends, he says,

> The beggar can hardly be noticed. It takes all the time of contemplation, sitting back in joy and sadness, fully intact in painful clarity, shattered beyond struggle, abandonment and the death of yet another loving and meaningful meeting, of years of togetherness in analytic distinction, to fully be in the bubble thin shadow that draws the fine line between the personal and the archetypal, to stand at the edge of the flattened earth, nearly falling off into the grand darkness of

the universe. The empty handed beggar is what remains, and
perhaps it is he who gives the final contribution, or maybe
not at all, to the most important part of the analysand's
journey—after the end of the interminable analysis.[21]

He likens this to the fourth and final stage of *ashrama* in the Hindu
tradition in which one becomes a homeless beggar at the culmination
of the arc of life. It is a most beautiful and true observation about the
end phase of a relationship in which the analytic couple have taken a
heroic journey toward the heart of individuation.

The timeless archetypal energies of enemy, cripple, and beggar are
reworked in the next book which integrates the archetypes within a
developmental context. In *The Cycle of Life: Themes and Tales of the
Journey*, Shalit places Jung's conceptualization of the transformations
of consciousness over the life span alongside life cycle theories, notably
those of Eric Erikson and Daniel Levinson. He also places his ideas
about the arc of life in relation to Greek myth (the three Morai who
spin one's fate—but not one's destiny—at birth) as well as biblical,
Talmudic, and Hasidic traditions, the Hindu Ashramas or four stages
of life, pre-Socratic Greek philosophy, Dante's *Divine Comedy*, and fairy
tales. Shalit's inspiration for articulating the developmental pathway
of consciousness, however, is clearly grounded in Jung's work, primarily
in his foundational essay, *The Stages of Life*, where he describes a life
cycle model for understanding human development as a progression
and regression of consciousness from womb to tomb.[22] This is a poetic
perspective, making extensive use of the metaphor of the sun's apparent
rise and fall over the course of the day to characterize four stages in the
arc of a full life: childhood, adulthood, midlife, and old age. Jung traces
the natural processes of emergence of the ego out of the unconscious
in infancy and early childhood and the sinking of the ego back into
the unconscious in old age. The in-between years are marked by an
always problematic consciousness that is inescapably at odds with itself,
plagued by what is left behind or discarded in the shadow as the ego
strives for adaptation and achievement. A return to the primordial
images that formed the groundwork for the initial development of
consciousness in childhood, and that operated all along in the
background, is the characteristic of the aged. As Shalit writes, "Jung
emphasizes life as a process of becoming conscious, which transforms
the experience of life into a living experience."[23]

Shalit's amplifications of Jung's work on understanding the life cycle
are substantial. He outlines the developmental progression through
the child, the puer/puella, the adult, and the senex. His talent for
integration and creative thinking is evident in bringing to bear on Jung's
thinking various psychoanalytic theorists—notably Freud, Klein, and
Winnicott—as well as myth, fairy tale, comparative religion,
etymology, and dream material. There is particular use made of the
myth of Prometheus and, again, the Oedipus story is explored (although
here the focus is not on the more well-known earlier years of Oedipus'
life as related in *Oedipus Rex* that were examined in *The Complex* but
the last years of his life as told by the ninety-year-old Sophocles in
Oedipus at Colonus.) This most tragic figure who had blinded himself
when he learned what he had done is guided by his daughter
Antigone as he wanders toward his last days decrying how his life
was shaped by a fate that was determined before he was even born.
Where this book shines is not in a dry recitation of the psychology
of transition through life's stages but in the sense of wonder and mystery
Shalit is able to articulate in relation to the problems of life all along
the journey. He writes,

> Consciousness pertains to knowing the suffering landscape that
> life provides, whether the landscape within the individual's
> private psyche, or the landscape of the soul and the matter in
> the world. Consciousness does not provide so much joy and
> pleasure, but rather for the depths, from which meaning and
> wisdom arise ... We are left with the questions blowing in the
> wind, to which the blowing in the wind, rather than the wind
> that has stopped blowing, may be the soul's main answer.
> "The wind is the pneuma hidden in the prima materia," says
> Jung. Individuation entails the extraction of the spirit that
> dwells in one's raw material, of detecting, awakening and
> engaging the energy that may be trapped in the matter. But
> the answer may, as well, drift in the water, flare in the fire, and
> ripen on the ground.[24]

The Cycle of Life illustrates dimensions of the developmental arc of
Shalit's own voice as a thinker and a writer. Reading his work as a whole
one sees a progression from the earlier to the more recent work in which
he becomes increasingly adept at moving from the description of a

patient's dream to mythical or biblical sources that amplify the dream material, to imaginative engagement with etymological roots in both English and Hebrew, bringing new and deeper understanding. One of my favorite examples of this in this book is Shalit's tracing of the dreams of a female scientist in her late sixties who, after a highly productive research career, is coming to terms with her own place as a link in the intergenerational chain when she is faced with the realization that the striving for perfection characteristic of her adult years must yield to a new consciousness that is driven more by the need for relatedness, particularly to her children and grandchildren, than the need for achievement. He links this woman's transformation to the biblical story of the wise King Solomon. Shalit's erudition is revealed in his capacity to not just relate the famous story of Solomon's decision to cut the baby in half as a way of discovering which of the two women is truly the mother but to relate another dimension of the Solomon story in which God shows up in Solomon's dream preceding the infant splitting incident and asks what he should give to the king. English translations of the response, Shalit notes, interpret Solomon's request as being for "an understanding heart" or "a wise heart"; however, Shalit explains that the original Hebrew translates more accurately as "a hearing heart," about which he then comments, "Wisdom comes from listening with your heart—not pure mind and intellect, but also not 'heart and nothing but heart.' Furthermore, *hear!* in Hebrew is shema!, the basis for mashmaot, which means *meaning.*"[25] He is describing the potential for hearing through our capacity for relatedness and emotion, and the necessity of doing this alongside our capacity to think about what we are feeling. He adds in a footnote that the "Shema" is often thought to be the most significant prayer in Judaism, ideally recited with the last breath of a dying person, and then goes on to explain that "a listening heart reflects the wisdom from the depths of the Self, that can guide us through what sometimes amounts to unbearable conflicts, limitations and divisions of the ego."[26] This idea of the hearing heart is a piece of wisdom from the ancestors which I find incredibly inspiring and useful. It goes along with another piece of biblical wisdom using the metaphor of the "circumcised heart" referred to in both Deuteronomy 30:6 and Isaiah, which can be understood as the cutting away of defensiveness, exposing the tender embodied spirit that is the core of our being.

CONCLUSION

Analytical psychology, like any school of psychology and psychotherapy, must continually assimilate new perspectives into the clinician's existing body of theory if it is to survive and remain potent. It needs to continually illustrate its effectiveness in understanding and articulating the human condition within an ever changing historical and cultural situation. Further, its insights must have the interpretive power to speak to the soul through both symbol and metaphor in ways that are simultaneously timeless and contemporary. If successful, such creative applications of theory yield new, more effective ways to understand the human condition and help those who are obviously suffering, as well as the existential suffering that afflicts—and, as James Hillman argued, "ensouls"— all of us. And, when most successful, the true psychologies—like great books—leave meaning open, raise questions that can never be fully answered, and help us become more complete for our encounter with them.

Erel Shalit's work deepens the context for all of us working as clinicians who are addressing issues of psyche and culture in the world today. He helps us both know and not know simultaneously, based not on the superiority or objective expertise of the analyst but on his or her ability to hear and speak from a hard-won knowledge of the human experience of uncertainty and suffering and from the position of being only a link in a chain of human and analytic generations that have come before and that are still to come, all caught in the complexities and mysteries of life. As a clinical writer the arc of his work holds the promise of still more thoughtful and evocative contribution to analytical psychology in the years ahead. Shalit is not the originator of a new theory but he is a unique synthesizer of Jung's original thinking and an amplifier of those seminal ideas in light of other theories of psychology, leading toward novel perspectives through explorations of religion, culture, myth, fairy tale, language, and politics. His books reflect his skill and experience as a clinician and thinker in the Jungian tradition. He succeeds in raising questions and helps us think about old problems in new ways, informed always by a listening heart.

> Dance me to your beauty with a burning violin
> Dance me through the panic till I'm gathered safely in
> Touch me with your naked hand or touch me with your glove
> Dance me to the end of love[27]

NOTES

1. Tom Cheetham, *Green Man, Earth Angel: The Prophetic Tradition and the Battle for the Soul of the World* (Albany, NY: State University of New York Press, 2005).

2. Tom Cheetham, *All the World an Icon: Henry Corbin and the Angelic Function of Beings* (Berkeley, CA: North Atlantic Books, 2012).

3. Erich Neumann, *Depth Psychology and a New Ethic* (New York: Harper and Row, 1969).

4. Joseph Henderson, "The Cultural Unconscious," *Proceedings of the Second International Congress for Analytical Psychology* (1964): 3–14.

5. Ari Shavit, *My Promised Land: The Triumph and Tragedy of Israel* (New York, NY: Spiegel and Grau, 2013).

6. Erel Shalit, *The Hero and His Shadow: Psychopolitical Aspects of Myth and Reality in Israel*, Revised (Carmel, CA: Fisher King Press, 2004, 2011), p. 117.

7. *Ibid.*

8. *Ibid.*, p. 161.

9. Erel Shalit, *Requiem: A Tale of Exile and Return* (Carmel, CA: Fisher King Press, 2010), p. 97.

10. *Ibid.*, p. 34.

11. *Ibid.*, p. 48.

12. Erel Shalit, *The Complex: Path of Transformation from Archetype to Ego* (Toronto: Inner City Books, 2002), p. 61.

13. *Ibid.*, p. 66.

14. Erel Shalit, *Enemy, Cripple & Beggar: Shadows in the Hero's Path* (Carmel, CA: Fisher King Press, 2008), pp. 57–58.

15. *Ibid.*, p. 137.

16. Sigmund Freud, "Lecture XXXI of the New Introductory Lectures in Psychoanalysis" in *The Complete Introductory Lectures on Psychoanalysis* (New York, NY: Norton, 1966), p. 544.

17. Shalit, *Enemy, Cripple & Beggar*, p. 106.

18. *Ibid.*, p. 112.

19. *Ibid.*, p. 198.

20. *Ibid.*, p. 199.

21. *Ibid.*, p. 204.

22. C. G. Jung, "The Stages of Life" (1931), in *The Collected Works of C. G. Jung*, vol. 8, ed. and trans. Gerhard Adler and R. F. C. Hull (Princeton, NY: Princeton University Press, 1966).

23. Erel Shalit, *The Cycle of Life: Themes and Tales of the Journey* (Carmel, CA: Fisher King Press, 2011), p. 15.

24. *Ibid.*, p. 180.

25. *Ibid.*, p. 176.

26. *Ibid.*, p. 177.

27. Leonard Cohen, "Dance Me to the End of Love" (on the CD *Various Positions*, 1984, Columbia Records).

Book Review

Jean Kirsch and Murray Stein, eds., *How and Why We Still Read Jung: Personal and Professional Reflections*. London and New York, NY: Routledge, 2013.

REVIEWED BY RODERICK MAIN

T he publications of C. G. Jung—including letters, seminars, and non-professional writings in addition to his *Collected Works*—already comprise well over thirty volumes, with many more planned. These publications span a period of more than sixty years, during which Jung underwent several major professional and personal transformations and witnessed and responded to some of the most turbulent political and cultural upheavals of the modern era. The range of influences drawn on and topics covered in his works is encyclopaedic and often arcane. The ideas he articulates frequently run athwart to both mainstream psychology and science and mainstream culture and religion. Moreover, in expressing his ideas Jung did not always prioritize clarity and precision; and for readers without German, most of what he writes can be read only through the inevitably distorting lens of translation.

Together, these factors can make reading Jung extremely challenging. Many would-be readers, even among those deeply attracted to Jungian ideas, either give up entirely or come to rely excessively on secondary expositions. The great value of Jean Kirsch and Murray Stein's edited collection of essays is that it provides a set of

Roderick Main, Ph.D., is a professor at the Centre for Psychoanalytic Studies and Deputy Dean (Education) for the Faculty of Social Sciences, University of Essex, UK. He is the author of *The Rupture of Time: Synchronicity and Jung's Critique of Modern Western Culture* (Brunner-Routledge, 2004) and *Revelations of Chance: Synchronicity as Spiritual Experience* (SUNY, 2007), the editor of *Jung on Synchronicity and the Paranormal* (Routledge/Princeton University Press, 1997), and the co-editor of *Myth, Literature, and the Unconscious* (Karnac, 2013).

compelling reasons and strategies for sticking with Jung's writings themselves, despite their difficulties.

There are, of course, many ways to read Jung and many reasons for doing so. In this volume we learn about the ways and reasons of nine Jungian analysts and three professors specializing in literature. Some have written more personally, others more professionally, whether as clinicians or academics (or both). But all have read Jung extensively and closely, and their reflections provide some rich and multi-faceted answers to the questions in the book's title.

In her introduction Jean Kirsch explains that the contributors were invited to write about their reading of Jung from a personal perspective. For many of the contributors this invitation seems to have matched what Jung's work invites them to do anyway: to respond to the written words subjectively as well as professionally or academically. In line with this Kirsch signals a theme that recurs throughout the volume: that reading Jung requires of the reader a willingness to be personally transformed.

The transformative effect of Jung's writing and a tactic for harnessing that effect are elaborated in Mark Saban's chapter, "Ambiguating Jung." Saban notes the ambiguity in Jung's writing style, which stems from Jung's dual commitment to what in *Memories, Dreams, Reflections* he refers to as his incommensurable No. 1 and No. 2 personalities. Saban suggests that this ambiguity is so fundamental to Jung's work that it should inform how we read him generally. Where Jung's writing is not overtly ambiguous, we as readers would do well to "ambiguate" it. In other words, whether in any particular text or passage Jung is writing predominantly in a No. 1 scientific mode or in a No. 2 imaginative and religious mode, we should always be alert to the other, less focal mode. Keeping these two modes in dialogue fosters individuation— and perhaps not only at the personal level. Saban argues that *Memories, Dreams, Reflections*, written largely from a No. 2 perspective, is Jung's own attempt to destabilize "all the sedimented dogma" that had accumulated around his No. 1 professional work and thereby allow his oeuvre as a whole to continue developing (p. 20).

Saban's basic proposition is neatly illustrated by Murray Stein's chapter, "A Lecture for the End of Time—'Concerning Rebirth.'" In his attentive reading of Jung's essay on rebirth, Stein, as from a No. 2 perspective, is alert to the way in which Jung himself creatively engages with the unconscious as well as inducts a similar meditative and transformative engagement in his readers. Yet at the same time, from a No. 1 perspective, Stein is sensitive to important but often-overlooked contextual information, such as the date the two parts of Jung's essay were originally presented (in the early days of the Second World War) and their relation to the work of the French scholar of Islam Louis Massignon, who had earlier spoken on the 18th Sura of the Koran at the same Eranos conference. This double awareness of Stein's approach reflects the double perspective to which Jung's core process of individuation—or "rebirth"—leads, dubbed by Stein "Dioscuri awareness": "a realization of oneself as one part human-all-too-human (ego identity) and one part transcendent and divine (archetypal self)" (p. 41). In conclusion, Stein can state explicitly what other contributors to the volume also imply: that "[Jung's] writings evoke the very processes spoken of in the texts" (*ibid.*).

In a similar spirit, Stan Marlan recounts how he has developed in his long engagement with Jung's alchemical texts an approach that he terms "daimonic reading," by which he means remaining open, while reading, to indications from dreams, fantasies, synchronicities, and other manifestations of the unconscious. Like Saban and Stein, he finds it impossible and undesirable to separate academic and personal modes of reading Jung.

In the chapter by Paul Bishop, "On Reading Jung in German: Jung's Significance for *Germanistik*," the focus shifts from the transformative effect of Jung's writings on their readers to the insights that Jung's distinctive depth psychological perspective can provide into the work of other modern authors, especially into their hidden archaic dimension. Thus Bishop comments on and extends Jung's interpretation of Hölderlin's poem "Patmos" as it is found in *Transformations and Symbols of the Libido* (1911-12/1952). From his more traditionally scholarly perspective, Bishop highlights the need to understand Jung's different styles—scientific, literary, and visionary—as well as his rich allusiveness, especially in relation to the German literary tradition. Despite the title of his chapter, Bishop focuses primarily on what survives translation in Jung's works.

Susan Rowland states explicitly that her concern is less with issues of translation and history—what Jung may really have said and meant—and more with readers' relationships to Jung's texts. In probably the boldest chapter in the volume, "Reading Jung for Magic:

'Active Imagination' for/as 'Close Reading,'" she argues that there is a deep affinity between Jung's process of active imagination and the close reading advocated by New Criticism, with possibilities of mutual enrichment for analytical psychology and literary theory. Further, invoking the concept of synchronicity, the tradition of Western esotericism, complexity theory, and the new field of biosemiotics, she argues that, in a more than metaphorical sense, both active imagination and close reading are forms of magic, practices that can non-locally both influence and be influenced by the cultural and natural worlds.

The archetypal criticism of the Canadian literary critic Northrop Frye was one of the academically most influential adaptations of Jung's thought by a thinker who was never an outright Jungian. In his chapter "Reading Frye Reading Jung" Craig Stephenson, keeping scholarly distance himself, tracks the ambivalence yet creativity of Frye's engagement with Jung.

For some readers access to Jung's work only becomes possible when Jung is viewed in relation to other thinkers, traditions, or disciplines. In her chapter "Tangled Up in Blue: A Reappraisal of Complex Theory" Betsy Cohen recounts how, for her, the deeper meanings behind Jung's deliberate ambiguity only began to open up when she read the philosopher Emmanuel Levinas and the scholar of Torah Avivah Zornberg.

Conversely, in the following chapter, "Chinese Modernity and the Way of Return," Shiuya Sara Liuh relates how it was reading Jung, specifically his "Commentary on 'The Secret of the Golden Flower,'" that enabled her to rediscover a relationship to aspects of traditional Chinese culture that had been repressed in the process of Chinese modernization. For Liuh, the inaccuracies in Jung's understanding and in the translation he used, as well as the unexceptional nature of the original Chinese text, are relatively unimportant compared with the illuminating and liberating power of Jung's symbolic, psychological reading of the text's spiritual content.

In contrast again, George Hogenson in his chapter "Philosophy, the Thinking Function, and the Reading of Jung" very much is concerned with scholarly accuracy. He outlines his own philosophically informed comparative reading of Jung vis-à-vis Freud, which highlights Jung's distinctiveness as a depth psychologist. Hogenson emphasizes the need to understand Jung's work as a whole, to recognise how rational it is for all its concern with the non-rational, and to be alert to the risks as well as potentials of its highly interdisciplinary character. He also illustrates, in his discussion of Jung's connection to Leibniz, the catalytic effect reading Jung can have in taking one down some important but neglected byways in the intellectual history of the West.

The religious aspect of Jung's thought is implicit in many of the chapters in the volume. Specific attention is turned to this aspect by David Tacey in his chapter "Jung: Respect for the Non-literal." Tacey highlights how, in a culture where myth and religion are devalued, Jung's metaphorical or symbolic approach allows for the possibility of "critical spirituality," for being a religious but non-literal thinker. He illustrates his argument with an analysis of Jung's preface to "Answer to Job."

Finally, Thomas Kirsch rounds the book off with his fascinating autobiographical chapter, "A Lifelong Reading of Jung." With reference to his own engagements with texts such as *Memories, Dreams, Reflections*, *Man and His Symbols*, and *Two Essays in Analytical Psychology*, he recounts how his reading of Jung was influenced by a variety of autobiographical factors, including having both parents as analysts, meeting Jung, and training in psychiatry and then in Jungian analysis. He especially echoes points made by other contributors regarding the need to read Jung through the unconscious, including being alert to synchronistic matching between what is read and what is experienced in life.

The variety of ways and reasons to read Jung evinced by the eleven essays in this volume is testimony to the continuing generative power of Jung's writings. Jung is read not just for his insight into psychological transformation (Saban, Stein, Marlan, Cohen, T. Kirsch) but also for the ways he can contribute to engagements with other disciplines, such as literary studies (Bishop, Rowland, Stephenson) or intellectual history (Hogenson), and to cultural understanding generally, on topics such as modernization (Liuh) or religion (Tacey).

While the essays all help to enrich one's reading of Jung, none claim that reading Jung is easy or can be made significantly easier. Rather, it often turns out that features which make reading Jung particularly challenging are also among the features that make his writings distinctive and valuable. For example, Jung's writings draw on and foster experiential as well as academic and scientific modes of knowing. In doing so, they broaden perspectives. But they also involve the reader's subjectivity in a process that is intrinsically transformative and as such, however implicitly, can make unwelcome ethical demands upon the reader.

Again, several of the contributors highlight Jung's ingrained view of the "doubleness" of the human condition—conscious and unconscious, rational and irrational, literal and symbolic, secular and religious, "No. 1" and "No. 2" personalities—and hence of the kind of awareness and cognition needed to engage with this doubleness: what Saban calls "ambiguation," Stein "Dioscuri awareness," Marlan "daimonic reading," and Tacey "critical spirituality." Such doubleness relentlessly undermines one-sided perspectives and fosters a view of the psyche and of psyche and nature as dynamic systems, deeply interconnected yet open-ended. This kind of subversion and dynamism can be unsettling as well as illuminating.

Further difficulties again are presented by the particular attention Jung pays to what gets marginalized by the prevalent rationalism of modern cultures. His writings about pre-modern, non-Western, and esoteric traditions (as discussed, for example, by Marlan, Bishop, Rowland, and Liuh) can be distinctly off-putting to readers whose thinking is aligned with post-Enlightenment rationality. Yet much of what is most fascinating, creative, and potentially transformative about Jung's writings stems from his attempt, from a modern perspective, to retrieve, integrate, and deploy something of value from these remoter traditions.

Implied by many of the essays, and explicitly stated by Hogenson (p. 165), is the importance of reading Jung "as a whole." This doesn't necessarily mean reading everything of Jung's that has been published—an overwhelming task that for most could probably only be accomplished at the cost of serious, distinctly "un-Jungian" imbalances elsewhere in their lives. What it surely does mean is having a rounded awareness of the range and diversity of Jung's writings, including not just their multi-faceted content but also their different voices, their numerous contexts and influences, their position in Jung's overall development, and the ways they fit or do not fit with other disciplines and discourses, in Jung's day or in our own. Together the essays in Kirsch and Stein's volume make an important contribution towards fostering such rounded awareness.

BOOK REVIEW

Craig E. Stephenson, ed., *Jung and Moreno: Essays on the Theatre of Human Nature*. London and New York, NY: Routledge, 2013.

REVIEWED BY ROBERT MACDONALD

In the *Dream Seminars* Jung recounts a dream where the dreamer is invited to the theatre by his brother-in-law and to dine afterwards. Jung interprets the theatre as "a psychotherapeutic institute [where the dreamer witnesses] the staging of his complexes—where all the images are the symbolic or unconscious representations of his own complexes."[1] The dinner engagement that follows the final curtain Jung sees as a consuming of those complexes.

In *Jung and Moreno* we read of an approach where the dream is embodied through action, the private theatre publicly staged within the temenos of a trusted group where members of that group take on the roles of the dream images, and the dreamer enters the staging of their psychological space in the spirit of "once-upon-a-time" storytelling.

The book comprises nine essays by psychodrama practitioners, most of them Jungian analysts who attended the Barz Psychodrama Institute Zumikon while training to be analysts at the C. G. Jung Institute Zürich. Although it is emphasized throughout the book that Jungian psychodrama operates as an adjunct to and is not a substitute for personal analysis, the essays draw us into the world of Jungian psychodrama and convey the unique benefits of this way of working. The book is rich in case material, without exception fascinating and

Robert Macdonald is a member of The Independent Group of Analytical Psychologists (IGAP) with a private practice in London, UK. He was formerly Head of Voice at the London Academy of Music and Dramatic Art where he taught the Alexander Technique for eighteen years. Website: www.robertmacdonald.org

lucidly written, which gives a fly-on-the-wall sense of what happens in a psychodrama.

Moreno was concerned with what binds human beings together. He posited a field that connects humans, one that precedes and runs deeper than the transference/counter-transference field. He wrote,

> *Tele* (from the Greek: far, influence into distance) is feeling of individuals into one another, the cement which holds groups together. ... Tele is a primary, transference a secondary structure. After transference vanishes, certain tele conditions continue to operate. Tele stimulates stable partnerships and permanent relations. It is assumed that in the genetic development of the infant tele emerges *prior* to transference.[2]

The essays are preceded by an excellent and thorough introduction by the editor, Craig Stephenson. He discusses the ethos of psychodrama and presents a theoretical framework in which to read the book, one that anticipates the tension between theory and practice that is held poignantly throughout. He introduces us to Moreno the man. His discussion of complexes and personification is illuminating. We learn of the three dimensional practice of Psychodrama: group psychotherapy, psychodrama, and sociometry—the subtle feeling for the group dynamic and the relationship between individuals within it.

Stephenson explains the theoretical differences between Jung and Moreno, "Moreno [who] locates experience of selfhood in an external field of interpersonal relatedness" and Jung who locates it intrapsychically.[3] Jung's therapeutic approach, for the most part, is a process of private introspection in the presence of an analyst. Moreno believed that being fixed in a role was a function of the group dynamic and working in a group was necessary to unfreeze those roles and revive what Moreno referred to as the "spontaneous element of being."

We learn of the process involved in Jungian psychodrama: the care with which a psychodrama enactment is constructed; the warming up stage when the collaborative energy of the group is awakened; the sensitive, sometimes urgent negotiation whereby the actor-protagonist (the person whose life experience will be explored) is chosen; and the skill with which the scene to be enacted is identified and focused on revealing archetypal themes. We meet the other players who participate in the psychodrama: the director who monitors the psychodrama ensuring balance between risk and restraint; the auxiliary ego who acts as a psychotherapeutic companion to the protagonist, supporting and occasionally challenging him to go deeper; and members from the group who are chosen by the protagonist to play key figures from the protagonist's life. The technique whereby role-players are modeled into those roles by the protagonist is discussed. We read of the structuring of the psychodrama and the creative sensitivity whereby the protagonist encounters unconscious aspects and is guided to make deeper associations. Role reversal, doubling, and mirroring are explained—processes that facilitate that deepening.

We will meet these roles again in the subsequent case histories: a woman curious about her blushing; a man exploring the circumstances that provoked his early life onset of asthma; the image of a "hole" and a growing interest to explore it; and a dream where the unfinished sculpted heads of the dreamer's parents relates to her wish to become a mother. A chapter on fairytale drama demonstrates the value of exploring archetypal narratives and their effect on personal material; a damaged father-son relationship is healed, an animus that can stand up to mother is sought, innocent child-guilt is lifted, and helpful animals are encountered. The use of psychodrama in one-to-one analysis recounts three enactments where a woman's relationship to an inner critic/demon lover becomes conscious. And we read of its application to musical performance where active imagination and allowing space and time for complexes, rather than shutting them out, lead to increased depth and expressiveness. The final essay is a touching personal testament to the value of psychodrama in life's journey.

A question arises around compromising the confidentiality of personal psychological material in a group situation. There is little said about the process of joining a psychodrama group but I sensed this is done with care and that what happens in the group remains there, kept secret and held as sacred. And of course this for Moreno is where the therapeutic value of the process lies—being held in a group. What is risked in terms of preserving confidentiality is gained in shared experience. And what about group members taking on roles of the protagonist's significant others? How can a role player know what someone's mother or father was like? Surely an inaccurate portrayal will unsettle the protagonist. The essays address these concerns convincingly. I was struck by the intuition of the players where more often than not they got it right. And when they didn't the process ensured that error led to a dialogue that clarified the protagonist's memory and deepened their experience of those past events.

I began reading with the question, what does psychodrama have to offer that sets it apart from a one-to-one analysis? That comparison faded as I became immersed in the world of psychodrama, where inner life is made concrete and reengaged with an embodied visceral experience. Memories are relived, significant others encountered, fantasies made flesh, and passages to the underworld personified:

> Psychodrama provides a chance to connect to body-ground, through trusting the urge to step into a drama, to present characters, to touch and move around the room. It is experienced first in breath, in lack of breath, with heartbeats, sweat, uneasiness, eagerness, postures, emotions.[4]

Hillman articulates the paradox "Do not act out; do not hold in"— its resolution to be found, he says, in acting in.[5,6] In psychodrama the distinction between "acting out" and "acting in" is blurred in the service of going deeper and differentiating between what was real and what were unconscious projections. Moreno distinguishes between two kinds of acting out: "*irrational, incalculable, acting out* in life itself, ... and *therapeutic, controlled acting out* taking place within the treatment setting."[7] The group imaginatively reconstructs the "real" and the protagonist is licensed to engage with the source of their resistance, meet defense mechanisms face to face, approach difficult feelings, and explore situations where the dangers of acting out are encrusted. The freedom to move between repression and acting out allows the complex, contained and guided by the imaginative response from the group, to find the way towards its center such that inner psychic processes are clarified, personal and archetypal material differentiated, and complexes become grounded in their psychic background. Through the re-enactment of memory a distinction is made "between what happened in the past and what happened as they re-experienced the past."[8] Personalization moves towards personification, engagement with the "real" reveals its symbolic background, and the role of archetypal forces in shaping memory is intimated.

Moreno first published on Spontaneity Theatre in the 1920s when the importance of mirroring and empathic attunement in childhood development and the therapeutic relationship were in their infancy.

In this, Moreno was at the forefront. In psychodrama mirroring is three-dimensional: person-to-person, individual-to-group, and group-to individual. From the warming up stage we get a sense of the giving and receiving that awakens the "feeling between" individuals and establishes the collective attunement where the protagonist can safely open, explore, and reveal.

The examples of role reversal are fascinating and its therapeutic potential compelling. In the initial enactment the protagonist has played himself, explored, and gone deeper. He then takes on the role of a significant other—say mother, father, younger brother—and by standing in their shoes looks back at himself, his protagonist role now played by another member of the group. He sees himself from an outsider's point of view, feels what it is like to be someone else in relationship to himself, even what it is like to be the recipient of his own projections! There is the option to switch back and forth: he plays himself, then again standing in the other's shoes, then back to the protagonist role. Finally the protagonist might stand out and witness the scene replayed by other members. There is an art of seeing here, where oscillating between different points of view leads to a wider perspective.

"Sharing" concludes the psychodrama when members of the group discuss their life experience and where it mirrors the protagonist's journey. The protagonist, having exposed his personal material, is not singled out. By recognizing shared complexes bridges are built between individuals, and consciousness of shared humanity binds the group together.

The book opened highlighting the differences between Moreno and Jung. As I read, their concern for the individual stood out and their different approaches were not opposed but rather complementary to achieving that end. An essay on the transference and counter-transference is placed appropriately towards the end of the book. While it revisits and articulates their different models of the psyche, at the same time it identifies what connects them by grounding both Jung's concept of *eros* and Moreno's *tele* in the deeper layers of the unconscious. Both men "... speak of the communication between co-unconscious states as the basis for the empathic relation between two or more people."[9]

Jung and Moreno is a fascinating and compelling testament to the therapeutic value of Jungian psychodrama and the integrity of its way of working. It is a feast of practical experience and theoretical reflection, full to the brim with inspiring guidance on working creatively with psychological material. It is said that psychodrama invites the unlived into life. Indeed this quest is shared by analytical psychology, and we read of some remarkable and moving examples in this book.

NOTES

1. C. G. Jung, *Dream Analysis: Notes of the Seminar Given in 1928–1930 by C. G. Jung*, ed. William McGuire (Princeton, NJ: Princeton University Press, 1948), p. 12.

2. J. L. Moreno, *Psychodrama, First Volume* (Beacon, NY: Beacon House, Inc., 1977), p. xi.

3. C. E. Stephenson, "Introduction," in C. E. Stephenson, ed., *Jung and Moreno: Essays on the Theatre of Human Nature* (London and New York, NY: Routledge, 2014), p. 4

4. S. Ness, "The True Time of Psychodrama: Reflections on a Jungian Psychodrama Group," in Stephenson, *Jung and Moreno*, p. 74.

5. J. Hillman, *Alchemical Psychology* (Putnam, CT: Spring Publications, 2014), p. 37.

6. Hillman, *Alchemical Psychology*, p. 37.

7. Moreno, *Psychodrama*, p. x.

8. W. Scategni, "Jung, Moreno and Dream Enactment," in Stephenson, *Jung and Moreno*, p. 99.

9. M. Graziosi, "Psychodrama and the Resolution of the Transference and Counter-transference," in Stephenson, *Jung and Moreno*, p. 143.

Book Review

Llewellyn Vaughan-Lee, ed., *Spiritual Ecology: The Cry of the Earth*. Point Reyes Station, CA: The Golden Sufi Center, 2013.

REVIEWED BY ANN KUTEK

T his is an anthology of twenty contributions from mainly American and US-based writers, whose perspectives range from First Nation and Sufi traditions through Buddhism and Christianity to General Systems Theory. Some of them are farmers and poets, others scientists or psychologists, or priests and philosophers. Significantly, there are no business moguls among them, and all share an inclination to listen and reflect on their discoveries. Their collective response to "the cry of the Earth" is a kind of multipartite consensus that is part poetic lament, part confessional, and part polemic. From the outset there is an assumption that humanity has somehow found itself severed from its previous spiritual and instinctual attachment to Nature and the planet. The editor, Llewellyn Vaughan-Lee, opens with a declaration that the Earth's perceived imbalance is not a problem out there but is deeply connected to the self and to man's forgetfulness of the sacredness of nature. Changes may be occurring involving unsustainable losses in communities of living organisms coupled with unfettered human activity around the globe. It is said that we are at the start of the sixth Great Extinction, but is it really ALL down to us, and what can be done about it?

Ann Kutek, B.A. (Hons.) Oxon. in PPE, Dip. Soc. Admin., Dip. S.W., C.Q.S.W., is a member of the British Psychotherapy Foundation (BPF)/British Jungian Analytic Association (BJAA), maintains a private practice, and has been published in journals and books since 1981. She was a manager in local government and the voluntary sector prior to becoming an analytical psychologist. Among her presentations have been papers on Translation in Montreal to the IAAP, on Climate Change to the Copenhagen Congress in 2013, and on Town Planning and Alchemy in London in 2014. She teaches at Birkbeck, University of London, at BPF, and in Poland where she supervises Polish IAAP routers.

Vaughan-Lee argues that the book gives no solutions, but is a response to this controversial dilemma. He urges that we need to redeem the split between spirit and matter by waking up and engaging in a spiritual journey to reclaiming our role as guardians of our heritage before the present spiritual and physical crisis reaches a "tipping point," a state of irreversible decline for the world as we know it. Indeed, one might be put in mind of the British Jungian analyst, Roderick Peters, who in 1987 observed, "Since the demise of alchemy, the eagle-like ascent of a scientific world view has de-animated matter so thoroughly that for most people the human body itself has become the last refuge of the divine matter."[1] His sentiment seems to chime with much of the book's content.

Chief Oren Lyons, faith-keeper of the Onondaga Nation exhorts people to get along and do the best they can by making peace with Mother Earth. Winona LaDuke, another American indigenous voice, rejects the American Dream, the corporate exploitation of land. She stresses the importance of place as teacher. Thomas Berry, a leading light in Earth-based spirituality, debunks the manifest sense of destiny and entitlement adopted by America's founding fathers and their descendants by describing them rather as a predator people on an innocent continent. This line of thought has been explored at much greater length by the geographer and physiologist, Jared Diamond (1998), in his ground-breaking book, *Guns, Germs and Steel.*[2] Berry's is a sobering vision of the Earth, a one-time project only. Another Berry, Wendell, draws on a mystical intelligence and lays out his creed in verse.

A brief Buddhist knell is sounded in Thich Naht Hanh's piece; no use blaming governments and corporations, he says. It's time for each of us to wake up and take action in our own lives. Chief Tamale Bwoya from Kenya passes on a message he received in a dream about the water-base-scale which records the sum of all human activity, and once this scale is upset, there will be a total cleansing, that is, demise of man and all living things in his care. This is a relentless dystopian vision.

Stanley and Loy's essay takes a broad-brush look at how our dichotomous brain may be behind the split between the intuitive and rational minds. Their supporting quotations come from Einstein and McGilchrist. They want to create a new story that brings together the best of science with the best of the non-dual spiritual traditions. They interpret the universe as a self-aware creative process which has made possible the wisdom and observations of poets like the XII century Sufi, Rumi. A cosmological view follows from Tucker and Swimme who tell us that only in the last century have the branches of science begun to weave together the story of an historical cosmos 13.7 billion years old. And, just as we are becoming conscious of how long it took to bring forth this abundance of life, it is dawning on us how quickly we are foreshortening its future flourishing. They pitch for an integrated story. Yet, informed by the recent swashbuckling book, *Sapiens: A Brief History of Humankind* by the Israeli author Harari (2014), one is tempted to view mankind's current behavior as inevitable, given how its dominance overcame five other human subspecies in the course of the planet's recent history.[3] Perhaps self-awareness in Homo sapiens counts for not much in the light of archetypal behaviors as Jung hypothesized or as Bion and others noted in group experiences.

The celebrated Vandana Shiva returns to the fruits of the Earth and the centrality of food as the web of life. The act of feeding as that of quenching thirst are sacred movements she tells us. All other human arrangements stem from this. In an eloquent and pithy essay, she berates the agro-chemical industry's role and the consequent extinction of farmers. She ends with the stark paradox: Climate change, erosion of biodiversity, and depletion of water are the consequences; if these costs were internalized, we could not afford to eat poisoned foods. A further paradox, if this is what it is, lies at the center of Susan Murphy's chapter, "The Koan of the Earth," typified in her Zen-inspired, "the softest thing on earth overtakes the hardest thing on earth." Satish Kumar, associated in Great Britain with Schumacher College, lends a Hindu perspective to his philosophical exposition. According to the principle of *yagna* we should celebrate the beauty, the abundance, and the grandeur of nature by replenishing what we have taken. It is part of living in harmony with nature, but humanity continues unabated to be at war with itself.

The eco-philosopher Joanna Macy refers to the overturning of the Western concept of self, which she believes to be co-extensive with the environment as is accepted in some Eastern societies. She calls it the "greening of the self." She, like others in this collection, refers to the conceptualizations of the Norwegian philosopher, Arne Naess.

Another couple of writers focus on the *Anima Mundi*, the soul of the earth—Geneen Marie Haugen, a wilderness wanderer; Jules Cashford, who describes the re-emergence of Gaia and links it to Jung's archetypal hypothesis; and Bill Plotkin, another author with a psychologist's background, who speaks of the West's adolescent pathogenic attitude. The alternative Plotkin proposes is a hierarchy of authentic adults and true elders, who might, like benevolent foster parents, mentor the vandal-like adolescents who are currently pillaging human culture.

Towards the end of the book the essays speak of shamanism, a return to ancient and archaic healing practices as explained by Sandra Ingerman, and consider the theology of Zoroastrianism and how it is still evident in contemporary Sufi practice through the words of Pir Zia Inayat Khan. The final contribution is from a Franciscan monk, Richard Rohr, who reminds us through scriptural references that the world is the incarnation of God, an echo of the earlier interview with the farmer and nun Sister Gillian MacGillis. The closing remarks by the editor are a consideration of the call to reawaken spiritually, to beware of adopting sustainability merely as a means of clinging onto a cherished materialism, and to respond instead with a recognition and respect for the sacred in our daily lives.

There are twenty-three endorsements inside the front of the book—perchance potential candidates for the sequel—and this volume, for all its variety, comes across as curiously homogenous, like the product of a conference. Yet it falls prey to fragmentation and compression; this feeling is augmented by the insertion of quotations preceding each chapter. The editing was possibly over ambitious, expecting the reader to change gear too often, calling for reserves of stamina and huge patience, which is a pity for some of the more memorable contributions. The language used brings some pieces into the tradition of religious tracts. In other chapters the themes are elegiac and haunting.

Overall, there is a sense of hurried exhortation and alarm in a format that could make it a difficult read for those not acquainted with or drawn to spiritual matters. One is then left with the following questions: is it an attempted "proof" of humanity's waywardness by calling on a cross-section of witnesses? Or, is it an appeal to those who could be accused of abusing their power in despoiling the Earth? Either way, the message is unlikely to reach them. The book may, however, appeal to some committed ecologists and those already advancing upon their own spiritual path, whether they are psychologically-minded or not. If it acts as a signpost, it may have served its editor's objective to some degree.

NOTES

1. Roderick Peters, "The Eagle and the Serpent," *Journal of Analytical Psychology* 32 (4, 1987): 359–86.

2. Jared Diamond, *Guns, Germs and Steel: A Short History of Everybody for the Last 13,000 Years* (London: Vintage, 1998).

3. Yoval Noah Harari, *Sapiens: A Brief History of Humankind* (London: Harvill Secker, 2014).

BOOK REVIEW

Dennis Patrick Slattery, *Creases in Culture: Essays Toward a Poetics of Depth*. Skiatook, OK: Fisher King Press, 2014.

REVIEWED BY SUSAN ROWLAND

C reases in Culture is an arresting title for poet and writer Dennis Patrick Slattery's new book of essays on subjects as rich and diverse as "psychic energy's portal to presence in myth, poetry and culture," to "motorcycles as myth and metaphor." "Creases" suggests both momentary imperfections but also those necessary folds that come about when an object is put to use. Creases trace presence, being, activity, and necessity. So too do these lucid and original essays trace a new sense of the *presence* of the embodied psyche resonating to the creative energy of archetypes while caught up in a reciprocal shaping with language and the material world.

C. G. Jung's psychology of the meaning-making presence of an archetypal inheritance in the soul could not be limited to psychotherapy, even for him. Jung became a psychologist of culture, even offering provocative formulations on the arts and artists. What he did not do, and what Slattery starts to offer here, is to examine the creases between psychic energy and structures within language. In a marvelously rich opening essay on myth, poetry and metaphor, Slattery explores with verve and persuasiveness what it means to call the psyche "poetic."

In particular, he suggests that psyche energy coalesces around metaphor. In effect, he says that metaphors in language "are then energy fields that bridge some quality between conscious and the unconscious,

Susan Rowland, Ph.D., is chair of the M.A. in Engaged Humanities and the Creative Life at Pacifica Graduate Institute. She has published widely on Jung, literary theory, and gender including the forthcoming *The Sleuth and the Goddess* to be published by Spring Journal Books in 2015.

and body-psyche."[1] When we read metaphors, we are materializing language by the way the mind is mobilized to explore meaning. Hence metaphor is a system of energy transfer between body, imagination, and word. Here is a deep exploration of psyche and archetypal liveliness in the written arts.

One important aspect of such work, building on post-Jungian innovations by James Hillman on archetype and language, is to start to rescue Jung's linguistic notion of the symbol from its relative neglect in both Jungian and literary studies. For as Slattery demonstrates, Jung's symbol by mode of metaphor slices through the disembodied poststructuralist account of literary language—one that has so influenced the humanities in the last three decades.

Crucially, Jung's archetypal image in words, or symbol, is neither fixed, nor determining, nor subject to determination by bodily energies, nor by social power. Rather the archetype provides a resistance to any one determinant of meaning while offering that "crease" of use, of response to actual psychic embodiment, that sparks language into contributing to being. A resonant metaphor in a poem leaps into life in the reader providing a crease, a momentary spark between psyches, bodies, and histories that may be widely separated in time and culture. We arc our imagination to the smell of the sea received and imagined by Homer.

Later in the book, Slattery invokes his poetic psyche-soma in an important treatment of Jung's *The Red Book* in "Thirteen Ways of Looking at a *Red Book*: C. G. Jung's *Divine Comedy*." Here is the liberation surely sought by Jung's radically experimental work. For in Slattery's deft poet's touch, the extended comparison with Dante's religious epic becomes a freeing of the possibilities incarnated in Jung's newly available text. As Slattery shows, it is important to take on the hardly subtle hint of medievalism in Jung's illuminated manuscript.

Yet, fortunately, Slattery's historical sense is tempered with his sensitivity to Jung's signature use of historicizing as a *psychological* style rather than dour essentialism. So the essay focuses on epic as a multi-voiced and cross-cultural genre that includes films such as *The Lord of the Rings* and the various series of *Star Trek*. Also an especial plus in this treatment of *The Red Book* is Slattery's appreciation for Jung's humor as productive of meaning, rather than the unfortunate adornment it is so often taken to be. In diagnosing Jung's text as a "redemptive epic text, comic in trajectory and Medieval in design that follows in part the structure of Dante's poem," Slattery of course embraces the dual sense of comedy.[2] While Dante is not known for his jokes, his work is comedy in the sense of circular toward an ending of redemptive bliss. For *his* times, argues Slattery, Jung rightly embeds humor more directly in order to propel the epic quest for psychic re-integration.

Towards the end of *Creases in Culture,* the book makes another important intervention into that neglected realm of literary and depth psychology theory working together. In "Poetics of Soul: *Revisioning Psychology* as Mythical Method," Slattery begins to explore the complex and challenging work of psychologist James Hillman. "Always a myth peers out from under theory's clothing," offers an essay in showing how the work of psychology as soul-making is also a gift to the literary-building of a life in narrative.[3]

Slattery's remarkable new book invites repeated reading as he too becomes a guide to soul-making, with words, with poetry. I will treasure the insights and sheer excitement of this book in its quest into the heart and imagination of our words.

NOTES

1. D. P. Slattery, *Creases in Culture: Essays Toward a Poetics of Depth* (Skiatook, OK: Fisher King Press, 2014), p. 17.

2. *Ibid.,* p. 87.

3. *Ibid.,* p. 187.

BIBLIOGRAPHICAL APPENDICES

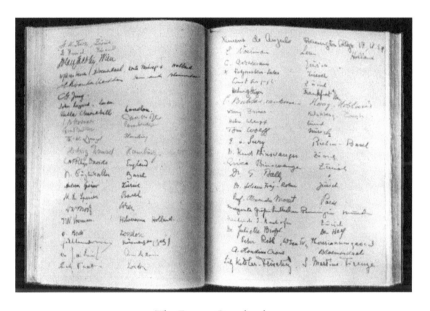

The Eranos Guestbook.
(Ph. Margarethe Fellerer. Eranos Foundation Archives)

APPENDIX I
LIST OF THE ERANOS YEARBOOKS (1933–2014)

Yoga und Meditation im Osten und im Westen—Fünfzehn Vorträge gehalten auf der Tagung in Ascona 14-26 August 1933, Eranos-Jahrbuch I / 1933, ed. Olga Fröbe-Kapteyn (Zürich: Rhein-Verlag, 1934).

Ostwestliche Symbolik und Seelenführung—Vorträge gehalten auf der Tagung in Ascona 20 August bis 1 September 1934, Eranos-Jahrbuch II / 1934, ed. Olga Fröbe-Kapteyn (Zürich: Rhein-Verlag, 1935).

Westöstliche Seelenführung—Vorträge gehalten auf der Tagung in Ascona 12-22 August 1935, Eranos-Jahrbuch III / 1935, ed. Olga Fröbe-Kapteyn (Zürich: Rhein-Verlag, 1936).

Gestaltung der Erlösungsidee in Ost und West (1)—Vorträge gehalten auf der Tagung in Ascona 6-14 August 1936, Eranos-Jahrbuch IV / 1936, ed. Olga Fröbe-Kapteyn (Zürich: Rhein-Verlag, 1937).

Gestaltung der Erlösungsidee im Judentum und im Protestantismus—Eranos-Vorträge von Heinz Westman und Paul Tillich—Ergänzungsband zum Eranos-Jahrbuch 1936, ed. Rudolf Ritsema (Ascona: Eranos Foundation, 1986).

Gestaltung der Erlösungsidee in Ost und West (2)—Vorträge gehalten auf der Tagung in Ascona 5-12 August 1937, Eranos-Jahrbuch V / 1937, ed. Olga Fröbe-Kapteyn (Zürich: Rhein-Verlag, 1938).

Vorträge über Gestalt und Kult der "Grossen Mutter"—Vorträge gehalten auf der Tagung in Ascona 8-15 August 1938—Mit 20 Kunstdrucktafeln, Eranos-Jahrbuch VI / 1938, ed. Olga Fröbe-Kapteyn (Zürich: Rhein-Verlag, 1939).

Vorträge über die Symbolik der Wiedergeburt in der religiösen Vorstellung der Zeiten und Völker—Vorträge gehalten auf der Eranos-Tagung in Ascona im August 1939, Eranos-Jahrbuch VII / 1939, ed. Olga Fröbe-Kapteyn (Zürich: Rhein-Verlag, 1940).

Zwei Vorträge über das Probleme der Trinitaet—Eranos 1940, ed. Olga Fröbe-Kapteyn (Ascona: privately printed, 1940).

Eranos 1941, ed. Olga Fröbe-Kapteyn (Ascona: privately printed, 1941).

Trinität, christliche Symbolik und Gnosis—Vorträge gehalten auf den Tagungen in Ascona im August 1940 und im August 1941, Eranos-Jahrbuch VIII / 1940–1941, ed. Olga Fröbe-Kapteyn (Zürich: Rhein-Verlag, 1942).

Das hermetische Prinzip in Mythologie, Gnosis und Alchemie—Vorträge gehalten auf der Tagung in Ascona 4-8 August 1942, Eranos-Jahrbuch IX / 1942, ed. Olga Fröbe-Kapteyn (Zürich: Rhein-Verlag, 1943).

Alte Sonnenkulte und die Lichtsymbolik in der Gnosis und im frühen Christentum—Vorträge gehalten auf der Tagung in Ascona 4-11 August 1943, Eranos-Jahrbuch X / 1943, ed. Olga Fröbe-Kapteyn (Zürich: Rhein-Verlag, 1944).

Die Mysterien—Vorträge gehalten auf der Tagung in Ascona 3-11 August 1944, Eranos-Jahrbuch XI / 1944, ed. Olga Fröbe-Kapteyn (Zürich: Rhein-Verlag, 1945).

Studien für C.G. Jung—Zur Idee des Archetypischen—Zum 70. Geburtstag von C.G. Jung [Studien zum Probleme des Archetypischen—Festgabe für C.G. Jung zum siebzigsten Geburtstag 26 Juli 1945], Eranos-Jahrbuch XII / 1945, ed. Olga Fröbe-Kapteyn (Zürich: Rhein-Verlag, 1945).

Der Geist—Vorträge gehalten auf der Tagung in Ascona 2-9 September 1945, Eranos-Jahrbuch XIII / 1945, ed. Olga Fröbe-Kapteyn (Zürich: Rhein-Verlag, 1946).

Geist und Natur—Vorträge gehalten auf der Tagung in Ascona 26 August bis 3 September 1946, Eranos-Jahrbuch XIV / 1946, ed. Olga Fröbe-Kapteyn (Zürich: Rhein-Verlag, 1947).

Der Mensch (Erste Folge)—Vorträge gehalten auf der Tagung in Ascona 18 bis 26 August 1947, Eranos-Jahrbuch XV / 1947, ed. Olga Fröbe-Kapteyn (Zürich: Rhein-Verlag, 1948).

Der Mensch (Zweite Folge)—Vorträge gehalten auf der Tagung in Ascona 23 bis 31 August 1948—Mit 9 Tafeln und 9 Abbildungen im Text, Eranos-Jahrbuch XVI / 1948, ed. Olga Fröbe-Kapteyn (Zürich: Rhein-Verlag, 1949).

Der Mensch und die mythische Welt—Vorträge gehalten auf der Tagung in Ascona 22 bis 30 August 1949—Mit 19 Abbildungen, Eranos-Jahrbuch XVII / 1949, ed. Olga Fröbe-Kapteyn (Zürich: Rhein-Verlag, 1950).

Aus der Welt der Urbilder—Sonderband für C.G. Jung zum fünfundsiebzigsten Geburtstag 26 Juli 1950, Eranos-Jahrbuch XVIII / 1950, ed. Olga Fröbe-Kapteyn (Zürich: Rhein-Verlag, 1950).

Mensch und Ritus—Vorträge gehalten auf der Eranos-Tagung in Ascona 21 bis 30 August 1950—Mit 2 Tafeln, Eranos-Jahrbuch XIX / 1950, ed. Olga Fröbe-Kapteyn (Zürich: Rhein-Verlag, 1951).

Mensch und Zeit—Vorträge gehalten auf der Eranos-Tagung in Ascona 20 bis 30 August 1951—Mit 6 Illustrationen und 6 Tabellen, Eranos-Jahrbuch XX / 1951, ed. Olga Fröbe-Kapteyn (Zürich: Rhein-Verlag, 1952).

Mensch und Energie—Vorträge gehalten auf der Eranos-Tagung in Ascona 20 bis 28 August 1952—Mit 16 Illustrationen und 8 Tabellen, Eranos-Jahrbuch XXI / 1952, ed. Olga Fröbe-Kapteyn (Zürich: Rhein-Verlag, 1953).

Mensch und Erde—Vorträge gehalten auf der Eranos-Tagung in Ascona 19 bis 27 August 1953—Mit 8 Kunstdrucktafeln, Eranos-Jahrbuch XXII / 1953, ed. Olga Fröbe-Kapteyn (Zürich: Rhein-Verlag, 1954).

Mensch und Wandlung—Vorträge gehalten auf der Eranos-Tagung in Ascona 19 bis 27 August 1954—Mit 10 Kunstdrucktafeln, Eranos-Jahrbuch XXIII / 1954, ed. Olga Fröbe-Kapteyn (Zürich: Rhein-Verlag, 1955).

Der Mensch und die Sympathie aller Dinge—Vorträge gehalten auf der Eranos-Tagung in Ascona 24 August bis 1 September 1955—Mit 10

Kunstdruckbildern sowie 22 Illustrationen und Tabellen im Text,
Eranos-Jahrbuch XXIV / 1955, ed. Olga Fröbe-Kapteyn (Zürich:
Rhein-Verlag, 1956).

Der Mensch und das Schöpferische—Vorträge gehalten auf der Eranos-
Tagung in Ascona 22 bis 30 August 1956—Mit einer Kunstdrucktafel
und einer Illustration im Text, Eranos-Jahrbuch XXV / 1956, ed.
Olga Fröbe-Kapteyn (Zürich: Rhein-Verlag, 1957).

Eranos-Index für die Jahrbücher I–XXV, 1933–1956, ed. Magda Kerényi
(Zürich: Rhein-Verlag, 1961).

Mensch und Sinn—Vorträge gehalten auf der Eranos-Tagung in Ascona
21 bis 29 August 1957—Mit 4 Kunstdrucktafeln, Eranos-
Jahrbuch XXVI / 1957, ed. Olga Fröbe-Kapteyn (Zürich:
Rhein-Verlag, 1958).

Mensch und Frieden—Vorträge gehalten auf der Eranos-Tagung in Ascona
14 bis 22 August 1958, Eranos-Jahrbuch XXVII / 1958, ed. Olga
Fröbe-Kapteyn (Zürich: Rhein-Verlag, 1959).

Die Erneuerung des Menschen—Vorträge gehalten auf der Eranos-Tagung
in Ascona 19 bis 27 August 1959, Eranos-Jahrbuch XXVIII / 1959,
ed. Olga Fröbe-Kapteyn (Zürich: Rhein-Verlag, 1960).

Mensch und Gestaltung—Vorträge gehalten auf der Eranos-Tagung in
Ascona 17 bis 25 August 1960, Eranos-Jahrbuch XXIX / 1960, ed.
Olga Fröbe-Kapteyn (Zürich: Rhein-Verlag, 1961).

Der Mensch im Spannungsfeld der Ordnungen—Vorträge gehalten auf
der Eranos-Tagung in Ascona 16 bis 23 August 1961, Eranos-
Jahrbuch XXX / 1961, ed. Olga Fröbe-Kapteyn (Zürich: Rhein-
Verlag, 1962).

Eranos-Index für die Jahrbücher XXVI–XXX, 1957–1961, ed. Magda
Kerényi (Zürich: Rhein-Verlag, 1965).

Der Mensch, Führer und Geführter im Werk—Vorträge gehalten auf der
Eranos-Tagung in Ascona 21 bis 29 August 1962, Eranos-Jahrbuch
XXXI / 1962, ed. Adolf Portmann (Zürich: Rhein-Verlag, 1963).

Vom Sinn der Utopie—Vorträge gehalten auf der Eranos-Tagung in Ascona 28 August bis 5 September 1963, Eranos-Jahrbuch XXXII / 1963, ed. Adolf Portmann (Zürich: Rhein-Verlag, 1964).

Das menschliche Drama in der Welt der Ideen—Vorträge gehalten auf der Eranos-Tagung in Ascona vom 19 bis 27 August 1964, Eranos-Jahrbuch XXXIII / 1964, ed. Adolf Portmann (Zürich: Rhein-Verlag, 1965).

Form als Aufgabe des Geistes—Vorträge gehalten auf der Eranos-Tagung in Ascona vom 18 bis 26 August 1965, Eranos-Jahrbuch XXXIV / 1965, eds. Adolf Portmann (Zürich: Rhein-Verlag, 1967).

Schöpfung und Gestaltung—Vorträge gehalten auf der Eranos-Tagung in Ascona vom 17 bis 25 August 1966, Eranos-Jahrbuch XXXV / 1966, ed. Adolf Portmann (Zürich: Rhein-Verlag, 1967).

Polarität des Lebens—Vorträge gehalten auf der Eranos-Tagung in Ascona vom 23 bis 31 August 1967, Eranos-Jahrbuch XXXVI / 1967, eds. Adolf Portmann and Rudolf Ritsema (Zürich: Rhein-Verlag, 1969.

Tradition und Gegenwart—Vorträge gehalten auf der Eranos-Tagung in Ascona vom 21 bis 29 August 1968, Eranos-Jahrbuch XXXVII / 1968, eds. Adolf Portmann and Rudolf Ritsema (Zürich: Rhein-Verlag, 1970).

Sinn und Wandlungen des Menschenbildes—Vorträge gehalten auf der Eranos-Tagung in Ascona vom 20 bis 28 August 1969, Eranos-Jahrbuch XXXVIII / 1969, eds. Adolf Portmann and Rudolf Ritsema (Zürich: Rhein-Verlag, 1972).

Man and Speech / Mensch und Wort / L'homme et le verbe—Lectures given at the Eranos Conference in Ascona from August 19ᵗʰ to 27ᵗʰ, 1970 / Vorträge gehalten auf der Eranos Tagung in Ascona vom 19 bis 27 August 1970 / Conférences données à la session d'Eranos à Ascona du 19 au 27 Août 1970, Eranos-Yearbook / Jahrbuch / Annales 39 / 1970, eds. Adolf Portmann and Rudolf Ritsema (Leiden: E.J. Brill, 1973).

The Stages of Life in the Creative Process / Die Lebensalter im schöpferischen Prozess / Les moments créateurs dans les saisons de la vie—Lectures given at the Eranos Conference in Ascona from August 18ᵗʰ to 26ᵗʰ, 1971 / Vorträge gehalten auf der Eranos Tagung in Ascona vom 18 bis 26 August 1971 / Conférences données à la session d'Eranos à Ascona du 18 au 26 Août 1971, Eranos-Yearbook / Jahrbuch / Annales 40 / 1971, eds. Adolf Portmann and Rudolf Ritsema (Leiden: E.J. Brill, 1973).

The Realms of Colour / Die Welt der Farben / Le monde des couleurs— Lectures given at the Eranos Conference in Ascona from August 23ʳᵈ to 31ˢᵗ, 1972 / Vorträge gehalten auf der Eranos Tagung in Ascona vom 23 bis 31 August 1972 / Conférences données à la session d'Eranos à Ascona du 23 au 31 Août 1972, eds. Adolf Portmann and Rudolf Ritsema, Eranos-Yearbook / Jahrbuch / Annales 41 / 1972 (Leiden: E.J. Brill, 1974).

Correspondences in Man and World / Die Welt der Entsprechungen / Le monde des correspondances—Lectures given at the Eranos Conference in Ascona from August 22ⁿᵈ to 30ᵗʰ, 1973 / Vorträge gehalten auf der Eranos Tagung in Ascona vom 22 bis 30 August 1973 / Conférences données à la session d'Eranos à Ascona du 22 au 30 Août 1973, Eranos-Yearbook / Jahrbuch / Annales 42 / 1973, eds. Adolf Portmann and Rudolf Ritsema (Leiden: E.J. Brill, 1975).

Norms in a Changing World / Normen im Wandel der Zeit / Avenir et devenir des normes—Lectures given at the Eranos Conference in Ascona from August 21ˢᵗ to 29ᵗʰ, 1974 / Vorträge gehalten auf der Eranos Tagung in Ascona vom 21 bis 29 August 1974 / Conférences données à la session d'Eranos à Ascona du 21 au 29 Août 1974, Eranos-Yearbook / Jahrbuch / Annales 43 / 1974, eds. Adolf Portmann and Rudolf Ritsema (Leiden: E.J. Brill, 1977).

The Variety of Worlds / Die Vielheit der Welten / La pluralité des mondes— Lectures given at the Eranos Conference in Ascona from August 20ᵗʰ to 28ᵗʰ, 1975/Vorträge gehalten auf der Eranos Tagung in Ascona vom 20 bis 28 August 1975/Conférences données à la session d'Eranos à Ascona du 20 au 28 Août 1975, Eranos-Yearbook / Jahrbuch /

Annales 44 / 1975, eds. Adolf Portmann and Rudolf Ritsema (Leiden: E.J. Brill, 1977).

Oneness and Variety / Einheit und Verschiedenheit / L'un et le divers—Lectures given at the Eranos Conference in Ascona from August 18ᵗʰ to 26ᵗʰ, 1976 / Vorträge gehalten auf der Eranos Tagung in Ascona vom 18 bis 26 August 1976 / Conférences données à la session d'Eranos à Ascona du 18 au 26 Août 1976, Eranos-Yearbook / Jahrbuch / Annales 45 / 1976, eds. Adolf Portmann and Rudolf Ritsema (Leiden: E.J. Brill, 1980.

Der Sinn des Unvollkommenen / The Sense of Imperfection / Le sens de l'imperfection—Vorträge gehalten auf der Eranos Tagung in Ascona vom 17 bis 25 August 1977 / Lectures given at the Eranos Conference in Ascona from August 17ᵗʰ to 25ᵗʰ, 1977 / Conférences données à la session d'Eranos à Ascona du 17 au 25 Août 1977, Eranos-Jahrbuch / Yearbook / Annales 46 / 1977, eds. Adolf Portmann and Rudolf Ritsema (Ascona / Frankfurt am Main: Eranos Foundation/Insel Verlag, 1981).

Zeit und Zeitlosigkeit / In Time and Out of Time / Le temps et ses frontières—Vorträge gehalten auf der Eranos Tagung in Ascona vom 23 bis 31 August 1978 / Lectures given at the Eranos Conference in Ascona from August 23ʳᵈ to 31ˢᵗ, 1978 / Conférences données à la session d'Eranos à Ascona du 23 au 31 Août 1978, Eranos-Jahrbuch / Yearbook / Annales 47 / 1978, eds. Adolf Portmann and Rudolf Ritsema (Ascona / Frankfurt am Main: Eranos Foundation / Insel Verlag, 1981).

Denken und mythische Bildwelt / Thought and Mythic Images / Image mythique et pensée—Vorträge gehalten auf der Eranos Tagung in Ascona vom 22 bis 30 August 1979 / Lectures given at the Eranos Conference in Ascona from August 22ⁿᵈ to 30ᵗʰ, 1979 / Conférences données à la session d'Eranos à Ascona du 22 au 30 Août 1979, Eranos-Jahrbuch / Yearbook / Annales 48 / 1979, eds. Adolf Portmann and Rudolf Ritsema (Eranos Foundation / Insel Verlag, Ascona / Frankfurt am Main, 1981).

Grenzen und Begrenzung / Extremes and Borders / Les extrêmes et la limite—Vorträge gehalten auf der Eranos Tagung in Ascona vom 20 bis 28 August 1980 / Lectures given at the Eranos Conference in Ascona from August 20th to 28th, 1980 / Conférences données à la session d'Eranos à Ascona du 20 au 28 Août 1980, Eranos-Jahrbuch / Yearbook / Annales 49 / 1980, eds. Adolf Portmann and Rudolf Ritsema (Ascona / Frankfurt am Main: Eranos Foundation / Insel Verlag, 1981).

Aufstieg und Abstieg / Rise and Descent / Descente et ascension—Vorträge gehalten auf der Eranos Tagung in Ascona vom 19 bis 27 August 1981 / Lectures given at the Eranos Conference in Ascona from August 19th to 27th, 1981 / Conférences données à la session d'Eranos à Ascona du 19 au 27 Août 1981, Eranos-Jahrbuch / Yearbook / Annales 50 / 1981, eds. Adolf Portmann and Rudolf Ritsema (Eranos Foundation / Insel Verlag, Ascona / Frankfurt am Main, 1982).

Das Spiel der Götter und der Menschen / The Play of Gods and Men / Les jeux des hommes et des dieux—Vorträge gehalten auf der Eranos Tagung in Ascona vom 18 bis 26 August 1982 / Lectures given at the Eranos Conference in Ascona from August 18th to 26th, 1982 / Conférences données à la session d'Eranos à Ascona du 18 au 26 Août 1982, Eranos-Jahrbuch / Yearbook / Annales 51 / 1982, ed. Rudolf Ritsema (Ascona / Frankfurt am Main: Eranos Foundation / Insel Verlag, 1983).

Physische und geistige Körperwelt / Material and Imaginal Bodies / Corps physiques et corps spirituels—Vorträge gehalten auf der Eranos Tagung in Ascona vom 17 bis 25 August 1983 / Lectures given at the Eranos Conference in Ascona from August 17th to 25th, 1983 / Conférences données à la session d'Eranos à Ascona du 17 au 25 Août 1983, Eranos-Jahrbuch / Yearbook / Annales 52 / 1983, ed. Rudolf Ritsema (Ascona / Frankfurt am Main: Eranos Foundation / Insel Verlag, 1984).

Die Schönheit der Dinge / Beauty of the World / La beauté sur la terre—Vorträge gehalten auf der Eranos Tagung in Ascona vom 22. bis 30. August 1984 / Lectures given at the Eranos Conference in Ascona from

August 22*nd* to 30*th*, 1984 / Conférences données à la session d'Eranos à Ascona du 22 au 30 Août 1984, Eranos-Jahrbuch / Yearbook / Annales 53 / 1984, ed. Rudolf Ritsema (Ascona / Frankfurt am Main: Eranos Foundation / Insel Verlag, 1986).

*Der geheime Strom des Geschehens / The Hidden Course of Events / Le courant caché des événements—Vorträge gehalten auf der Eranos Tagung in Ascona vom 21 bis 29 August 1985 / Lectures given at the Eranos Conference in Ascona from August 21*st* to 29*th*, 1985 / Conférences données à la session d'Eranos à Ascona du 21 au 29 Août 1985*, Eranos-Jahrbuch / Yearbook / Annales 54 / 1985, ed. Rudolf Ritsema (Ascona / Frankfurt am Main: Eranos Foundation / Insel Verlag, 1987).

*Spiegelung in Mensch und Kosmos / Human and Cosmic Mirroring / L'homme et le cosmos en miroir—Vorträge gehalten auf der Eranos Tagung in Ascona vom 20. bis 28. August 1986 / Lectures given at the Eranos Conference in Ascona from August 20*th* to 28*th*, 1986 / Conférences données à la session d'Eranos à Ascona du 20 au 28 Août 1986*, Eranos-Jahrbuch / Yearbook / Annales 55 / 1986, ed. Rudolf Ritsema (Ascona / Frankfurt am Main: Eranos Foundation / Insel Verlag, 1988).

*Wegkreuzungen / Crossroads / La croisée des chemins—Vorträge gehalten auf der Eranos Tagung in Ascona vom 19 bis 27 August 1987 / Lectures given at the Eranos Conference in Ascona from August 19*th* to 27*th*, 1987 / Conférences données à la session d'Eranos à Ascona du 19 au 27 Août 1987*, Eranos-Jahrbuch / Yearbook / Annales 56 / 1987, ed. Rudolf Ritsema (Ascona / Frankfurt am Main: Eranos Foundation / Insel Verlag, 1989).

*Gleichklang oder Gleichzeitigkeit / Concordance or Coincidence / Résonance ou simultanéité—Mit Inhaltsverzeichnis 1–1933 bis 57–1988 / With a Table of Contents 1–1933 to 57–1988 / Avec une table alphabétique 1–1933 à 57–1988—Vorträge gehalten auf der Eranos Tagung in Ascona vom 17 bis 25 August 1988 / Lectures given at the Eranos Conference in Ascona from August 17*th* to 25*th*, 1988 / Conférences données à la session d'Eranos à Ascona du 17 au 25 Août 1988,*

Eranos-Jahrbuch / Yearbook / Annales 57 / 1988, ed. Rudolf Ritsema (Ascona / Frankfurt am Main: Eranos Foundation / Insel Verlag, 1990).

Chou Yi—The Oracle of Encompassing Versatility—Volume I: Hexagrams 1–30—Provisional Edition for the Use of Participants in the Eranos Round Table Conferences—Eranos Yi Ching Project, Part I, 1, Eranos-Jahrbuch / Yearbook / Annales 58 / 1989, eds. Rudolf Ritsema and Stephen L. Karcher (Ascona: Eranos Foundation, 1990).

Chou Yi—The Oracle of Encompassing Versatility—Vol. II: Hexagrams 31–64—Provisional Edition for the Use of Participants in the Eranos Round Table Conferences—Eranos Yi Ching Project, Part I, 2, Eranos-Jahrbuch / Yearbook / Annales 59 / 1990, eds. Rudolf Ritsema and Stephen L. Karcher (Ascona: Eranos Foundation, 1990).

Chou Yi—The Oracle of Encompassing Versatility—Vol. III: Supplementary Materials and Concordance—Provisional Edition for the Use of Participants in the Eranos Round Table Conferences—Eranos Yi Ching Project, Part I, 3, Eranos-Jahrbuch / Yearbook / Annales 60 / 1991, eds. Rudolf Ritsema and Stephen L. Karcher (Ascona: Eranos Foundation, 1991).

The Yi Ching and the Ethic of the Image—Presentations of the 1992 Eranos / Uehiro Round Table Session, Ascona, Switzerland, October, 1992—Eranos Yi Ching Project, Part II, 1, Eranos-Jahrbuch / Yearbook / Annales 61 / 1992, ed. Stephen L. Karcher (Ascona / Putnam, CT: Eranos Foundation / Spring Journal, Inc., 1993).

I Ching—The Classic Chinese Oracle of Change—The Divinatory Texts with Concordance—Eranos I Ching Project, Part I, 4–6, Eranos-Jahrbuch / Yearbook / Annales 62 / 1993–63 / 1994–64 / 1995, eds. Rudolf Ritsema and Stephen L. Karcher (Ascona / Shaftesbury, Dorset / Rockport, MA / Milton, Brisbane: Eranos Foundation / Element Books, Ltd., 1994).

The Shadow of Perfection—Presentations of the 1995 Eranos / Uehiro Round Table Session, Ascona, Switzerland, May, 1995, Eranos-Jahrbuch / Yearbook / Annales 65 / 1996, eds. James G. Donat and Jay

Livernois (Ascona / Woodstock, CT: Eranos Foundation / Uehiro Foundation / Spring Journal, Inc., 1996).

Gateways to Identity—Presentations of the 1996–97 Eranos Round Table Sessions, Ascona, Switzerland—Eranos I Ching Project, Part II, 2, Eranos-Jahrbuch / Yearbook / Annales 66 / 1997, eds. James G. Donat and Jay Livernois (Ascona / Putnam, CT: Eranos Foundation / Spring Journal, Inc., 1997).

Chroniclers and Shamans—Presentations of the 1997–98 Eranos / Uehiro Round Table Sessions, Ascona, Switzerland—Eranos I Ching Project, Part II, 2, Eranos Yearbook 67 / 1998, eds. James G. Donat and Jay Livernois (Ascona / Woodstock, CT: Eranos Foundation / Uehiro Foundation / Spring Journal, Inc., 1998).

The Magic of the Tortoise—Eranos I Ching Project, Part II, 2, Eranos Yearbook 68 / 1999, eds. James G. Donat and Jay Livernois (Ascona / Putnam, CT: Eranos Foundation / Spring Journal, Inc., 1999).

Eranos Reborn—The Modernities of East and West—Perspectives on Violence and Aggression—Emerging Images of Humanity—The Legacy Tour—Presentations of the 2006, 2007, and 2008 Eranos Conferences, of the 2007 Fetzer at Eranos Conference, and of the 2008 Pacifica at Eranos Conference, Eranos & Monte Verità, Ascona, Switzerland, Eranos Yearbook 69 / 2006–2007–2008, eds. John van Praag and Riccardo Bernardini (Ascona / Einsiedeln: Eranos Foundation / Daimon Verlag, 2010).

Love on a Fragile Thread / L'amore sul filo della fragilità—Presentations of the 2011 Eranos Conference, of the 2008–2011 Fetzer Institute Dialogues at Eranos, and of the 2010–2011 Eranos-Jung Lectures, Eranos, Monte Verità, and San Materno Theater, Ascona, Switzerland / Presentazioni del Convegno di Eranos 2011, dei Dialoghi del Fetzer Institute a Eranos del 2008–2011 e delle Eranos-Jung Lectures del 2010–2011, Eranos, Monte Verità e Teatro San Materno, Ascona, Svizzera, Eranos Yearbook / Annale 70 / 2009–2010–2011, eds. Fabio Merlini, Lawrence E. Sullivan, Riccardo Bernardini, and Kate Olson (Ascona / Einsiedeln: Eranos Foundation / Daimon Verlag, 2012).

Beyond Masters—Spaces without Thresholds / Dopo i maestri: spazi senza soglie—Presentations of the 2012 Eranos Conference and Eranos-Jung Lectures, Eranos & Monte Verità, Ascona, Switzerland / Presentazioni del Convegno di Eranos e delle Eranos-Jung Lectures del 2012, Eranos e Monte Verità, Ascona, Svizzera / Eranos Yearbook / Annale 71 / 2012, eds. Fabio Merlini and Riccardo Bernardini (Ascona / Einsiedeln: Eranos Foundation / Daimon Verlag, 2014).

Soul between Enchantment and Disenchantment / L'anima tra incanto e disincanto—Proceedings of the 2013 and 2014 Eranos Conferences and Eranos-Jung Lectures, Eranos & Monte Verità, Ascona, Switzerland / Atti dei Convegni di Eranos e delle Eranos-Jung Lectures del 2013–2014, Eranos e Monte Verità, Ascona, Svizzera / Eranos Yearbook / Annale 72 / 2013–2014, eds. Fabio Merlini and Riccardo Bernardini (Ascona / Einsiedeln: Eranos Foundation / Daimon Verlag, 2015).

APPENDIX II
LIST OF THE ERANOS ROUND TABLE SESSIONS
(1990–2002)

Dream and Oracle: The Language of the Yi Ching, Eranos *I Ching* Project, October 25–28, 1990

Dream and Oracle: The Language of the Yi Ching, Eranos *I Ching* Project, April 18–21, 1991

Dream and Oracle: The Language of the Yi Ching, Eranos *I Ching* Project, May 30–June 2, 1991

Images of the Unknown, Eranos *I Ching* Project, September 26–30, 1991

Oracular Language and the Fabric of Meaning, Eranos *I Ching* Project, October 24–27, 1991

Images of the Unknown, Eranos *I Ching* Project, May 28–31, 1992

Images of the Unknown, Eranos *I Ching* Project, June 25–28, 1992

Healing Images: Divination and Therapeutics, Eranos *I Ching* Project, September 17–20, 1992

In Dreams begin Responsibilities: The Ethic of the Image, Eranos *I Ching* Project, October 29–November 1, 1992

The Shadow of Perfection, Eranos *I Ching* Project, May 25–28, 1995

Begegnung mit dem Unbekannten: Eine praktische Einführung in den I Ging, Eranos *I Ching* Project, October 5–8, 1995

Di fronte al profondo: un'introduzione alla pratica dell'I Ching, Eranos *I Ching* Project, 19–22 ottobre 1995

Medical Diagnosis and the Destiny of the Individual, Eranos *I Ching* Project, May 16–19, 1996

Traditional Ties and Global Nets: Individual Uprooting and the Search for Cultural Identity, Eranos *I Ching* Project, October 17–20, 1996

Di fronte al profondo: pratica dell'I Ching con la nuova traduzione italiana Eranos, Eranos *I Ching* Project, October 23–27, 1996

L'anima nell'abitazione, Eranos *I Ching* Project, May 8–11, 1997

Chroniclers and Shamans: Historical Events and Archetypal Images, Eranos *I Ching* Project, June 5–8, 1997

Di fronte all'ignoto: lettura dei testi oracolari nell'I Ching di Eranos, Eranos *I Ching* Project, September 11–14, 1997

The Interplay of Individual and Collective Identity, Eranos *I Ching* Project, October 23–26, 1997

Percorso di approfondimento I Ching I: Pratica approfondita dell'I Ching con la traduzione italiana Eranos, Eranos *I Ching* Project, November 15–16, 1997

Percorso di approfondimento I Ching II: Pratica approfondita dell'I Ching con la traduzione italiana Eranos, Eranos *I Ching* Project, February 21–22, 1998

Percorso di approfondimento I Ching III: Pratica approfondita dell'I Ching con la traduzione italiana Eranos, Eranos *I Ching* Project, April 18–19, 1998

Filling the Gaps: Creative Imagination in Scientific Theory, Eranos *I Ching* Project; May 20–24, 1998

La magia della tartaruga: sessione di approfondimento dell'I Ching di Eranos, Eranos *I Ching* Project, June 12–14, 1998

Introduzione all'I Ching di Eranos, Eranos *I Ching* Project, June, 11, 1998

From Polarity to Complementarity: Dilemmas in Science and Gender Identity, Eranos *I Ching* Project, October 21–25, 1998

Il flusso continuo del tempo e il millennio prorompente, Eranos *I Ching* Project, May 12–16, 1999

Politik und Wirtschaft: Wesen und Grenzen der Machbarkeit, Eranos *I Ching* Project, September 8–12, 1999

Begegnung mit dem Unbekannten: Ein psychologischer Zugang zum Orakelbuch I Ching, Eranos *I Ching* Project, October 7–10, 1999

Constellating Synchronicity: Fate and the Ethical Dimension of Oracle [with Uehiro Foundation], Eranos *I Ching* Project, October 27–31, 1999

The Two Sides of the Looking Glass: Psyche and Matter, Eranos *I Ching* Project, October 11–15, 2000

Nella corrente del grande fiume: sogno e I Ching, Eranos *I Ching* Project, October 19–22, 2000

Lo specchio del presente, Eranos *I Ching* Project, June 1–4, 2001

Unknown Gods / Dèi ignoti: The Spirit of this Place, Eranos *I Ching* Project, June 13–17, 2001

Unknown Gods / Dèi ignoti: Riflessi nello specchio oscuro, Eranos *I Ching* Project, September 19–23, 2001

Unknown Gods / Dèi ignoti: Called or Not Called [with Uehiro Foundation], Eranos *I Ching* Project, October 3–7, 2001

Orakelbefragung als Besinnung auf das Hier und Jetzt; Einer psychologischer Zugang zur neuen deutschen Übersetzung der Orakeltexte des Yi Jing (I Ging), Eranos *I Ching* Project, November 15–18, 2001

Beyond Consolidated Forms: Emergence of Change, Eranos *I Ching* Project, November 20–24, 2002

APPENDIX III

LIST OF THE PROCEEDINGS OF THE ASSOCIAZIONE AMICI DI ERANOS (1990–2012)

Auferstehung und Unsterblichkeit, Eranos Neue Folge I/1990, eds. Erik Hornung and Tilo Schabert (München: Wilhelm Fink, 1993).

Strukturen des Chaos, Eranos Neue Folge II/1991, eds. Tilo Schabert and Erik Hornung (München: Wilhelm Fink, 1994).

Wanderungen, Eranos Neue Folge III/1992, eds. Fritz Graf and Erik Hornung (München: Wilhelm Fink, 1995).

Die Macht des Wortes / Il Potere della Parola / Pouvoirs de la Parole / The Power of Words, Eranos Neue Folge IV/1993, eds. Tilo Schabert and Rémi Brague (München: Wilhelm Fink, 1996).

Anfänge, Eranos Neue Folge V/1994, eds. Tilo Schabert and Detlev Clemens (München: Wilhelm Fink, 1998).

Die Wahrheit der Träume / La Verità dei Sogni / The Truth of Dreams / La Vérité des Rêves, Eranos Neue Folge VI/1995, eds. Gaetano Benedetti and Erik Hornung (München: Wilhelm Fink, 1997).

Schuld, Eranos Neue Folge VII/1996, eds. Tilo Schabert and Detlev Clemens (München: Wilhelm Fink, 1999).

Kulturen des Eros, Eranos Neue Folge VIII/1997, eds. Tilo Schabert and Detlev Clemens (München: Wilhelm Fink, 2001).

Die Sprache der Masken, Eranos Neue Folge IX/1998, eds. Tilo Schabert (Würzburg, Königshausen + Neumann, 2002).

Das Ordnen der Zeit, Eranos Neue Folge X/1999, eds. Tilo Schabert and Matthias Riedl (Würzburg, Königshausen + Neumann, 2003).

Pioniere, Poeten, Professoren. Eranos und der Monte Verità in der Zivilisationsgeschichte des 20 Jahrhunderts, Eranos Neue Folge XI/2000, eds. Matthias Riedl and Alexandra Tischel (Würzburg, Königshausen + Neumann, 2004). Italian edition: *Eranos. Monte Verità. Ascona*, eds. Elisabetta Barone, Adriano Fabris, and Flavia Monceri (Pisa: ETS, 2003).

Propheten und Prophezeihungen / Prophets and Prophecies, Eranos Neue Folge XII/2001, eds. Matthias Riedl and Tilo Schabert (Würzburg, Königshausen + Neumann, 2005).

Die Menschen im Krieg, im Frieden mit der Natur / Humans at War, at Peace with Nature, Eranos Neue Folge XIII/2003, eds. Tilo Schabert and Matthias Riedl (Würzburg, Königshausen + Neumann, 2006).

Religionen: Die Religiöse Erfahrung / Religions: The Religious Experience, Eranos Neue Folge XIV/2004, eds. Matthias Riedl and Tilo Schabert (Würzburg, Königshausen + Neumann, 2008).

Gott oder Götter? / God or Gods?, Eranos Neue Folge XV/2005, eds. Tilo Schabert and Matthias Riedl (Würzburg, Königshausen + Neumann, 2009).

Die Stadt: Achse und Zentrum der Welt / The City: Axis and Centre of the World, Eranos Neue Folge XVI/2006, eds. Matthias Riedl and Tilo Schabert (Würzburg, Königshausen + Neumann, 2009).

The Eranos Movement, Eranos Neue Folge XVII/2012, eds. Tilo Schabert (Würzburg, Königshausen + Neumann, 2015; forthcoming).

APPENDIX IV
LIST OF THE PROCEEDINGS OF THE VEREIN ZUR FÖRDERUNG DER WISSENSCHAFTLICHEN TAGUNGEN VON ERANOS (2001–2014)

Der Mensch und sein Widersacher, Eranos 2001–2002, eds. Erik Hornung and Andreas Schweizer (Egg: Fotorotar AG, 2003; rpt. Basel, Schwabe).

Die Weisheit der Schlange, Eranos 2003–2004, eds. Erik Hornung and Andreas Schweizer (Basel: Schwabe, 2005).

Schönheit und Mass, Eranos 2005–2006, eds. Erik Hornung and Andreas Schweizer (Basel: Schwabe, 2007).

Bilder des Unerkennbaren, Eranos 2007–2008, eds. Erik Hornung and Andreas Schweizer (Basel: Schwabe, 2009).

Jenseitsreisen, Eranos 2009–2010, eds. Erik Hornung and Andreas Schweizer (Basel: Schwabe, 2011).

Feuer und Wasser, Eranos 2011–2012, eds. Erik Hornung and Andreas Schweizer (Basel: Schwabe, 2013).

Heilige Landschaft, Eranos 2013–2014, eds. Erik Hornung and Andreas Schweizer (Basel: Schwabe, 2015).

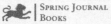

New: Jung at Eranos

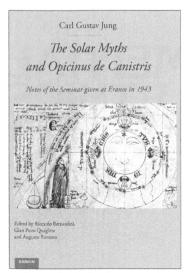

Carl Gustav Jung

The Solar Myths and Opicinus de Canistris

Notes of the Seminar given at Eranos in 1943

Edited by Riccardo Bernardini, Gian Piero Quaglino and Augusto Romano

Carl Gustav Jung

The Solar Myths and Opicinus de Canistris

Edited by Riccardo Bernardini, Gian Piero Quaglino, and Augusto Romano

Carl Gustav Jung held an 'extemporaneous' seminar on The Solar Myths and Opicinus de Canistris at the 1943 Eranos Conference. This book presents all known material about the seminar, including the notes taken by Alwine von Keller and Rivkah Schärf Kluger, and the outline that Jung himself prepared for his seminar. Opicinus de Canistris (1296–c. 1352) was an Italian priest and cartographer. His medieval cartography includes historical, theological, symbolic and astrological references along with a curious anthropomorphism, which depicted continents and oceans with human features. Jung recognized this as a projection of Opicinus' inner world and interpreted the maps as mandalas, where the integration of the shadow, the dark principle, was missing. (200 pages, hardcover, illustrated, ISBN 978-3-85630-756-1)

Eranos Yearbook 71: 2012
Beyond Masters –
Spaces without Thresholds

edited by Fabio Merlini
and Riccardo Bernardini

The 71st volume of the Eranos Yearbooks, *Beyond Masters – Spaces Without Thresholds*, gathers the lectures presented at the 2012 Eranos Conference, "On the Threshold – Disorientation and New Forms of Space," together with the talks given on the occasion of the 2012 Eranos-Jung Lectures seminar cycle, "The Eclipse of the Masters?" (416 pages, hardcover, color illustrations, ISBN 978-3-85630-754-7)

ERANOS
YEARBOOK
2012

Beyond Masters –
Spaces without Thresholds
Dopo i maestri:
spazi senza soglie

Edited by
Fabio Merlini and Riccardo Bernardini

NOS

Lightning Source UK Ltd.
Milton Keynes UK
06f2358170816

UK00022B/732/P